DOCTRINE

**MARK DRISCOLL &
DR. GERRY BRESHEARS**

Doctrine
© 2021 by Mark Driscoll & Dr. Gerry Breshears

ISBN:
978-1-7374103-5-5 (Print)
978-1-7374103-6-2 (E-Book)

Cover art designed by Jonathan Thomas and Frank Thomas; inside artwork designed by Jonathan Thomas. Unless otherwise indicated, scripture quotations are from The Holy Bible, English Standard Version, copyright 2001 by Crossway Bibles, a publishing ministry of Good News Publishers. Used by permission. All rights reserved.

All emphases in Scripture quotations have been added by the author.

No part of this publication may be reproduced, stored in a retrieval system, or transmitted in any form by any means, electronic, mechanical, photocopy, recording, or otherwise, without the prior permission of the publisher, except as provided for by USA copyright law.

CONTENTS

CHAPTER 1: TRINITY (GOD IS) 1

CHAPTER 2: REVELATION (GOD SPEAKS) 27

CHAPTER 3: CREATION (GOD MAKES) 61

CHAPTER 4: IMAGE (GOD LOVES) 89

CHAPTER 5: FALL (GOD JUDGES) 119

CHAPTER 6: COVENANT (GOD PURSUES) 149

CHAPTER 7: INCARNATION (GOD COMES) 175

CHAPTER 8: CROSS (GOD DIES) 203

CHAPTER 9: RESURRECTION (GOD SAVES) 231

CHAPTER 10: CHURCH (GOD ACTS) 251

CHAPTER 11: WORSHIP (GOD TRANSFORMS) 281

CHAPTER 12: KINGDOM (GOD REIGNS) 309

NOTES 337

ABOUT THE AUTHORS 354

CHAPTER 1: TRINITY

"GOD IS"

And when Jesus was baptized, immediately he went up from the water, and behold, the heavens were opened to him, and he saw the Spirit of God descending like a dove and coming to rest on him; and behold, a voice from heaven [God the Father] said, "This is my beloved Son, with whom I am well pleased."
MATTHEW 3:16–17

My wife Grace and I met in high school at the age of seventeen. I played baseball; she was a sprinter on the track team. After running track for a few years, one day Grace was surprised to learn that she had been poorly coached. Apparently, to get the fastest start to a race, thereby setting up every step of the race, it is important to begin at the starting line with your feet in the correct position. For a few years, Grace had her feet in the wrong position at the starting line. In every race for her first season, she literally started off on the wrong foot. This slowed down her speed and meant that all of her steps were not in the correct order. Eventually, a helpful coach got her set correctly in the blocks and she ended up making it to the state semifinals her senior year.

You cannot overstate the importance of getting the first step right on any journey. As we begin our run through 12 big doctrines of the Bible, the first step really matters. Otherwise, you could go to the wrong direction, drift off course, or trip over your own feet.

Some theological statements start with mankind. For example, something called the Five Points of Arminianism starts with human freedom of the will, and the Five Points of Calvinism starts with human sinfulness. But, is focusing on mankind the best first step in the pursuit of God? Probably not.

Many systematic theology textbooks start with revelation and how God speaks to us through the Scriptures. This is not a bad first step, but is it the best first step?

Like a coach trying to get your feet right at the starting line, we will begin with God. Here's what we find in the starting blocks of the Bible, "In the beginning, God..." We begin this book where the Bible begins - God. Everything right begins with God. Everything wrong begins with no God, or some false god(s), which we will now study.

THEOLOGY IS THE STUDY OF GOD

Theology literally means the "study of God". Varying religions and philosophies have vying proposed understandings of what the truth is about God. In an effort to help you understand many of the most prominent perspectives on God, we will now explore the various ways that people get started on the wrong foot in their study of God so that we can then get started on the right foot.

Atheism

Atheism comes from the negative a-, which means "no," "not," or "without," and theos, which means "god". Basically, atheism is the belief that there is no God. Related to atheism are the beliefs that there is no devil, no supernatural realm, no miracles, no absolute moral truth over all cultures, and nothing beyond the material world, so therefore people do not have souls and there is no possibility of spiritual life after physical death. Curiously, atheism is historically a relatively new concept.

The word atheism does not exist in the Old Testament language of Hebrew. Moreover, the Old Testament generally assumes that everyone believes in the existence of God saying, "The fool says in his heart, 'There is no God.'"[a]

Agnosticism

In stating that there is no god, atheism must prove that God does not exist; this requires that we have complete knowledge, which is impossible. Consequently, agnosticism has become more popular with doubters of the existence of a God or gods. Agnosticism is derived from a-, meaning "without," and Gnosticism or gnosis, meaning "knowledge." An agnostic does not know about or is ignorant about God. Agnosticism asserts that while we can examine the physical world, we have no access to the spiritual world and therefore can never know if a God or gods exist.

Agnosticism overlooks the possibility that if God exists, He could reveal Himself to us and thereby make Himself known. This is precisely what the Bible teaches.

---

[a] Psalm 14:1; 53:1

TRINITY: GOD IS

Jesus "descended from heaven."[a] In Jesus, "the Word became flesh and dwelt among us, and we have seen his glory, glory as of the only Son from the Father, full of grace and truth."[b] Jesus says of Himself, "Whoever has seen me has seen the Father."[c] Jesus came down from heaven and revealed God to us in order to clear the fog of agnosticism so that we can see God clearly.

Deism

Deism teaches that a god made the universe but then left his creation alone and has no dealings with it a bit like an absentee landlord. With god absent, deism teaches that the world runs by natural laws that god established to govern his creation. Subsequently, miracles are impossible because the universe is a closed system, and god does not intervene in his creation or overrule his natural laws.

Perhaps the most noted and consistent deist was President Thomas Jefferson (1743–1826). He sat down in the White House with a razor in one hand and the Bible in the other and cut out those parts of Scripture that he decided were untrue. The result was The Philosophy of Jesus of Nazareth, or The Life and Morals of Jesus of Nazareth. Only one in 10 Scripture verses survived, zero miracles were considered factual, and the resurrection of Jesus was systematically cut from the pages of Scripture.

The inconsistencies with deism are many, including the fact that they deny miracles yet affirm the great miracle of creation by God. Furthermore, Jesus is not only the Creator God of the universe, but also the ongoing Sustainer God who contradicts the central tenet of deism: "For by him [Jesus] all things were created, in heaven and on earth, visible and invisible, whether thrones or dominions or rulers or authorities—all things were created through him and for him. And he is before all things, and in him all things hold together."[d]

Finite Godism

Finite Godism teaches that a god does exist but with limitations, such as not being all-knowing (omniscient) or all-powerful (omnipotent). The motivation behind finite godism is to explain how a good god could coexist with all of the evil and injustice in the world. Finite godism seeks to explain the goodness of a god and evil in the world by stating that, while this god is good, this god is limited and unable to stop evil in the world.

The problems with finite godism are many. First, a finite god would need a greater infinite God to enable its continued existence. Second, past and present evil does not negate the fact that the all-powerful, infinite God will one day bring evil to an end, as Scripture teaches. Third, the existence of evil does not in any way disprove the infinite wisdom and power of God. Fourth, a finite god is simply

---

[a] John 3:13; 6:38 [b] John 1:14 [c] John 14:9 [d] Col. 1:16–17

of no help at all; such a helpless god cannot truly help us in our time of need and is therefore unworthy of devotion.

Jesus answers the question motivating the belief in finite godism. At the cross of Jesus, we witness the darkest hour of history. At the hands of an unjust legal system, surrounded by chants of a bloodthirsty mob, the greatest person who has ever lived, Jesus Christ, was brutally murdered. In that moment, it appeared that God was in fact finite as He did nothing to intervene and stop the injustice. Yet, three days later, Jesus rose from the grave, defeating evil. God demonstrated Himself not as powerless but powerful. Therefore, through the life, death, and resurrection of Jesus, the question "Where is God when it hurts?" is answered: God is good and powerful and at work through Jesus Christ to bring about victory and life, even though what appears at first glance is nothing more than defeat and death.

Pantheism

Pantheism is derived from pan, which means "all" and theism, which means "god." Pantheism is the belief that all is god or that the material world is itself god or divine. Based upon monism, which is the belief that all reality is one interrelated being, the god of pantheism is impersonal. Pantheism is popular in Hinduism and some forms of Buddhism along with New Spirituality (also called New Age-ism), Christian Science, Unity Church, Scientology, and Theosophy. Pantheism is widely advocated in the worldview of Star Wars, where God is not a person but rather an impersonal force that envelopes and includes each of us. Earth religions like Wicca or Gaia see the planet as a living substance and call for people to worship it as our mother.

In pantheism there are no miracles because God is not beyond this world or able to override it. It is also said that pain, matter, and evil are unreal illusions, which does not make any sense after you stub your toe leaving yoga class.

Pantheism has many other shortcomings, including denying that the universe had a beginning when both Big Bang cosmology and the Second Law of Thermodynamics say otherwise, declaring the physical world to be an illusion, and an inability to explain how a world without intelligence or morality brought both into existence. Pantheism is clearly refuted in Romans 1:25: "They [people who do not know God] exchanged the truth about God for a lie and worshiped and served the creature rather than the Creator, who is blessed forever! Amen." We should worship the Creator instead of His creation, as pantheism encourages.

Panentheism

Panentheism comes from pan ("all") + in + theism ("god"), which together mean "all in god." Not to be confused with pantheism, panentheism teaches that a god figure is part of or in creation so that, in a way, creation is akin to this god's body, which houses his spirit. In panentheism, the god is seen as existing in two polarities, existing in one form as a present reality and existing in another form

TRINITY: GOD IS

as a future possibility. It is said that this god is growing, maturing, and evolving from his current state to his potential state, not unlike humanity. As a result, it is said that this god is both finite and infinite, and eternal without a beginning yet not eternal and with a beginning. Contradicting itself, panentheism therefore teaches that this god made himself, which would require him to exist before he existed. Furthermore, panentheism says that this god figure is presently imperfect but ever learning, growing, and changing to become more and more perfect.

Despite the self-contradictions of panentheism, it was held in the ancient world by men such as Plato. Tragically, some who profess to be Christian have also adopted the false understanding of God postulated by panentheism. This includes some feminist theologians and Marxist theologians, process theology, and some forms of open theism stressing the immanence of God over His transcendence and the changing of God over His immutability.

Panentheism does not agree with the God of the Bible. Some of God's attributes, include His unchanging immutability, His eternal perfection, His sovereignty over creation, His infiniteness, and His independence of the world rather than dependence upon it.

Polytheism

Polytheism comes from poly, which means "many," and theism, which means "god." Polytheism says there is more than one god. Religions adhering to polytheism include Hinduism, Confucianism, Shintoism, Taoism, Jainism, ancient Greek mythology, Mormonism, Scientology, and the Unification Church.

The idea of polytheism is a little like a large shopping mall where you go to the store that carries your product at the best price, so there are a lot of gods, spiritual beings, that are more or less equal but with different specialties. You bring your offering to get what you want from that god. Clearly, the Bible acknowledges that many people worship false gods. There is only one true God, Yahweh, the Creator of heaven and earth[a] and all other "gods" no more than powerful angels, spiritual beings who can turn staffs into snakes[b] but are "nothings" when compared to Yahweh.[c]

Other gods

The Old Testament clearly states that there is only one God.[d] The New Testament is in full agreement.[e] The Bible also teaches that there is no one like

---

[a] 2 Chron. 15:3; Jer. 10:10; John 17:3; 1 Thess. 1:9; 1 John 5:20-21 [b] Ex. 7:11-12
[c] Deut. 32:21; 1 Sam. 12:21; Ps. 96:5; Isa. 37:19; 41:23-24, 29; Jer. 2:11; 5:7; 16:20; 1 Cor. 8:4; 10:19-20 [d] Deut. 4:35, 39; 6:4-5; 32:39; 1 Sam. 2:2; 2 Sam. 7:22; 22:32; Ps. 86:8-10; Isa. 37:20; 43:10; 44:6-8; 45:5, 14, 21-22; 46:9
[e] John 5:44; Rom. 3:30; 16:27; 1 Cor. 8:4-6; Gal. 3:20; Eph. 4:6; 1 Tim. 1:17; 2:5; James 2:19; Jude

God.[a] Thus, claiming to be like God is a satanic lie.[b]

However, demons (fallen spirit beings) may also pose as gods and elicit worship, possibly even through counterfeit signs, wonders, and miracles. This happens throughout the book of Exodus where the Kingdom of God and Satan's kingdom of the "gods" are vying for supremacy in a cosmic showdown.[c]

- Exodus 12:12 - "I will pass through the land of Egypt that night, and I will strike all the firstborn in the land of Egypt, both man and beast; and on all the gods of Egypt I will execute judgments: I am the Lord."
- Exodus 18:10-11 - Jethro said, "Blessed be the LORD, who has delivered you out of the hand of the Egyptians and out of the hand of Pharaoh and has delivered the people from under the hand of the Egyptians. Now I know that the LORD is greater than all gods."
- Exodus 20:3 - "You shall have no other gods before me."

These "gods" are very powerful fallen angels and other spirit beings who rebelled against God. They revile the real God and want to replace him with gods. Practically, this means that there are incredibly powerful demonic spirits—with names such as Baal, Chemosh, Molech, Brahman, Jezebel, Allah, Mother Earth, Mammon (money), and Aphrodite (sex)—that are wrongly worshiped by multitudes as gods. One major theme of the Bible is that God creates, and Satan counterfeits. False gods are behind false religions lead by false teachers who perform false miracles - all schemes to lead people astray from the real God to the false gods.

From the beginning, God's people have lived with constant pressure to accept other religions and "gods" as equally worthy of worship as the God of the Bible. Too many times people are like Solomon and divide their devotion between God and the "gods".[d] To embolden us, the Bible presents stirring stories of faithful followers like Shadrach, Meshach, Abednego, and Daniel who would not compromise their devotion to God despite facing opposition and persecution.[e]

Monotheism

Monotheism teaches that there is only one personal God who is separate (transcendent) from the universe, though involved in it (immanent). As a result, many people have regarded Christianity as just one of many monotheistic religions along with Judaism and Islam. In one sense, Christianity is monotheistic, as it does believe in one God. Yet, upon further investigation, the Bible is not impressed with mere monotheism because God's objective is not that we simply believe in one God. As James 2:19 says, "You believe that God is one; you do well. Even the demons believe—and shudder!" The God of Christianity as revealed in the Bible

---

[a] Ex. 8:10; 9:14; 15:11; 2 Sam. 7:22; 1 Kings 8:23; 1 Chron. 17:20; Ps. 86:8; Isa. 40:18, 25; 44:7; 46:5, 9; Jer. 10:6–7; Mic. 7:18 [b] Gen. 3:5; Isa. 14:14; John 8:44 [c] Deut. 32:17; Ps. 106:37; 1 Cor. 10:18–22; Gal. 4:8 [d] 1 Kings 11 [e] Dan. 3,7

is one God who exists in the Trinitarian community of Father, Son, and Spirit. No other religion shares the concept of the Trinity with Christianity. Now that we have eliminated ways we can get started on the wrong foot, we can now get started on the right foot by learning about the one true God.

WHAT IS THE TRINITY?

God is Father, Son, and Holy Spirit. One God. Three persons. While the word Trinity does not appear in the Bible, this One-who-is-Three concept very clearly does. As an aside, the Bible also does not include the word Bible. The word Trinity is a shorthand way of summarizing complex biblical truth. It was likely first used by the church father Tertullian (AD 155-220). To say that God exists as a Trinity does not mean that there are three Gods, or that one God merely manifests himself as either the modes of Father, Son, or Holy Spirit on various occasions.

The Westminster Confession of Faith (1647) summarizes the doctrine by saying, "In the unity of the Godhead there be three persons, of one substance, power, and eternity: God the Father, God the Son, and God the Holy Ghost."

For our purposes, we will use the following definition: The Trinity is one God who eternally exists as three distinct persons—Father, Son, and Spirit—who are each fully and equally God in eternal relation with each other.

To say that each member of the Trinity is a "person" does not mean that God the Father or God the Spirit became human beings. Rather, it means that each member of the Trinity thinks, acts, feels, speaks, and relates because they are persons and not impersonal forces. Further, each member of the Trinity is equally God, which means that they share all the divine attributes (e.g. eternity, omniscience, omnipotence, and omnipresence), which we will explore in later chapters.

The Father, Son, and Spirit are equally declared throughout Scripture to be God. We will get to know more each Person of the Godhead, starting with the Father.

GOD THE FATHER

Innumerable Scriptures clearly and emphatically declare the Father to be God.[a]

In the history of Christianity and all the cults and religions that have erred from biblical truth, there has never been any noteworthy false teaching denying the deity of God the Father, because it is so obviously clear throughout the entirety of Scripture.

However, one reason there has been an underemphasis on God the Father in many Christian circles is because of a father wound. The father wound is an

---

[a] John 6:27; 17:3; 1 Cor. 8:6; 2 Cor. 1:3; Eph. 1:3; 1 Pet. 1:3

DOCTRINE

unhealed hurt from a physical or spiritual father or father figure in our life. Fathers fail us, and unless we forgive them and invite God the Father to heal our father wound, we remain burdened instead of unburdened, broken instead of healed, and made bitter instead of made better.

People with an unhealed father wound can have a wrong and warped view of God. Our view of God is often a projection or rejection of our imperfect earthly dad onto God. Here are some specific examples:

Atheism says I have no Father.

Agnosticism says I may or may not have a Father, but I've never met Him, I don't know who or where He is, and I don't really care to find out.

Deism says I have a Father but, like my dad who abandoned me when I was little, He lives far away and we don't have a relationship.

Extreme reformed theology says I have a Father who is a distant, controlling, and not very relational, domineering dad.

Extreme Arminian theology says I have a Father who is passive and lets me make my own decisions to do whatever I want, like my earthly dad who stayed on the sidelines of my life.

Extreme liberal theology says I have a Father who acts more like an enabling older sibling and does not tell me what to do but helps me do whatever I want, even if it's foolish or rebellious.

Extreme feminist theology says that we don't need a Father since men are dangerous and harmful, so we should instead move on and be happy to be spiritually raised by a single parent and worship God as Mother.

God the Father is largely forgotten. In too many evangelical, reformed, and Bible churches the focus is on Jesus Christ, the Son of God. In too many Pentecostal and Charismatic churches, the focus is on God the Holy Spirit. Books are written on the Son and Spirit, but hardly anything is written on the Father. Sadly, the Mormons and Muslims are the ones filling the gap and talking a lot about their demonic, counterfeit views of their "god" as father. This might explain the growth of the Mormon cult and allure of Islam to young men around the world.

According to the Bible, when we look at Jesus, we see God the Father. revealed.[a] Jesus says, "Whoever has seen me has seen the Father."[b]

When the Bible says that people, including Jesus, are God's image bearers, it means that people are made to mirror. A mirror's only job is to reflect accurately. A mirror does not exist to create any images but only reflect. When the Bible says Jesus "is the image of the invisible God"[c] it means that the character of the Father is reflected perfectly in the life of the Son. In Jesus we see the Father heart of God.

To heal the father wound, you need to forgive the earthly physical and spiritual father(s) who have failed you. This forgiveness will remove the demonic foothold that bitterness brings. Jesus promised "I will not leave you as orphans."[d] The Holy Spirit was sent to heal the father wound and bring adoption and sonship. "For

---

[a] John 1:18 [b] John 14:9 [c] Col. 1:15 [d] John 14:18

all who are led by the Spirit of God are sons of God. For you did not receive the spirit of slavery to fall back into fear, but you have received the Spirit of adoption as sons, by whom we cry, 'Abba! Father!' The Spirit himself bears witness with our spirit that we are children of God, and if children, then heirs—heirs of God and fellow heirs with Christ."[a]

As you walk away from the demonic spirits of the father wound, and by the Spirit walk with the Father, you will experience radical life change. Although you may be a Christian, even a devout and seasoned Christian, you may have not yet made the full journey from Jesus to the Father. Jesus said, "I am the way, and the truth, and the life. No one comes to the Father except through me."[b]

The Holy Spirit brings you to Jesus. Then, Jesus brings you to the Father. The Spirit convicts you of sin and brings you to Jesus for the forgiveness of sin. Jesus forgives your sin and then brings you to the Father for healing. Many Christians understand conviction and forgiveness but have not yet experienced the Father's healing. To be a Christian is to experience the fullness of "adoption as sons."[c]

When a child gets adopted, they adapt to having a father and spend time getting to know their new father and family. To become a Christian is to get a new family (the church), a new big brother (Jesus), and a new Father (God).

The Old Testament talks a lot about fathers, including genealogies listing generations of dads. God is referred to as Father roughly 15 times, and those few occasions are in reference to God's relationship with the nation of Israel, and not warm and personal communication to an individual. Everything changes with the coming of Jesus Christ. His favorite title for God is Father and, in the four Gospels alone, He calls God His Father roughly 165 times, specifically using the word abba translated in most Bibles as "Father".

A theological dictionary says that "the uniqueness of Jesus' teaching on this subject is evident for several reasons. For one, the rarity of this designation for God is striking. There is no evidence in pre-Christian Jewish literature that Jews addressed God as "Abba". A second unique feature about Jesus' use of abba as a designation for God involves the intimacy of the term...Abba was a term that not only small children used to address their fathers, it was also a term that older children and adults used. As a result, it is best to understand Abba as the equivalent of "Father" rather than "daddy" since "Father" connotes the respectful intimate family meaning better than "papa" or "daddy".[1]

GOD THE SON AND GOD THE SPIRIT

Jesus is also repeatedly declared to be God throughout the Scriptures by both

---

[a] Rom. 8:14-17 [b] John 14:6 [c] Gal. 4:5

others[a] and Himself, without apology or correction.[b] Jesus was ultimately put to death for declaring Himself to be God, a declaration that, if untrue, would have been a violation of the first commandment and a blasphemous sin.[c]

In addition to the Father and Son, the Holy Spirit is clearly called God throughout the Scriptures. In the Old Testament, He possesses the attributes of God, which reveals his divinity; He is creator,[d] eternal,[e] omnipotent (all-powerful)[f], omniscient (all-knowing)[g], and omnipresent[h]. In the New Testament, the Holy Spirit is also clearly declared God.[i]

Furthermore, the Holy Spirit is not merely an impersonal force but a person who can be grieved[k], resisted[m], and insulted[n]. The personhood of the Holy Spirit explains why Jesus speaks of Him as a personal "He" and not an impersonal "it."[o]

Importantly, though one God, the Father, Son, and Spirit are distinct persons. The Father and Son are referenced as two unique persons in frequent salutations of letters in the New Testament[p], as well as in other Scriptures.[q] Scripture is also clear that Jesus and the Holy Spirit are not the same person.[r] Likewise, the Father is not the Holy Spirit.[s] Jesus was repeatedly clear that He and the Father are distinct persons but one God, saying, "I and the Father are one"[t] and "we are one."[u] We will study in greater detail the person and work of Jesus Christ and the Holy Spirit in later chapters.

WHAT IS THE TRINITARIAN GOD OF THE BIBLE LIKE?

Perhaps the Bible's best-known Trinitarian statement is 1 John 4:8, "God is love."

The Trinity is the first community of friends and the ideal for all friendly communities. That community alone has not been stained by the selfishness of sin. Therefore, in the diversity of God the Father, Son, and Spirit is perfect unity as one God that communicates truthfully, loves unreservedly, lives connectedly, serves

---

[a] Matt. 28:9; John 1:1–4, 14; 5:17–18; 8:58; 10:30–38; 12:37–41; cf. Isa. 6:9–11; 20:28–29; Acts 20:28; Rom. 1:3–4; 9:5; 1 Cor. 8:4–6; Gal. 4:4; Phil. 2:10–11; Col. 1:16–17; 2:8–9; 1 Tim. 6:15; Titus 2:13; Heb.1:8; 1 John 5:20; Rev. 1:8, 17–18; 17:14; 19:16; 22:13–16 [b] Matt. 26:63–65; John 5:17–23; 8:58–59; 10:30–39; 19:7 [c] Matt. 26:64–66; Mark 14:62–64; John 8:58–59; 10:30–31 [d] Gen. 1:2; Ps. 104:30 [e] Heb. 9:14 [f] Mic. 3:8; see also Acts 1:8; Rom. 15:13, 19 [g] Isa. 40:13–14; see also 1 Cor. 2:10 [h] Ps. 139:7 [i] Acts 5:3–4; see also John 14:16; 2 Cor. 3:16–18 [k] Eph. 4:30 [m] Acts 7:51 [n] Heb. 10:29 [o] John 14:17, 26; 16:7–14 [p] Rom. 1:7; 1 Cor. 1:3; 2 Cor. 1:2; Gal. 1:3; Eph. 1:2; 6:23; Phil. 1:2; 1 Thess. 1:1; 2 Thess. 1:1–2; 1 Tim. 1:1–2; 2 Tim. 1:2; Titus 1:4; Philem. 3; James 1:1; 2 Pet. 1:2; 2 John 3 [q] John 3:17; 5:31–32; 8:16–18; 11:41–42; 12:28; 14:31; 17:23–26; Gal. 4:4; 1 John 4:10 [r] Luke 3:22; John 14:16; 15:26; 16:7; 1 John 2:1 [s] John 14:15, 15:26; Rom. 8:11, 26–27; 2 Cor. 1:3–4; Gal. 1:1 [t] John 10:30 [u] John 17:11

TRINITY: GOD IS

humbly, interacts peaceably, and serves selflessly. Or, to say it another way, God is like a perfect relational Family and the model for all families that make up the human family.

Love is spoken of roughly eight hundred times throughout Scripture. In stating that "God is love," the Bible reveals the Trinitarian God of the Bible as simultaneously the definition, example, and source of true love.

To declare that God is love is to confess that God is Trinitarian. In the very nature of God there is a continuous outpouring of love, communication, and oneness because God is a relational community of love. For example, during his earthly life, Jesus frequently spoke about the deep love between him and God the Father in terms that are intended to convey to us the concept of God as a loving family:

- "The Father loves the Son and has given all things into his hand."[a]
- "The Father loves the Son and shows him all that he himself is doing."[b]
- "I do as the Father has commanded me, so that the world may know that I love the Father."[c]

In the Old Testament the most sacred name for God is Yahweh. Yahweh is a distinctly proper name for the God of the Bible. Sacred, it is never used to refer to any pagan gods; neither is it used in regard to any human. It is reserved solely for the one true God alone. The name Yahweh appears some 6,823 times in the Old Testament, as He is the focus and hero of the Scriptures.

The third commandment[d] warns us not to use His name in a vain or thoughtless manner. Even more it means that we carry God's name in the world, and we must not live in such a way that we dishonor or blaspheme it. Thus, Leviticus 24:16 commanded that anyone who used it in a blasphemous manner was to be put to death. Worried, people stopped writing or speaking that name. Consequently, when reading the Old Testament Scriptures, Jews did not speak the name Yahweh but replaced it with 'Edonai ("Lord," often transliterated from the Hebrew as "Adonai"). The ancient Hebrew Bible had only consonants, so the name of God was written as YHWH. When your translation has the word "LORD," in all capital letters, you know this is the personal name of God, YHWH.

Sometime between AD 600 and AD 900 the rabbis put dots and dashes around the ancient consonants so people would be able to see the vowels. When they came to the divine name YHWH, they added vowels from 'Edonai. This was transliterated as JeHoWaH. There is nothing wrong with the name Jehovah, but it is not the name God gave Moses and his people.[e]

In light of the unprecedented power, might, and glory of Yahweh, it is also amazing to consider how He chose to reveal Himself to His people in Exodus

---

[a] John 3:35 [b] John 5:20 [c] John 14:31 [d] Ex. 20:7 [e] Ex. 3:14

34:6-7 which is the most quoted passage in the Bible:

The LORD, the LORD, a God merciful and gracious, slow to anger, and abounding in steadfast love and faithfulness, keeping steadfast love for thousands, forgiving iniquity and transgression and sin, but who will by no means clear the guilty.

This description of the entire Trinity is so packed that we must consider each truth it reveals.

1. Yahweh, the Trinitarian God of the Bible, is a person with the name "LORD." In the Old Testament, God's people were surrounded by the Assyrians, Babylonians, Phoenicians, Philistines, and other nations that each had separate gods. These demonic false gods ruled over a people and a place but did not rule over all people and all places as the Lord of the Bible does. The same can be said of the New Testament, wherein God's people were also in a world "full of idols,"[a] and even our own day, when spirituality is popular but very few spiritual people know the Lord who rules over all spirits and spiritualities.

2. Yahweh, the Trinitarian God of the Bible, is a relational Person. He has a name so we can know and speak with Him.

3. Yahweh, the Trinitarian God of the Bible, is compassionate to hurting and suffering people. He sees our lives, knows our frailty, and responds with compassion.

4. Yahweh, the Trinitarian God of the Bible, is helpful. Not only does God rule over us and have compassion on us, but God is also at work for us. Our God is a servant who delights in humbly serving the people He has made; He does so not because He has to but because He longs to, as an outworking of His goodness.

5. Yahweh, the Trinitarian God of the Bible, is slow to anger. Unlike the ancient Greek and Roman gods who are irritable and volatile, the God of the Bible has a long wick and is patient with us.

6. Yahweh, the Trinitarian God of the Bible, is lovingly faithful, shown by the wonderfully powerful Hebrew word *khesed*. It speaks of the constant, passionate, overflowing, relentlessly pursuing, extravagant, limitless, trustworthy, and merciful love of our God. It speaks of His caring provision coming from His magnanimous mercy.

7. Yahweh, the Trinitarian God of the Bible, is dependable and truthful. He never fails and He never lies. As a result, He alone is fully worthy of faith, trust, and devotion, because He alone will always keep his promises.

8. Yahweh, the Trinitarian God of the Bible, is forgiving. God is keenly aware of our sin. Yet, in His loving mercy, He is willing and able to forgive repentant sinners.

---

[a] Acts 17:16

TRINITY: GOD IS

9. Yahweh, the Trinitarian God of the Bible, is just. In the end, no one who lives in sin and rejects his offer of loving relationship through forgiven sin will have any excuse. God is altogether holy and good, and because He is just, He cannot and will not excuse or overlook sin that is not repented of to Him in relationship with Him.

This revelation of God takes on extraordinary depth because the Lord gave it in the context of Israel's horrific betrayal and sin when they worshiped the golden calf.[a] Yahweh, the Trinitarian God of the Bible, is a person who is compassionate, helpful, slow to anger, loving, dependable, forgiving, and just to ill-deserving sinners. He is the one we see in the God-man, Jesus Christ. John tells us He is full of grace and truth.[b] This is an unmistakable allusion to Exodus 34:6-7. John is saying that Jesus Christ is full of Yahweh, come to earth to reveal the Father.

DOES THE TRINITY APPEAR IN THE OLD TESTAMENT?

The opening lines of Scripture reveal God in a most surprising and Trinitarian way:

In the beginning, God created the heavens and the earth. The earth was without form and void, and darkness was over the face of the deep. And the Spirit of God was hovering over the face of the waters.[c]

We see both God the Father and the Spirit of God involved in creation. Just a few verses later, God speaks of Himself with plural pronouns: "Then God said, 'Let us make man in our image, after our likeness.'"[d] This points to some sort of complexity in the unity of God just as in Genesis 1:2 where we see "God" and the "Spirit of God". When you see the Trinitarian understanding of Genesis 1:1-2, everything falls into place as the plural reference is to the godhead.

We also find the three persons referred to in many other Old Testament passages. One of the most important is: "The Spirit of the Lord GOD is upon me, because the LORD has anointed me to bring good news to the poor."[e] We see the "Spirit," the "me" who is anointed (which is Messiah Jesus), and the "LORD" (God the Father). We read that Jesus began His public ministry by reading this passage and identifying himself as the "me" of Isaiah 61:1, saying, "Today this Scripture has been fulfilled in your hearing."[f]

We also see the Trinity in this Old Testament passage:

In all their affliction he [the Father] was afflicted, and the angel of his presence [the Son] saved them; in his love and in his pity he redeemed them; he lifted them up and carried them all the days of old. But they rebelled and grieved his Holy Spirit; therefore he turned to be their enemy, and himself fought against them.[g]

The "angel of the LORD" is another puzzling phenomenon in the Old Testament, but it makes sense when you realize it is coming from a Trinitarian

---

[a] Ex. 32 [b] John 1:14 [c] Gen. 1:1-2 [d] Gen. 1:26 [e] Isa. 61:1 [f] Luke 4:18-21 [g] Isa. 63:9-10

perspective.[a] In Genesis 16 "the angel of the LORD" finds Hagar and speaks to her. Then, in 16:13, Hagar "called the name of the LORD who spoke to her," El Roi, which means, "You are a God of seeing." Is this the LORD (Yahweh) or the angel (which means "messenger") or "word" of the LORD? The conundrum is solved when we realize this is the second person of the Trinity, the eternal Son who became incarnate in Jesus. He came down to comfort and bless Hagar at the spring. She recognized that it was God who had appeared to her in love. In the New Testament, when Jesus comes in the flesh, He again comforts and commands a troubled, non-Hebrew woman by a spring.[b] This was the Samaritan woman, and she, too, recognized that God had appeared to her.

Lastly, the Old Testament reveals in advance the divine Son who will come as the Messiah, God coming to save sinners and crush sin on behalf of God the Father:

- The LORD [Father] says to my Lord [Son]: "Sit at my right hand, until I make your enemies your footstool."[c]
- And now the Lord GOD [Father] has sent me [Son], and his Spirit.[d]
- ...there came one like a son of man [Son], and he came to the Ancient of Days [Father] and was presented before him. And to him was given dominion and glory and a kingdom, that all peoples, nations, and languages should serve him; his dominion is an everlasting dominion, which shall not pass away, and his kingdom one that shall not be destroyed.[2e]

From the beginning of the Bible, we see the Trinity, as well as other key doctrines, appearing in bud form. As the Scriptures continue to reveal God, what is called progressive revelation, the bud opens bit by bit. The Old Testament people of God looked forward to the coming of the Spirit-anointed Son who would reveal the Father more completely. Then they would understand more of this mysterious promise of the one who is God but differs from the Father, who will be anointed by the divine Spirit who is neither Father nor Son.

DOES THE TRINITY APPEAR IN THE NEW TESTAMENT?

The New Testament continues and deepens the revelation of God, living and active in three fully divine persons and we get glimpses into the inner, heavenly life of Father, Son, and Spirit (what theologians call the immanent or ontological Trinity)[3].

Scripture focuses on the historical acts which reveal the Trinity (what

---

[a] See Gen. 22:11, 15; Ex. 3:2; Num. 22:22-35; Judg. 6:11-22; 13:3-21; Zech. 3:1-6 [b] John 4 [c] Ps. 110:1. Gen. 19:24; Ps. 45:6-7; Isa. 48:6-7; Hos. 1:6-7; Zech. 3:2; and Mal. 3:1-2 are some of the other Old Testament passages where two beings are distinguished and both are called Lord or God [d] Isa. 48:16 [e] Dan. 7:13-14

TRINITY: GOD IS

theologians call the economic Trinity). This reveals to us how the Trinity always works in unison as a model of unity and diversity.

The New Testament reveals more of the Trinity doing the work of creation, speaking of the role of the Father[a], Son[b], and Spirit[c].

In the Gospels, the entire Trinity is involved in Mary's conception of Jesus. Luke 1:35 says, "The angel answered her, 'The Holy Spirit will come upon you, and the power of the Most High [Father] will overshadow you; therefore the child to be born will be called holy—the Son of God [Jesus].'"[4]

At the baptism of Jesus, we witness one of the clearest pictures of the Trinity. Matthew 3:16-17 says:

When Jesus was baptized, immediately he went up from the water, and behold, the heavens were opened to him, and he saw the Spirit of God descending like a dove and coming to rest on him; and behold, a voice from heaven said, "This is my [Father] beloved Son, with whom I am well pleased."

All three persons of the Trinity are present, and each one is doing something different: the Father is speaking, and the Son is being anointed and empowered by the Holy Spirit to be the Messiah.

Jesus' Great Commission is also Trinitarian. Matthew 28:19 says, "Go therefore and make disciples of all nations, baptizing them in the name of the Father and of the Son and of the Holy Spirit." Baptism is in one name and three persons, an unmistakably Trinitarian formula. In addition, Acts 1:7-8 says, "He [Jesus] said to them, 'It is not for you to know times or seasons that the Father has fixed by his own authority. But you will receive power when the Holy Spirit has come upon you, and you will be my witnesses...'"

The entire Trinity is also involved in our salvation, but with distinct roles:

- In love he [the Father] predestined us for adoption as sons through Jesus Christ, according to the purpose of his will, to the praise of his glorious grace, with which he has blessed us in the Beloved [Jesus]. In him [Jesus] we have redemption through his blood...In him [Jesus] you also, when you heard the word of truth, the gospel of your salvation, and believed in him [Jesus], were sealed with the promised Holy Spirit.[d]
- ...the foreknowledge of God the Father, in the sanctification of the Spirit, for obedience to Jesus Christ...[e]
- When the goodness and lovingkindness of God our Savior [Father] appeared, he saved us, not because of works done by us in righteousness, but according to his own mercy, by the washing of regeneration and renewal of the Holy Spirit, whom he poured out on us richly through Jesus Christ our Savior.[f]

God the Father planned and predestined our salvation. God the Son came to

---

[a] Acts 17:24; 1 Cor. 8:6 [b] John 1:2; 1 Cor. 8:6; Col. 1:16 [c] Matt. 1:18-20; John 3:5; 1 Cor. 6:11; Titus 3:5; see also Gen. 1:2; Ps. 33:6; 104:30; Isa. 40:12-14 [d] Eph. 1:4-13 [e] 1 Pet. 1:2 [f] Titus 3:4-6

die on the cross in our place for our sins. God the Holy Spirit takes up residence in Christians to regenerate us and ensure our final salvation. The entire Trinity is clearly at work in our salvation.

Furthermore, the entire Trinity is involved in the bestowing of our spiritual gifts for ministry: "Now there are varieties of gifts, but the same Spirit; and there are varieties of service, but the same Lord [Jesus]; and there are varieties of activities, but it is the same God [the Father] who empowers them all in everyone."[a]

When New Testament authors sum things up they often also use Trinitarian formulas:

- The grace of the Lord Jesus Christ and the love of God [the Father] and the fellowship of the Holy Spirit be with you all.[b]
- There is one body and one Spirit—just as you were called to the one hope that belongs to your call—one Lord [Jesus], one faith, one baptism, one God and Father...[c]
- Praying in the Holy Spirit, keep yourselves in the love of God, waiting for the mercy of our Lord Jesus Christ...[d]

Finally, Jesus himself describes the Trinity: "Believe me that I am in the Father and the Father is in me... And I will ask the Father, and he will give you another Helper, to be with you forever, even the Spirit."[e]

WHAT IS THE HISTORY OF THE DOCTRINE OF THE TRINITY?

A Christian is a member of the universal church which includes everyone from every nation, culture, language, and race whose saving faith is in Jesus Christ. A Christian is part of a tremendous family heritage and comes to the Scriptures along with all of God's people from throughout all of the church's history. Despite many differences, Catholic, Orthodox, and Protestant Christians confess together that the God of the Bible is Trinitarian.

The earliest Christians were Jewish believers. They believed that there is only one God, and that this God is Yahweh, the God of Abraham, Isaac, and Jacob. It is important to note that the early Christians continued to affirm their belief in one God. But they also confessed belief in Father, Son, and Spirit. While the Apostles' Creed was not written by the 12 disciples, it is ancient, dating back to the second century. It begins, "I believe in God the Father," continues with "and in the Lord Jesus Christ," and culminates with "I believe in the Holy Spirit."

Tertullian, who converted to Christianity just before AD 200 and defended Christianity prolifically until he died around AD 220, initiated the use of the Latin words *Trinitas*, *persona*, and *substantia* (Trinity, person, and substance or essence) to express the biblical teaching that the Father, Son, and Holy Spirit are one in divine essence but distinguished in relationship as persons within the inner life of

---

[a] 1 Cor. 12:4-6; see also Eph. 4:4-6 [b] 2 Cor. 13:14 [c] Eph. 4:4-6 [d] Jude 20-21
[e] John 14:11, 16-17

TRINITY: GOD IS

God Himself.

Three major ecumenical councils are noteworthy in tracing the development of the doctrine of the Trinity. These gatherings of church leaders discussed major theological issues for the purpose of recognizing what the church did and did not believe. One reason councils were called was to respond to heretical teaching. The Council of Nicaea (AD 325) included some 300 bishops, many of whom bore the scars of persecution, and was convened primarily to resolve the debate over Arianism, the false teaching that Christ was a creature, an angel who was the highest created being, but not God. The Council of Nicaea concluded that the Son was one substance (*homoousios*) with the Father. The Logos, who was incarnate in Jesus of Nazareth, is God Himself. He is not like God but is fully and eternally God.

The confirming of Christ's deity at the Council of Constantinople (AD 381) extended the discussion to the identification of the Holy Spirit within the Godhead. Constantinople expanded the Nicene Creed, making the creed fully Trinitarian, and officially condemned Arianism. It also solidified the orthodox doctrine of the full humanity of Jesus Christ. The Council of Chalcedon (AD 451) focused on the relationship of Christ's humanity to his divinity (known as hypostatic union) and issued the formula of Chalcedon, which became the orthodox statement on the person of Christ. Hypostatic union means that Jesus is one person with two natures and therefore simultaneously fully God and fully human.

The contributions of the councils to the doctrine of the Trinity can be summarized under four headings:

1. One Being, Three Persons. God is one being and has one essence. There is no God but the triune God who exists eternally in three distinct persons: Father, Son, and Holy Spirit. The whole God is in each person, and each person is the whole God. Threeness of person is not just a matter of action or revelation but of eternal being.

2. Consubstantiality. One identical divine substance is shared completely by the Father, Son, and Holy Spirit. Any essential characteristic that belongs to one of the three is shared by the others. Each of the three divine persons is eternal, each almighty, none greater or less than another, each God, and yet together being but one God.

3. Perichoresis. There is a loving interrelation, partnership, or mutual dependence of the three persons (also called circumincession or interpenetration). Some define this in terms of dance, leading to all sorts of strange speculations. But this is a mistake that comes from a misunderstanding of Greek language. Dance looks the same in its transliteration but is spelled differently in Greek. Since all three persons are fully God and the whole God is in each of the three, it follows that the three mutually indwell or contain one another, as Jesus said: "Just as you, Father, are in me, and I in

you."[a] This oneness of indwelling is not just in their functioning in this world but even more foundationally in their eternal existence as Trinity.
4. The Order of the Persons. There is a clear order of the relations between the three fully divine persons: from the Father through the Son by the Holy Spirit.

As the doctrine of the Trinity developed, theologians struggled to explain the eternal relationships of the Trinity. What differentiates Father from Son from Spirit? Using philosophical methodology, they worked backward from God's economic working in the world to define His eternal relationships. The Bible says the Father sent the Spirit to conceive Jesus in the womb of Mary.[b] Jesus is therefore referred to as the "only begotten [*monogenes*] Son."[c]

Theologians extended this begetting in history back into the eternity of the Trinity and posited that the Son is eternally begotten of or generated by the Father. Similarly, they went from Jesus' historical promise to His disciples, "I will send to you from the Father, the Spirit of truth, who proceeds from the Father,"[d] to posit that the Spirit eternally proceeds from the Father. Thus, the Nicene Creed (325) defined the Son as "begotten of the Father." The First Council of Constantinople (381) added that the Holy Spirit "proceeds from the Father." This formulation was confirmed at the Council of Chalcedon (451).

Theologians of the Western church often extended the procession phrase to read that the Holy Spirit "proceeds from the Father and the Son [*filioque*]." This revision of the Nicene Creed was made at the Third Council of Toledo (589) and was officially endorsed in 1017. This insertion of a single Latin word to an ecumenical creed caused a crisis of authority that eventually led to the split between the Eastern Orthodox churches and the Western Roman church in 1054. The subtle theological points were far less responsible for the split than the ecclesiastical power struggle over the authority of the pope much like a burned dinner is followed by a divorce where the meal is not entirely to blame.

The attempt to define the past eternal relations in the immanent or ontological Trinity seems like straining to bring certainty out of a mystery. First, God has given us no revelation of the nature of their eternal relations. We should follow the command of the Bible: "The secret things belong to the LORD our God"[e] and refuse to speculate. Second, the Apostles' Creed defines the Son as "begotten, not made." The point was that something begotten was of the same substance as the one who does the begetting. But the term "begotten" could never be defined with any clarity, so it was of little use. Third, begotten unavoidably implies a beginning of the one begotten. That would tragically lend support to the Arian heresy that the Son is a created being and not the Creator God. For these reasons, we omit the creedal terms "begotten" and "proceeds" from our definition of Trinity. We appreciate the creeds but keep Scripture above them in authority.

---

[a] John 17:21 [b] Luke 1:31–35; Matt. 1:20 [c] John 1:14, 18; 3:16, 18; Acts 13:33; Heb. 1:5; 5:5; 1 John 4:9; 5:1 [d] John 15:26 [e] Deut. 29:29

TRINITY: GOD IS

To summarize, we stand with the universal Trinitarian definition of the church to confess that God is one God, eternally existing in three persons - Father, Son, and the Holy Spirit.

WHY SHOULD WE STUDY THE DOCTRINE OF THE TRINITY?

Many Christians find the doctrine of the Trinity difficult to understand. Yet, Jesus himself urges us to love God with both our heart and mind which means that deep worship sometimes requires deep thinking in addition to deep feeling.[a]

J.I. Packer says: "The historic formulation of the Trinity...seeks to circumscribe and safeguard this mystery (not explain it; that is beyond us), and it confronts us with perhaps the most difficult thought that the human mind has ever been asked to handle. It is not easy; but it is true."[5] Practically speaking, studying the Trinity helps believers appreciate their great salvation, which is frequently described in Paul's writings as the work of the triune God.[6]

As we grow to more deeply understand the saving plan of God the Father, the sacrifice of Jesus Christ, and the sealing of the Holy Spirit, we become more intimately thankful to each member of the Trinity for their work for us, in us, and through us. Christians should study the doctrine of the Trinity because God has given the church a great blessing in truthfully revealing something so glorious about Himself; namely, He is triune. If He reveals this to us, He must consider it important and valuable for our relationship.

To have a real relationship, both parties need to be both known and loved. The same is true of our relationship with God. The Trinitarian God loves us deeply and allows Himself to be known so that we can respond by loving Him. Not only is the Trinity relational, but they also want us to love God and others so that the life of the Trinity flows into all of our relationships. This point cannot be overstated. For too long people have struggled with their relationships and found theology to be the boring pursuit of academics arguing over impractical things that often don't matter much. True biblical theology is the study of our loving and relational God for the purpose of cultivating our love and relational health with Himself and others. When theology is removed from relationships, it drifts from its Trinitarian purpose. When the New Testament repeatedly exhorts "sound" doctrine, that word for sound means to be healthy as the point of knowing God is to become healthy through a loving relationship with God and then having healthy loving relationships with others.[b] Simply put, to be biblical, you must be relational.

Sinclair Ferguson keenly points out in John 13-17 that it is before Jesus goes to the cross that He has the most to say to His disciples about the Trinity and His relationship to the Father and to the Spirit.[7] Christ's final words to his disciples before going to the cross were to explain, in part, the doctrine of the Trinity. Since the doctrine of the Trinity was so important for Jesus to stress at such a

---

[a] Matt. 22:37; Mark 12:30; Luke 10:27 [b] 1 Tim. 1:10, 6:3; Titus 1:9, 2:1

pivotal moment in history, we are right to assume that it is also imperative for us to understand the person and work of the entire Trinity.

We are further blessed when we study the Trinity because we then learn how the cross enables believers to share the unity and love that exist eternally between the Father and the Son[a], and how the cross, resurrection, and ascension of Christ bring to us the full power and knowledge of the Holy Spirit so that we are invited into new life with the Trinity.[b]

WHAT ARE THE MAJOR DOCTRINAL ERRORS REGARDING THE TRINITY?

Many heresies have arisen throughout the history of the church that deny the basic assertions of the doctrine of the Trinity, which are these:
1. God is three persons.
2. Each person is fully God.
3. There is one God.[8]

Like a game of tug-of-war, the tendency is for either the three-ness or the oneness of God to be overly stressed at the expense of the other, resulting in heretical false teaching.

The three main heresies that contradict the doctrine of the Trinity are modalism (the persons are ways God expresses himself, as in Oneness or Jesus Only theology), Arianism (the Son is a creature and not divine, as with Jehovah's Witnesses), and tritheism (there are three distinct gods, as in Mormonism and Hinduism).

Admittedly, the doctrine of the Trinity is complicated. Therefore, the only way to accurately discern what a professing Christian believes about the Trinity is to talk with people directly and hear what they actually believe. We must not fall into the heritage of Christian fundamentalism and condemn people based on secondhand reports or their associations. As an example, controversy erupted when I spent some hours, including a public conversation, on the Trinity with Bishop T.D. Jakes some years ago. Perhaps the world's most famous living pastor, he graciously explained how, as a newer Christian, he was taught by pastors who did not believe in the Trinity, but after years of studying the Bible, his views had changed. People learn as they grow and although the doctrine of the Trinity is an essential Christian doctrine that I preach at The Trinity Church where I pastor, we need to not rush to judgment of others without first understanding both what the Trinity is and what someone actually believes. However, if any of the following counterfeits are held, they need to be identified as error.

---

[a] John 17:11, 22–26 [b] John 14:16–17, 26; 15:26; 16:13

TRINITY: GOD IS

Modalism

Modalism teaches that God is successively Father, Son, and Holy Spirit; he is not simultaneously Father, Son, and Holy Spirit. Modalism is a heresy that does not view the Father, Son, and Holy Spirit as three particular persons in relation but merely as three modes or manifestations of the one divine person of God. It is said, God revealed Himself successively in salvation history, first as Father (creator and lawgiver), then as Son (redeemer), and finally as Spirit (sustainer and giver of grace).

For a modalist, the God of the Old Testament is manifested as the Father. In the incarnation, God was manifested in Jesus. Then, after the resurrection and ascension of Christ, God came in the mode of the Holy Spirit. However, the baptism of Jesus and Jesus' prayer in the garden of Gethsemane reveal clearly that the three persons converse with each other simultaneously.

Some heretical groups adopt a "Jesus only" formula for baptism and thus what they refer to as one-ness theology. They affirm both that their God is one and that Jesus is fully God. But they deny that there are three divine persons. The United Pentecostal Church is the largest one-ness group in America. They officially deny the doctrine of the Trinity, saying:

In distinction to the doctrine of the Trinity, the UPCI holds to a oneness view of God. It views the Trinitarian concept of God, that of God eternally existing as three distinctive persons, as inadequate and a departure from the consistent and emphatic biblical revelation of God being one...Thus God is manifested as Father in creation and as the Father of the Son, in the Son for our redemption, and as the Holy Spirit in our regeneration.[9]

In other words, the Son of God is the manifestation of the Father in the flesh. The Son is not eternal, nor pre-existent. Jesus is the Father and the Son: Father in His divinity and Son in His humanity. Hence, the Trinity is wrongly said to be a misunderstanding of the biblical teaching.

Arianism

In Arianism (based upon the teaching of Arius), the central characteristic of Arian thought was that because God is one, Jesus could not have also been truly God. In order to deal with the scriptural testimony to the exalted status of Christ, Arius and his followers proposed that Jesus was the highest created being of God. So, although Christ was fully human, he was not fully God. Arius' teaching was condemned as heretical at the Council of Nicaea in AD 325.[10]

Arianism is the official teaching of the Jehovah's Witnesses cult, which was founded in 1881 by Charles Taze Russell. They teach that there is no biblical basis for the doctrine of the Trinity. They teach that there is one solitary divine being from all eternity. This divine being is Jehovah God, the creator and preserver of the universe and all things. Jehovah's Witnesses essentially believe what Arius taught in the third century; namely, that Christ is not God but rather God's first created creature. Thus, for them, Jesus is the Old Testament archangel Michael.

Neither is the Spirit divine but rather more of a cosmic force of Jehovah.

Tritheism

Tritheism teaches that the Trinity consists of three equal, independent, and autonomous beings, each of whom is divine. Tritheism stresses the plurality of the Godhead. Many human analogies for the Trinity actually convey tritheism instead. Examples include the erroneous analogy that the Trinity is like an egg with the three parts of yolk, white, and shell.

Mormonism believes that the Trinity is three separate gods; the Father is an exalted man who became a god, Jesus is the first spirit-child between God the Father and His wife, and the Holy Spirit is another spirit-child of the Father and His wife. They teach that none of the three persons of the Trinity are eternal or almighty God. The Son and the Spirit are not truly equal with the Father since they are His spirit-children. They also say there are many gods of many worlds. These three are just the gods of this world, the gods we relate to.

One theologian has refuted these three main heresies well:

The doctrine of the Trinity does not on the one hand assert that three persons are united in one person, or that three beings in one being, or that three Gods in one God (tri-theism); nor on the other hand that God merely manifests Himself in three different ways (modalism); but rather that there are three eternal [personal] distinctions in the substance of God.[11]

Alarmingly, every generation has some who fall into the same errors that have surrounded the doctrine of the Trinity throughout the church's history. These people are prone to question, if not renounce, the doctrine of the Trinity. It is important for each generation of Christians, particularly Christian leaders, to be able to lovingly and winsomely define and defend the doctrine of the Trinity because no less is at stake than the issue of who God is.

WHAT ARE THE PRACTICAL IMPLICATIONS OF THE TRINITY?

Indeed, while that which is hypothetical, theoretical, and philosophical may be interesting to a few people, only that which is practical is of service to all people. Subsequently, we have chosen to close this chapter with some practical implications of the doctrine of the Trinity.

First, Trinitarian life is humble. The doctrine of the Trinity is so complex and wonderfully mysterious that it humbles us. While God can be known truly, he cannot be known fully. This forces us to be humble in our understanding of God and establishes a precedent in our thinking to allow room for mystery, as we indeed see and know in part, as Scripture states.[a]

Second, Trinitarian life is loving. When 1 John 4:7 says, "Love is from God," it is revealing that love emanates from the Trinitarian community of God. Trinitarian

---

[a] 1 Cor. 13:12

TRINITY: GOD IS

love includes love for God, family, friend, neighbor, stranger, and even enemy. This is because, even though we were enemies of God, estranged by sin, Jesus came to be our neighbor, loved us as a friend, died for our sins to make us family, and shared with us God's love.

Third, Trinitarian life is worshipful. We are to live all of our life to the Father, through the Son, by the power of the Spirit.

Fourth, Trinitarian life is relational. John 1:1 says, "In the beginning was the Word [Jesus], and the Word was with God [Father], and the Word was God." In the original Greek, John is saying that God the Father and God the Son were proverbially face-to-face in eternity past. This is the language of friendship, which compels us to live face-to-face with others in companionship and relationship. This is why Christians practice hospitality to strangers and why we participate in the life of a local church as we live face-to-face with their spouses and children. All of this is to practice for the day when, as Paul says, we too will see Jesus "face to face."[a]

Fifth, Trinitarian life is unified and diverse like a healthy family. Greek Christian theologians are fond of describing the Trinity with the term perichoresis. As the three persons of the Trinity are mutually indwelling, or permeating one another, we are deeply connected as God's human family, yet we retain our own identity. The term Christian is a bit like a last name that reveals the connection between all family members.

Sixth, Trinitarian life is submissive. As we hear Jesus teaching us to pray, "Your will be done,"[b] and Himself praying, "Not my will, but yours, be done,"[c] while sweating like drops of blood from anxiety caused by His looming his crucifixion, we learn to submit ourselves to the will of the Father by the Spirit like the Son.

Seventh, Trinitarian life is joyful. Tim Keller explains:

To glorify something or someone is to praise, enjoy, and delight in them. When something is useful you are attracted to it for what it can bring you or do for you. But if it is beautiful, then you enjoy it simply for what it is. Just being in its presence is its own reward. To glorify someone is also to serve or defer to him or her. Instead of sacrificing their interests to make yourself happy, you sacrifice your interests to make them happy. Why? Your ultimate joy is to see them in joy.[12]

What Keller is rightly saying is that the Trinity is the place of the greatest joy that has ever been or ever will be; each member delights in the others and pours Himself out continuously for the good of the others in unparalleled joyful healthy relationship. Indeed, another synonym for the Trinity is Happy.

The God of the Bible is in Himself eternally personal, emotional, and relational. Some religions teach that God made people to cure his loneliness; conversely, the fact is that God as a Trinitarian community was never without loving community. Rather, He is a relational God who welcomes us into relationship with Himself.

In closing, the Trinity is not a doctrine to be philosophized beyond the teachings of Scripture but rather a humble, loving, worshipful, relational, diverse,

---

[a] Ibid. [b] Matt. 6:10 [c] Luke 22:42

submissive, and joyful life to be entered into by the Spirit through the Son to the Father.

God is good. God made you. God made this world as a home for you to live in and have a loving and life-giving relationship with Him, the rest of His earthly family of human beings, along with His spiritual family of spirit beings.

This is why we are starving for refreshing relationships. We want someone to love us and that we can love, someone who we can trust and can trust us, we want someone to speak with and hear from. What we really need is a Someone. Your relationship with God is supposed to be your first priority, source of healthy living, and model for all your other relationships. Your relational needs are God-sized. Even a good friend is a bad God. There is no relationship with anyone that can replace your relationship with God. If you follow the deepest longings of your soul, they will lead you back to the God who made you for a relationship with Him.

Admittedly, the doctrine of the Trinity is complex to comprehend. Sadly, various analogies have been used to try and explain the Trinity in physical terms such as water, ice, and mist. The problem with these kinds of analogies is that they are physical and not relational. Perhaps the best way to consider how God can be three persons but one is to consider that, in the covenant of marriage, a husband and wife, though two distinct persons, are supposed to be "one".[a] In fact, the same Hebrew word *echad* used for the husband and wife is also referred to as the Trinitarian God of the Bible in the refrain which ancient Jewish believers said three times a day, "The Lord, our God, the Lord is one."[b] You were made from relationship, made for relationship, and are made by relationship which explains why God speaks to us as we will study next.

QUESTIONS FOR PERSONAL JOURNALING AND/OR SMALL GROUP DISCUSSION

1. Besides the Lord, who would you consider the most faithful person in your life? How can you thank them today?
2. Which member of the Trinity are you most familiar with? Which member(s) of the Trinity are you least familiar with? What could you do to become equally familiar with all three?
3. When you think about God, what are the most common characteristics that come to mind? Spend a few moments thinking of practical ways that God has shown His love to you.
4. Take a few moments in prayer and thank God the Father, God the Son, and God the Spirit each for something unique they have done for you.
5. Is there someone who first taught you about the Trinity, or perhaps helped

---

[a] Gen. 2:24 [b] Deut. 6:4

you best understand that doctrine? Is there any way you could thank them today for serving you in that way?
6. As you face the day before you, take a moment to invite the Holy Spirit to empower you so that you can live a life like Jesus to the glory of God the Father. This will help you behave godly and wise even in the midst of trial or tragedy.
7. Do you believe any heresies regarding the Trinity? Is there anyone you know who believes any heresies regarding the Trinity? In addition to praying for them, is there anything you can do to help them come to believe the truth about the Trinity?
8. Since God is relational and made us for relationships, take some time today to pray for the people closest to you and encourage them by thanking them.

CHAPTER 2: REVELATION
"GOD SPEAKS"

So also no one comprehends the thoughts of God except the Spirit of God. Now we have received not the spirit of the world, but the Spirit who is from God, that we might understand the things freely given us by God.
1 CORINTHIANS 2:11a –12

As a boy, I was raised in a Catholic Church. Rather than carrying a Bible to church, most everyone just picked up the books that were in each pew containing some Scripture readings, prayers, and songs. These books were left at the church building, and so my assumption as a child was that those things were for church, but not for the rest of life outside the church.

At home, our family had an enormous Bible that sat on our coffee table, but it was large enough to serve as its own coffee table. On the front was a picture of Jesus with long beautiful hair wearing a white dress and sensible sandals and, if memory serves me correct, hanging out with sheep. Despite seeing that Bible every day, I never remembering opening it as the Jesus on the cover was, frankly, not a depiction of any man I wanted to follow or become like. I assumed I knew the gist of what the Bible said – be a good person and you will be fine and go to Heaven – so I did not feel any urge to dig deeper.

In high school, I considered myself to be a moral young man who did believe in God but did next to nothing to grow spiritually other than uttering a rote memorized prayer when I felt bad to lift some of my guilt. Things started to change when I met a pastor's daughter. We became friends, and she was quickly my most favorite person. Since our first date on March 12, 1988, I am happy to report that she remains my favorite person on the planet.

DOCTRINE

Grace bought me a really nice Bible as a graduation present. It had a genuine leather cover with my name embossed on it. Some months later in college at a state university, seemingly every professor and class referenced the Bible, Jesus, and Christianity – negatively. Out of curiosity, I started reading the Bible. In all honesty, I disagreed with a lot of what I read. The good religious folks like me were the bad guys who killed Jesus. Furthermore, considering myself a good person, the thought that all people were sinners, not essentially good, and could only be saved from Hell by God's help was offensive. The rules against things like sex outside of marriage also seemed like boring, outdated rules that we'd moved past.

Like many people, I did not know the Bible but assumed I knew the gist. Reading it for myself, I did not agree with much of it. Eventually, I concluded that my real problem with the Bible was one of authority. Since the Bible and I disagreed on a lot of things, one of us would need to change. Kind of like the kids' game "chicken" where two kids run at each other to see who is the bravest, the chicken is the one who jumps out of the way at the last moment to avoid the collision. I was in a game of chicken with the Bible. Either I would try and ignore it or edit it in an effort to move it out of my way. Or I would be the one to change position, move, and let the Bible have authority to determine my life course.

Eventually, I was the proverbial chicken. I concluded the Bible was right, and when I disagreed, I was wrong. I accepted the Bible as perfect revelation from God and that I had no right to change it, as its' purpose was to change me. Since that decision, every day of my life I have been devoted to studying and teaching the Bible not as a word about God from people, but rather the Word of God that is from God and for people. In the remainder of this chapter, it is our hope to help you understand the concept of divine revelation in general, and the Bible in particular.

WHAT IS REVELATION?

People have a seemingly insatiable appetite for information and communication. From cell phones to televisions, e-mail, radios, smart phones, Websites, blogs, social media, meetings, online video chats, books, magazines, newspapers, movies, songs, text-messages, face-to-face conversations, etc., people want to know and be known. Why? Our God communicates, as Genesis 1 tells us no less than ten times, "God said" and made us in His likeness to communicate with Him and each other.

In our deluge of data, the daunting question is, how do we hear the voice of God? Does God speak internally through our spirit? Does God speak externally through a holy man such as a guru or prophet? Does God speak through ancient wisdom or collected tradition? Or perhaps, God does not speak at all because God is not a person but a mute force, distant and disinterested in us?

Core to Christianity is the belief that God speaks through revelation, teaching us perhaps the two most important things we can learn: 1) who God is and 2) who we are. The opposite of divine revelation from God is human speculation about God. As we receive and believe God's revelation by faith, the power and presence of God are unleashed to transform us to become more like Jesus Christ. Revelation culminates in mission to tell the world about God in the same way that someone who has fallen deeply in love cannot stop talking about the person they enjoy and introducing him or her to everyone they know.

HOW DOES GOD REVEAL HIMSELF?

When talking with someone, generally the best way to understand what they are saying is to see their face and hear their words. This is because people communicate meaning in multiple ways at once. In the same way, God communicates to us in two ways all the time. These are called general revelation and special revelation.

General Revelation
God reveals Himself to everyone everywhere through general revelation. General revelation includes creation, common grace, providence, and conscience.

Concerning creation, Psalm 19:1,4 says, "The heavens declare the glory of God, and the sky above proclaims his handiwork...Their voice goes out through all the earth, and their words to the end of the world." Isaiah 6:3 proclaims, "The whole earth is full of his glory!" Romans 1:19-20 adds, "For what can be known about God is plain to them, because God has shown it to them. For his invisible attributes, namely, his eternal power and divine nature, have been clearly perceived, ever since the creation of the world, in the things that have been made." Through creation—the heavens and earth, flower and fly, galaxy and quark—God has made Himself and his power, love, and glory known. People everywhere see His wisdom, majesty, power and divine nature, justice, and goodness.[a]

Among the most awe-inspiring aspects of creation is the human body. Every doctor, mother who births a child, grandparent who holds a grandchild, and person reading this with eyes God made sending data to the brain God designed should be brought to worshipful wonder. Psalm 8:3-4 says, "When I look at your heavens, the work of your fingers, the moon and the stars, which you have set in place, what is man that you are mindful of him, and the son of man that you care for him?"

Regarding common grace, among the first to use the term was Augustine (AD 354-430) because it is for everyone and therefore common to all human beings. Through common grace, God reveals His love to all people, though not in a saving way. God's common grace includes the water we drink, food we eat, sun we

---
[a] Psalm 104; Ps. 8:1; Rom. 1:20; Rom. 2:14-15; Acts 14:17

enjoy, and rain we need, as God is good to the sinner and saint alike.[a]

God's common grace allows even those who despise him to learn and make gains in science, philosophy, technology, education, medicine, etc. God's common grace allows societies to flourish, families to exist, cities to rise up, and nations to prosper.[b] Common grace also allows people who are not connected to God to live decent, moral lives as Good Samaritan(s), though their deeds are not in any way done to God's glory as acts of worship. The result of God's common grace is that life is far better than would otherwise be possible if sinners were simply left to themselves. Everyone experiences the grace of God to varying degrees, no matter how sinful they are, because God is loving, good and is determined to do good in love. Anyone who has laughed, held a baby, enjoyed the warmth of the sun on their face, gone for a swim, eaten a good meal, or watched a sunset has enjoyed a measure of God's common grace.

Externally, God's common grace is experienced in providence and miracle. God is good, sovereign, and the good things we enjoy in our life are from Him. Just as you get work done with two hands, consider God as metaphorically also working with two hands. On one hand, God works through miracles that are visible revelations of His person and power. Many people have God show up supernaturally in their lives at some point – something often not understood until we have been saved and look back in faith.

On the other hand, God works through providence that are invisible revelations of His person and power. Some people wrongly attribute the cause of God's providence to luck, fate, chance, or karma. The truth is, God is at work in the lives of people who do not know it and do not know Him. Acts 14:17 says, "he did not leave himself without witness, for he did good by giving you rains from heaven and fruitful seasons, satisfying your hearts with food and gladness."

Internally, God also reveals Himself generally through the conscience He gave us. Most everyone knows it is wrong to murder, lie, and commit adultery, because God has written His morality on human hearts.[c] Additionally, God the Holy Spirit convicts the whole world of sin, righteousness, and judgment.[d] Even sinners know to give good gifts to their children because God created us as His image bearers with a conscience that serves as a moral compass.[e] While some people ignore or break their conscience, the fact that others see their violation of what is right and good serves only to reinforce the fact that through the conscience God has revealed Himself as holy and just. Additionally, people innately appeal to conscience every time they want justice or decry something as wrong or unfair.

Positively, general revelation means that all people know God in a general way. As a result, Romans 1 says that those who "suppress" the truth of God made known through general revelation are "without excuse"; subsequently, their

---

[a] Ps. 65:9; 104:14; Matt. 5:45 [b] E.g., Ex. 31:2-11; 35:30-35 [c] Rom. 2:14-15 [d] John 16:8-11 [e] Matt. 7:11

damnation is deserved.[a] His goodness and kindness shown to all should lead people to repentance of sin and relationship with Him.[b] Those who follow the truth path of general revelation can enjoy further special revelation about God that can lead to eternal life.[c] Innumerable examples could be given, but some include God bringing missionaries to an unreached people group open to the gospel, God sending dreams and visions of Jesus to Muslims in countries otherwise closed to the gospel, and even sending an angel to communicate the gospel of Jesus Christ. In short, we trust the goodness of our sovereign God to deal justly with all people and find creative ways to reveal Himself to them.

Special Revelation

For anyone to have a saving knowledge of God requires that, in addition to general revelation, they also must receive and believe special revelation. While general revelation is good and true, it is not sufficient for someone to know that God became a man and died on a cross in our place for our sins.

Christians have always believed that God is real, personal, and relational. We believe it is only by God's gracious self-revelation that anyone comes to know him. God revealed Himself supremely through the incarnation, where the second person of the Trinity humbly entered into human history as the God-man Jesus Christ. During His earthly ministry, Jesus was led and empowered by the third member of the Trinity, God the Holy Spirit. That same Holy Spirit also inspired the writing of the Holy Bible to speak to us about Jesus Christ and regenerate Christians to receive special revelation from the Bible about Jesus.

God continues to reveal Himself today, primarily through the divinely inspired, inerrant, and authoritative Bible. The Bible is uniquely and solely God's completely trustworthy revelation to us today. Scripture is the court of highest authority for Christians and their leaders, by which any alleged revelation from God is to be tested.

Christian belief stands or falls with the Bible. New Testament scholar Darrell Bock puts it like this in an interview I conducted with him:

You can't talk about Christianity without the Scripture. If you take Scripture away, you won't have much left. Although you might have a belief in God and might know a little bit about who Jesus is, you wouldn't know very much. That's a starting point and a reference point for all of us. Not that we're worshiping the Book, but we're engaged with the concepts that put us in proper relationship to God.[1]

Because the Bible is so central to what Christians believe, at some point each of us has to settle what we think about the Book. Most disagreements between Christians and non-Christians come down to whether or not we think the Bible is true. A non-Christian might consider a few parts of the Bible curious. They might

---

[a] Rom. 1:18–32; 2:5–6, 8–9; John 3:19 [b] Rom. 2:4 [c] Acts 10:1–7; Rom. 2:7, 10; 10:15–18

write some of its words on a sticky note for inspiration. They accept some points but not others. They approach the Bible like a salad bar: "I'll take that, I'll leave that, I'll take that, I'll leave that." But for Christians, the Bible is fully true. It is not a salad bar. It is a boxed lunch—take it or leave it.

When Christians make enormous claims about the Bible, they are in fact simply restating what the Bible says about itself. The Bible asserts that God authored the entire book down to every word. It also claims God did this through human authors. These authors retained their own style, voice, perspective, and cultural distinctives, yet God uniquely inspired them to write down what He wanted recorded with complete accuracy. This is different from the Koran or Book of Mormon, for example, which adherents of Islam and Mormonism claim were the result of someone taking dictation. This makes the Bible unique from, superior to, and in authority over everyone and everything else on the earth, because when the Bible speaks, God speaks.[2]

WHAT ARE THE SCRIPTURES?

Scripture is God speaking his truth to us in human words. The New Testament writers claim that the Old Testament is sacred Scripture, which literally means "writing."[a] The word Bible comes from the Greek word for book. Holy Bible means "Holy Book." It was written in three languages (Hebrew, Greek, and a bit in Aramaic) over a period of more than fifteen hundred years by roughly forty authors (of varying ages and backgrounds) on three continents (Asia, Africa, and Europe).

The Protestant Canon of the Bible contains 66 separate books. 39 books, approximately three-quarters of the Bible, are in the Old Testament, which is a record of God's speaking and working in history from when he created Adam and Eve, up until about 450 BC. In the period between the two testaments, people waited for the coming of the Messiah into human history. The 27 books of the New Testament begin with the four Gospels, which record the life, death, burial, resurrection, and return to Heaven of Jesus, and then proceed to instruct Christians and churches about how to think and live for God.

The Bible is a library of books compiled as one Book, showing a divine unity and continuity. This point is illustrated by the fact that the New Testament has roughly 300 explicit Old Testament quotations, as well as upwards of 4,000 allusions to the Old Testament. In many ways, the Old Testament is a series of promises that God makes, and the New Testament is the record of their fulfillment, and the anticipation of the final fulfillment of the remaining promises at Jesus' Second Coming.

---
[a] Matt. 21:42; 22:29; 26:54, 56; Luke 24:25–32, 44–45; John 5:39; 10:35; Acts 17:2, 11; 18:28; Rom.1:2; 4:3; 9:17; 10:11; 11:2; 15:4; 16:26; 1 Cor. 15:3–4; Gal. 3:8, 22; 4:30; 1 Tim. 5:18; 2 Tim. 3:16; James 4:5; 2 Pet. 1:20–21; 3:15–16

REVELATION: GOD SPEAKS

The Bible is the best-selling book of all time. The Old Testament was originally written on papyrus—a form of paper made out of reeds. By the time the New Testament was written, parchments (prepared animal skins) were also used.[a] The pages were put together into scrolls.[b]

Chapters and verses were added to provide addresses (not unlike those on our homes) that help us find particular sections. In 1205, Stephen Langton, a theology professor who became the archbishop of Canterbury, began using Bible chapters. In 1240, Cardinal Hugo of St. Cher published a Latin Bible with the 1,189 chapter divisions that exist today. Robert Stephanus, a Protestant book printer, was condemned as a heretic for printing Bibles. As he fled with his family to Geneva on horseback, he arbitrarily made verse divisions within Langton's chapter divisions. His system was used for the first English Bible (The Geneva New Testament of 1557) and became today's system of 31,173 verses. The Bible's chapters and verses were not applied with any consistent method and, while helpful, they are not authoritative. Because the Bible was not intended to be read in bits and pieces, reading verses out of context can lead to serious misunderstanding. Thus, rightly interpreting particular sections of Scripture requires paying attention both to the immediate context and the overall context of all of Scripture.

HOW IS JESUS THE HERO OF THE BIBLE?

The opening line of Scripture introduces us to its Hero, God, who is revealed throughout the rest of the pages of Scripture. In the closing line of the New Testament, we are reminded that our hope is in "The grace of the Lord Jesus". Thus, the written Word of God reveals to us the incarnate ("in human flesh") Word of God, Jesus Christ. Without the written Word, we cannot rightly know the incarnate Word.

The Old and New Testament are about Jesus Christ – anyone can read the Bible, but only someone who reads it in the Spirit comes to this rightful conclusion. Some prefer the New Testament to the Old Testament because they wrongly believe that only the New Testament is about Jesus. However, Jesus Himself taught that the Old Testament was primarily about Him while arguing with the theologians in his day. In John 5:39-40 Jesus says, "You search the Scriptures [Old Testament] because you think that in them you have eternal life; and it is they that bear witness about me, yet you refuse to come to me that you may have life." The Bible is not just principles to live by, but a Person to live with.

Following His resurrection, Jesus opened the Old Testament to teach about Himself: "Beginning with Moses and all the Prophets, he interpreted to them in all the Scriptures the things concerning himself."[c] Likewise, in speaking to his disciples, Jesus said, "These are my words that I spoke to you while I was still with you, that

---

[a] 2 Tim. 4:13 [b] Ezra 6:2; Ps. 40:7; Luke 4:17, 20 [c] Luke 24:27

DOCTRINE

everything written about me in the Law of Moses and the Prophets and the Psalms must be fulfilled."[a] We then read that he "opened their minds to understand the Scriptures."[b] Jesus' own words about Himself as the central message of the Old Testament are pointedly clear. He said in Matthew 5:17-18, "Do not think that I have come to abolish the Law or the Prophets; I have not come to abolish them but to fulfill them. For truly, I say to you, until heaven and earth pass away, not an iota, not a dot, will pass from the Law until all is accomplished." Jesus repeated this fact throughout his ministry by saying he "fulfilled" particular Scriptures.[c] To correctly interpret Scripture, you will need to connect its verses, concepts, and events to Jesus.

The Old Testament predicts the coming of Jesus in a variety of ways to prepare people. The New Testament reflects back on the life of Jesus, particularly in the four Gospels, and reports the results of Jesus' life and ministry, particularly in the Epistles.

The Old Testament uses various means to reveal Jesus, including promises, appearances, foreshadowing types, and titles. First, the Old Testament teaches about Jesus in the numerous prophetic promises given about him. More than one-quarter of the Old Testament was prophetic in nature, promising future events. No other world religion or cult can present any specific prophecies concerning the coming of their prophets. However, in the Old Testament, we see hundreds of fulfilled prophecies extending hundreds and sometimes over a thousand years into the future, showing God's foreknowledge of and sovereignty over the future.

Second, the Old Testament teaches about Jesus through appearances that He makes before His birth, also called Christophanies. Examples include walking with Abraham, wrestling with Jacob, appearing to Moses, joining Shadrach, Meshach, and Abednego in the fiery furnace, and calling Isaiah into ministry.[d] Other examples may include "the angel [messenger] of the LORD," who is sometimes identified as God.[e] This angel provided the sacrifice in Isaac's place and spoke and journeyed with Moses.[f]

Third, types are Old Testament representative figures, institutions, or events that foreshadow Jesus. Examples include Adam, who foreshadows Jesus the second Adam; the priesthood, prefiguring Jesus as our high priest; David and other kings, prefiguring Jesus as the King of kings; Moses and the prophets, prefiguring Jesus as our ultimate prophet; animal sacrifices, prefiguring Jesus as the sinless Lamb of God slain for our sins; the temple, prefiguring God's presence dwelling among us in Jesus; shepherds reminding us sheep that Jesus is our Good Shepherd; judges, foreshadowing Jesus as the final judge of all people; and many others, such as Jesus the true bread, true vine, and true light.

---

[a] Luke 24:44 [b] Luke 24:45 [c] E.g., Matt. 26:56; Luke 4:20-21; 22:37 [d] Gen. 18; cf. John 8:56; Gen. 32:30; Ex. 3:2-6; cf. John 8:58; Dan. 3:24-25; Isa. 6:1-5; cf. John 12:41 [e] Judg. 6:11-21; 13:22 [f] Gen. 22:9-14; Ex. 3:14; 23:20-21; cf. John 8:56-59

We also see people in the Old Testament who perform various kinds of service that is analogous to the service that Jesus performs perfectly. Unlike the first Adam, Jesus Christ is the Last Adam who passed his test in a garden and in so doing imputed his righteousness to us to overcome the sin imputed to us through the sin of the first Adam. Jesus is the true and better Abel who, although he was innocent, was slain and whose blood cries out. When Abraham left his father and home, he was doing the same thing that Jesus would do when He left heaven. When Isaac carried his own wood and laid down his life to be sacrificed at the hand of his father Abraham, he was showing us what Jesus would later do. Jesus is the greater Jacob who wrestled with God in Gethsemane and, though wounded and limping, walked away from his grave blessed. Jesus is the greater Joseph who serves at the right hand of God the King and extends forgiveness and provision to those of us who have betrayed him, using His power to save us for loving reconciliation. Jesus is greater than Moses, standing as a mediator between God and us, bringing us the new covenant.

Like Job, innocent Jesus suffered and was tormented by the Devil so that God might be glorified, while His foolish friends were no help or encouragement. Jesus is a king greater than David; He has slain our giants of Satan, sin, and death, although in the eyes of the world He was certain to face a crushing defeat at their hands. Jesus is greater than Jonah in that He spent three days in the grave, not just in a fish, to save a multitude even greater than Nineveh. When Boaz redeemed Ruth and brought her and her despised people into community with God's people, he was showing what Jesus would do to redeem his bride, the church, from all the nations of the earth. When Nehemiah rebuilt Jerusalem, he was doing something similar to Jesus, who is building for us a New Jerusalem as our eternal home. When Hosea married an unfaithful wife that he continued to pursue in love, he was showing us the heart of Jesus, who does the same for His unfaithful bride, the church.

We also see various Old Testament events preparing people for the coming of Jesus Christ. For example, in the Exodus account of Passover, the people placed blood over the doorframe of their home with hyssop (a common herb bundled for cleaning), and no one was to leave their home until the morning. Death would not come to any home marked with lamb's blood. Peter says our salvation is given by Jesus Christ and "sprinkling with his blood."[a]

Fourth, there are many titles for God in the Old Testament that refer to Jesus Christ as God. In Daniel 7:13–14, God is called the "son of man," and Jesus adopted that as his favorite title, using it some 80 times in the four Gospels. Jesus is the Suffering Servant that was promised in Isaiah.[b] Jesus is also known by many other Old Testament titles for God, including first and last, light, rock, husband or

---

[a] 1 Peter 1:2 [b] Isa. 42:1–4; 49:1–7; 52:13–53:12; cf. Phil. 2:1–11

bridegroom, shepherd, redeemer, savior, and the Lord of glory.[a]

To properly understand the Old Testament, we must connect it to the person and work of Jesus. This should not be done in an allegorizing manner where arbitrary meanings foreign to Scripture are assigned to Old Testament words and images, thereby changing their meaning. Rather, the meaning of the Old Testament includes symbolism and identity that are most fully revealed in Jesus.

Unless Jesus is the central message of the Scriptures, errors abound. The most common is moralizing. Moralizing is reading the Bible not to learn about Jesus but only to learn principles for how to live life as a good person by following the good examples of some people and avoiding the bad examples of others. That kind of approach to the Scriptures is not Christian, because it treats the Bible like any other book with moral lessons that are utterly disconnected from faith in and salvation from Jesus and life empowered by the same Holy Spirit of Jesus.

WHO WROTE THE BIBLE?

As part of His teaching ministry, Jesus often taught his students (disciples) about the future. On a few occasions He promised the day He would leave them and send the Holy Spirit to perfectly remind them of His life and teachings, so that they could write and teach accurately and truthfully to complete the Bible.[b]

The human authors of the Bible include kings, peasants, philosophers, fishermen, poets, statesmen, a doctor, and scholars. The books of the Bible cover history, sermons, letters, songs, and love letters. There are geographical surveys, architectural specifications, travel diaries, population statistics, family trees, inventories, and numerous legal documents.

Unlike any other book, the Bible is a book written by both God and man. Hundreds of times the Bible says, "thus says the Lord", and uses similar statements nearly 4,000 times. It was not co-authored, however, as is what you are reading. It was not God and humans collaborating, or a human writing a draft with God making revisions, or God giving ideas that the human authors put into words. They were not words dictated to humans, as is falsely claimed with the Koran. The Bible is not human writings that become divine when the reader discovers spiritual meaning in them, as it is said of many Eastern religious writings. It is not one of many books containing the religious insights of ancient sages, as many liberals teach.

People who were providentially prepared by God, and motivated and superintended by the Holy Spirit, spoke and wrote according to their own personalities and circumstances in such a way that their words are the very Word

---

[a] Isa. 41:4, 44:6, 48:12; cf. Rev. 1:17, 2:8, 22:3; Ps. 27:1; cf. John 1:9; Ps. 18:2, 95:1; cf. 1 Cor. 10:4, 1 Pet. 2:6-8; Hos. 2:16, Isa. 62:5, cf. Eph. 5:28-33, Rev. 21:2.; Ps. 23:1, cf. Heb. 13:20; Hos. 13:14, Ps. 130:7, cf. Titus 2:13, Rev. 5:9; Isa. 43:3, cf. John 4:42; Isa. 42:8, cf. 1 Cor. 2:8 [b] John 14:25-26; 16:12-15

REVELATION: GOD SPEAKS

of God.[a] God's supernatural guidance of the writers and their situations enabled them to perfectly receive and communicate all God would have us know for His glory and our salvation.

We call this divine inspiration. Putting it a bit more technically, the writings themselves have the quality of being God-breathed. It is not the authors or the process that is inspired, but the writings.

The belief that God wrote Scripture in concert with human authors whom He inspired to perfectly record His words is called verbal (the very words of the Bible) plenary (every part of the Bible) inspiration (are God-breathed revelation).[b] Very simply, this means that God the Holy Spirit inspired not just the thoughts of Scripture but also the very details and exact words that were perfectly recorded for us as Scripture.

When we say verbal, we believe that the very words are inspired and important, chosen by God, so every word does matter. That's why Jesus can say "not an iota, not a dot" of the Bible can be ignored.[c] We cannot limit the divine inspiration to concepts that God put in the mind of human authors who did their best to put those ideas into words. Rather, His revelation comes to us in those exact words.

When we say plenary, we mean there are no parts of the Bible we don't believe or won't teach, preach or obey. We cannot be like Thomas Jefferson, who brazenly sat down in the White House with a razor in one hand and a Bible in the other and cut out the portions he rejected. We also cannot be like those who are more subtle than Jefferson and simply ignore parts of the Bible as primitive, dismiss them as outdated, or explain them away with human reasoning. Paul shows us the proper attitude toward Scripture in 2 Timothy 3:16-17:

All Scripture is breathed out by God and profitable for teaching, for reproof, for correction, and for training in righteousness, that the man of God may be competent, equipped for every good work.

The very words of Scripture are miraculous revelation. Every part of Scripture is God's Word to us, the product of his creative breathing, just as the world, humans, and apostles were.[d] It is not helpful because it is the voice of our God who loves you, cares for you, converses with you, counsels you, comforts you, and confronts you. To get a word from God, all you have to do is open the Word of God.

2 Peter 1:19-21 echoes Paul's words:

We have something more sure, the prophetic word, to which you will do well to pay attention as to a lamp shining in a dark place, until the day dawns and the morning star rises in your hearts, knowing this first of all, that no prophecy of Scripture comes from someone's own interpretation. For no prophecy was ever

---

[a] Jer. 1:5, Gal. 1:15; 1 Cor. 2:13; 2 Tim. 3:16, 2 Pet. 1:20–21; Mark 12:36, 1 Cor. 14:37 [b] Matt. 4:4, 1 John 1:1–3; Matt. 5:17, Rom. 15:4, 2 Tim. 3:16 [c] Matt. 5:18 [d] Ps. 33:6; Gen. 2:7, Job 33:4; John 20:22

DOCTRINE

produced by the will of man, but men spoke from God as they were carried along by the Holy Spirit.

The Bible is not just made up like a fairy tale. Its authors were carried along by the Holy Spirit as a boat is carried by a breeze that fills its sails. Because the Scriptures come from God, they perfectly reveal things no human could know. For example, the writers of the Old Testament could not have made up prophesied details such as a virgin birth in the tiny town of Bethlehem hundreds of years in advance.[a] If God had not moved them, they could not have seen the future in such detail. The God who knows and rules the future also reveals it in Scripture.

The biblical authors consciously knew they were writing Holy Scripture. Paul said in 1 Corinthians 14:37, "The things I am writing to you are a command of the Lord." He had the courage to give them a commandment from Jesus and then put his own command right alongside it, as having equal authority.[b] Paul quotes the Old Testament as Holy Scripture: "For the Scripture says, 'You shall not muzzle an ox when it treads out the grain,'" and then he quotes Luke right alongside it, saying, "The laborer deserves his wages."[c] Peter also compares the letters of Paul to "other Scriptures."[d]

Taken all together, the Scriptures make incredible truth claims. The Scriptures are given by God's inspiration; the very words of God; all we need to know God; a perfect guide for life; pure; true; trustworthy; perfect; effective; powerful; not to be taken from or added to; for everyone; the standard by which all teaching is to be tested; to be obeyed. Speaking poetically, the Scriptures also claim to be sweet like honey; a lamp to guide our life; food for our soul; a fire that purifies and a hammer that breaks us; a sword; a seed for salvation planted in us; milk that nourishes us.[e]

WHAT IS THE CANON OF SCRIPTURE?

The canon of Scripture is the collection of books that God has chosen, and the Church has recognized, as having divine authority in matters of faith and doctrine. The term comes from the Greek word *kanon* and the Hebrew word *qaneh*, both of which mean "a rule," or "measuring rod." The canon is an authority to which other truth claims are compared and by which they are measured. To speak of canonical writings is to speak of those books that are regarded as having divine authority. They are the books of our Bible.

The 39 books of the Old Testament and 27 books of the New Testament

---

[a] Isa. 7:14, Mic. 5:2 [b] 1 Cor. 7:10, 12 [c] 1 Tim. 5:18 [d] 2 Pet. 3:15-16 [e] 2 Tim. 3:16, 2 Pet. 1:19-21; 1 Thess. 2:13; Luke 16:29, 31; Prov. 6:23; Ps. 12:6, 119:140; Ps. 119:160, John 17:17; Prov. 30:5-6; Ps. 19:7; Isa. 55:11; Heb. 4:12; Deut. 4:2, 12:32; Rom. 16:25-27; Acts 17:11; James 1:22; Ps. 19:10; Ps. 119:105; Jer. 15:16; Jer. 23:29; Eph. 6:17, Heb. 4:12.; James 1:21;1 Pet. 2:2

graciously preserved by God in the Bible are the inspired Word of God. The Protestant church recognized that these books constitute the complete canon inspired by God and received them as uniquely authoritative because they are God speaking to his people. F. F. Bruce says:

One thing must be emphatically stated. The New Testament books did not become authoritative for the Church because they were formally included in a canonical list; on the contrary, the Church included them in her canon because she already regarded them as divinely inspired, recognizing their innate worth and generally apostolic authority, direct or indirect. The first ecclesiastical councils to classify the canonical books were both held in North Africa—at Hippo Regius in 393 and at Carthage in 397—but what these councils did was not to impose something new upon the Christian communities but to codify what was already the general practice of those communities.[3]

Time after time, Jesus and His apostles quoted from this distinctive body of authoritative writings. They designated them as "the Scripture," "the Scriptures," "the holy Scriptures," "the sacred writings," and so forth.[a] They often introduced their quotations with "It is written"; that is, it stands firmly written.

We call these authoritative writings the Old Testament. Jewish people call them the Tanakh, an acronym formed from the first letters of Torah (Law), Naviim (Prophets), and Ketubim (Writings). We see this idea when Jesus explained to His disciples "everything written about me in the Law of Moses and the Prophets and the Psalms must be fulfilled."[b] It is important to note that the Tanakh includes the same material as the Protestant Old Testament, though they arrange the books differently.[4]

Beginning 250 years before Christ, Greek-speaking Jews living in Alexandria translated the Old Testament into Greek, calling it the Septuagint. For some unknown reason, they changed the content of several books, added many books, and rearranged the order of the books.

Early Jewish Christians followed Jesus and used the same Old Testament books as found in the Hebrew Bible today, the canon that was formally ratified in a meeting of rabbis at Javneh in 90 AD. It is an astonishing fact that all Jews, and all branches of Christianity, agree that these books are canonical, the very word of God. While other books were added in the Septuagint, these 39 books were and are universally accepted.

But as the center of Christianity moved away from Jerusalem and Christians read and worshiped more in Greek than Hebrew, the books of the Septuagint were widely used. There was a long and complicated debate about the validity and status of these books. Eventually the Roman Catholic Church adopted many of the books of the Septuagint into its Latin version, called the Vulgate. They referred to them as deuterocanonical, which means secondary canon. The Eastern

---

[a] John 7:38, Acts 8:32, Rom. 4:3; Matt. 21:42, John 5:39, Acts 17:11; Rom. 1:2; 2 Tim. 3:15 [b] Luke 24:44

Orthodox Church included more books in their canon than the Roman Church. As the Reformers attempted to rid the church of many tradition-based, Bible-less teachings and get back to the Bible, they also rejected the deuterocanonical books, calling them the Apocrypha. They kept the ordering of the Vulgate but returned to the authoritative books of Jesus, the Hebrew-speaking Jews, and the original Christians.

Today the Eastern Churches and the Catholic Churches accept different versions of the Apocrypha while Protestants remain with the books accepted by Hebrews then and now. It should be noted that accepting the Apocrypha would have no significant impact on the doctrinal teaching of the church. The errors of the Catholic Church came from using Apocryphal texts as seeds for speculation rather than from the teachings of the texts themselves.

The early church immediately recognized most of the books of the New Testament as canonical. The four Gospels, written to preserve and spread the story of Jesus to the whole church, were received gladly and universally, as were the writings of Paul, including 1 Timothy, 2 Timothy, and Titus (also known as the Pastoral Letters). Acts, 1 John, 1 Peter, and Revelation were also universally recognized. However, Hebrews remained in dispute for several centuries, especially in the West, because of the anonymity of its author. The status of James, 2 Peter, 2 John, 3 John, and Jude fluctuated according to church, age, and individual judgment and are occasionally omitted from canonical lists. Some works of the apostolic fathers, such as the Epistle of Barnabas, the Shepherd of Hermas, and the first and second epistles of Clement are sporadically cited as potentially Scripture but are not included in formal canonical lists.

In the fourth century, the church moved to settle the issues of the New Testament canon. In the East it was done in the Thirty-Ninth Paschal Letter of Athanasius in AD 367. In the West, the canon was fixed at the Council of Carthage in AD 397.

Was the New Testament canon disputed? Not really. Virtually all the books were immediately accepted. Did the church canonize the books? Not at all. Rather, they recognized and confirmed their canonical status. J.I. Packer writes:

The Church no more gave us the New Testament canon than Sir Isaac Newton gave us the force of gravity. God gave us gravity, by His work of creation, and similarly He gave us the New Testament canon, by inspiring the individual books that make it up.[5]

How did the church know which books ought to be recognized as canonical? What were the criteria for canonicity? They used three primary criteria:
1. Conformity to "the rule of faith." Did the book conform to orthodoxy, Christian truth recognized as normative in the churches?
2. Apostolicity. Was the writer of the book an apostle or did the writer of the book have immediate contact with the apostles? All but a few New

Testament writers were eyewitnesses to the events they recorded.[a] Though not eyewitnesses, Luke received his information from Paul and numerous eyewitnesses, while Mark received his information from Peter, who was an eyewitness. James and Jude were closely associated with the apostles in Jerusalem and were probably Jesus' brothers, which would have also made them eyewitnesses.[b]

3. Catholicity. Did the book have widespread and continuous acceptance and usage by churches everywhere?

In considering the great agreement surrounding the canon of Scripture, scholars have said:

The fact that substantially the whole church came to recognize the same twenty-seven books as canonical is remarkable when it is remembered that the result was not contrived. All that the several churches throughout the Empire could do was to witness to their own experience with the documents and share whatever knowledge they might have about their origin and character. When consideration is given to the diversity in cultural backgrounds and in orientation to the essentials of the Christian faith within the churches, their common agreement about which books belonged to the New Testament serves to suggest that this final decision did not originate solely at the human level.[6]

CAN I TRUST THAT MY BIBLE IS GOD'S WORD?

If you have a good modern translation of the Bible, then you have almost exactly what the ancient authors wrote. It is amazing that people try to argue that we cannot trust the Bible because we do not have the original copies. The same is true of Plato, Sophocles, Homer, or Caesar Augustus.

Until the middle of the twentieth century, our oldest copies of the Old Testament dated from about AD 900. We knew the extreme care the rabbis used to copy the sacred text before they destroyed the worn one. But still, the copies we had were historically distant from the original (called the *autographa*). But then in 1947 the Dead Sea Scrolls were discovered at Qumran. Suddenly we had copies of much of the Old Testament that were more than 1,000 years older than our previous oldest copies, including some 40,000 ancient inscriptions. From these fragments more than 500 books have been reconstructed, including some Old Testament books, such as a complete copy of Isaiah.

A comparison of the Qumran manuscript of Isaiah with the Masoretic text from AD 1000 showed the most minor variations, mostly spelling (like the American honor and the British honour) or stylistic changes such as adding a conjunction. Checking the pivotal text of Isaiah 53, we find that out of the 166 words in that chapter, only one word is really in question, and it does not at all change the

---

[a] John 19:35; 20:30–31; Acts 1:1–3, 9; 10:39–42; 1 Cor. 15:6–8; 1 Pet. 5:1; 2 Pet. 1:16; 1 John 1:1–3 [b] 2 Tim. 4:11; Luke 1:1–4; 1 Pet. 5:13

meaning of the passage. The Qumran text added the word "light" after "he shall see" in verse 11. It's a word that was implied but not actually written. Our confidence in the text was confirmed.

In the case of the New Testament, we have more than 20,000 handwritten manuscripts in Greek, Latin, Syriac, Coptic and other ancient languages including almost 6,000 Greek manuscripts with fragments written no later than 50 years after the original books and letters. In addition, we have more than one million quotations of the New Testament by church fathers. This is truly amazing because the Bible was copied onto fragile materials like papyrus. The copies weren't stored anywhere that protected them from the elements, but in God's providence they still survived.

As we compare copies of both Old and New Testament, we do find variations, but most of the variations in the many handwritten copies involve spelling, word order, or style. We would expect such minor human error no matter how careful the scribes were. Less than 1 percent of all the variations have anything to do with doctrine, and no doctrine is affected by any variation.

Lastly, Jesus himself used copies and translations. He trusted them, so we should too, especially when the science of textual criticism has confirmed that our text is accurate. Because we have so many manuscripts to check, we are virtually certain that the text of the New Testament is 99.5% textually pure.[a][b] In the entire text of 20,000 lines, only 40 lines are in doubt (about 400 words), and even Bible critics agree that none of these affects any significant doctrine.[c]

CAN SCRIPTURE BE WRITTEN TODAY?

The only people who could write Scripture were prophets and apostles—people who were witnesses of God's revelation in Jesus, or authors like Luke who based his Gospel on eyewitness testimony and on the report of the apostles who were eyewitnesses.[d]

Books of the Bible cannot be written today for two primary reasons. First, the Old Testament ended with the prophet Malachi promising that the next major event in redemptive history would be the coming of John the Baptist, preparing the way for Jesus.[e] Four hundred years followed during which time no book of the Bible was written until John came, as promised.[f] Likewise, the New Testament ends with its final book, Revelation, telling us that no other books of the Bible are to be written following it, as the Bible is completed as we await Jesus' Second Coming.[g]

Today, we are like God's people in the days between Malachi's promise and

---

[a] Geisler, Norman L., Nix, William E., A General Introduction to the Bible (Chicago: Moody Press, 1986), 475 [b] Blomberg, Craig. Can We Still Trust the Bible?: An Evangelical Engagement With Contemporary Questions (Brazos Press, 2014). [c] Ibid. [d] Luke 1:1-4; Acts 1:1-3, 9 [e] Mal. 3:1; 4:5-6 [f] Luke 1:11-17 [g] Rev. 22:18-19; Rev. 22:20-21

Jesus' coming. We know the future but are awaiting its coming. We do not need any more Scripture, but rather the fulfillment of the promises we have already received.

Second, the Bible says that Jesus is God's final word to us and that we should not add anything to the Bible.[a] Furthermore, we have no need for any new book of the Bible because we already have all we need for faith and godliness. If there were some knowledge that all Christians desperately needed, God would certainly not have waited some 2,000 years to reveal it while His people sat in the darkness of partial knowledge.

Simply stated, the canon of Scripture is closed. No books, not even a word, will be added to the Bible. John's warning at the end of Revelation (22:18-19) applies to the Bible as a whole:

I warn everyone who hears the words of the prophecy of this book: if anyone adds to them, God will add to him the plagues described in this book, and if anyone takes away from the words of the book of this prophecy, God will take away his share in the tree of life and in the holy city, which are described in this book.

This does not mean that God's special revelation has ceased. God still speaks to people and groups, albeit not in apostolic, inspired, canonical revelation. Examples include such things as predictive prophecies, audible speech, dreams, visions, angelic visits, and the like that Scripture itself speaks of.

In dealing with any alleged extra-biblical revelation, we must follow the biblical cautions. We must be neither gullible nor skeptical. On one hand, 1 Thessalonians 5:20-21 says we must "not despise prophecies," but instead, "test everything; hold fast what is good." 1 John 4:1 says, "Beloved, do not believe every spirit, but test the spirits to see whether they are from God, for many false prophets have gone out into the world."

The following six biblical guidelines are for testing those who allege to have extra-biblical revelation, including prophesy:

1. Are they loyal to the Lord?[b]
2. Is their word consistent with the Bible?[c]
3. Is what they describe or predict accurate?[d]
4. Is their character Christlike?[e]
5. Does their word build up and encourage the church in truth?[f]
6. Do Spirit-filled church leaders affirm their word?[g]

WHY IS SCRIPTURE AUTHORITATIVE?

Holy Scripture is God speaking. That simple but profound statement is why

---

[a] Heb. 1:1-2; Deut. 4:2, 12:32, Prov. 30:5-6 [b] Deut. 13:1-11; 18:20 [c] Deut. 13:1-11, 1 Kings 13:15-18 [d] Deut. 18:22 [e] Jer. 23:9-40, Mic. 3:5-10 [f] 1 Cor. 14:3 [g] 1 Cor. 14:29

Christians believe that Scripture is our highest authority by which all other lesser authorities are tested. Practically, this means that lesser courts of reason, tradition, and culture are under the highest court of truth, which is divinely inspired Scripture.

By contrast, the Roman Catholic and Eastern Orthodox churches teach that Scripture is a part of the larger pool of revelation that the church uses in its teaching. For them, authority is not in the Bible itself, but in the teaching office of the church.

Others appeal to the so-called Wesleyan Quadrilateral: *Wesley believed that the living core of the Christian faith was revealed in Scripture, illumined by tradition, vivified in personal experience, and confirmed by reason. Scripture [however] is primary, revealing the Word of God "so far as it is necessary for our salvation."*[7]

In practice, though, the Bible often becomes just one of four major sources of authority to be balanced. Thus, when contemporary critical theories of the Bible start to be taken seriously, the Bible often is judged by other authorities.

The central development of the Protestant Reformation was the return to Scripture as supreme authority. The Reformers coined the slogan "sola Scriptura" (sometimes prima Scriptura) to summarize this conviction. Nothing judges Scripture. It judges everything else. As followers of Jesus, we take the same stance He did and receive the Bible alone as infallible, inerrant truth from God with full authority over our lives.

The Bible is a living book of God authoritatively speaking as a perfect Father to children He dearly loves about how to live godly lives. For example, it commands us to "put away falsehood" and "speak the truth with [our] neighbor," not as arbitrary rules of conduct but as church family members who are "members one of another."[a] It is a story of what is best in God's loving family of the Spirit. It is the story of the God of redemption rescuing us from rebellion, brokenness, sin, and death. Its authority is that in these inspired words we find how to connect with the forgiving and transforming power of the death and resurrection of Jesus.

IS THE BIBLE SUFFICIENT OR ALL I NEED FOR LIFE WITH GOD?

The Protestant Reformers' slogan "sola Scriptura" means that Scripture alone is our court of highest authority. This should not be confused with "solo Scriptura", which is the erroneous belief that truth is to be found only in Scripture and nowhere else. Scripture itself speaks of lesser courts of lower authority that Christians should obey; we should submit to the authority of pastors, government, and parents up to the limits of disobeying the highest authority of Scripture.[b]

The Bible itself models the fact that there is at least some truth outside of the

---

[a] Eph. 4:25 [b] Heb. 13:17; cf. 1 Tim. 5:17–20; 1 Pet. 2:13–15; cf. Acts 4:19; 5:29; Rom. 13:1, 5; cf. Acts 16:35–40

Bible when it occasionally quotes other books, such as the *Book of Jashar* and the *Book of the Wars of the Lord*.[a] In quoting them, the Bible is not saying that they should be included as sacred Scripture but rather that they do contain some truth. Likewise, a mechanic, doctor, or computer programmer does not have to consult Leviticus to turn a brake drum, perform open-heart surgery, or make an addition to a software program.

Regarding the sufficiency of Scripture, the Bible and the Bible alone teaches a complete Christian worldview that includes what we need to know about God, how to come into relation with him, who Jesus is and what he did for our salvation, and what will happen at the end of history. One example is perhaps most clarifying in understanding the sufficiency of Scripture. Jesus tells the story of a man who died in unbelief and was suffering in torment. Jesus explains how a man in anguish had a conversation with Abraham across a chasm that separated those who had died in faith from those who had died in unbelief in the days prior to Jesus opening heaven. The man in anguish was concerned for his five brothers who remained alive and in unbelief. Luke 16:29–31 reports:

Abraham said, "They have Moses and the Prophets; let them hear them." And he said, "No, father Abraham, but if someone goes to them from the dead, they will repent." He said to him, "If they do not hear Moses and the Prophets, neither will they be convinced if someone should rise from the dead."

Jesus was emphatically clear that the Scriptures alone are sufficient for all that is needed to know God and enjoy His salvation. As Abraham said in Jesus' story, the Scriptures are even clearer and more compelling than the testimony of a man returned from death to give a personal report of the consequence for dying in unbelief.

WHY ARE THERE DIFFERENT TRANSLATIONS OF SCRIPTURE?

For centuries the Eastern church had the Bible only in Greek. The Western church had the Bible only in Latin. Since most people were not fluent in these languages, they were unable to read the Bible themselves. One of the great developments of the Protestant Reformation was to return the Bible to the people in their own language. Martin Luther and John Wycliffe are just two of the men who risked their lives to translate the Bible into German and English. William Tyndale was charged with heresy and condemned to death for translating the Bible into English. According to Foxe's Book of Martyrs, he "was tied to the stake, strangled by the hangman, and afterwards consumed with fire," simply because he wanted people to be able to read the Bible.[8]

Today, part of the Bible has been translated into at least 2,454 languages, at least one of the two Testaments exists in at least 1,168 languages, and the full Bible is available in at least 438 languages.[9] During the past four centuries there

---
[a] Josh. 10:13, 2 Sam. 1:18; Num. 21:14

have been hundreds of English Bible translations, and dozens are actively used today. They fall into three major categories.

1. Word for Word Translations

Word-for-word translations (or formal equivalence translations) emphasize the patterns of the words and seek "as far as possible to capture the precise wording of the original text and the personal style of each Bible writer...Thus it seeks to be transparent to the original text, letting the reader see as directly as possible the structure and meaning of the original."[10] The goal is precision like one would expect in other important communications, such as legal documents, marriage vows, or contracts.

Word-for-word translations have advantages for studying because of their closeness to the original, though they sometimes become a bit stilted stylistically because the biblical languages use different patterns of grammar and expression from English. Among the best contemporary word-for-word translations is the English Standard Version (ESV). The King James Version (KJV) is also a word-for-word translation and remains the best-selling English translation. It sounds very reverent to many people, but it is difficult for some people to read because it uses old English when the Greek New Testament was, in fact, written in the common language of ordinary people. Other good word-for-word English translations include the New King James Version (NKJV) and the New American Standard Bible (NASB).

2. Thought-for-Thought Translations

Thought-for-thought translations (also called dynamic equivalence or functional equivalence) attempt to convey the full nuance of each passage by interpreting the Scripture's entire meaning and not just the individual words. Such versions seek to find the best modern cultural equivalent that will have the same effect the original message had in its ancient cultures.

A favorite thought-for-thought modern English translation, the New International Version (NIV), is also the most popular. Others include the New Living Translation (NLT) and the Contemporary English Version (CEV).

3. Paraphrase Translations

Paraphrased translations put the emphasis on readability in English. Therefore, they pay even less attention to specific word patterns in an attempt to capture the poetic or narrative essence of a passage. Examples of paraphrased translations include The Message (MESSAGE), The Living Bible (TLB), The Passion Translation (TPT) and The Amplified Bible (AMP).

All faithful Bible translations try to achieve a balance of four elements:
1. Accuracy to the original text as much as possible
2. Beauty of language
3. Clarity of meaning

4. Dignity of style

While some translations are better than others, each has various strengths and weaknesses. Furthermore, rather than fighting over translations, Christians should praise God for every good translation, study multiple translations, and trust God the Holy Spirit to use them to transform our lives as we enjoy them.

For serious study we encourage comparing a formal equivalence translation, a dynamic equivalence translation, a good Catholic translation (New American or New Jerusalem Bible), a Jewish translation of the Old Testament, and a translation into a language other than English. That will enable you to get behind ambiguities of particular wordings or interpretations in translation.

We would encourage you to use the English Standard Version or another good word-for-word translation as your primary study tool, while also using other translations as secondary resources. Noted theologian and ESV general editor J.I. Packer reflected, "I find myself suspecting very strongly that my work on the translation of the ESV Bible was the most important thing that I have done for the Kingdom, and that the product of our labors is perhaps the biggest milestone in Bible translation in the past fifty years or more."[11]

While Christians should enjoy multiple good translations, they must be careful of corruptions. Corruptions are counterfeit and deceptive "translations" of Scripture that undermine the very teaching of Scripture. These include the Jehovah's Witness' New World Translation, written to eliminate the deity of Jesus Christ. Just like demons masquerade as angels, some brazen lies masquerade as biblical truth.

ARE THERE GOOD ANSWERS TO COMMON OBJECTIONS TO THE BIBLE?

In a research project that culminated in the book *Christians Might Be Crazy*, I commissioned researchers to discover the primary objections and questions regarding Christianity among the unchurched (people without church history), and the dechurched (people who used to go to church but no longer do). The research included more than 900,000 phone calls, survey interviews with 1,000 people, and eight focus groups (male and female) in four major American cities that resulted in over 400 pages of transcribed conversations about the Bible and Christianity. Regarding the Bible, the following objections appeared most frequently.

"The Bible has been edited by too many people."

People in every focus group said the Bible has undergone so many changes throughout its history that we no longer have access to its original message. One man echoed many saying, "The people that are obeying it to the letter of the words, they might not be following what Jesus really said because it's been passed down from so many different people, so many different scholars. It's been edited by too many people. So, do we really know what the word of God in the Bible is? We don't, there's no way to know."

In the days before the printing press and electronic files, trained scribes copied manuscripts letter by letter to preserve and disseminate them. While critics object that we do not possess the original autograph, the ancient age and quantity of copies we do have on hand means we are nevertheless certain of the Bible's original message.

As far as New Testament documents, Dr. Darrell Bock said in an interview with me, "We have access to literally thousands of manuscripts and fragments that are used in translating the Bible, not a long chain of degraded translations…" And "We have over 5,800 Greek manuscripts of one sort or another."[12]

There are another 15,000 copies in other ancient languages. This compares with fewer than a dozen copies of most ancient works. Tragically, opponents of Scripture have attacked its trustworthiness by falsely stating that our current English translations are built upon poorly transmitted copies. However, the bibliographical test of Scripture emphatically refutes this argument. This test determines the historicity of an ancient text by analyzing the quantity and quality of copied manuscripts, as well as how far removed they are from the time of the originals, the autographs mentioned earlier. In the next section we will examine this fact in greater detail.

The quantity of New Testament manuscripts is unparalleled in ancient literature. There are about 5,800 Greek manuscripts and about 15,000 manuscripts in other languages.

As the following chart illustrates, both the number of transmitted manuscripts we possess of Scripture and their proximity in date to the autographs are unparalleled when compared to other ancient documents.[13]

Author	Work	Date Written	Earliest MSS	Time Gap	Manuscripts
Homer	Iliad	800 BC	c. 400 BC	400	1,757
Herodotus	History	480-425 BC	10th C.	1,350	109
Sophocles	Plays	496-406 BC	3rd C. BC	100-200	193
Plato	Tetralogies	400 BC	895	1,300	210
Caesar	Gallic Wars	100-44 BC	9th C.	950	251
Livy	History of Rome	59 BC-AD 17	Early 5th C.	400	150
Tacitus	Annals	AD 100	1st half: 850, 2nd: 1050 (AD 1100)	750-950	2+31 15th C.
Pliny, the Elder	Natural History	AD 49-79	5th C fragment: 1; Rem. 14th-15th C.	400 (750)	200

REVELATION: GOD SPEAKS

Author	Work	Date Written	Earliest MSS	Time Gap	Manuscripts
Thucydides	History	460-400 BC	3rd C. BC (AD 900)	200 (1,350)	96
Demosthenes	Speeches	300 BC	Some fragments from 1 C. BC (AD 1100)	1,100+ (1400)	340
New Testament		AD 50-100	AD 130 (or less)	40	5,795

In our interview, Dr. Darrell Bock adds, "If we're going to discount the text of the New Testament, we should shut down our classics departments in universities around the country. We would have to reject the content of most of the works we use to understand ancient history. The idea that we don't know the text of the New Testament documents is simply something close to crazy. We've got by far more manuscript evidence for the text of the New Testament than any other ancient work. And it's by miles, it's not just close."[14]

Additionally, we find that "the vast majority of these variations involve mere changes in spelling, grammar, and style, or accidental omissions or duplications of letters, words, or phrases," according to New Testament scholar Craig Blomberg.[15] "Overall, 97 to 99 percent of the original Greek New Testament can be reconstructed beyond any reasonable doubt. Moreover, no Christian doctrine is founded solely, or even primarily, on any textually disputed passage."[16]

The Bible is not a collection of fables and legends assembled over long periods of time. The book we hold in our hands faithfully reflects what God spoke through the original authors.

In our interview, Bock highlighted a second faulty assumption about the transmission of Scripture. "Many people think the Bible was written in some ancient language long ago but has since been translated and re-translated over and over into so many different languages that we cannot trust it anymore. The reality is that teams of translators/scholars painstakingly go back to the original Greek and Hebrew to create Bibles in English and other tongues of people around the world. These linguistic experts have as much or more schooling than many rocket scientists, and their work is open to evaluation by anyone who wants to wade into the details."[17]

"The Bible says..."

People often judge the Bible based on what they think it says. Here is a sample of some of the claims we heard in our focus groups:

"You're supposed to sell your first daughter into slavery." The Bible says no such thing.

"Give a man a fish, and he'll eat for a day, and teach a man to fish and

DOCTRINE

he'll be fed forever." Literary types think they can trace back to the story "Mrs. Dymond" by Anne Isabella Thackeray Ritchie (1837–1919).[18]

"The Old Testament character Job [had sex with] his daughters. Incest is allowed according to the Bible." Actually, the Bible repeatedly condemns incest, and the exceptionally righteous man Job did no such thing. Our participant might have been thinking of Lot's daughters, who got their dad drunk in an effort to get pregnant (Gen. 19:30–38). That episode is a horrific story that illustrates the principle that the Bible often *describes* behaviors it never *prescribes*. It often records awful events as a warning, not as a recommendation on how to live.

"The Bible teaches Jesus was born on Christmas." In fact, the Bible makes no attempt to clarify the date Jesus was born. The traditional observance of Jesus' birth on December 25 started during the reign of the Roman emperor Constantine (AD 306–337).

"The Bible is full of contradictions."

This is no small complaint. Why should anyone agree with a book that can't agree with itself? One woman spoke for many when she said the Bible had no shortage of passages that say completely opposite things. She felt it was "mindboggling" that anyone believes the Bible.

People who make these claims are often simply parroting what they have heard. So, when they say "contradictions," it is more than fair for you to say, "Show me." But we also have to be honest. While the Bible claims to be true, trustworthy, perfect, and God-breathed, it does not claim to always be easy to understand.

2 Peter 3:15-16 (NLT) says, "And remember, our Lord's patience gives people time to be saved. This is what our beloved brother Paul also wrote to you with the wisdom God gave him—speaking of these things in all of his letters. Some of his comments are hard to understand, and those who are ignorant and unstable have twisted his letters to mean something quite different, just as they do with other parts of Scripture. And this will result in their destruction."

Peter packs a lot into those words. He declares that the letters Paul wrote as "Scripture" alongside other Bible books, showing that Paul's writings—13 or 14 (there's a debate on who wrote Hebrews) of the 27 books in the New Testament—were accepted as sacred as soon as they were written. Peter had to admit that even though Paul wrote with God-given wisdom, his letters contained comments that were tough to understand. Nevertheless, people are not free to interpret this, or any passage of Scripture, however they want. Already some "ignorant and unstable" people were twisting Paul's writings and other Scriptures, resulting in their destruction.

If it appears that there is a contradiction in Scripture, we should first dig deeply into our Bible to see if what appears to be an error is, in fact, not an error once we have examined it more closely.[19] In the end, it is perfectly reasonable to say that we do not have an answer for every question, we are always learning so the answer might come later, or when we get to heaven the answer will be clear. With our three pound fallen brains, humility requires that we begin by assuming we may be wrong or simply not understand many things in and out of the Bible.

As Christians, we trust that God makes clear the true essentials of our faith, a principle called the perspicuity of Scripture. We also humbly admit that sometimes the Bible feels challenging because we don't like what it says. Our problem often is less that we don't understand what it says and more that we don't agree or don't want to obey. This is especially true of sexual sin, as the Bible is a lot clearer than many people had hoped. Thankfully, there are entire books that reason through the toughest points of Scripture.[20]

"The New Testament was largely written by people who didn't even know Jesus."

A woman in Austin exposed a common attitude toward Bible accounts, claiming the New Testament was written by people who had never met Jesus, "To me Jesus is this guy who lived and then they wanted to create a religion around him and so they changed the end of what they call the Old Testament, the Torah, and built this new religion."

Earlier in this chapter, we established the fact that the New Testament is testimony from eyewitnesses to Jesus' life and ministry. The Bible also says that upward of 500 witnesses saw Jesus risen from death at one time, and most were still alive and willing to testify about it publicly at the time.[a]

These details are intensely relevant. Devout Jews who believed that the act of worshiping a false god would damn them to Hell forever started worshiping their friend, brother, and son as God. Many were tortured and died as martyrs without one of them ever recanting that Jesus was God who rose from death. Additionally, many of the historically verifiable early church leaders such as Polycarp, who was martyred for his testimony of Jesus, were disciples of the Apostles.

Some people imagine that a chronological gap between Jesus' life and the writing of His story made room for corruption, legends, and myths to develop. In actuality, the time between the New Testament events and their recording is very short, especially compared with other ancient documents. Paul wrote 1 Corinthians 15:1-8 about Jesus' resurrection, within about 25 years. Eyewitnesses were alive to object if what Paul wrote and the church taught were historically inaccurate. The earliest surviving manuscript fragment of the New Testament—from the Gospel of John—dates to about AD 130, within decades of when John penned his Gospel in AD 70-100. New Testament scholar Daniel Wallace reports that a fragment of Mark may date to the first century, even earlier than the one from John.[21]

---

[a] 1 Cor. 15:1-8

"There are some stories that are kept in and some stories that were kicked out."

Participants across our focus groups believed that many early Christians played fast and loose with the facts about Jesus, including only select details when they compiled the Bible. A woman in Austin said, "They put together the whole New Testament so there's [sic] some stories that are kept in and some stories that were kicked out. I think some of the real history is in there. I just don't think we have all of the story." A San Francisco woman shared, "I've heard the Vatican hides sections of the Bible that portray Jesus in a more negative light." And another Austin woman noted, "In the Bible there's [sic] 26 original gospels. Only four of them got put in the Bible. I think that maybe there's [sic] more to that."

Our focus groups repeatedly mentioned Dan Brown's novel The Da Vinci Code, which popularized the idea that there were numerous competing "gospels" and church leaders chose their favorites and rejected others, including the Gospel of Thomas, the Gospel of Barnabas, the Gospel of Philip, or even the Gospel of Judas. Whenever these "other gospels" get bursts of media attention, it seems to challenge the credibility of the Bible. There are a couple obvious reasons these "other gospels" are unreliable as genuine history about Jesus.

Dan Brown built much of the storyline of his best-selling book, The Da Vinci Code, on the premise that the church selected the four canonical Gospels from 80 similar books.[22] The others, it is said, were stamped out by "a Church that had subjugated women, banished the Goddess, burned non-believers, and forbidden the pagan reverence for the sacred feminine."[23]

In fact, however, even by the most generous count, there are fewer than thirty "gospels." Only the canonical Gospels date from the first century. The earliest of the others was written more than 100 years after Jesus lived. Most of them are dated at least 200 years after Jesus. Contrary to false accusation, not one of these "lost gospels" was hidden by the church. Furthermore, no "lost" gospels have been discovered. All of the discovered books were referred to in the church fathers' writings because they knew of their existence but simply did not consider them sacred Scripture. Some older or more complete copies of them have been discovered, most significantly in the Egyptian Nag Hammadi site. 2 Peter 1:16 rightly calls these kinds of claims about lost gospels and suppressed teachings about Jesus "cleverly devised myths" with no basis in fact or reality.

There is no reason to be concerned about any lost gospels containing truth that we need about God. Anyone curious about their truthfulness should simply read them. The Gospel of Philip purportedly says that Jesus and Mary Magdalene were married. In fact, it says, "And the companion of the [...] Mary Magdalene, [...] her more than the disciples [...] kiss her on her [...]. The rest of [...]. They said to him, 'Why do you love her more than all of us?'" (The ellipses in brackets indicate where the papyrus is broken and lost.) To say the least, this is extremely slender evidence for Jesus' marriage that some purport, even if this very late, clearly Gnostic gospel was accepted as authentic, which it is not.

The Gospel of Thomas is one of the earlier and most widely affirmed Gnostic gospels. It is not a gospel in the sense of a narrative that tells the story of Jesus. Rather, it consists of 114 sayings attributed to Jesus, some of which clearly parallel sayings in the canonical Gospels.

But that is where the similarity ends. It was written at least a century after the four biblical Gospels, long after the eyewitnesses to Jesus Christ were dead. It clearly reflects Gnostic theology built on a belief system that despised earthly and material realities and exalted the "higher" spiritual plane. The "god" of Thomas is a second-rate angelic being who rebelliously created this physical world. Humans are presented as spiritual beings ensnared in a wretched physical body. The only attention given to the humanity of Jesus was when trying to excuse it. The canonical Gospels, however, provide a very different picture of Jesus: a man who is fully human, in body and spirit, and who had disciples and friends, both male and female.

To make the differences between the real Gospels in the Bible and the Gnostic Gospel of Thomas clear, just read its final adage where only men can enter Heaven:

Simon Peter said to him, "Let Mary leave us, for women are not worthy of life." Jesus said, "I myself shall lead her in order to make her male, so that she too may become a living spirit resembling you males. For every woman who will make herself male will enter the kingdom of heaven." (114)

Regarding the wrongly termed "lost gospels," New Testament scholar Craig Blomberg has said:

In no meaningful sense did these writers, church leaders, or councils "suppress" Gnostic or apocryphal material, since there is no evidence of any canon that ever included them, nor that anyone put them forward for canonization, nor that they were known widely enough to have been serious candidates for inclusion had someone put them forward. Indeed, they would have failed all three of the major criteria used by the early church in selecting which books they were, at times very literally, willing to die for—the criteria of apostolicity (that a book was written by an apostle or a close associate of an apostle), coherence (not contradicting previously accepted Scripture), and catholicity (widespread acceptance as particularly relevant and normative within all major segments of the early Christian community).[24]

To be fair, there are a handful of other ancient books that have some good content. The Shepherd of Hermas and the Didache were appreciated by the early church and are akin to some popular Christian books today. Helpful like C.S. Lewis? Yes. Bible? No. Only a few individual churches and teachers wanted them included in the canon. Simply, they were not accepted because they were not God's Word for his whole church.

From the very earliest days, the church knew which books were God's inspired Word for them in the same way that a child knows who their parent is in a crowd. They read them, studied them, obeyed them, lived them, and passed them on. We should do the same without adding anything to the Scriptures. Proverbs 30:5-6 says, "Every word of God proves true; he is a shield to those who take refuge in him. Do not add to his words, lest he rebuke you and you be found a liar."

"Christianity borrowed from ancient religions."

"If you look at Egyptian cultures," said Kirk from the Phoenix focus group, "there's the story of a virgin birth in there somewhere, and if you look at it even further..." That was one assertion among many, that Christianity stole its best ideas from outside sources.

The easiest way to decide if early believers indeed borrowed key elements like the resurrection from other ancient religions is to read those supposed sources. The story about a corn god died, was buried, and came back to life as new crops is not exactly the Jesus story. Neither is the yarn about Osiris and Isis, Egypt's ultimate power couple. In the oldest version of the myth, the divine Osiris is killed and dismembered, with his body parts scattered across Egypt. His wife, Isis, retrieved every last piece—save for his phallus, which unfortunately had been gobbled up by fish. Isis made a gold phallus and sang a song to bring Osiris back to life. Osiris then impregnated Isis, and she gave birth to the new king, Horus. And did we mention that Isis was Osiris' sister?

It is hard to see how we should consider myths like these as inspiration for stories of the death, burial, and resurrection of Jesus Christ, which is an actual historical event attested to by eyewitnesses. After thoroughly researching ancient beliefs about resurrection, theologian N. T. Wright concludes: "Nobody in the pagan world of Jesus' day and thereafter actually claimed that somebody had been truly dead and had then come to be truly, and bodily, alive once more."[25]

Edwin Yamauchi has immersed himself in no less than 22 languages and is an expert in ancient history, including Old Testament history and biblical archaeology, with an emphasis on the interrelationship between ancient near Eastern cultures and the Bible. He is widely regarded as an expert in ancient history, early church history, and Gnosticism. He has published over 80 articles in more than three dozen scholarly journals and has been awarded eight fellowships. His writing includes contributing chapters to multiple books, as well as books on Greece, Babylon, Persia, and ancient Africa. After a lifetime of careful academic study on this issue, Yamauchi has concluded that there is no possibility that the idea of a resurrection was borrowed because there is no definitive evidence for the teaching of a deity resurrection in any of the mystery religions prior to the second century.[26]

In fact, it seems that other religions and spiritualities stole the idea of a resurrection from Christians! For example, the resurrection of Adonis is not spoken of until the second to fourth centuries.[27] Attis, the consort of Cybele, is not referred to as a resurrected god until after AD 150.[28]

Some have postulated that the taurobolium ritual of Attis and Mithra, the Persian god, is the source of the biblical doctrine of the resurrection. In this ritual, the initiate was put in a pit, and a bull was slaughtered on a grating over him, drenching him with blood. However, the earliest this ritual is mentioned is AD 160, and the belief that it led to rebirth is not mentioned until the fourth century. Princeton scholar Bruce Metzger has argued that the taurobolium was said to have the power to confer eternal life only after it encountered Christianity.[29]

In summary, whatever similarities might exist between points of Jesus' story and ancient religions, it is far more likely that the other faith borrowed from Christianity than vice-versa.

WHAT ARE THE MAJOR REASONS CHRISTIANS BELIEVE THE BIBLE?

We believe that what the Bible teaches is true, so we come to the Bible with what J. I. Packer calls "an advance commitment to receive as truth from God all that Scripture is found on inspection actually to teach."[30] In the same way, the wives we love who have only been good to us throughout our years together get the benefit of the doubt when they tell us something – because of their character we begin by assuming that what they say to us is loving and true.

We believe that all that the Bible teaches is truth from God, whether statements of fact about earth, heaven, humans, or God, or moral commands, or divine promises. This has been the universal affirmation of the church until the time of the Enlightenment, when acceptance in the secular academy led some biblical scholars to base their conclusions on culturally misguided reason rather than on revelation and reality.

The affirmation of the truthfulness of the Bible is tied to the character of God. God is a truthful God who does not lie.[a] Therefore, because God is ultimately the author of Scripture, it is perfect, unlike every other uninspired writing and utterance.

Taken altogether, inerrancy is the shorthand way of summarizing all that the Scriptures say about Scripture. Inerrant means that the Scriptures are perfect, without any error. The doctrine of inerrancy posits that because God does not lie or speak falsely in any way, and because the Scriptures are God's Word, they are perfect.[b] As a result, the entire Bible is without any error.[c]

The Bible claims to be wholly true and therefore inerrant. We find such explicit statements in passages such as 2 Samuel 7:28, "O Lord GOD, you are God, and your words are true"; Psalm 19:7–10, which uses words such as perfect, sure, right, pure, true, and righteous; Psalm 119:42–43, 142, 151, 160, 163, which uses the specific word truth or true; and John 17:17, "Your word is truth." Second Timothy 3:16 rightly says, "All Scripture is breathed out by God."

Unlike the Bible, however, those of us who read and study it, are not inerrant in our understanding of it. The Bible itself gives us much cause for humility as we

---

[a] Heb. 6:18; Titus 1:2 [b] 1 Sam. 7:28; Titus 1:2; Heb. 6:18 [c] Num. 23:19; Ps. 12:6; 119:89; Prov. 30:5–6

approach the Scriptures because:
- God's thoughts are much loftier than ours[a]
- God has secrets that He has not revealed to anyone[b]
- Sometimes we see the truth as if through a dirty and fogged window[c]
- We are prone to resist God's truth because it forces us to repent, and sometimes we are simply hard-hearted[d]
- We know in part[e]
- Some parts of the Bible are just hard to understand[f]

A telling example of the Bible's accuracy is in the transliteration of the names of foreign kings in the Old Testament as compared to contemporary extra-biblical records, such as monuments and tablets. The Bible is accurate in every detail in the 36 instances of comparison, a total of 183 syllables. To see how amazing this is, Manetho's ancient work on the dynasties of the Egyptian kings can be compared to extra-biblical records in 140 instances. He is right 49 times, only partially right 28 times, and in the other 63 cases not a single syllable is correct! The Bible's accuracy is shown not only in the original work but in its copies as well.[31]

Luke correctly identifies by name, title, job, and time such historical individuals as Annas, Ananias, Herod Agrippa I, Herod Agrippa II, Sergius Paulus, the Egyptian prophet, Felix, and Festus.[g] Political titles were very diverse and difficult to keep straight since every province had its own terms and, worse yet, the terms constantly changed. Yet Luke gets them right: a proconsul in Cypress and Achaia, the undeserved title Praetor in Philippi, the otherwise unknown title of Politarchs in Thessalonica, Asiarchs in Ephesus, and "the chief man" in Malta.[h]

The descriptions of local custom and culture are equally accurate. As John Elder states:

It is not too much to say that it was the rise of the science of archaeology that broke the deadlock between historians and the orthodox Christian. Little by little, one city after another, one civilization after another, one culture after another, whose memories were enshrined only in the Bible, were restored to their proper places in ancient history by the studies of archaeologists...Contemporary records of biblical events have been unearthed and the uniqueness of biblical revelation has been emphasized by contrast and comparison to newly discovered religions of ancient peoples. Nowhere has archaeological discovery refuted the Bible as history.[32]

This affirmation of the truthfulness of the Bible is exactly the attitude of Jesus himself. Frederick C. Grant, who is not any sort of fundamentalist Christian, acknowledges that the New Testament consistently takes "for granted that what is

---

[a] Isa. 55:9 [b] Deut 29:29 [c] 1 Cor. 13:12 [d] Rom. 1:18–19 [e] 1 Cor. 13:9 [f] 2 Pet. 3:15–16 [g] Acts 4:6; Acts 23:2; Acts 12:1–3, 20, 23; Acts 25:13–26:32; Acts 13:7; Acts 21:38; Acts 23:23–24:27; Acts 24:27 [h] Acts 13:7, 18:12; Acts 16:12, 20ff., 35ff; Acts 17:6, 9; Acts 19:31, 35; Acts 28:7

written in Scripture is trustworthy, infallible and inerrant. No New Testament writer would ever dream of questioning a statement contained in the Old Testament."[33]

Those parts of the Old Testament that are most commonly rejected as error are also those sections of Scripture that Jesus clearly taught. This includes the literalness of Genesis 1 and 2, Cain and the murder of Abel, Noah and the flood, Abraham, Sodom and Gomorrah, Lot, Isaac and Jacob, the manna, the wilderness serpent, Moses as lawgiver, the popularity of the false prophets, and Jonah in the belly of a great fish.[a]

In matters of controversy, Jesus used the Old Testament as His court of appeals.[b] On many occasions where an Old Testament teaching was questioned, Jesus simply believed the clear teaching of Old Testament Scripture and defended Himself by saying, "it is written."[c]

Some of the most common critiques launched at the Old Testament are in regard to authorship, but Jesus actually named the authors of some Old Testament books. For example, many Old Testament "scholars" boldly claim that Moses did not pen any of the first five books of the Bible, or that two or three authors penned Isaiah, none of whom was actually Isaiah. But Jesus taught that Scripture was authored by Moses, Isaiah, David, and Daniel.[d]

Following Jesus' example, while New Testament authors often refer to the Old Testament in a rather general way, they also feel confident to appeal to the smallest detail. In Matthew 22:29–33, Jesus' argument rests on the present tense of "to be" in Exodus 3:6. Matthew 22:41–46 refers to the use of "Lord" in Psalm 110:1. In John 10:34, Jesus' argument comes from the Old Testament use of the word "gods."[e] Galatians 3:16 rests on the singularity of the Old Testament word translated "seed" or "offspring."[f]

The standard for true prophecy was complete truthfulness, which is why Elijah was affirmed as a prophet: "Now I know that you are a man of God, and that the word of the LORD in your mouth is truth."[g] Can the standard for the Bible be any less, if it is truly prophetic?

Because Scripture is God speaking to us as our Father, we also believe Scripture usually speaks accurately in ordinary language. Bible writers use popular language rather than technical terminology. So, they say, "the sun had

---

[a] Matt. 19:4–5, Mark 10:6–8; Matt. 23:35, Luke 11:50-51; Matt. 24:37–39, Luke 17:26–27; John 8:56; Matt. 10:15, 11:23–24, Luke 10:12, 17:29; Luke 17:28–32; Matt. 8:11, Luke 13:28; 2John 6:31, 49, 58; John 3:14; Matt. 8:4, 19:8, Mark 1:44, 7:10, 10:5, 12:26, Luke 5:14, 20:37, John 5:46; 7:19; Luke 6:26; Matt. 12:40 [b] Matt. 5:17–20; 22:29; 23:23; Mark 12:24 [c] Matt. 4:4, 6, 10; 11:10; 21:13; 26:24, 31; Mark 1:2; 7:6; 9:12–13; 11:17; 14:21, 27; Luke 2:23; 4:4, 8,10, 17; 7:27; 10:26; 19:46; 22:37; John 2:17; 6:31, 45; 8:17; 10:34 [d] Mark 7:10; Matt. 13:14, Mark 7:6; Mark 12:36; Matt. 24:15 [e] Ex. 4:16; 7:1; 22:28; Ps. 138:1 [f] Gen. 12:7; 15:3; 17:19 [g] 1 Kings 17:24

risen,"[a] or refer to "the four corners of the earth."[b] There are figures of speech like "the trees of the field shall clap their hands."[c] There are also summaries, such as the Sermon on the Mount and Peter's sermon at Pentecost, of events for which we do not have full transcriptions.[d] Sometimes, the Bible also gives us rounded numbers rather than exact head counts of, for example, the number of men killed each day during a war.[e] To interpret the Bible accurately we must consider it carefully. Thus, we interpret historical accounts, figures of speech, approximations, summaries, and such according to the author's intent, taking care lest our cultural and personal presuppositions distort our interpretation.

This does not mean there are no questions to explore. My (Gerry's) biggest question revolves around the numbers in Numbers. Compared to archaeological estimates, they are too big by a factor of 10. There are several proposals for what is going on, but at this point, we don't know. A few decades ago, I also had questions about Jericho. According to the best archaeological reports, it was uninhabited from about 1600 BC to about 1200 BC. The Bible says the walls came tumbling down about 1440 BC. That would be hard if the city was already destroyed. But as excavations were done in a different part of the ancient site, a thick layer of ash containing grain was discovered. Dating by three different methods showed a burn date of (try to guess before you look!)—1440 BC.[34]

HOW DOES OUR VIEW OF SCRIPTURE AFFECT OUR LIFE?

God speaks to us through the Scriptures as a perfectly loving Father. Christians worship God, not the Bible. But the Bible informs us of who God is and how we are to live in His love as worshippers. As a result, we come to the Bible for transformation, not just for information.

We agree with Luther, "When the Scripture speaks, God speaks." Because Scripture is God speaking to us, we memorize, meditate, study, teach, and share His truth. Everything in life and ministry is guided by the truth of Scripture. Everything good is a result of the truth of biblical revelation being used by God the Holy Spirit to change our character to be more like Christ.

Sooner or later we all have to settle what we think about the Bible. We shouldn't make that decision based on hearsay or speculation, but on what the Bible actually is, what it says, and does. Other people can't determine our opinion. We each must make a decision. Scholar and friend Wayne Grudem has spent his life studying and teaching the Bible, and watching people wake up to what the Bible is all about. He describes how that happens in an interview I conducted:

"Hundreds of millions of people throughout history have begun to read the Bible with an open mind and then said, 'Wow, this book speaks to my heart like

---

[a] Gen. 19:23; Mark 16:2 [b] Isa. 11:12; Rev. 7:1; 20:8 [c] Isa. 55:12 [d] Matt. 6:34; Acts 4:4 [e] Judg. 20:44–47

no other book I have ever read. This is unlike any other book. These are the very words of God.'" The Bible itself claims to be God's words in written form. And that is our starting point. *"Am I going to believe that claim?"* Grudem asks. *"I think the only way for people to evaluate that is to give some serious time to reading the Bible and studying it and seeing if it rings true as being the word of God. Do I hear the voice of my Creator speaking in it when I read it?"*[35]

When the Bible says that the god of this world has blinded the minds of unbelievers[a], it means that they really can't see what we see. We might nag them. We might talk down to them. We might holler at them. But that's like yelling at a colorblind guy about what's on a painting. Yelling will not make him see.

The ability to see the truth of the Bible is not an intelligence issue. It's a condition issue. We should bring the same compassion and respect we would show anyone who is physically blind. If you know someone who is spiritually blind, buy them a nice Bible. Put the person's name on it and give it to them like Grace did for me. Then pray that the Holy Spirit opens their understanding as they read it. Why? Because we need God to get involved in this. It takes a miracle as big as Jesus healing a blind guy. The good news? He still heals the blind.

QUESTIONS FOR PERSONAL JOURNALING AND/OR SMALL GROUP DISCUSSION

1. Take a few moments today to thank God for choosing to reveal Himself to you and recount some of the ways He has done so (e.g. the Bible, godly Bible teachers, general revelation, etc.).
2. Which Old Testament Bible story reminds you the most of Jesus Christ?
3. If you could pick one book of the Bible to study, which would it be? Why don't you commit to taking some months to study it?
4. Do you feel like you are getting enough time reading the Bible? What changes could be helpful for increasing your Bible reading time?
5. What is the last Bible verse that you memorized? Which one should you memorize next?
6. How does the unity of the Bible across so many cultures, centuries, and authors reveal that God is ultimately responsible for all of its' content?
7. Is there any part of Scripture that you have struggled to believe and need to devote some time to studying in depth?
8. Is there any book or author that you are capable of elevating too close to God's Word in authority?
9. Is there a big issue or decision in your life right now that requires you to study God's Word in order to face it?
10. Who do you know that needs a nice Bible? What Bible could you buy them?

---

[a] 2 Cor. 4:4

CHAPTER 3: CREATION

"GOD MAKES"

In the beginning, God created the heavens and the earth.
GENESIS 1:1

When I was a little boy, before my four siblings were born, my dad worked out of town a lot. My parents were married at a young age and birthed me when they were just over twenty years old. To pay the bills, my hardworking construction worker dad had to sometimes take some jobs out of town, sleep in his truck, and send the money to me and my mom.

For fun, my mom would load me up in an old Chevy car and take me up to the mountains to explore God's creation. She often told me, "Marky we need a Jeep." Many years later, as we started to have five kids of our own, the seed planted in my imagination by my mom came to mind and so I bought a Jeep. Today, I am driving my second Jeep around Scottsdale, Arizona where we live and minister. During the winters, the weather is spectacular with big blue skies, warm sunny weather, and jaw dropping sunsets exploding with color. It is life-changing to have the top off the Jeep all winter to enjoy God's creation and take the Jeep up into the mountains to find hidden places of beauty that God created for us to explore and enjoy.

Since moving to the desert, my life has drastically changed. For most of my life, I suffered from a bad case of Seasonal Affective Disorder (S.A.D.). The wet, cold dark winters took a serious physical toll every year. My doctor said that no medication would help and that I simply needed to be outside enjoying God's creation under the light of the sun and my body would heal itself by God's design. Since relocating to the desert and driving around all winter in the Jeep with the top off, my health has been completely transformed. My wife Grace likes to joke that I am solar powered as I enjoy the healthiest and most enjoyable season of my life. I have learned in a very personal and practical way that God made this world as a gift for us to live in and, apart from enjoying God's creation, it is nearly impossible to be healthy.

According to the Scriptures, creation is a gift from a loving Creator God. From the bodies we inhabit, the air we breathe, the sun we bask in, the food we eat, the flowers we pick, the water we drink, the ground we walk upon, and the pets we love, to the pleasures we enjoy and destinations we visit on vacation, life is filled with good gifts for us to steward and enjoy. As we now learn about creation, the main goal is to learn to love the Creator.

WHAT HAVE CHRISTIANS HISTORICALLY BELIEVED ABOUT CREATION?

Christians have always believed in creation. There was little debate over the nature or date of creation until the last couple of centuries. However, science began gaining credibility through the great advances in the so-called Age of Reason (also called The Enlightenment or Modernism) developed in the 18th century. Science increasingly became identified with the physical-centered, naturalistic worldview that stood in direct opposition to the spirit-centered, theistic worldview of the Bible. What was presented as scientific evidence became a weapon used by opponents of Christianity to attack the biblical worldview with great cultural success.

Unfortunately, many Christians began to accommodate themselves to naturalism and rationalism. Classic Christian liberalism began to dominate the church in Europe in the 19th century and in America going into the 20th century. A group of biblical Christian scholars published a series of books called "The Fundamentals" in an attempt to define and defend biblical Christianity against this widespread compromise with liberalism. As the debates developed, controversies about the date and nature of creation arose among biblical Christians. Fundamentalism became defensive and suspicious of compromise and the controversies often became acrimonious and remain so today as even secondary and tertiary issues are warred over.

Thankfully, even this creation controversy can be yet another gift to us from God, compelling us to more deeply ponder his creative works and thereby grow to more clearly savor his Word, see his grace, and sing his praises. Before turning to the opening pages of Genesis where creation commences, a few prefatory comments are in order.

First, there is no conflict between Christianity and experimental science. This is because the Christian worldview, which believes that God created the world with natural "laws" and orderliness, is what undergirds the entire scientific enterprise. For example, inductive reasoning and the scientific method are based on the assumption of the regularity of the laws of nature. This means that scientists assume that water will boil tomorrow under the identical conditions that it does today. Without this kind of regularity, we could not learn from experience, including the experiences of scientific testing. This also helps to explain why, in cultures where creation is said to be an illusion or disorderly chaos because it was not created by an orderly God, the sciences have not historically flourished; indeed, the scientific method depends upon the kind of underlying worldview that a creating and providentially ruling God of the Bible provides.

Second, there is total conflict between Christianity and scientific naturalism, the belief that all phenomena can be explained in terms of presently operating natural causes and laws. The only true knowledge is that which comes through observable experiments. This negates even the possibility of the supernatural or miraculous as, by definition, those are not repeatable and controllable events. When natural science is the arbiter of all truth claims, religion becomes superstition and God, spirit, and choice are omitted from discussion.[1]

Third, the Bible in general, and the book of Genesis in particular, was not written with the intention of being a scientific textbook. Rather, it is a theological narrative written to reveal the God of creation, which means its emphasis is on God and His relationship with humanity and not on creation. Genesis is far more concerned with the questions of who made creation and why He made creation than exactly when and how He did. Therefore, as Galileo said, "The Holy Ghost intended to teach us how to go to heaven, not how the heavens go." This explains why the lengthiest treatise of creation in all of Scripture, Genesis 1 and 2, is only a few pages of our Bible. It is as if the story of Scripture opens with the panoramic view of creation and then the camera quickly focuses in on the creation of our first parents and the history that ensues.

Fourth, one's view of the date or exact details of creation should not be the litmus test for Christian faithfulness. Within Christian theology there are open- and closed-handed issues. Biblical authority is a closed-handed issue. Christians receive what the Bible actually teaches as truth from God to be believed and obeyed. Regarding creation, a Bible-believing Christian must reject such things as the atheistic evolutionists' claims that there is no God, and that creation is not a gift but rather an epic, purposeless accident. Nevertheless, Bible-believing Christians can and do disagree over the open-handed issues, such as exactly how God made the heavens and the earth, whether the six days of Genesis 1-2 are literal 24-hour days, and the age of the earth. These sorts of issues must remain in the open hand as these are not about the Who but instead the how of creation.

WHAT DOES THE BIBLE SAY ABOUT CREATION?

The first book of the Bible, Genesis, takes its name from its first words, "In the beginning," as genesis means "beginning." The book of Genesis in general, Genesis 1-3 in particular, records the beginning of creation and human history. Moses penned Genesis in roughly 1400 BC as the first of a five-part book called the Pentateuch, meaning "book in five parts". The Genesis account of creation was likely directly revealed to Moses by the same Holy Spirit who was present in Genesis 1:2, since Moses was not present for the creation event. Genesis is not an exhaustive treatment of early history but rather a theologically selective telling of history that focuses on God and mankind while omitting such things as the creation of angels or the fall of Satan and demons in heaven.

The first line of Genesis says, "In the beginning, God created the heavens and the earth."[a] The two subsequent chapters of the Bible are devoted to speaking about creation. Brilliantly, the Bible opens with the one true, eternal God as both the author and subject of history and Scripture. Consequently, everything else in history and Scripture is dependent upon God and is only good when functioning according to His intentions for it from creation.

Only in the last century has evidence forced the natural sciences reluctantly to agree with what Scripture has always taught: the universe had a beginning. It is an amazing testimony to the truth of Scripture. The scientific consensus that the universe had always been pretty much as it currently is (Steady State) was so strong that Einstein overrode the implications of his theory of general relativity and added a cosmological constant to make them consistent with the prevailing view. The opening phrase "In the beginning" speaks of an inauguration of a history, a space and a time when the Lord worked. Implicitly, it anticipates an end, a time when He will bring history to an end and create a new heavens and a new earth.[b]

In Genesis 1:1, the word used for "created" is the Hebrew word bara, which means "creation from nothing". The other Hebrew word used in a creative sense in Genesis is *asah*, translated "make" or "made". This very common word is used in the creative sense[c] which means "to fashion or shape," or "to make something suitable," such as making loincloths out of fig leaves[d] or making the ark.[e] *Bara* emphasizes the initiation of an object, whereas *asah* emphasizes the shaping of an object. Along with statements where God does initial creation like the heavens and the earth[f], the only other things *bara'd* are the living creatures[g] and human beings.[h] When people create, we are doing *asah*, not *bara*. We can take things that God has given us such as seed and land to plant crops and harvest food, but in so doing we are not creating food from nothing but rather creating it from the gifts given to us by God in creation.

In the creation account, we see that God created (*bara*) "the heavens and the earth". This phrase could be more literally translated "the skies and the land," since the heavens are not the place where God lives, but the place where stars move[i] and birds fly.[k] The Hebrew word *eretz*, usually translated "earth," in Genesis 1 does not mean the planet but the land under the water[m], separated

---

[a] Gen. 1:1 [b] Isa. 65:17; 2 Pet. 3:13; Rev. 21:1 [c] Gen. 1:7, 16, 25, 26, 31; 2:2, 3, 4, 18; Ps. 86:9; 95:5; 96:5 [d] Gen. 3:7 [e] Gen. 8:6 [f] Gen. 1:1; 2:3, 4 [g] Gen. 1:21 [h] Gen. 1:27; 5:1, 2 [i] Gen. 1:14 [k] Gen. 1:21 [m] Gen. 1:2

from water[a], where vegetation grows[b] and animals roam.[c] Elsewhere in Scripture it usually means the Promised Land. The phrase "skies and land" is a Hebraic way of saying "everything"[d] from the skies above to the earth below, like saying from top to bottom or head to toe, including space-time, mass-energy, and the laws that govern them. In other places in Scripture, the phrase includes the sun and moon, which could in turn mean that the sun and moon were created as a part of this first creation.[e]

The land or earth is "without form and void". Many read this as primordial space, but it is eretz, land or earth in Gen. 1:2 before God prepared them for humans. Ancient Greek cosmology said that what originally existed was essentially a formless hunk of mud, which God then formed from chaos into cosmos. This ideology has had great sway in many Christian interpretations of Genesis 1:2, including the first English translation of the Bible overseen by William Tyndale, which translated it as "void and empty," thereby sadly setting in motion a precedent for many future Bible translations and Bible commentators, including Martin Luther.[2]

However, the same language for "without form (*tohu*) and void (*bohu*)" used in Genesis 1:2 is used elsewhere in Scripture in reference to uninhabited land. Examples include Deuteronomy 32:10, which speaks of "a desert land, and in the howling waste (*tohu*) of the wilderness." Isaiah 45:18 says that God "formed the earth and made it (He established it; He did not create [*bara*] it empty [*tohu*], He formed it to be inhabited!)." Perhaps the closest parallel is Jeremiah 4:23 where God prophesied the future state of Judah, a nation doomed to exile by its sin: "I looked on the earth, and behold, it was without form and void; and to the heavens, and they had no light." Here, "without form and void" does not mean chaos, but it means empty of humans because it was not yet ready for human life; "no light" may not mean there is no sun but that the land is without the life of God's blessing.

Similarly, in Genesis 1:2 "without form and void" is the condition of the land before God made it good, filling it with light and life. The best understanding is not that God created primordial chaos and formed earth out of it, but that God created everything out of nothing and that the land existed for some unstated period of time in a desert-like, empty state suitable for plants and animals but not human flourishing. The dawn of God's light signals the arrival of his blessing. Then, God took six literal days to prepare the land for human habitation, as recorded in Genesis 1–2. This work is forming (*asah*) already-existing material, not creating (*bara*) from nothing. Historically, this view goes all the way back to Augustine.

The creation of heavens and earth in the first verse is a concrete, historical, scientific fact. But the text simply does not tell us when it happened, only that it was

---

[a] Gen. 1:10 [b] Gen. 1:11–12 [c] Gen. 1:20–24 [d] Isa. 44:24; 65:17; Jer. 10:10–16; Eph. 3:9; Col. 1:16–17; Rev. 21:1 [e] Isa. 13:10; Joel 3:15–16

DOCTRINE

sometime before the preparation of the land for humans to dwell with God. "In the beginning" means that there was an inauguration, but not when that moment was. Therefore, Genesis 1:1 leaves open both the possibilities of a young and an old earth.

The creation account goes to great lengths to make it clear that the God who created (*bara*) everything according to the first verse is the same God who prepared (*asah*) the land for humans to dwell with him in the remainder of Genesis 1 and 2. The God of creation is also the God of covenant relation.

WHERE DID CREATION COME FROM?

The opening line of Scripture clearly reveals that creation comes from God.[a] Genesis 1 and 2 further reveal God as a prophet who both made creation and prepared it for us solely by the power of His word. This is indicated by the repeated phrases, "And God said" and "Let there be" or "Let the . . ."[b] When God spoke, creation obeyed His command, as is repeatedly demonstrated by the phrase "And it was so." After each act of creating, God pronounced the perfectly sinless nature of His creation with the phrase "And God saw that it was good".

Therefore, original creation came not from preexisting matter but rather out of nothing, by God's word.

The Bible teaches that God made creation ex *nihilo* (Latin for "out of nothing"). Hebrews 11:3 says, "By faith we understand that the universe was created by the word of God, so that what is seen was not made out of things that are visible." This doctrine is important because it negates the possibility of naturalistic evolution and an eternal universe. While God did not make creation from any preexisting matter or the proverbial hunk of mud, creation did come into existence and was prepared for human inhabitation by the powerful word of God.

It is curious that God did not create from nothing on each of the six days of creation. Still, God did speak as both a prophet and poet on each day. Furthermore, there is a set pattern to God's words in Genesis 1. It is as follows:

1. Announcement: "And God said."
2. Commandment: "Let there be."
3. Separation: God separated the day and night, water and land, animals and plants.
4. Report: "And it was so."
5. Evaluation: "And God saw that it was good."

In this pattern we see that God's word is living, active, and powerful, and that it accomplishes what He decrees. Later, God explicitly declares this fact in Isaiah 55:11: "So shall my word be that goes out from my mouth; it shall not return to me empty, but it shall accomplish that which I purpose, and shall succeed in the thing

---

[a] Gen. 1:1 [b] Gen. 1:3, 6, 9, 11, 14, 20, 24, 26

for which I sent it." The rest of Scripture confirms that creation was prepared for us by God's powerful word.[a]

Indeed, Genesis 1 portrays God's word as the most powerful force in all of creation. God's word brings order, makes things good, creates an environment in which life can exist, separates things, comes with unparalleled authority, and accomplishes exactly what God intends. Therefore, we are not to dismiss, disdain, or distort God's word, as it is the source of understanding.

In summary, God brought creation out of nothing and prepared it for us because he cares for us as Jeremiah 10:16 says, "Not like these is he who is the portion of Jacob, for he is the one who formed all things, and Israel is the tribe of his inheritance; the LORD of hosts is his name." As Francis Schaeffer pointed out about this verse, creation was made and lovingly prepared for us by a loving and personal "He," not an impersonal, unloving "it."

HOW IS CREATION A WITNESS TO GOD'S EXISTENCE?

Some years ago, our family drove up to visit the Grand Canyon. As we approached the rim, we stopped as a sense of overwhelming wonder gripped each of us. Surrounding us were throngs of people from around the world who had traveled to stand in front of something that made them feel small and awestruck in the presence of something glorious that was much bigger than us that stood before we were born and would continue long after we were gone. At this moment, it dawned on me that everyone who visits the Grand Canyon is ultimately looking for God, whether they know it or not. The same is true for everyone who stops to feel the sun or a breeze on their face, looks up at a sunset, or hikes into the mountains for the good of their soul. When we feel in the presence of something that makes us feel small and in awe, we begin to experience the wonder of worship.

Christian philosophers have long sought to start with creation to move backwards to introduce people to the Creator. Among the most popular are the arguments from the highest ideal (ontological argument), intelligent design (teleological argument), first cause (cosmological argument), time (Kalam argument), and morality (axiological argument). Each of these arguments is complex and can be presented in multiple ways. Generally speaking, these philosophical arguments are each inductive in form, meaning they reason from what God has done to an understanding of who God is. The one exception is the ontological argument, which is a deductive argument. To help you consider the merits of these arguments, we will summarize each briefly.

Ontological Argument from Highest Ideal
The philosopher Anselm of Canterbury first formulated the argument from

---

[a] Ps. 33:6, 9; 148:5; 2 Pet. 3:7

the highest ideal, also called the ontological argument (*ontos* means "being"). The ontological argument seeks to prove the existence of God by reasoning that human beings, regardless of their culture or period in history, continually conceive of a perfect being that is greater than they are—so great that no greater being can be conceived of. This perfect being is God. The argument follows that since the human mind is only able to conceive of that which actually exists, God must exist because we would not be able to conceive of God unless there was God. Likewise, everything else that we conceive of, from automobiles to the color blue, does exist. Therefore, our idea about this perfect, highest being called God is derived from the actual existence of this God. This argument is rooted in Exodus 3:14, where God reveals Himself to Moses as "I am who I am."

Historically, this argument for the existence of God has been highly controversial. Its defenders include René Descartes and Benedict Spinoza. Its critics include Christian Thomas Aquinas and atheist David Hume. While not without merit, this argument's complexity and controversy make it perhaps not the most compelling argument for God's existence in comparison to the inductive arguments that we will now explore.

Teleological Argument from Design

The teleological argument (*telos* means "purpose" or "design") seeks to convince from the amazing harmony in all of creation that the world has been ordered by an Intelligent Designer, who is God. In its simple form, the argument contends that when we see something that is designed, we rightly assume that an intelligent designer created it. Further, the more complicated something is, the more intelligent the designer must have been.

Classic advocates of the teleological argument from design include Christian philosophers Thomas Aquinas and William Paley. Paley's watchmaker analogy stated that if you came across something as complex as a watch, you would rightly assume that an intelligent designer made it. Likewise, as we walk through the world, we continually encounter things made with far greater complexity than a watch, such as the eye you are using to read these words. Biochemistry professor Michael Behe made similar points in his argument for "irreducible complexity": that certain biological systems, like an eye, are too complex to have evolved from simpler predecessors.[3] They had to come into existence as complete systems. Therefore, we are logically compelled to believe that these things were intelligently designed by God.

The teleological argument is found Psalm 19:1: "The heavens declare the glory of God, and the sky above proclaims his handiwork" and Romans 1:20: "[God's] invisible attributes, namely, his eternal power and divine nature, have been clearly perceived, ever since the creation of the world, in the things that have been made."

Regarding our bodies, Psalm 139:13–14 says, "For you formed my inward parts; you knitted me together in my mother's womb. I praise you, for I am fearfully and wonderfully made. Wonderful are your works..." Further findings in science continually increase our understanding of the wondrous complexity of our body, including the fact that just one human DNA molecule holds roughly the same amount of information as one volume of an encyclopedia.

God Himself even used teleological reasoning. Beginning in Job 38, God peppers Job with 64 questions about the design of creation, including: "Where were you when I laid the foundation of the earth? Tell me, if you have understanding." As an aside, God's questioning of Job was God seeking in love to bring Job to the understanding that, just as God had a purposeful design for His creation, so too He had a purposeful design in mind for Job's suffering.

In recent decades, the "fine-tuning argument" has also gained prominence as a form of the teleological argument. Proponents note that these basic physical constants must fall within very narrow limits if intelligent life is to develop. For example, our world's constant gravitational force, the rate of universe expansion, the average distance between stars, the nature of gravity, earth's distance from the sun, earth's rotation period, and even our carbon dioxide levels are so finely tuned for life on our planet that no logical explanation other than God is tenable. Collins says:

"When you look from the perspective of a scientist at the universe, it looks as if it knew we humans were coming. There are 15 constants—the gravitational constant, various constants about the strong and weak nuclear forces, etc.—that have precise values. If any one of those constants was off by even one part in a million, or in some cases, by one part in a million, the universe could not have actually come to the point where we see it. Matter would not have been able to coalesce, there would have been no galaxy, stars, planets, or people."[4]

Cosmological Argument from First Cause

The cosmological argument comes from the word cosmos, which means "orderly arrangement." The word was purportedly first used to explain the universe by the 6th C. BC Greek philosopher Pythagoras. The argument from first cause asserts that, for every effect, there is a cause. (This is referred to formally as the law of causality.) Therefore, the material world must have a beginning, and that beginning must be outside of the material world to cause it to come into existence. The first cause, also called the uncaused cause, is God. On this point, the astronomer Fred Hoyle claimed that "the probability of life arising on earth (by purely natural means, without special divine aid) is less than the probability that a flight-worthy Boeing 747 should be assembled by a hurricane roaring through a junkyard."[5]

Throughout history this argument has been popular with many non-Christian thinkers such as Plato, Aristotle, the Muslim philosopher Al-Farabi, and Jewish thinker Moses Maimonides. Noteworthy Christians advocating the cosmological argument include Augustine, Anselm, Descartes, and Aquinas. They have reasoned that, in addition to the material world, immaterial things such as emotions and

DOCTRINE

intelligence are simply not possible apart from a God who created the world in general and humans in particular. Simply, the cause of our emotions and thoughts cannot be emotionless and unintelligent matter. Therefore, we must have been created by an emotional and intelligent God, which explains our feelings and thoughts.

The cosmological argument for creation from a first cause is rooted throughout Scripture. The biblical creation story tells us that an eternal, necessary first cause (God) created the universe and all that is in it. God is eternal and independent and is therefore separate and apart from His dependent creation as the necessary first cause.[a] The first two chapters of Genesis report that God eternally existed before any aspect of creation and that God alone is the Creator and cause of our world.

In explaining how God is the cause of creation, it is common to hear the phrase *ex nihilo*. *Ex nihilo* is Latin for "out of nothing" and is commonly used to explain how God made creation out of nothing. Hebrews 11:3 says, "By faith we understand that the universe was created by the word of God, so that what is seen was not made out of things that are visible."

Opponents of this argument have sought to negate its claims by offering alternatives to the concept that the world had a cause and a beginning. For example, solipsists suggest that the world is simply an illusion. Nevertheless, they hypocritically look both ways before crossing a busy street. Some have argued that the world is self-created, which seems as illogical as coming home to find a new smart phone already connected to all of your accounts and believing that it created itself, downloaded its software, and connected itself to the internet. Others have reasoned that the material world came from nothing and was made by nothing, which also seems illogical because no-thing cannot create a-thing. Believing that matter and energy sprang from nothing requires a leap of faith more giant than believing that creation is the work of God.

Finally, others have opposed the argument from first cause by suggesting that the universe is eternal. Most scientists believe that the universe is winding down to an eventual end based upon the Second Law of Thermodynamics and the Big Bang Theory, which state that it likewise had a beginning. This leads us to the argument from time, which we will examine next. As a curious historical footnote, even the great father of evolution, Charles Darwin, was clear in "On the Origin of Species" that he remained convinced that God existed in agreement with the cosmological argument.

Kalam Argument from Time
The basic Kalam argument is that the existence of time necessitates a beginning as a reference point from which time proceeds. This reference point would have to be outside of time to begin time, and that eternal reference point is God, who is

---

[a] Ps. 90:2

outside of time but initiated time. To put it another way, the universe is not eternal and therefore must have a beginning. Behind that beginning must be a cause that is eternal, or apart from time. Therefore, the cause of time and creation is God.

This argument relies heavily on the Second Law of Thermodynamics, which affirms that the universe is running out of usable energy and is therefore winding down to an end. Practically, this means that since the universe will have an end, it is not eternal and must have also had a beginning. Also used in support of this argument is Big Bang cosmology, which states that the universe had a beginning and has been expanding ever since and is therefore not eternal.

The argument from time was formulated by Muslim philosophers such as Al-Farabi and Al-Ghazali and is now popular among Muslims, Jews, Protestants, and Catholics who teach that the existence of time is evidence for God. The argument does have merits and is helpful, but it does not prove that God is personal or intelligent. Neither does it determine the nature of God as deistic, pantheistic, or monotheistic. Therefore, by itself the Kalam argument can help us believe in a god but cannot clearly articulate any specific information about the nature of God.

Axiological Argument from Morality

The axiological argument takes its title from the word axios, which means "judgment." The argument from morality contends that everyone, regardless of his or her culture, has an innate understanding of right and wrong. Simply, all sane people know that such things as rape and murder are wrong.

But where do these universal morals that exist in each of us come from? God has made us with a conscience that helps us navigate through life as responsible moral beings, though we often ignore the conscience He has given us. When we argue that the way something is is not the way it "ought" to be, the moral argument proponents would say we are not merely appealing to law, but ultimately to God, who is the giver of the moral law implanted in our consciences. Speaking of non-Christians, Romans 2:15 says, "the work of the law is written on their hearts, while their conscience also bears witness, and their conflicting thoughts accuse or even excuse them." Simply, when we feel bad about what we have done or what someone else has done, we are bearing witness that God is the Lawgiver and has put an understanding of His law in our conscience.

The axiological argument was formalized by the philosopher Immanuel Kant and used by the great Christian thinker C. S. Lewis. Lewis insightfully noted that when we have been sinned against, we often appeal to the universal laws that define right and wrong, assuming that there is an authority above the person who acted unjustly toward us. We also anticipate that somehow everyone else will agree with our understanding of right and wrong because we know that they have a conscience in them, which explains why we appeal to it.

One of the beautiful results of the moral law is that it permits us to have a righteous anger. Because there is both a Lawgiver and Law, we are able to rise above the incessant postmodern pluralism that says that there is no Law but only cultural perspective on morality. Because the axiological argument is true, we do not have to accept evil atrocities and injustices committed in culture; instead, as human beings we can appeal to the higher authority of God the Lawgiver who sits over all cultures in authority. This explains, for example, why Nazi Germany was stopped for violating God's unchanging laws regarding human dignity and not merely accepted as a law unto itself. Curiously, at the Nuremberg trials, one of the more common appeals by those on trial was that there was no Lawgiver or Law, and that they were simply obeying the law of their nation. In response, the axiological argument was given because human beings were made with a sense of right and wrong by a moral God who is our Lawgiver. Other glorious examples of the practical outworking of the axiological law are Abraham Lincoln's and William Wilberforce's battles against slavery, as well as Martin Luther King Jr.'s fight for civil rights from religious convictions.

In conclusion, taken together as a cumulative case, the various arguments for God's existence reveal that God exists; He is the Intelligent Designer, the powerful cause of all creation, apart from time but at work in time, and morally good.

WHAT DOES CREATION REVEAL ABOUT GOD?

Genesis 1:1 reveals that "in the beginning, God created." In the same way that a piece of music reveals something of the composer and artwork reveals something of the artist, so too creation reveals something of the Creator. In this way, creation is a form of general revelation.[a] Therefore, examining creation reveals 14 glorious truths about God as Creator.

1. God is the only God. The opening line of the Bible does not say, for example, "In the beginning, nothing made everything," or "In the beginning, Creator and creation were one and the same as they had been throughout eternity," or even "In the beginning, the gods made the heavens and the earth." No, the opening line of the Bible says, "In the beginning, God created." Likewise, Isaiah 45:18 says, "For thus says the LORD, who created the heavens (he is God!), who formed the earth and made it…'I am the LORD, and there is no other.'"
2. Our personal Creator God is Trinitarian.[b] Genesis 1:26 reveals that the Creator God is the Trinity: "Then God said, 'Let us make man in our image, after our likeness.'" Therefore, when Genesis says that God is the creator, it speaks of the entire Trinity. This fact is confirmed in the rest of Scripture, revealing that the Father created[c], the Son created[d], and the Spirit created.[e]
3. God is eternally uncaused. This means that God eternally existed before creation, that God is not created, and that creation is not eternal like God.

---

[a] Ps. 19:1–2; Rom. 1:20 [b] We discussed this topic in further detail in chapter 1
[c] Ps. 19:1; Acts 17:28; 1 Cor. 8:6 [d] John 1:1–3, 10; Col. 1:16–17 [e] Gen. 1:2; Job 26:13

4. God is living. Life in general and human life in particular does not spring forth from the "it" of unliving matter. Rather, God is living, and He makes life and, as we will see in the next chapter, He breathes his life into human beings to give us life.
5. God is independent. While the rest of creation is dependent upon God, God himself is uncaused, independent, and without need, lack, want, or dependence upon anyone or anything. Everything apart from God is created by God and dependent upon God so that it simply would not have come into existence or continue to exist without God. This is precisely what Paul preached: "The God who made the world and everything in it, being Lord of heaven and earth, does not live in temples made by man, nor is he served by human hands, as though he needed anything, since he himself gives to all mankind life and breath and everything."[a] Because God is independent, He alone can truly and purely love; since He does not need us, His interactions with us alone are of pure motive.
6. God is transcendent, separate from His creation. There is a clear demarcation between Creator and creation that does not exist in pantheism, panentheism, radical environmentalism, Wicca, or the New Spirituality.
7. God is immanent. Not only is God transcendent over creation, but contrary to the deists' claim, He is also actively at work in His creation, sustaining and providentially ruling over it.
8. God is personal. Because God is personal, He made mankind in a personal way and gives to us personality and personhood. God is a personal "He" not an impersonal "it". Apart from a personal God, there is no way to explain human personhood.
9. God is powerful. In creation, God's power is seen in the fact that He made everything from nothing by Himself and that He rules over creation, even suspending natural laws as He wills to perform miracles and supernatural feats.
10. God is beautiful. Whereas God could have created air filtration machines, He instead chose to create trees. Whereas God could have chosen to cast creation in black and white, He instead chose to paint from a vast palette of colors. Why? Because God is gloriously beautiful, and creation reflects His beauty with ceaseless displays of breathtaking splendor.
11. God is holy. God is without evil, and creation originally reflected His holy purity until it was marred and stained by demonic and human sin. Our holy God moves in His sin-marred creation to make it pure. In re-creation, God will again restore all creation to a holy state, when He lifts the curse and removes its effects forever.
12. God is a prophet. It was through speaking that God brought creation into existence by His word. Similarly, God also kindly uses the preaching of His

---

[a] Acts 17:24–25

Word to bring forth life.
13. God is gracious. We see the grace of God in creation as He blesses His creation, including the man and woman, whom He makes in His image and likeness. From the opening pages of Scripture to its final line in Revelation 22:20–21, God speaks words of grace, saying, "'Surely I am coming soon.' Amen. Come, Lord Jesus! The grace of the Lord Jesus be with all. Amen."
14. God is a sovereign King. As Creator, God is king over all that is made, including Satan, demons, mankind, planets, stars, suns, moons, animals – everyone and everything everywhere. All of creation comes from God, is ruled by God, belongs to God, and will give an account before God, who is without peer.

In sum, we see that God is not a faceless intelligent designer of the universe, but the living Lord, Yahweh, who alone created everything so we could live in loving relation with Him now and forever. From the first words of the Bible, the Lord is distinguished from the gods of the nations. The other gods—demons, really—are created beings that can't create anything.[a] All they can do is counterfeit what God creates, but as God's children, we can know and enjoy all that God has created for us to enjoy.

WHAT ARE THE VARIOUS CHRISTIAN VIEWS OF CREATION?

Among Bible-believing Christians, there are at least four primary interpretations of the creation account in Genesis 1-2. Personally, we find the first view to be the most persuasive biblically. But, as Paul says, we now see only in part, and one day in Jesus' presence we will know in full, and we will all be in complete agreement on this and other matters. Until that day, may we worship our Creator together and graciously discuss and debate our differences without unnecessarily dividing over them.

In all these models, there is agreement that "God created the heavens and the earth", meaning He created the universe. There is disagreement on how He did this work.

All models agree that microevolution, change as organisms adapt to their environment, is a scientifically verifiable fact but disagree if God used macroevolution, the emergence of new types of organisms different from their ancestral organisms in accomplishing His creative work.

In all the models other than No. 3, there is agreement that the days of Genesis 1 are six sequential 24-hour days. There is disagreement on what the six days describe.

Most scholars agree that there is a literary pattern in the structured narrative of Genesis 1, but disagree if this portrays a sequence of creative events or is just a literary framework for revealing the creation theology:

---

[a] Deut. 32:17; 1 Cor. 10:19–21; Col. 1:16

CREATION: GOD MAKES

Cycle	Forming	Filling
1	Day-Night	Sun-Moon
2	Heavens-Waters	Fish-Birds
3	Dry Land	Earth Animals-Humans

View 1: Historic Old-Earth Young Humanity Creationism

The word used for "beginning" in Genesis 1:1 is *re'shit* in Hebrew, which marks a starting point for what comes afterwards. There is no gap between verses 1 and 2. Rather verse 1 begins the Genesis story telling us that the God who created everything is the same God who creates His image bearers and the Promised Land where He will live with them. What God created in the first verse existed for an undefined period of time (which could be anywhere from a moment to billions of years) before God began the work of preparing the uninhabitable land for the habitation of mankind. The preparation of the uncultivated land and the creation of the first human beings, Adam and Eve, occurred in the six literal 24-hour days of Genesis 1, as echoed in Exodus 20:11. This view leaves open the possibility of an old earth, six literal days of creation, and a young humanity on the old earth. It does have the biblical difficulty since it appears that sun and moon are created on day four rather than before the story begins. In protest, some will argue that death did not come until human sin, but this might refer to human death only. For example, before Adam and Eve sinned, if they or an animal ate a plant, would that plant not die? If a leaf fell off of a tree, would that leaf have not died?[6]

View 2: Young-Earth Young Humanity Creationism

In this view, God created the entire universe, including Adam and Eve, in six literal 24-hour days. As it seeks to be faithful to its reading of the biblical text, this view affirms that the entire universe is less than 10,000 years old. It interprets the data of science in terms of inspired Scripture, refusing to compromise God's teaching about the date and divine methods of creation with naturalistic scientific theories. It does have some biblical difficulties, such as the creation of sun and moon on day four while there is evening and morning on the first three days.[7]

View 3: Old Earth Creation or Intelligent Design (no evolution involved)

The "days" of Genesis 1 are analogies of God's workdays, setting a pattern for our rhythm of work and rest. They are understood in the same sense as "in that day" of Isaiah 11:10-11. They represent periods of God's historical supernatural activity in preparing and populating the earth as a place for humans to live, love, work, and worship. These days are broadly consecutive periods of indiscriminate length from a human point of view. The biblical difficulty is that the days have evenings and mornings, so they would naturally be 24-hour days.[a]

---

[a] Proponents include Hugh Ross: "Reasons to Believe" and Stephen Meyer: "Discovery Institute"

View 4: Evolutionary Creation

In this view, God used the planned and purpose-driven natural process of evolution to do His creative work of the universe and life. Genesis 1 uses the six sequential 24-hour days of the Sabbath rhythm as a literary framework to reveal the theology of creation. The universe is a creation that is completely dependent for its continued existence on the sustaining power of the triune God of the Bible. God's design is shown in the finely tuned physical laws and the biological processes necessary for life to evolve through transitions, which would be impossible without God's involvement, culminating in humans with their incredibly complex brains and minds paired together in full image of God's personhood. Humans evolved from pre-human ancestors, and, over a period of time, the image of God and human sin were gradually and mysteriously manifested. While embracing the methodological naturalism of experimental science, which searches for natural rather than supernatural processes, it decisively rejects metaphysical naturalism, which denies the existence of God and the supernatural. It has biblical difficulties in that it usually does not hold Adam and Eve as literal parents of the human race though the New Testament takes this as literal history.[a] It also has difficulties in explaining how one species can actually transition into another as Genesis 1:21, 24, 25 all speak of God making fish, birds, and animals "according to their kinds".[b]

ARE THE SIX DAYS OF CREATION LITERAL 24-HOUR DAYS?

While the four Christian views of creation listed above are possible, the question remains, which is probable? To answer that question, we have to deal with the very important issue of whether the six days of creation listed in Genesis 1 are in fact literal 24-hour days of creation.

As an aside, it is curious that the names we currently use for the days of our week come from paganism and their named for false gods honored on their particular day of the week. Sunday means "Sun's day", Monday means "Moon's day", Tuesday means "Tiu or Twia's day", Wednesday mean's "Woden's day" named after "Odin", Thursday means "Thor's day", Friday means "Freya's day", and Saturday means "Saturn's day".

Those Christians who argue for a metaphorical view of the six days of creation, the so-called day-age views, rightly point out that the word used for day in Hebrew (*yom*), often refers to an extended period of time that is more than a literal 24-hour day.[c] Nonetheless, if we read the Scriptures, it seems apparent that the six days of creation in Genesis 1 are literal 24-hour days for two reasons.

---

[a] Matt. 19:4-6; Rom 5:12-14; Heb. 4:4-7; 2 Pet 2:4-5 [b] Proponents include Biologos, John Walton, Francis Collins, John Lennox, Philip Johnson, Tim Keller, and Michael Behe [c] Ps. 20:1; Prov. 11:4, 21:31, 24:10, 25:13; Eccl. 7:14

CREATION: GOD MAKES

First, each day is numbered so that there is a succession of days. Further, each day is described as having a morning and evening, which is the common vernacular for a day.[a] These details in Genesis 1 clearly indicate that the days are literal.

Second, in Exodus 20:8–11, God says:

"Remember the Sabbath day, to keep it holy. Six days you shall labor, and do all your work, but the seventh day is a Sabbath to the LORD your God. On it you shall not do any work, you, or your son, or your daughter, your male servant, or your female servant, or your livestock, or the sojourner who is within your gates. For in six days the LORD made heaven and earth, the sea, and all that is in them, and rested on the seventh day. Therefore the LORD blessed the Sabbath day and made it holy."

God says that He made (*asah*, fashioned or shaped, rather than *bara*, created from nothing) creation in six days and on the seventh day He rested. Additionally, His work and rest are to be the precedent for us and why God's people in the Old Testament had a seven-day week with a Sabbath day.

Evolutionary creationism, using the Literary Framework View sees the days as 24-hour days of the weekly rhythm, which Moses used to tell the creation story. However, they are not days of creation as Exodus 20:11 teaches. Genesis 1-11 is a narrative of origins cast in the worldview of ancient peoples rather than a record of actual historical events. The ancient intellectual categories of the inspired writers were employed in the process of God's inspired description of creation.

We hold to historic creationism, which emphasizes that the first two chapters of Genesis, God's inspired and inerrant Word, tell us that the God who created everything (angels, space-time, mass-energy, sun, moon, and stars, and all species of animals) prepared the land for human habitation in six literal 24-hour days. At the end of those days, he shaped dust and breathed the breath of life into it, creating Adam. From Adam's rib, God created the woman. They were created to be in relationship with each other and with God as living Creator and loving Lord and first human beings, the parents of us all.

Nonetheless, there have been ongoing debates by Jesus-loving, Bible-believing scholars throughout the history of the church regarding whether the days of creation were literal 24-hour days. So long as one's position on this issue does not become the litmus test for Christian orthodoxy, ongoing spirited study and discussion can be helpful to God's people; it can force them to build their unity around what they do agree on, such as the fact that the Trinitarian God of the Bible created the heavens and the earth and lovingly fashioned them as a gift to us and home for us in which to worship and enjoy Him.[8]

---

[a] Gen. 1:5, 8, 13, 19, 23, 31

HOW OLD IS THE EARTH?

There has been no shortage of attempts to determine and defend a particular age of the earth.

For many Christians, the Bible's teaching seems pretty simple: the earth was created on the first of the six 24-hour days of Genesis, which culminated with the creation of Adam, the first human. Adding up the genealogies in Genesis puts the age of the earth at about 6,000 years.

Other Christians, ancient and contemporary, have not seen the creation account in strict historical terms. They focus on God as creator rather than on six literal days and think we should not try to specify the age of the earth.

Still others seek to integrate the general scientific consensus—that the earth is around 4.5 billion years old—into their theology. They adapt their view of the Bible to accommodate science and teach that the earth must be old.

Archbishop James Ussher dated creation precisely to 4004 BC According to traditional Judaism, the year 2020 AD is actually year 5,780 of creation. The Jewish year of creation is Gregorian year 3761 BC Both Ussher and Jews used the biblical genealogies (e.g., Genesis 5 and 10) and added up the number of years between Adam, Noah, and Abraham to arrive at their creation dates. That they differ somewhat on their dates indicates the difficulty of achieving high accuracy. Still, the method cannot be merely dismissed if one holds to inspired and inerrant Scripture. Jews, Ussher, and many Christians agree within a couple hundred years because of indications within the genealogies in Genesis 5 and 11. They differ, however, from the genealogies of Jesus in Matthew 1 and Luke 3, which show line of descent rather than specific lengths of time in each generation. The Genesis genealogies do not have large gaps. If one follows Scripture, Adam, the first human, was created about 6,000 years ago.

However, believing in a recent Adam does not require a young earth. If one sees the days other than six 24-hour days, then the age of the earth is not a biblical teaching. Those who agree with us that the Genesis days are 24-hours long still may not hold that Scripture mandates a young earth. The creation of planet earth may not have been during those six days.

Many believe that Genesis 1:1 is a brief summary of an unspecified period of time—perhaps a minute or billions of years, since the Hebrew word for beginning, like its English translation, refers to inauguration rather than to a specific timeframe—that preceded the six literal days of Genesis during which God prepared Eden on the already-created earth as the dwelling place of mankind.

In the end, we believe the date of the earth cannot be a closed-handed issue. It seems to us that those who strongly advocate either young- or old-earth dates are inferring a position from the Bible that the Bible simply does not state unequivocally. It must also be admitted that the age of the earth is not of great concern in the Bible. The great authors of the Bible, including David, Isaiah, and Paul, and Jesus himself, never referred to the age of the earth, even though they asserted God as Creator.

As Augustine rightly said, the Bible is not a scientific textbook seeking to answer the ever-changing inquiries of science but rather a theological textbook seeking to reveal God and the means by which he saves us. What the Bible actually teaches is inerrant truth from God that must be believed, but it does not teach everything we want to know. We must be courageous to receive and teach unashamedly what it does say as closed-handed issues[a] but humble enough to let unclear and unrevealed matters be open-handed issues, avoiding unprofitable controversies.[b]

The question persists as to how we deal with the widespread scientific consensus that the earth is 4.5 billion years old and certainly appears to be old, even to nonscientists. Many solutions have been offered, including the following:

1. Though the earth appears old to most scientists, it is in fact young, and the scientists are simply mistaken. Admittedly, Christians who hold this view are considered unscientific and even unintelligent by the watching world, but they retort that it is better to believe Scripture than the ever-changing theories of scientists.
2. The earth appears old because it was made mature, like Adam was. If we had seen Adam and Eve just after they were created (remember, they were mature enough to be commanded to be fruitful and rule the earth), and asked them how old they were, we would have been astonished at their answer.
3. The flood in Genesis 6-9 covered the earth universally, which compressed the geological layers and rearranged the topography so greatly that the earth appears to be old, especially when we assume geologic processes take long periods of time.
4. The earth is in fact old, and the days mentioned in Genesis 1 and 2 are not literal 24-hour days but rather extended periods of time.
5. The earth may be, or likely is, old. As our examination of Genesis 1:1 revealed, God created the earth during an indefinite period of time before the six days of Genesis. That could in fact have been billions of years ago, which would explain the seemingly old age of the earth. Then, in six literal days God prepared the earth for the creation of mankind and on the sixth day made the first man and woman.

We find this last view quite compelling for five reasons. (1) It maintains a literal six-day interpretation of Genesis 1, which seems to be the point of the chapter. (2) It defines key terms biblically rather than scientifically. The word translated "heavens" is better understood as "skies"; "earth" (planet) as "land" (Promised Land); and "without form and void" (primordial chaos) as "uncultivated" and "uninhabited." (3) It teaches that the first humans appeared recently so that human

---

[a] 2 Tim. 2:15, 3:16–17; Titus 1:9; Jude 3   [b] Deut. 29:29; 2 Tim. 2:23; Titus 3:9

life on the earth is young even if the earth is old. (4) It was the most common view of early Christians, such as Augustine, and did not fall out of favor until the rise of modern science. (5) It correlates with the findings of the scientific world from a biblical worldview. The teachings of the Bible always have priority in our theologizing, but of the possible biblical views, we prefer this view that explains the most data with the fewest difficulties.

While there is great debate about the age of the earth, there is much more agreement between the biblical and scientific data on the age of the first true Homo sapiens, that is, true humans who lived in villages and practiced agriculture. Scientists generally date the origin of true Homo sapiens to less than 10,000 years ago, even as they date other human-like beings much older. Even those people who are committed to naturalistic evolution and an old earth agree with the biblical data that, while the earth may be old, human life as we know it is relatively young. Their studies are now concluding that there was a first human female ("mitochondrial Eve") and a first human male ("Y-chromosomal Adam"). Therefore, even the most conservative Bible scholars and the most unbelieving naturalistic scientists agree that human life as we know it, that is humans with villages, gardens, and temples, is, at most, roughly 10,000 years old.

HOW DOES CREATIONISM DIFFER FROM NATURALISM?

The bottom line in the debate about the origins of our world and life therein is that it either comes from God (creationism) or somehow came into existence apart from God (naturalism). Dr. George Wald, Professor of Biology at Harvard University, and recipient of the 1971 Nobel Prize in Biology said, "When it comes to the origin of life, we have only two possibilities as to how life arose. One is spontaneous generation arising to evolution; the other is a supernatural creative act of God. There is no third possibility...Spontaneous generation was scientifically disproved one hundred years ago by Louis Pasteur, Spellanzani, Reddy and others. That leads us scientifically to only one possible conclusion – that life arose as a supernatural creative act of God...I will not accept that philosophically because I do not want to believe in God. Therefore, I choose to believe in that which I know is scientifically impossible, spontaneous generation arising to evolution."[9]

Naturalism, associated with atheism, views creation as merely the product of time, energy, and chance. As Carl Sagan famously said, "The Cosmos is all that is or ever was or ever will be."[10] Or, to say it another way, the ultimate explanation of everything from life to love is to be found in particle physics, string theory, and whatever governs the elements of the material world, as there is nothing beyond the physical world and its atoms.

Likely the most famous proponent of naturalism is Charles Darwin (1809–1892), an English naturalist who founded the modern theory of evolution. He published his proposal in the 1859 book "On the Origin of Species by Means of Natural Selection, or the Preservation of Favoured Races in the Struggle for Life". The lengthy original title is often shortened to "On the Origin of Species", both because of its length and racist overtones. While it seems that Darwin never disbelieved in the existence of a God of some kind, his evolutionary theory has been used in an effort to explain the origin of human life apart from God. In fact, atheist Richard Dawkins says that "although atheism might have been logically tenable before Darwin, Darwin made it possible to be an intellectually fulfilled atheist."[11]

As Christians, we freely accept the experimentally verified fact of micro-evolution—that species can and do adapt to their environments. In fact, micro-evolution may be simply yet another evidence of the goodness and mercy of God upon his creation, since it helps a species adapt to its environment so as to help protect it from predators. However, Christians are not free to accept the thesis of atheistic, naturalistic-evolution—that one species can evolve into another species entirely by random application of natural processes.

Although it reigns as the dominant paradigm for over 100 years, the theory of natural evolution continues to be questioned by both Christian and non-Christians. Antony Flew, the preeminent philosopher of atheism, abandoned his failed theory in 2004.[12]

Thomas Nagel, an atheistic philosopher, argues that the materialist version of evolutionary biology fails because it cannot account for the existence of mind and consciousness. He suggests scientists need an entirely different kind of theory to explain the emergence of life, and in particular conscious life.[13]

The reasons for the lack of confidence in naturalistic evolution are many, but the following are some of the most implausible leaps of faith that it makes, all of which require at least as much faith as believing in an eternal creator God.

1. Naturalistic evolution purports that nothing made everything, also called spontaneous generation. Essentially, no-thing causes every-thing to spring into existence, although this is not considered a miracle because there is no God. Francis Collins, who headed the Human Genome Project, says, "I can't imagine how nature, in this case the universe, could have created itself. And the very fact that the universe had a beginning implies that someone was able to begin it. And it seems to me that had to be outside of nature."[14]

    Naturalistic evolution is put in a quandary between the undeniable evidence that the universe had a beginning and the equally undeniable principle that nothing comes from nothing. Most scientists give credence to the big bang theory, which states that there was some sort of initial incident that set in motion events that in time led to the formation of the world as we know it; thus, the big bang accounts for the continual expanding of the universe. Stephen Hawking wrote: "Almost everyone now believes that the universe, and time itself, had a beginning at the big bang."[15] While Christians would see Big God rather than big bang, the point in either case is that the universe is not eternal but had a beginning.

In desperation to avoid the quandary of a universe with a beginning, they speculate that there might be an infinite number of invisible parallel universes stretching back into eternity, without a shred of evidence to support their imagining. How can they criticize Christians for being people of blind faith? We have all the historical evidence for Jesus and His resurrection to support our faith, while they have absolutely nothing for their mythology.

2. Naturalistic evolution purports that chaos made order. The basic telling of the history of the universe according to atheistic naturalism is that the orderliness of our universe is the result of cataclysmic disorder, chaos, and chance that together resulted in great orderliness. As a general rule, our life experiences confirm to us that great chaos and disorder do not, in and of themselves, lead to harmonious order. On this point, the astronomer Fred Hoyle "claimed that the probability of life arising on earth (by purely natural means, without special divine aid) is less than the probability that a flight-worthy Boeing 747 should be assembled by a hurricane roaring through a junkyard."[16]

Additionally, Stephen Hawking has said, "The odds against a universe like ours emerging out of something like the big bang are enormous. I think there are clearly religious implications."[17] Furthermore, Hawking admitted, "It would be very difficult to explain why the universe would have begun in just this way except as the act of a God who intended to create beings like us."[18] This conclusion agrees with the teleological argument which we studied previously.

3. Naturalistic evolution purports that impersonal matter made personal humanity. Naturalists have reasoned that, in addition to the material world, immaterial things such as emotions and intelligence are simply the result of impersonal, unfeeling, and unintelligent matter. How can matter that does not feel create people who weep? How can matter that does not think create not only the physical organ of the brain but the mental thoughts that accompany it? How can impersonal matter create a person with an identity and personality?

Indeed, the burden of proof is on the naturalist to explain the untenable, whereas the Christian simply states the biblical fact that our personal, passionate, and infinitely brilliant God made us with bits of his glory in our heart, mind, and personality. Furthermore, if our views of justice and morality were nothing more than neurochemistry hardwired into us, then we would lose the right to be morally outraged at such things as genocide, rape, murder, and racism. When we deny the dignity of humanity as created in God's image, we saw off the moral branch upon which we sit to defend it.

4. Naturalistic evolution purports to be unbiased science. But faith beyond any

evidence is still required. Attempts to trace a possible genetic line of transition from one species to another or explain intermediate forms which could survive have so far been fruitless. Further, the atheistic naturalists continue to reject any possibility of the hand of God in the making of the world. This is, as Romans 1:18 states, because they suppress the truth due to hardness of heart against God. As Harvard professor Richard Lewontin said, "We are forced by our a priori adherence to material causes to create an apparatus of investigation and a set of concepts that produce material explanations."[19] He continues to insist that this "materialism is absolute, for we cannot allow a divine foot in the door."[20]

In addition, Nobel laureate Steven Weinberg says, "I personally feel that the teaching of modern science is corrosive of religious belief, and I'm all for that!"[21] He goes on to say: "From my own point of view, I can hope that this long sad story will come to an end at some time in the future and that this progression of priests and ministers and rabbis and ulemas and imams and bonzes and bodhisattvas will come to an end, that we'll see no more of them. I hope that this is something to which science can contribute and if it is, then I think it may be the most important contribution that we can make."[22] Evolutionary biologist Jerry Coyne wrote "Faith Versus Fact: Why Science and Religion Are Incompatible" to make his point that science must be limited to what can be known from empirical study and that anything else is superstition. But it is impossible to take him seriously when he completely ignores the historical arguments for Jesus' resurrection done by scholars such as Gary Habermas, Larry Hurtado, and N.T. Wright or the failure of naturalistic science to explain origin of life and consciousness. Coyne's naturalistic conclusion is "in reality we're puppets performing scripted parts written by the laws of physics."[23]

Yet, if all we are is simply the result of time and chance, and our thoughts are no more than the random collision of matter, why should we trust our minds to tell us anything truthful or to be a trustworthy guide in scientific discovery? On this point, the prominent atheistic philosopher Thomas Nagel asks if we can have any "continued confidence in reason as a source of knowledge about the nonapparent character of the world? In itself, I believe an evolutionary story tells against such confidence."[24]

Indeed, there is no conflict between experimental science and Christian faith. However, there is a conflict between Christianity and atheistic naturalism, because it will not allow the possibility of a Creator God. Christians should not, however, in any way abandon the sciences; instead, they should pursue them with great vigor and faith to learn more about God through what He has made as an act of worship to Him.[25]

Tragically, there has been much misreporting about the historical relationship between Christianity and science. Thus, we want to refute some powerful yet untrue myths that have caused some to wrongly see Christianity as suppressing the truth while science pursues it.[26]

The first myth is that, prior to Christopher Columbus's first voyage, Christians thought the world was flat. The truth is that, more than 800 years before Columbus's voyage, Bede the church historian taught that the earth was round, as did Thomas Aquinas. Furthermore, Sacrobosco's book De Sphaera, written around 1231, was the standard manual for elementary astronomy until the Renaissance. That work described a spherical earth some two centuries before Columbus.

The second myth is that when Copernicus wrote that the earth revolved around the sun, his conclusions were a revolutionary, and previously untaught, concept. The truth is that Copernicus was taught the essential fundamentals leading to his model by his Scholastic professors, that is, Christian scholars who developed the model gradually over the previous two centuries.

The third myth is that the "scientific revolution" of the seventeenth century invented science as we know it because Christianity had lost the power to prevent it. The truth is that 300 years before Newton, a Scholastic cleric named Jean Buridan anticipated Newton's first law of motion, that a body in motion will stay in motion unless otherwise impeded. It was Buridan, not an Enlightenment luminary, who first proposed that the earth turns on its axis. Furthermore, science flourished only in Europe, where the worldview was shaped by Christianity. Many civilizations had alchemy, yet only Christian-influenced Europe developed chemistry. Likewise, astrology was practiced everywhere, but only in Europe did it become astronomy.

In closing, we would commend those whom God has gifted to love Him with all their mind and to do so in the sciences to God's glory and their joy, as has always been the case with God's people.

WHAT DIFFERENCE DOES THE DOCTRINE OF CREATION MAKE FOR YOUR LIFE?

The Bible teaches that creation in general and human life in particular were made by God, belong to God, exist for God, are restless apart from God, and will return to God. Disbelief in the doctrine of creation logically causes people to believe that we came from no one, are alive on the earth for nothing, and that we die to go nowhere. The renowned atheistic philosopher Bertrand Russell summarizes this worldview:

"That Man is the product of causes which had no prevision of the end they were achieving; that his origin, his growth, his hopes and fears, his loves and his beliefs, are but the outcome of accidental collocations of atoms; that no fire, no heroism, no intensity of thought and feeling, can preserve an individual life beyond the grave; that all the labours of the ages, all the devotion, all the inspiration, all the noonday brightness of human genius, are destined to extinction in the vast death of the solar system, and the whole temple of Man's achievement must inevitably be buried beneath the debris of a universe in ruins—all these things, if not quite beyond dispute, are yet so nearly certain, that no philosophy which rejects them can hope to stand. Only within the scaffolding of these truths, only on the firm foundation of the unyielding despair, can the soul's habitation henceforth be safely built."[27]

We agree, the only logical option apart from the biblical doctrine of creation is the tragic "firm foundation of the unyielding despair." Similarly, when Richard Dawkins was asked if his view of reality made him depressed, he replied, "I don't feel depressed about it. But if somebody does, that's their problem. Maybe the logic is deeply pessimistic, the universe is bleak, cold and empty. But so what?"[28]

As a pastor who has preached the funerals of suicide victims and prays often with teenage women who continually cut themselves and comes from a long family history of depression so severe that it often results in mental insanity and self-medication with alcoholism, I could not fathom encouraging people to build their lives on "unyielding despair" because "the universe is bleak, cold, and empty" only to disregard their pain and tears by saying "So what?"

Indeed, if no Savior is coming to rescue us, and there is no better place to which we can escape at the end of this life, then once the pain of this life gets too much to bear, we should simply hasten the inevitable. Tragically, many do.

People who do not understand the doctrine of creation and the doctrines that relate to it want to die. Some die a little bit at a time, weeping until they are empty and can no longer muster any tears. Others medicate themselves with prescriptions; antidepressants are now the most sold category of medicine, and depression is the most common diagnosis. Still others self-medicate with sex, food, alcohol, drugs, gambling, entertainment, video games, Internet surfing, and anything else that can serve as a diversion from the "unyielding despair".

What is even sadder than this sadness is the tragic fact that we have not learned from history and show no sign of doing so anytime soon. Anglican bishop N. T. Wright has wisely said:

"There are three basic ways (with variations) in which we can imagine God's space and ours relating to one another...Option One is to slide the two spaces [heaven where God dwells and earth where we dwell] together...Since God, as seen in this option, doesn't hide in a corner of his territory but fills it all with his presence, God is everywhere, and—watch this carefully—everywhere is God. Or, if you like, God is everything, and everything is God. This option is known as "pantheism." It was popular in the ancient Greek and Roman worlds of the first century...it has become increasingly popular in our own times...The main obligation on human beings then is to get in touch with, and in tune with, the divinity within themselves and within the world around."[29]

Wright goes on to explain that it is difficult for people to believe there is divinity in literally everything, including cancer, bugs, and hurricanes. So, the subtle variation of panentheism has become more popular. Panentheism teaches that God is in everything. Wright says:

"The problem with pantheism, and to a large extent panentheism, is that it can't cope with evil. Within the multigodded paganism out of which pantheism grew, when something went wrong you could blame it on a god or goddess who was out to get you. ...But when everything (including yourself) shares in, or lives within, divinity, there's no higher court of appeal when something bad happens. Nobody can come and rescue you. The world and 'the divine' are what they are, and you better get used to it. The only final answer (given by many Stoics in the first century, and by increasing numbers in today's Western world) is suicide."[30]

Option two, Wright says, is to hold the two spaces of Heaven and earth firmly apart with great distance between God and us. This, of course, is the teaching of deism. As Wright says, "Human beings should get used to being alone in the world. The gods will not intervene, either to help or to harm."[31] He goes on to explain that in the ancient world, if you were rich, powerful, healthy, successful, and the like, with a good home to live in, good food to eat, and slaves to tend to your every whim, you were often fine with the idea that you were on your own and that there was no divine help at your disposal. On the other hand, "if, like the great majority of the population, your life was harsh, cruel, and often downright miserable, it was easy to believe that the world where you lived was dark, nasty, and wicked in its very essence and that your best hope was to escape it...by death itself (there we go again)."[32]

Finally, option three, Wright says, is not that Heaven and earth are one and the same (pantheism and panentheism) or completely separated (deism), but rather that God in varying ways interlocks His heaven with His creation. We see this throughout the Old Testament: Jacob saw a ladder coming down from heaven; a pillar of cloud by day and a pillar of fire by night led God's people in the wilderness; and the Tent of Meeting traveled with God's people as a portable meeting place between heaven and earth until they had the temple where the ark of the covenant was kept in the Most Holy Place, which is a sort of interlocking place between heaven and earth. Wright goes on to say that, for the Christian, "the creation of the world was the free outpouring of God's powerful love...And, having made such a world, he has remained in a close, dynamic, and intimate relationship with it, without in any way being contained within it or having it contained within himself."[33]

Therefore, the doctrine of creation sets the stage for the coming of Jesus Christ as our Creator entered His creation. Jesus comes to connect Heaven and earth through Himself as the mediator between the two. As we will see in coming chapters, He comes on a rescue mission to save us from "unyielding despair" by dying for us, placing His own Spirit in us, and promising to return one day to rescue us from death and creation from decay so that life is no longer "bleak, cold, and empty." Indeed, just as He took a barren wasteland and prepared it for our first parents, He will again prepare creation for His people, and rather than saying "so what?" to our pain, the Bible promises that He will wipe every tear from our eyes with nail-scarred hands that understand our need for hope beyond this broken, fallen, weeping world.

QUESTIONS FOR PERSONAL JOURNALING AND/OR SMALL GROUP DISCUSSION

1. Is there a particular view of creation that you subscribe to? How confident do you feel in that position?
2. What is your favorite place you have ever been in God's creation? Why?
3. When you get to Heaven, what questions do you hope to have answered about creation that Genesis simply does not clearly answer?
4. When we care for someone, we make great efforts to prepare a place for them to dwell safely. This is what God did for us in creation. What aspect(s) of God's creation do you most appreciate because of His attention to detail?
5. Why do you think it is important to leave room for mystery in the Christian faith and sometimes say, "I don't know for certain"?
6. Do you think the earth is likely old or young? Why?
7. Think of any Christians you may know who work in the various fields of science (e.g. medicine, engineering, chemistry) and pray for their work and ministry today.
8. What aspect of God's creation (e.g. the human body) do you find most amazing? Spend a moment thanking God for that aspect of His creation.
9. What difference does it make in your life to know that there is a personal Creator God who loves you and has come to rescue you from this fallen world? How would your life be different if you did not believe this?
10. In thinking about Creation, and Jesus returning to erase sin and the curse by bringing a New Creation, what are you most looking forward to in eternity?

CHAPTER 4: IMAGE

"GOD LOVES"

God said, "Let us make man in our image, after our likeness..." So God created man in his own image, in the image of God he created him; male and female he created them.
GENESIS 1:26–27

When I first started dating Grace as a teenager in high school, her Uncle John was the closest thing she had to a grandfather. Uncle John was an older man with no children of his own and Grace and her uncle loved each other dearly. Sadly, his wife Gladys developed Alzheimer's and lived in a full-time care facility because he could no longer care for her. She could not remember who she was or who her husband was.

Nevertheless, every single day, Uncle John would go out to breakfast and have fresh fruit boxed up to take to Gladys. At least once every day, he would lovingly sit and visit with his wife who had completely forgotten their identities. He knew who she was, but she had no idea who either of them was. Despite this painful reality, Uncle John faithfully visited his wife every day until he passed.

I wonder if God often feels like Uncle John. He is present in the lives of the members of His beloved bride, the church, but day after day, we forget who He is and who we are in relationship to Him.

As Christians, we're a lot like Gladys. We have a condition. We're continually forgetting who God is and who we are and are filling that void by placing our identity in pretty much anything else. One question is far-reaching, belief-revealing, life-shaping, and identity-forming. How you answer determines your identity and your testimony. Tragically, few people – even few Bible-believing, Jesus-loving

Christians – rightly answer that question.

"Who am I?"

If you had to pick one word to describe who you are, what would that word be? Would you define yourself by your life stage - child, single, married, divorced, widow, parent, or grandparent? Would you define yourself by your performance - smart or dumb, beautiful or not so much, tough or weak, loved or hated, responsible or irresponsible, organized or messy, winner or loser, joyful or depressed, etc?

"Who am I?"

Your answer to that question is identity-forming and therefore life-shaping. How you see yourself is your identity. Our culture talks about identity as self-image or self-esteem. As Christians, we do not define ourselves by ourselves, but rather find ourselves in relationship with God. Perhaps the two most important things we can learn in the Bible is who God is and who we are. The Bible tells us first who God is and then tells us who we are in relationship with God.

It is crucial to know your identity because it determines what you do. When you know who you are, you know what to do. Knowing your identity is the primary thing that changes everything.

WHAT IS THE BASIS OF UNDERSTANDING WHO WE ARE?

Who do you think you are? Where do we even start to answer that enormous question? Let's start at the beginning. You are an image bearer of God.

Genesis, the book of beginnings, 1:26-27 reports, "God said, 'Let us make man in our image, after our likeness. And let them have dominion over the fish of the sea and over the birds of the heavens and over the livestock and over all the earth and over every creeping thing that creeps on the earth.' So God created man in his own image, in the image of God he created him; male and female he created them."

The Trinitarian God, who lives in eternal friendship, created us to image Him. God uniquely honors humanity in this way. He's made nothing else in His image. Practically, this means that God made us to image, or reflect Him, as a mirror does. And in a world where we're encouraged to spend much time gazing at ourselves in a mirror, it's helpful every time we look in the mirror to be reminded that we're made to mirror God to others. He created us to reflect His goodness and glory in the world around us, like Moses, who radiated the glory of God after being in God's presence.[a] You were created by God, are on the earth to image and glorify God, and when you die, if you are in Christ, you will be with God forever, imaging and glorifying Him perfectly in a sinless state.

The question of identity is one that humans have struggled with since Satan's conversation with our first parents. Only by seeing ourselves rightly and biblically

---

[a] Ex. 34:30

between God and the animals can we have both humility and dignity. There alone are we as God intended us to be. By understanding our position under God as created beings, we should remain humble toward and dependent upon God. By understanding our position of dominion over creation, we embrace our dignity as morally superior to animals.

Ludwig von Feuerbach was a 19th century atheist who curiously declared that God did not make us but rather we made God as a figment of our imagination. Students of his thinking include Karl Marx, who applied this politically, Sigmund Freud, who applied this psychologically, and Friedrich Nietzsche, who applied this philosophically. Conversely, in Genesis 1-2 we see that we did not create God, but rather God created us in His image and likeness.

Admittedly, the number of verses in Scripture clearly declaring that God made human beings in His image and likeness (also commonly referred to by the Latin phrase *imago Dei*) are few.[a]

However, it is not enough simply to search the Bible for the phrase "image of God". Sinclair Ferguson writes, "While statistically the phrase is infrequent, the interpretation of man which it enshrines is all-pervasive."[1]

There are 12 vital truths revealed in the fact that we were made in the image and likeness of God. Taken together, they provide the essence of a biblical anthropology, or view of humanity from God's intention as our Creator, that has massive implications for virtually every discipline from anthropology to sociology, politics, and philosophy.

1. We were created by the Trinity. Augustine was fond of noting that the plural language of Genesis 1:26, "Let us make man in our image, after our likeness," means we were created by the Trinity. We are to understand ourselves not as autonomous individuals but rather as image bearers made for four categories of relationship. Theologically, we are to live in relationship with God. Psychologically, we are to live in relationship with ourselves, knowing who God intends for us to be. Socially, we are to live in relationship with other people, in community. Environmentally, we are to live in relationship with all that God has put under our dominion, including animals.

2. We were created as persons by a personal God. Unlike the rest of creation, which was made solely by God's word, God formed us by his proverbial hands and then breathed life into us to speak to us.[b]

3. God originally made mankind without sin. Genesis 1:31 calls our first parents "very good" in comparison to the rest of creation, which God simply called "good." Ecclesiastes 7:29 says, "God made man upright." Therefore, all human sin is fully the responsibility of sinners and not of God our Creator. In addition, all the effects of sin and the curse were not originally part of the world God created for us in love.

---

[a] Gen. 1:26-27, 5:1-3, 9:6; 1 Cor. 11:7; James 3:9 [b] Gen. 2:7

DOCTRINE

4. God blesses us.[a] God is good and does not need to be prompted or compelled to give grace; rather, He delights in doing so and does so without request.
5. Unlike the animals who were made according to their "own kind," we are made in the "image of God." Human life is distinct from and superior to all other created things. We are altogether unique with special dignity, value, and worth.
6. God gives commands to us because He made us as moral image bearers. We can know right and wrong, and we can respond to God with moral obedience as an act of faith in love.
7. God made us curious adventurers and granted us permission to explore His creation through everything from a telescope to a microscope.[b] We have an insatiable curiosity that begins at birth and continues throughout life as we seek to experience and learn, travel the world, and explore every nook of creation.
8. God created us to be creative and make culture.[c] This explains the innate love people have for everything from fashion to film, music, theater, architecture, painting, photography, dance, storytelling, and the like.
9. God created us to be reproductive and have children.[d] This explains why people long to be parents and consider children a great blessing.
10. God made us with meaningful work to do.[e] This explains why there is an innate drive in most people to work.
11. God created us as His image bearers, but not because He needed us in any way. He bestowed on us the dignity of being His image bearers solely for our benefit, not His own. The church father Irenaeus explains, "God formed Adam, not as if He stood in need of man, but so that He might have someone upon whom to confer His benefits."[f] Similarly, Lactantius said, "It cannot be said that God made the world for His own sake. For He can exist without the world...It is evident, therefore, that the world was constructed for the sake of living beings, since living beings enjoy those things that it consists of."[g]
12. God created us to live *coram Deo*, "before the face of God" as friends. This Latin phase was commonly used by theologians throughout church history to explain the Christian life. Practically speaking, we were created to live all of life in the presence of God, under the authority of God, according to the Word of God, by the power of God, to the glory of God. Nothing in our life is secular or separated from the sight of God because all of life is sacred.

After God created our first parents in His image and likeness, they, unlike the rest of creation, related to God in a unique way. For starters, mankind was

---

[a] Gen. 1:28 [b] Ibid. [c] Ibid. [d] Ibid. [e] Gen. 2:15–17 [f] Irenaeus, Haer. 4.14.1
[g] Lactantius, Inst. 7.4

not made to live independent of God but rather dependent upon God. One theologian says, "The relationship between God and man was not one between equals. Nor was it one of autonomy. Man is dependent upon God for the blessings of life and sustenance; and man is accountable to God in the areas of service and obedience!"[2] Furthermore, the relationship between God and our first parents is not only one of dependence, but also of grace. Dr. John Piper says, "Before sin entered the world, Adam and Eve experienced God's goodness not as a response to their demerit (since they didn't have any) but still without deserving God's goodness. You can't deserve to be created. You can't deserve, as a non-being, to be put into a lavish garden where all your needs are met by a loving Father. So even before they sinned, Adam and Eve lived on grace. And God's will for them was that they live by faith in future grace – God's daily, fatherly care and provision."[3]

Like a child is dependent upon a parent to care for them and speak to them, so is our relationship with God from the Garden. We were given the ability to communicate with God and one another that no other creature was given. We can hear God's Word and live in light of revelation from Him. Even in their sinless state, our first parents were dependent upon God and needed to hear from God and be in His presence. Thus, in our sinful and fallen state, we even more desperately need to hear from and be with God. Thankfully, this is possible because, unlike lower creation, such as plants and animals, our relationship with God is tethered with words – He speaks to us through Scripture and other forms of revelation, and we speak to Him in such things as prayer and song.

As thinking beings, we are able to interpret and make meaning out of the revelation we receive. Simply, we can think, ponder, consider, probe, and learn unlike anything else God has made. For us to correctly understand and apply the revelation we receive, we must seek to love God with all our mind so that the facts we receive can be not just mental information, but information that contributes to our moral transformation.

As worshipers, revelation and interpretation culminate in exaltation. Because they were image bearers, our first parents were created to worship God in thought, word, deed, and motive. All of their life was supposed to be lived in light of who God is, what God does, and what God says. They were supposed to interpret all of this revelation and respond to God in ways that would both bring him glory and them joy as they were doing what He created them to do.

WHAT DOES IT MEAN THAT WE ARE GOD'S IMAGE?

The Bible is clear that men and women, unlike the rest of creation, are made in the image of God.[a] Furthermore, the Bible repeats this truth after sin enters the

---

[a] Gen. 1:26-27

DOCTRINE

world, which means that even though sin has stained and marred us, we remain God's image bearers.[a]

The word image is often translated "idol." An idol is something that makes the invisible God visible. Admittedly, the Bible renounces idolatry emphatically, repeatedly, and forcefully. Therefore, we want to be clear that we are not endorsing idolatry. Nonetheless, to image the real Trinitarian God of the Bible is to make Him visible to the world as the Holy Spirit reflects the character of God off the children of God as their witness to the world. 2 Corinthians 3:17-18 says it this way, "Now the Lord is the Spirit, and where the Spirit of the Lord is, there is freedom. And we all, with unveiled face, beholding the glory of the Lord, are being transformed into the same image from one degree of glory to another. For this comes from the Lord who is the Spirit."

To image God is to "mirror" His invisible attributes to the world, somewhat like Moses, who radiated the glory of God after being in God's presence. Therefore, we are not to reflect sinful Adam, the culture, or even ourselves to the world. All persons are God's image in a basic sense, but Christians image him more than non-Christians and mature Christians do so even more.[b]

Furthermore, image is both personal and relational. By personal, we mean that we as individual worshipers must continually ask whether we are good reflections of our God. By relational, we mean that churches, families, and Christian communities must continually ask whether they are good reflections of God to one another and the world.

This understanding of our created purpose (and subsequently one source of our joy) is radically different from the world's understanding of being true to oneself, or simply reflecting one's sin nature to the world. In fact, this understanding of imago Dei is even radically different from many Christian teachings about why we exist.

We are not empty cups needing to be filled by God as is commonly said. Rather, we are broken mirrors that need to be put back together by God, beginning with our regeneration and continuing every day in our sanctification, so that we can better and better reflect God.

Imaging God practically means mirroring both his moral and non-moral likeness. Mirroring God's moral likeness means exercising decision-making power, having dominion over lower creation, living in social relationships with others, feeling our emotions, loving, serving, and communicating. Mirroring God's non-moral likeness means using our intellect and reason to think and that we can be creative with the materials God has created; it also includes our immortality as will live spiritually even after dying physically.

In an effort to explain God according to Scripture, theologians have distinguished between His unshared attributes that belong to Him alone (incommunicable attributes), and God's shared attributes, which He bestows upon

---

[a] Gen. 5:1-3; 9:6; James 3:9 [b] Rom. 8:29, 2 Cor. 3:18, Col. 3:10

IMAGE: GOD LOVES

us to a lesser degree than He possesses them (communicable attributes).

Before examining God's attributes as revealed in Scripture, two points are important. First, God's attributes are not merely attributed to Him, but they are qualities inseparable from his very being. In every way that God exists, He exists without limit, that is, in perfection. Second, we know God by our experiences through relationship with him: when we recognize his presence all around us, when we recognize His provision in our lives, when we confess our sins and accept His grace to live by faith. In His loving friendship, we come to a fuller realization of who He truly is as revealed in Scripture.

Unshared Attributes
1. Omnipresence: God is everywhere at all times.[a]
2. Omniscience: God has complete and perfect knowledge of all things, including the past, present, future, and everything actual or potential.[b]
3. Omnipotence: God is all-powerful and able to do all that He wills.[c]
4. Immutability: God does not change in his essence, character, purpose, or knowledge but does respond to people and their prayers.[d]
5. Eternality: God has no beginning or end and is not bound by time, though He is conscious of time and does work in time.[e]
6. Sovereignty: God is supreme in rule and authority over all things,[f] though He does allow human freedom.[g]

Shared Attributes
1. Holiness: God is absolutely separate from any evil.[h] We mirror God when we hate sin and love holiness by repenting of our sin and fighting against sin in the world.
2. Love: God alone is perfectly good and loving, and He alone is the source for all goodness and love.[i] We mirror God when we love God and others, starting with our families, friends, fellow believers, and extending love and dignity to strangers for hospitality and even enemies.
3. Truth: God is the source of all truth. He is the embodiment of truth.[k] We mirror God when we believe truth over lies and speak truthfully as an act of worship.

---

[a] Deut. 31:6; Ps. 139:7-12; Prov. 15:3; Jer. 23:24; Col. 1:17 [b] Ps. 139:1-6; 147:5, Isa. 40:12-14; 46:10; Heb. 4:13 [c] Job 42:2; Ps. 147:5; Matt. 19:26; Eph. 3:20 [d] Num. 23:19, Ps. 102:27; Mal. 3:6; Rom. 11:29; Heb. 13:8; James 1:17 [e] Ps. 90:2, 93:2, 102:12; Eph. 3:21 [f] 2 Sam. 7:28; 1 Chron. 29:10-13; Ps. 103:19; Rom. 8:28 [g] Gen. 50:21-22 [h] Ex. 3:5; Lev. 19:2; Ps. 5:4-6; 99:5; Isa. 6:3, 8:13, 57:15; Hab. 1:12-13; 1 Pet. 1:14-19; 1 John 1:5 [i] Ex. 34:7; Ps. 84:11; John 3:16; Gal. 5:22; Eph. 2:4-7; 1 John 4:8-16 [k] Num. 23:19; John 14:6, 17:17; 2 Cor. 1:20; Titus 1:2

4. Righteousness: God does not conform to a standard of right and wrong, but right and wrong flow from his character.[a] We mirror God as we fight oppression, injustice, and evil and pursue justice – particularly for those without power, such as the unborn, sick, poor, marginalized, defenseless, and abused.
5. Mercy: God does not give some people what they deserve, because He is loving and gracious.[b] We mirror His mercy when we forgive those who sin against us and do good to those who do evil in an effort to bring them to God for help.
6. Beauty: God is beautiful, and His creation reflects His beauty. God made men and women in His image and likeness to also create works of beauty.[c] We mirror God when we create and enjoy beauty in a holy way, such as by stewarding God's beautiful creation (including our own bodies and health), enjoying the arts, and even painting the walls of our home in thanks to God who gives us both color and eyes to see it.

WHAT DOES IT MEAN THAT WE WERE MADE MALE AND FEMALE?

In Genesis 1, God declared what He made "good," except for the man and woman, which He declared "very good". The only thing that we are told is not good before sin and the Fall is Adam's being alone.[d] Even in a sinless state we were made for human contact, friendship, and love. Even though Adam had God above him and creation beneath him, he lacked an equal with whom to be in relationship, one who would enable him to function like the Trinity in covenantal partnership as "one".

God's answer to Adam's lack was creating Eve as Adam's wife and helper.[e] It is important to note that the word "helper" does not denigrate Eve; in fact, God is also referred to as our helper.[f] The first woman was taken from the side of the man, as she belongs alongside him in partnership, not behind him in denigration (chauvinism) or in front of him in domination (feminism). It may also explain why cuddling alongside her man is the favorite pastime of many a bride, as it is, for her, a sort of homecoming. Though the woman was taken from the man, in the sexual consummation of marriage, the two again become one.

While God is not engendered, He does reveal himself as Father and comes to us as the God-man Jesus Christ, the Son of God. Nonetheless, He makes both men and women in his image. Practically, this means that though they are in some ways different, the man and woman are equal in dignity, value, and worth by virtue of the fact that they are equally God's image bearers.

Important to note is that God created the covenant of marriage; thus, He alone

---

[a] Gen. 18:25; Ex. 34:7; Deut. 32:4; Acts 17:31; Rom. 2:11 [b] Ex. 34:6-7; Matt. 18:23-35; Rom. 12:8; Eph. 2:4-7; Titus 3:5 [c] Ps. 27:4, 50:2; Eccles. 3:11; Isa. 33:17 [d] Gen. 2:18 [e] Gen. 2:19-25 [f] E.g., Ps. 10:14; 118:6-7; Heb. 13:6

defines what it is. His definition of one man and one woman, husband and wife for life, as one flesh, eliminates the alternatives such as bestiality, homosexuality, fornication, polygamy, adultery, and the like. At the first wedding, God brought the woman to the man, gave her away as her Father, and officiated the ceremony as their pastor. Upon seeing his bride for the first time, Adam responded to her beauty by singing her a song. Adam's poetic words to his bride on their wedding day are the first recorded words of any human being.

Genesis 2:24 then explains how a man can overcome his state of being single, which is not good. First, a man should leave his parents' care and be responsible for himself. Second, a man should marry a woman he loves and who loves him and the Lord. Third, their marriage should be intimate in every way including sexual consummation, and they should spend the rest of their life becoming "one" as the Trinitarian God is "one."[4] Both Jesus and Paul repeat this process throughout the New Testament as the pattern God intends for marriage and sexuality.[a]

Also important is that, in the creation account, God establishes an order to the covenant of marriage and organizes the family with the husband as the head (singular headship) and husband and wife as the leaders (plural leadership). This is evidenced in five ways:

1. God creates Adam first and then brings Eve to him.[b]
2. The woman is helper meaning she joins her strength to his to accomplish God's command to work and guard the garden, which was given to Adam first.[c]
3. Although the woman sinned first, God came calling for the man first.[d]
4. It is Adam's sin that is imputed to the human race because he is our head, and that sin can be removed only by Jesus, who is called "the last Adam."[e]
5. Echoing the creation account of our first parents, the Bible repeatedly declares that husbands are to lovingly lead their homes as Christ-like heads caring for and considering their wives, and wives are to respect their husbands as co-leader in the family.[f]

This does not mean that a husband is in ultimate authority. God is, and other authorities are over the man, such as the state and church governments. Nor does it mean that a wife does not have independent thoughts or seek to influence her husband, or must obey her husband's command to sin, or is less intelligent or competent than her husband. This does mean that a husband and wife are equal with complementary roles (like a left and right hand that work together). Like Jesus' emotional discussion with the Father in the Garden of Gethsemane, wives give their feelings, desires and trusts to their husbands.[g] Like the Father responding

---

[a] Matt. 19:5; Mark 10:7-8; Eph. 5:31 [b] Gen. 2:7, 21-23; 1 Cor. 11:8-9; 1 Tim. 2:13 [c] Gen. 2:15-17, 18 [d] Gen. 3:8-9 [e] Rom. 5:12-21; 1 Cor. 15:45 [f] Gen. 2:18; cf. Gen. 5:2; 1 Cor. 11:2-16; 14:33-34; Eph. 5:21-33; Col. 3:18; 1 Tim. 2:11-15; Titus 2:3-5; 1 Pet. 3:1 [g] Mark 14:32-26

DOCTRINE

to the groaning of His people, husbands hear, remember the covenant, look on, are concerned for, and come to help their wives.[a]

Christian marriage is supposed to reflect something of the Trinity and the gospel, where Jesus pursues us in love and takes responsibility for us as an example to husbands and fathers. For this to happen, believers should marry believers and not unbelievers.

Tragically, sin has caused much pain and misunderstanding surrounding marriage, culminating in the gender wars or the battle of the sexes. The only healthy way forward is for husbands and wives to be filled with the Spirit and committed to doing all that the Bible counsels because the God who made us male and female, and made marriage, knows how to make marriage succeed. This starts by celebrating our God-given genders, the God-given covenant of marriage between one man and one woman, sexual pleasure within marriage, sex without shame, and our spouse as our standard of beauty not to be compared to anyone else. This is how things were until sin, and how things can increasingly be because of the forgiveness of sins and new life in the Spirit.

WHAT ARE THE ASPECTS OF OUR HUMANITY?

The Scriptures speak of human beings in many ways and terms that, when understood together, give us a thorough picture of the aspects of our humanity.[5]

First it describes humans as one being in two parts – material/physical and immaterial/spiritual.[b] Furthermore, the material part of our being does affect our immaterial part, and vice-versa.[c] For example, the Bible reports that the disciples' bodily fatigue overcame their willing immaterial spirits and that a Christian can change the actions in their material body by having a renewed, immaterial mind.[d]

Many in our world, especially atheists, reduce humans to nothing more than electro-chemical machines determined by our genetics and worldly circumstances without freedom, dignity, or purpose.[6] This is sadly common in biological sciences, medicine, and education. Others reduce humans to their minds or consciousness, making the body temporary, evil, or even unreal. This was developed from roots in Hindu and Greek philosophy by such 19th century idealists as Berkeley, Kant, Hegel, and into 20th century existentialism and the New Age (also called New Spirituality). It became mythic with Star Wars, is promoted by Oprah, and pervades much contemporary self-help advice and corporate leadership training.

<u>Aspects of Our Humanity in the Old Testament</u>

The Bible speaks of the **soul** (*nepesh*). *Nepesh* refers to the person as a creation in relation to God rather than immortal, immaterial substance. The term

---

[a] Ex. 2:23-25, 3:7-10 [b] Gen. 2:7; Psa 104:29; 146:4; Eccl. 12:7; Matt. 10:28; Luke 23:46; 2 Cor. 4:16-5:8; James 2:26 [c] Matt. 26:41; 2 Cor 12:7 [d] Matt. 26:42; Rom. 6:12-13, 19, 12:1-2; 1 Cor. 9:27

is occasionally used for God. In the broadest sense, it connotes all biological life. Both humans and animals are called living *nepesh* in Genesis, which simply means "living creature." It is not that people possess souls but that we are souls.

The Bible speaks of **spirit** (*ruach*) in reference to God, people, and animals. The basic meaning is "wind" or "breath" especially when speaking of the Holy Spirit. In humans it can mean "mind,"[a] "resolve,"[b] or "will"[c]. None of these comes from humans themselves, but from God who breathed life into dust in creation to make us alive.

The Bible speaks of **flesh** (*basar*), one-third of the time in reference to animals and never to God. It refers to what humans share with animals in contradistinction to God. Most often, it means flesh as characteristic of bodily existence.[d] It often stands for the human body as a whole – a concept for which Hebrew has no distinct word.[e] Flesh in the Old Testament has none of the sinful connotations that we find in Paul's usage throughout the New Testament to speak of our proclivity to wrongdoing.[f]

The Bible speaks of **blood** (*dam*) in reference to the physical life of humans and animals.[g] Subsequently, shedding blood is shedding life.[h]

Lastly, the Bible speaks of the **heart** (*leb*) and almost always in reference to humans. Only rarely does it refer to the anatomical heart. The heart is the focus of the personal life—the reasoning, responding, deciding self. It is the deepest center of the human person, the driving force, and the most fundamental values from which our actions and attitudes come.[i] It is so deep that only God fully knows it.[k] The heart is the source of the deepest wishes and desires[m] and decisions of the will.[n] The heart is the center of the intellectual and rational functions that we usually ascribe to the mind.[o] It appears 100 times in Proverbs alone, and the distinction between head and heart is totally foreign in the Old Testament.[p] A godly person is a person after God's own heart.[q]

Aspects of Our Humanity in the New Testament

The constellations of words and images in the New Testament that speak of aspects of our humanity are, generally speaking, broken into the categories of the inward and outward person.[r] Our outward existence is visible, physical, and world-oriented, and primarily involves our physical body. Conversely, our inward existence is invisible, spiritual, and God-oriented, and involves our mind, heart, and spirit. Importantly, these are both aspects of one person and not independent entities that operate apart from the others. Nonetheless, the New Testament does distinguish, though not divide, these aspects of our humanity.

---

[a] Ezek. 11:5 [b] Jer. 51:11 [c] Isa. 19:3 [d] Job 10:11; Ps. 78:39 [e] Num. 8:7; Ps. 38:3 [f] Deut. 5:26; Ps. 56:4; Jer. 17:5, 7 [g] Ps. 72:13-14; Prov. 1:16, 18 [h] Gen. 9:4-6 [i] Prov. 4:23 [k] 1 Sam. 16:7 [m] Gen. 6:5; Ps. 14:1, 21:2 [n] Ex. 7:22; Josh. 14:8 [o] 1 Kings 3:9, 12 [p] Prov. 23:7 [q] 1 Sam. 2:35; 13:14 [r] Rom. 7:22; 2 Cor. 4:16; Eph. 3:16

When the New Testament speaks of the **body** it is referring to the physical aspect of a person or animal.[a] In this way, the body is our outward existence in contrast to our inward existence.[b] Humans are created to be embodied for all eternity.

The **soul** (*psuche*) for Paul throughout the New Testament is neither the immortal in a person nor only the immaterial part of the person.[c] Instead, the soul in Paul's thinking refers to the whole person created by God with an inner life of motive, thought, feeling, and the like. At times, Paul also speaks of the soul negatively, as that part of our being that is stained and marred by sin or lived without God in view.[d]

When the Bible speaks of the human **spirit** (*pneuma*) it describes our inner being as juxtaposed with our outer being[e] and is sometimes equivalent to the soul[f], flesh[g], and sometimes contrasted with that which is soulish.[h]

When the New Testament speaks of the **heart** (*kardia*), as Jesus often does, it is speaking of human beings as emotional with feelings, intellectual with thoughts, volitional with a will, moral with decisions, and spiritual with worship. It is therefore used to denote that which is central and vital in human nature.

By **mind** (*nous*), the New Testament speaks of the human person as knowing, thinking, judging, self-determining, and responsible. In many contexts, mind connotes one's outlook on life, or what is called "worldview" today. Fundamentally, it refers to the rational activity of the person and is not exalted as the *summum bonum* of our being but rather a very vital and helpful part of our person.

In speaking of the **conscience** (*suneidesis*), the New Testament is referring to the capacity of universal moral judgment. The primary role of our conscience is to give warning when an action violates it. While modern thinking sees conscience as a reliable standard of morality, the Bible sees it as a tool to be trusted only when it is enlightened by God the Holy Spirit.

In summary, while the Bible speaks of aspects of our humanity in various terms, it is not in as neat and tidy a manner as some would prefer. And in an effort to answer the question on which this section is based, a debate has ensued over what is called dichotomy and trichotomy.

Dichotomy teaches that we are basically two parts – that which is material and physical, and that which is immaterial and spiritual. Christian dichotomists note that the Bible does distinguish our existence into the two major groupings of material and immaterial[i] and note that upon death we are only two parts that are separated until our resurrection.[k] They also note that "soul" and "spirit" are terms

---

[a] 1 Cor. 13:3; 2 Cor. 10:10; Gal. 6:17 [b] Rom. 12:1; Heb. 13:15–16 [c] Rom. 2:9, 11:3, 13:1 [d] 1 Cor. 2:14, 15:44 [e] Rom. 8:10; 1 Cor. 7:34 [f] Philem. 1:17 [g] 2 Cor. 2:13, 7:5 [h] 1 Cor. 2:14, 15:44 [i] Rom. 8:10; 1 Cor. 7:34 [k] Eccles. 12:7; Matt. 10:28; Luke 23:46; Acts 7:59; James 2:26

the Bible often uses interchangeably.[a]

Trichotomy agrees with dichotomy, with a notable exception. Unlike the dichotomist who sees the spirit and soul as usually synonymous terms in the Bible, trichotomists say that we have a spirit with God-consciousness and a spiritual capacity through which we relate to God in addition to a soul with affections, desires, reason, emotions, will, and self-consciousness. Although the trichotomist view is largely rooted in Greek philosophy, those Christians arguing for the trichotomist position do appeal to Scripture.[b] We do see places where a distinction is made between the spirit and soul[c] and do see that the Holy Spirit works with the human spirit.[d]

It is our conviction that the Bible reveals the aspects of our being according to the dichotomist view – an inner life that is spiritual and an outer life that is physical. Furthermore, we believe that it is best to minister out of the personal view, where we are dealing with a whole person, not merely aspects of someone, to best serve them.

Practically, this means that if someone has a chemical or hormonal imbalance that would benefit from medication or needs an operation for cancer, they should not be derided for not having enough faith, as if every issue is solely a spiritual issue. Conversely, sometimes people are depressed and struggling for spiritual, not physical, reasons; in these cases, rather than giving them a pill, we need to help them grow in the gospel and lovingly limp with them as empathetic friends.

We must minister to people physically by considering their health and diet and exercise, emotionally with love and compassion, intellectually by answering their questions biblically, volitionally by appealing to their will for obedience, familially by dealing with issues related to their family of origin and current family dynamics, as well as socially by dealing with the social network and interpersonal relationships both in and out of the church.

This is all necessary because the aspects of our being are not isolated but instead impinge upon and affect one another because we are whole persons. A woman struggling with serious depression serves as one example. Some of her trouble seemed physical (she had a long family history of clinically diagnosed depression and high rates of suicide), emotional (she was discouraged because loved ones had recently died), intellectual (she was struggling to understand how God related to her depression and wrongly assumed Christians were always supposed to be happy), volitional (she was not choosing to pray or read Scripture regularly), familial (she was hurting because her spouse had recently committed adultery), and social (she was hurting, as she had recently moved to our city from another state and thus lost close connection with her friends). For her, like most people, there is not one answer that addresses one aspect of her being but rather

---

[a] Gen. 41:8; Ps. 42:6; Eccles. 12:7; Matt. 6:25, 20:28, 27:50; Luke 1:46–47; John 12:27, 13:21 [b] Luke 1:46–47; Phil. 1:27; 1 Thess. 5:23; Heb. 4:12 [c] Matt. 20:28; 27:50 [d] Rom. 8:16

answers that address all the aspects of her being and explains why ministry can be messy.

HOW DO PSYCHOLOGY AND ANTHROPOLOGY DEFINE HUMAN LIFE?

Unlike today, there was a day in which people did not think of themselves in primarily individual terms. Instead, what it meant to be a person was largely defined by one's relationship to such communities as family, history, parents, ethnicity, nationality, city, religion, and trade. This was consistent with the fact that we know each person of the Trinity not by isolating them but rather by seeing them in relationship with one another at work in our world and for our salvation.

However, everything changed in the days of the church father Augustine. In writing his book *Confessions*, he set in motion a historical trajectory that has forever changed how we answer the question of what it means to be human. Augustine did not look outward to his social network but rather inward to his feelings, convictions and longings. This elevated the importance of the autonomous individual in understanding the essence of humanity.

Many years later, the Christian philosopher René Descartes built on Augustine's concept of the person as an autonomous individual and defined the essence of what it means to be human in terms of the mind. He synthesized this with his statement, "I think, therefore I am."

Building on Augustine and Descartes, arguably the greatest American theologian, Jonathan Edwards, taught that the autonomous reasoning individual can be saved and improved by God's grace to God's glory.

The influential non-Christian philosopher Jean-Jacques Rousseau then taught that the essence of what it means to be human is that the autonomous reasoning individual can be improved by self-acceptance and self-love; thus, we are to look in to self and not out to God for our identity and betterment. According to his teaching, we are not sinners needing God's acceptance and love, but rather good people needing to accept ourselves and love ourselves.

Subsequently, the influential American psychologist William James said that the autonomous reasoning individual can be improved by self-acceptance and self-love aided by psychology. One's hope was then to be found in a trained professional and not ultimately the power of God's Spirit. This ideology that human beings are essentially machines that can be worked on by psychology led to the trained professional as the key to self-improvement.

Finally, American psychologist Abraham Maslow said that the autonomous reasoning individual is improved by self-acceptance and self-love aided by psychology to self-actualization, which is the defining principle of what it means to be human. Being true to yourself has replaced being true to the character of God.

Thus, the historical reasons for the current poor, prevailing perspective on personhood are obvious, but we still need to understand what God teaches about who we are as human beings. This is incredibly important, as one rabbi has said:

"We become what we think of ourselves...What determines one's being is the image one adopts."[7]

Therefore, the nearly millennium-and-a-half transition from Augustine to today has resulted in the commonly held belief that God does not save us for His glory and to make us part of His people, the church, to grow in holiness. Rather, we essentially save ourselves through loving and accepting ourselves and heeding the counsel of professionals. The ultimate goal of this is not that we would glorify God, but rather that we would achieve our potential, experience our greatness, or, in theological terms, live for our own glory as worshipers of ourselves, being all we can be, experiencing all we can experience, and doing all we can do. The self has replaced God as the center of human life.

Sociologist Christian Smith says that the true religion of most people in the West today, regardless of what religion they profess to participate in, is moralistic therapeutic deism.[8] By moralistic, he means we are good individuals who can get better, not sinners who need actual salvation. By therapeutic, he means that it is counseling and therapy, not God or the church, that enable our betterment. By deism, he means that God the Holy Spirit is not really involved in our lives; we are essentially on our own with the occasional exceptions of God answering a prayer we send Him or sending us a pithy insight to aid our betterment.

WHAT ARE COMMON CHRISTIAN ERRORS REGARDING THE IMAGE OF GOD?

There are, generally speaking, three broad categories of Christian errors regarding the doctrine of image. The first is not maintaining the rightful place of humanity in God's created order. The second is reductionism that seeks to make one part of our humanity the defining aspect of what it means to be human. The third is defining what it means to be God's image bearers in terms of something we do rather than who we are. We will deal with each category of error in succession.

First, error occurs regarding the doctrine of image when there is a failure to maintain the theological tension that Scripture does. Genesis 1 and 2 (especially 1:26) reveals that mankind was made under God in and over the rest of creation. Generally speaking, nearly every error in anthropology puts us up to be divine like God or pushes us down to be animals like the rest of creation.

The former is common when human sinfulness is overlooked and/or there is an erroneous belief that we are somehow part of the divine, common in pantheism and panentheism, as if we had at least a spark of divinity within us.

The latter is common when humans are seen as little more than highly evolved animals who should follow our desires for power and indulgence. This explains why, for example, such things as sexual sin are celebrated in our culture. If we are little more than animals with no moral compass above our instinctual drives, then we should act like animals and not feel bad about it. We do well to dominate and cancel others and satisfy every passion. This explains everything from gluttony to sexual perversion and commitment to radical environmentalism, and animal rights activism placing humanity at or near the same level of plants and animals. Examples of this error include the occasional legal efforts to extend human rights to animals.

Second, numerous errors emerge when it is believed that rather than being God's image bearers in total, we bear the image of God in some specific part of us. This is called the substantive view and has been the predominant position historically. One theologian writes that in this mode of thought, the *imago Dei* refers to "something within the substantial form of human nature, some faculty or capacity man possesses" that distinguishes "man from nature and from other animals."[9]

The truth is that it is not just a part of us that bears God's image while the rest of us does not. Instead, we are in totality (mind, body, soul, etc.) the image of God. When a part of us is thought to be the image of God, or at least the defining aspect of what it means to be human, it is lifted up above the rest of our person in various ways.

For some, we are entirely material so that our body alone is the totality of our humanity. Those holding this belief deny any immaterial or spiritual aspect to our being, such as a soul. Atheism and a denial of life after death are common beliefs related to this position.

For others, it is the mind and our ability to reason, communicate, learn, and the like that is the defining aspect of what it means to be human. This kind of belief was perhaps most popular during the era of modernity, which was marked by rationalism.

Perhaps the most popular error for those religiously and spiritually oriented is the belief that the soul alone is the defining aspect of what it means to be human. Even Bible teacher John Calvin erred by elevating the immaterial soul as what the Bible means by *imago Dei*. In some Eastern religions (e.g. Sikhism, Bahái', Hinduism) our physical body has little worth, which explains why meditation and yoga are used in an effort to connect with one's soul and disconnect from one's body.

Quite popular since the Romantic period is the belief that the essence of our humanity is to be found in our emotional feelings. In this ideology, to be human is to be most deeply connected to one's feelings and the worst of sins is to not be true to one's emotions. This kind of thinking is promulgated teaching about self-love and self-esteem. The result is that we are defined not as much by God's love for us and creating of us, but rather by our love for ourselves and creating our own identity. Some even try in vain to Christianize this thinking by saying that learning to feel love for ourselves allows us in turn to love God, when the Bible says God loves us first.[a] Furthermore, the practical implication of this teaching is that we must

---

[a] 1 John 4:10

be true to our feelings over and above God's commands. This excuses much sin in the name of being true to oneself, which is often simultaneously being untrue to God.

Lastly, as psychologists such as B. F. Skinner have become popular, it is increasingly common for people to define themselves in light of their environment. This teaching says that who we are is in large part the result of our environment so that, generally speaking, we are victims of environmental conditions beyond our control. In popular terms, this explains why people are prone to blame their genes, father, socio-economic background, media, personality type, and the culture for who they are and how they act. In some ways, this is little more than a more nuanced and mature version of the blame-shifting that our first parents did when God confronted them about their sin in Eden. The problem with each of these errors is found in Romans 1:25, which defines idolatry as worshiping anything created. By taking an aspect of our being (e.g., body, mind, soul, emotions, environment) and elevating it to be the defining aspect of what it means to be human, we are guilty of worshiping that part of our being instead of seeing ourselves as one whole person who bears God's image to worship Him.

The third error regarding *imago Dei* occurs when we define our humanity in terms of things we do. Called the functional view, it emphasizes a human function, usually the exercise of dominion over creation.[10] The problem with this view is that those who are not able to function as most people do would logically be considered somehow less human than the rest of us. Yet, the unborn, sick, comatose, elderly, infirm, and the like are as much image bearers of God as those who can do certain things.

In sum, we believe five things regarding the *imago Dei*. (1) Human beings alone are God's image bearers. (2) As God's image bearers, human beings are under God and over lower creation, and great error arises when they are pulled up toward God or pushed down toward animals. (3) Human beings are the image of God, and this fact is not reduced to any aspect of their person or performance. (4) As God's image bearers, human beings have particular dignity, value, and worth. (5) As God's image bearers, humans were made to mirror God as an act of worship, which is only possible as we turn toward God.

WHEN DOES HUMAN LIFE BEGIN?

Because human beings are God's image bearers and bestowed with particular dignity, value, and worth, the question of when life begins is incredibly important. The importance of this question is amplified because of the widespread practice of abortion and the issue of whether it is in fact the taking of a human life and therefore murder.

Scientifically and medically, it is beyond debate that human life begins at conception. From the initial joining of sperm and egg, the tiny baby is alive, distinct from its mother, and living and growing as a human.[11]

While the ability to express humanity and personhood changes throughout the life cycle, human essence and human personhood are innate to the living being. No matter how tiny or weak, humans deserve support and protection because they are God's image bearers. Princeton professor and former member of the President's Council on Bioethics, Robert P. George, says:

Human embryos are not...some other type of animal organism, like a dog or cat. Neither are they a part of an organism, like a heart, a kidney, or a skin cell. Nor again are they a disorganized aggregate, a mere clump of cells awaiting some magical transformation. Rather, a human embryo is a whole living member of the species Homo sapiens in the earliest stage of his or her natural development. Unless severely damaged, or denied or deprived of a suitable environment, a human being in the embryonic stage will, by directing its own integral organic functioning, develop himself or herself to the next more mature developmental stage, i.e., the fetal stage. The embryonic, fetal, child, and adolescent stages are stages in the development of a determinate and enduring entity—a human being—who comes into existence as a single-celled organism (the zygote) and develops, if all goes well, into adulthood many years later. But does this mean that the human embryo is a human person worthy of full moral respect? Must the early embryo never be used as a mere means for the benefit of others simply because it is a human being? The answer...is "Yes."[12]

Scripture confirms human life does begin at conception and an unborn baby is an image bearer of God. Psalm 51:5 says we are both image bearers and sinners from conception, "Behold, I was brought forth in iniquity, and in sin did my mother conceive me." God called both Isaiah and Jeremiah for prophetic ministry from their mothers' wombs.[a] Furthermore, Luke 1:15 said that John the Baptizer "will be filled with the Holy Spirit, even from his mother's womb".

Perhaps the most extensive section of Scripture on human life in the womb is Psalm 139:13–16:

For you formed my inward parts;
you knitted me together in my mother's womb.
I praise you, for I am fearfully and wonderfully made.
Wonderful are your works;
my soul knows it very well.
My frame was not hidden from you,
when I was being made in secret,
intricately woven in the depths of the earth.
Your eyes saw my unformed substance;
in your book were written, every one of them,
the days that were formed for me,
when as yet there was none of them.

---

[a] Isa. 49:1b; Jer. 1:5

Christians have always followed the teaching of the Old Testament Jews, that abortion of a preborn child and ending the life of a born child are both murderous sins. The Didache, an ancient manual for church instruction says, "You shall not commit murder...You shall not procure abortion, nor commit infanticide."[13] Some will argue that there is a difference between a child in a mother's womb and one outside of it, yet the early church saw both as equally living people and the taking of life in either state as equally murderous.

The medical doctor, Luke, writes more of the New Testament than anyone. The Holy Spirit who knows life in the womb says the following through Dr. Luke who uses the same Greek word in every verse below:

- ...when Elizabeth heard the greeting of Mary, the **baby** [John the Baptizer] leaped in her womb.[a]
- ...the **baby** [John the Baptizer] in my [Elizabeth's] womb leaped for joy.[b]
- ...you will find a **baby** [Jesus] wrapped in swaddling cloths and lying in a manger.[c]
- ...they went with haste and found Mary and Joseph, and the **baby** [Jesus] lying in a manger.[d]
- Now they were bringing even **infants** to him [Jesus] that he might touch them.[e]
- He [Pharoah] dealt shrewdly with our race and forced our fathers to expose their **infants**, so that they would not be kept alive.[f]

Scripture uses the same word (*brephos*) for Elizabeth's unborn child (John the Baptizer), newborn baby Jesus, and also for the children brought to Jesus along with kids killed in the Old Testament. A child in the womb and a child singing and dancing around Jesus in worship are equally human beings who bear the image of God. Not to extend legal protections to preborn children because of age, size, or phase of development is a grievous discrimination and injustice akin to racism, sexism, and ageism.

WHY DO CHRISTIANS OPPOSE ABORTION?

When Grace and I first met in high school, I was strongly in favor of abortion and the eugenics ideology of Thomas Malthus that was held by Margaret Sanger, the founder of Planned Parenthood. I wrongly believed less fit people should be sterilized, not permitted to conceive and encouraged, if not required, to abort and won debates on the issue in high school and college classes.

Grace was a Bible-believing pastor's daughter who was consistently pro-life. I won most of our arguments from a rhetorical point of view, but she was right, and I was wrong. Today, as we parent our five wonderful children together, I cannot even fathom what I was thinking. As a new Christian, the Bible completely

---

[a] Luke 1:41 [b] Luke 1:44 [c] Luke 2:12 [d] Luke 2:16 [e] Luke 18:15 [f] Acts 7:19

transformed my mind on this issue.

Behind abortion is racism that began with Nazi mastermind Malthus who brought death in concentration camps to reduce minority populations and Sanger who brought death in clinics, both in an effort to reduce minority populations. Yes, clinics are little concentration camps. Trying to promote social Darwinism, Sanger set up the first clinics in the poorest and most ethnic neighborhoods to reduce the "less fit".[14]

Theologian Wayne House says, "In 1933 the magazine for Planned Parenthood, known in Sangers [sic] day as Birth Control Review, actually published 'Eugenic Sterilization: An Urgent Need,' by Ernst Rudin, Hitlers [sic] director of genetic sterilization and founder of the Nazi Society for Racial Hygiene."[15] Furthermore, later that same year the magazine "published an article by E. A. Whitney, entitled 'Selective Sterilization,' which strongly praised and defended Nazi racial programs."[16]

Sanger saw birth control as the most effective way to eradicate "feebleminded" people, whose mental ability was less than that of a 12-year-old.[17] Sanger also said, "Birth control appeals to the advanced radical because it is calculated to undermine the authority of the Christian churches. I look forward to seeing humanity free someday of the tyranny of Christianity no less than Capitalism."[18]

Today, abortion providers continue the racism as out of the roughly million abortions a year in the United States, the majority of abortions are for minority populations.

Here is a summary of the eight core biblical truths that pertain to the issue of abortion:

1. God is the Creator and Author of human life.[a]
2. God made humanity in His image and likeness, making human life unique and sacred.[b]
3. God intends for human beings to fill the earth.[c]
4. God confirmed that life begins at conception and declares that an unborn baby is a sacred life.[d]
5. God knows us from our mother's womb.[e]
6. God declares that when human life is taken without just cause (i.e., capital punishment, just war, self-defense), the sin of murder has been committed.[f]
7. God is sovereign over the womb and can ultimately open and close it as He wills.[g]
8. Children are a blessing from God to be provided and cared for by parents

---

[a] Gen. 1–2; Deut. 32:39; Ps. 139:13–16 [b] Gen. 1:27; James 3:9 [c] Gen. 1:28, 9:1 [d] Exod. 1:16–17, 21:22–25; Lev. 18:21; Jer. 7:31–32; Ezek. 16:20–21; Mic. 6:7; Matt. 2:16–18; Acts 7:19 [e] Jer. 1:5; Job 10:9–12, 31:15; Ps. 119:73; Eccles. 11:5 [f] Gen. 9:5; Exod. 20:13 [g] Gen. 20:18, 29:31, 30:22; 1 Sam. 1:5–6; Isa. 66:9; Luke 1:24–25

as well as extended family and the church, including those who are adopted as Jesus was.[a]

Writing for Fox News I said, "Of all the Ten Commandments, number six is the only one that our nation has codified into law. 'You shall not murder.' Since 1973, legal abortions in America have taken the lives of 55 million people...That total of 55 million lives equals 17.5% of the country's current population, is greater than the population of any state in the Union, and is greater than the population of 219 of the world's countries including South Africa, South Korea, Spain, Australia, Argentina, and Canada. Fifty-five million is about the same as the population of the 25 smallest states and Washington D.C. combined."[19]

I included my interview with Dr. John Piper about his conversation with an abortion doctor. Piper said, "Before I could get my first of 10 arguments out of my mouth, [the doctor] said, 'Look, I know I'm killing children.'" Piper was astounded and asked the man to explain why he would do such a thing. "To be honest, my wife wants me to because it's a matter of justice for women [and] the lesser of two evils in her mind."[20]

Additionally, the Bible assumes that an unborn baby is a human life and assigns the death penalty for anyone who takes an unborn life because it is murder. Exodus 21:22-25 says:

When men strive together and hit a pregnant woman, so that her children come out [the Hebrew term is <u>yasa</u>, a live birth—not <u>shakal</u>, the typical term for miscarriage], but there is no harm, the one who hit her shall surely be fined, as the woman's husband shall impose on him, and he shall pay as the judges determine. But if there is harm, then you shall pay life for life, eye for eye, tooth for tooth, hand for hand, foot for foot, burn for burn, wound for wound, stripe for stripe.

God came to earth as a baby, but He grew up to become a man who died on the cross to forgive any and all sins – including the taking of an unborn life. For Christians, this debate hits close to home. Mary was probably a teenager, poor, possibly uneducated, living in a small rural town. She got pregnant out of wedlock in a highly religious cultural context. If she walked into a clinic today, we know what she would be encouraged to do. But Mary gave birth to God. Jesus came into the world through the womb of a woman who fits the stereotype of someone who "should" get an abortion. Thankfully, Mary courageously brought Jesus into the world so that He could save the world from death.

HOW IS THE BIBLE THE ONLY REAL DEFENSE OF HUMAN EQUALITY?

World religions did not come up with the idea of equal rights. Nor did it originate in a secular, non-religious outlook.

---

[a] Gen. 1:28a; Ps. 127:3-5, 128:3-4; Matt. 18:5-6; Mark 9:36-37, 10:16; 1 Tim. 5:8

No major faith apart from Christianity mandates a deep commitment to the equality of all people. In every other religion, certain individuals and classes rank higher than others on a ladder of spiritual attainment. They are more enlightened, more holy, further along in paying their karmic debt, closer to the divine by virtue of their good works, and so on. And the result can be horrific inequities. In Hindu culture, for example, the caste system made untold masses unequal and untouchable. In Muslim culture, sharia law gives women and outsiders nothing resembling the rights and privileges of the male faithful. Eric Metaxas, author of *Amazing Grace: William Wilberforce and the Heroic Campaign to End Slavery*, sums it up this way in an email interview I conducted:

In India, the concept of caste is a perfect example of how some cultures today believe and act upon the belief that some human beings are inherently better than other human beings. In many Muslim countries today, a Jew or Christian is viewed as subhuman, and they are routinely called "monkeys and pigs" and thought to be fit for extermination or slavery. Subjection breeds ignorance and pain. When you ask yourself, "Do the religions of the world contribute to equality?" the honest answer is no.

The foundation of a dominant secular worldview— evolution—leads to the conclusion that some are more fit than others. Some deserve to be winners, and losers deserve to die. And by placing animals and human beings on a continuum of development, evolution has given rise to racist views that some individuals, peoples, and races are more advanced than others. In a debate I participated in on ABC Nightline, Deepak Chopra, for example, referred to myself and some other people as "primitive."

Similarly, Charles Darwin himself wrote a famous book that you may have not known the full title of, *On the Origin of Species by Means of Natural Selection, or the Preservation of Favored Races in the Struggle for Life*. Darwin also wrote, "At some future period, not very distant as measured by centuries, the civilised [sic] races of man will almost certainly exterminate, and replace, the savage races throughout the world."[21] An evolutionary view of humanity cannot lead to equality because some races are more evolved and fit than others who are less evolved and fit hence the survival of the fittest.

During the 20th century alone, some 170 million people were killed by other human beings.[22] Of those, roughly 130 million died at the hands of those holding an atheistic and evolutionary ideology.[23] Stalin killed 40 million people, Hitler killed six million Jews and nine to 10 million others (mainly Christians), and Mao killed some 70 million Chinese.[24] In addition to this number could be added the more than one billion people worldwide who were aborted and killed in the wombs of their mothers during the 20th century alone.

Comparatively, roughly 17 million people were killed by professing Christians in 20 total centuries of Christian history. No Christian today lauds them or calls them heroes apart from cases of self-defending preservation. So, in all of history, those proclaiming but possibly not professing Christian faith have killed only a tiny fraction of the number of people that atheists and followers of other religions have killed in one century.

Unlike human religions and philosophies, the Bible espouses equality:
- Do not show partiality to the poor or favoritism to the great."[a]
- Showing partiality is never good.[b]
- ...there is not Greek and Jew, circumcised and uncircumcised, barbarian, Scythian, slave, free...[c]
- ...show no partiality as you hold the faith in our Lord Jesus Christ...[d]

The equality of all human beings is a biblical idea that has touched societies around the globe and been adopted even by our most vocal opponents.

Scholar Nancy Pearcey points out that eminent atheist Friedrich Nietzsche credited Christianity for the concept of equality. In *The Will to Power*, he wrote, "Another Christian concept...has passed even more deeply into the tissue of modernity: the concept of the 'equality of souls before God.' This concept furnishes the prototype of all theories of equal rights."[25] Pearcey cites radical atheist postmodern philosopher Richard Rorty who admits that "the idea of universal human rights was a completely novel concept in history, resting on the biblical teaching 'that all human beings are created in the image of God.'" Pearcey comments: "Rorty admits that atheists like himself have no basis for human rights within their own worldview. He calls himself a 'freeloading atheist' because he is fully aware that he is borrowing the idea of rights and human dignity from the Christian heritage."[26]

Whether others acknowledge it or not, this basic Christian belief has driven the fight for equal rights throughout history. Pearcey maintains that the success of many secular movements advocating equality today derives from "a beauty and an appeal that comes from their origin in a biblical worldview." Arguments are ripped from their Christian context, redefined, and distorted, but they retain a measure of their original power.[27] She says, "The only reason that movements for equality are making headway today is that they borrow their best lines from Christianity."[28]

Christians broke ground on the battle for racial equality. Why? The Bible teaches that every person is created by God in His image and descended from one family and have the same first parents. Each has the opportunity to be adopted into a spiritual family with God as Father and Jesus as big brother.

Eric Metaxas describes similar Christian involvement in bringing down slavery in England and the British Empire in the early 1800s in an email interview I conducted:

It was Christians who fought passionately to end the slave trade and slavery itself. William Wilberforce and other Christians stood against secularists and for African slaves precisely because they believed that all men are brothers and all

---

[a] Lev. 19:15 (NIV) [b] Prov. 28:21 (NLT) [c] Col. 3:11 (ESV) [d] James 2:1 (ESV)

human beings are created in the image of God. Those who did not believe the Bible thought that notion a joke and thought the darker-skinned races to be as obviously inferior to the light-skinned races as dogs were superior to rats or bugs.

Scholar Wayne Grudem added in a personal interview that fully two-thirds of the leaders of the American abolitionist movement were Christians preaching that slavery should end. In more recent years, it was Christians like Rosa Parks, Jackie Robinson, and Martin Luther King Jr. who used biblical imagery and language to move a nation to stand against racial injustice, as Metaxas pointed out in our interview.

Christians across time and geography have followed Jesus' example of welcoming all peoples. Today, Jesus is worshiped among more races and cultures in more languages than anyone in history. There is simply no organization of any kind that has as much diversity as Christianity because the Bible teaches that we all equally bear God's image.

WHAT HAPPENS WHEN WE DON'T IMAGE GOD?

We were made by God to mirror Him. When we do not mirror Him, we mirror someone else. This simple fact explains much of our fascination with celebrities, social media, and an increasingly unhealthy, unhappy, and unholy world.

Dr. Drew Pinsky is a regular television expert on human addiction, behavior, and culture. Some years ago, I flew to Los Angeles and co-hosted his call-in radio show *Loveline*. My wife Grace and I were also interviewed by him on his television programming regarding marriage and sexuality from a Christian perspective.

In our conversations, he said something profound. I do not believe he is a Christian, but as a professional following the facts, he arrived at an amazing conclusion that agrees with the Bible, culminating in a book called The Mirror Effect. His thesis is that celebrities model behavior and then people mirror it. This explains such things as social media influencers and the insatiable appetite to know everything about famous people from the food they eat to clothes they wear, cars they drive, surgeries they have and adult home movies they film.

This frenzy has created celebrities that are more dysfunctional by the day, and media that is more invasive by the minute. Today, to be famous, you do not need to have any virtue or accomplish anything honorable or helpful. Pinsky says, "Celebrities today are as likely to be recognized for their bodies, rap sheets, and rehab stints as they are for their talents. That's because the behavior of today's celebrities is much more dramatically dysfunctional than it was a decade ago."[29]

Why?

To get attention, or worship, to use a Bible word, people need to do something shocking, dangerous, self-destructive, or socially taboo. As "gods" they model behavior that their followers then mirror. If a famous person wears a clothing brand, sales go up. If a famous person drinks a type of liquor, others buy it at the bar to make a social statement. If a famous person does drugs, has a sex change operation, and lets everyone peer in on their life with a reality television show, their followers will get high, go under the knife, and let us watch via social media and YouTube. Super-celebrities create their own brands and products to sell their followers as a form of tithing to their gods and goddesses. This is exactly how we got the entire Kardashian family.

Pinsky refers to this mirror effect as, "Dysfunctional behavior, usually in four specific areas: body image, hypersexuality, substance abuse and addiction, harmful acting out."[30]

Normal people are not shocking enough to get much attention. Abnormal people are shocking enough to get much attention. Once we've watched someone do something a few times, that behavior becomes normalized. So, if you are a celebrity, very quickly you are no longer interesting unless you do something more extreme. Likewise, a nobody wanting to become somebody needs to just do something crazier than everyone else. This explains the ever-devolving porn industry that seems bent on digging a hole to Hell as fast as possible while counting clicks and cashing checks.

For older folks, the Internet, social media, and normalizing of what was considered immoral and undesirable for past generations is now normalized and incredibly tempting for younger generations. Pinsky says, "Adolescents in particular are at high risk for mirroring such dangerous behavior…"

- 3.7% of all female adolescents suffer from anorexia
- 4.2% suffer from bulimia
- 46% of teens aged 15-19 have had sex at least once
- 25% of teens have a STD
- 28% of teens admit to consuming alcohol
- 10% of 12th graders use the prescription Vicodin for non-medical reasons
- 10% of 8th graders use marijuana[31]

These statistics are worsening as all of these behaviors become normalized due to the mirror effect. Whether it's celebrities online or the cool kids in school, a few are modeling behavior that the majority are mirroring.

Making matters worse is social media. Pinsky says, "These unmonitored sites… invited users to create new personae whose connection with their real lives were often tenuous at best, a high-tech version of what psychiatric professionals call a pseudo-self, a classic social coping mechanism among narcissists."[32] Not only do celebrities create fake identities; they do not know who they are. Consumed by themselves and their image and response of fans, this is the breeding ground to encourage and multiply narcissism where people want to be like God and have as many people as possible be their followers and imitators or, to use Bible words, converts and worshippers.

We were made to mirror God. When we do not mirror God, we mirror people. This is idolatry. Romans 1:25-32 explains this in detail. First, "they exchanged the truth about God for a lie and worshiped and served the creature rather than the Creator". Second, the brakes come off behavior once "God gave them up to dishonorable passions." Third, this celebrity-modeling and people-mirroring causes sexual perversion: "For their women exchanged natural relations for those that are contrary to nature; and the men likewise gave up natural relations with women and were consumed with passion for one another, men committing shameless acts with men..." Fourth, as sin escalates, the result is a culture marked by even school curriculum that brainwashes: "A debased mind to do what ought not to be done." Fifth, in addition to sexual unhealth, all of life and culture is "filled with all manner of unrighteousness, evil, covetousness, malice...envy, murder, strife, deceit, maliciousness." Sixth, the worst offenders become popular as the celebrity followers "are gossips, slanderers, haters of God, insolent, haughty, boastful, inventors of evil, disobedient to parents, foolish, faithless, heartless, ruthless." Seventh, they will then have parades for shameful things that trend online as, "not only do them but give approval to those who practice them." Lastly, this celebrity idolatry is not hidden or discreet as we literally call celebrities our idols and have reality television shows where normal people can seek to become celebrity idols themselves.

Jonathan Edwards said that those we idolize, we eventually demonize. Pinsky says the same thing, "The same instincts that drive us to want to mimic these celebrities, however, can also compel us to try to tear down the very idols we create. This urge to destroy what we cannot have often takes the shape of indulging in 'harmless' gossip about celebrities whose behavior makes us uncomfortable. This, in turn, fuels the tabloid madness – delivering constant new episodes of the latest celebrity train wrecks in progress."[33] The end result of this demonic and destructive cycle is modern western culture, and the only hope is to stop mirroring created beings and start mirroring God our Creator.

HOW DOES SATAN ATTACK OUR IDENTITY?

What you do flows from who you are. As Christians, we live *from* our identity, not *for* our identity. We are defined by who we are *in* Christ, not what we do or fail to do *for* Christ. Christ defines who we are by who He is and what He's done for us, in us, and through us. Understanding this information is the key to your transformation. When you know who you are, you know how to live. Only if your identity is rooted in your relationship with God above the ever-changing circumstances of your life can your identity be life-proof and get you through any and every situation.

Satan declares war on our identity because he knows it is perhaps the surest way to wreck the relationship between us and our God. Satan refused to accept his God-given identity and instead sought to form a new identity apart from God. He tempts us to do the same, which is demonic. God created you with an identity, and Satan wants you to instead live out of some counterfeit identity.

The demonic war on identity started when our first parents, Adam and Eve, encountered the serpent who was "more crafty" than anything else made by God.[a] The serpent started by attacking the very identity of God, "But the serpent said to the woman, 'You will not surely die. For God knows that when you eat of it your eyes will be opened, and you will be like God, knowing good and evil.'"[b]

As a Christian, you must base your identity upon two things, perhaps the most important things you can learn studying the Bible: (1) who God really is and (2) who God says you really are. It is no surprise that demonic attack starts on those two fronts with Satan giving a counterfeit identity for God and you. If you have a wrong view of God, and/or who you are in relation to God, then everything in your life spins out of control, as it did for Adam and Eve.

Satan wanted them to achieve an identity by rebellion and living apart from God so that, "you will be like God." Just prior, "God said, 'Let us make man in our image, after our likeness'…So God created man in his own image, in the image of God he created him; male and female he created them."[c] God made us in His "likeness" and all we need to do is receive this identity. When Satan tempted our first parents to become "like God", he was lying because they were already made in God's likeness and all they needed to do was trust that fact by faith.

Satan tried this same trick on Jesus. Luke 4:1-13 says Jesus spent 40 days, "being tempted by the devil." Then, "The devil said to him, 'If you are the Son of God'". Satan was attacking Jesus' identity as the Son of God. Just prior, at Jesus' baptism, God the Father said, "You are my beloved Son; with you I am well pleased."[d]

There is no authority in all of creation equal or superior to God the Father. When He says Jesus is the Son of God, that is a forever fact. With the Trinity present at Jesus' baptism, the Holy Spirit comes down to empower Jesus to live out His God-given identity and now does the same for Christians.

Do you also see how Jesus would work from the identity received from the Father and not work for an identity achieved by Himself? Before Jesus preached a sermon, performed a miracle, or cast out a demon, the Father was "well pleased" with Him. The same is true of you. You are a child of God, and that identity is secure. You can work from that identity with joy and gladness, knowing the Father's love is secure.

Demonic forces frequently attack Christians in the area of their identity, but most of us are unaware of it. Like a poker player with a "tell," Satan's subtle behavior is detectable. When speaking to Adam, Jesus, and you, the demonic realm speaks in the second person word you. To Adam and Eve, Satan said, "*You will not surely die,*" and "*you will be like God.*" When speaking to Jesus, Satan said twice, "*If you are the Son of God.*"

When you speak of yourself, you use the first-person pronoun "I." When someone else speaks to you, they use the second person pronoun "you". When

---

[a] Gen. 3:1 [b] Gen. 3:4-5 [c] Gen. 1:26 [d] Luke 3:22

a physical being talks to us in the second person, we easily recognize that we are being spoken to by someone else. But when a spiritual being talks to us in the second person, we have to decide if we are hearing from God or the devil and his demons. Sometimes, when a demon does speak to us, we can easily overlook the fact that we are being spoken to by a demon because they are unseen.

Here are some examples of common attacks on the identity of believers by Satan which are counterfeit lies seeking to undermine the truth of who God says His people are:

- You are worthless.
- You are a failure.
- You got what you deserved.
- You will never change.
- You are hopeless.
- You are disgusting.
- You are not a real Christian.
- God is sick of you.
- If people knew what you were really like, they would all hate you.
- You are probably going to Hell.
- You should kill yourself.

These sorts of things are demonic. Our Father does not say things like this to any of His kids.

Tragically, some people overlook the demonic and think they are saying awful things to themselves. They wrongly assume negative self-talk and a low self-image when the truth is, they are under attack. This leads to self-contempt.

Even worse, some people confuse the demonic messages as a Word from God. This leads to God-contempt, as Satan is so tricky that he will try to get you to believe that his attack is actually from your Heavenly Father.

When you receive a message regarding your identity in the second person, you need to test it by the Word of God. Jesus did this. When Satan attacked Jesus' identity, He kept quoting Scripture because truth casts out lies and light casts out darkness. Jesus kept saying, "It is written..." and quoting Scripture. Jesus did not get defensive or coerced into an argument. Jesus let the battle be between the enemy of God and the Word of God because that's a battle where the Word always wins.

If you forget this when the enemy attacks your identity, you will end up like the sad story of Gladys. You will have a God who loves you and is present with you every day like a husband, but you will not remember who He is or who you are.

HOW DOES THE HOLY SPIRIT HELP JESUS AND US IMAGE GOD?

Next time you look into a mirror, remind yourself that Jesus Christ was the perfect mirror of God the Father to the world. Jesus alone has imaged God perfectly. Many New Testament Scriptures, and even Jesus Himself, declare this:

- Christ, who is the image of God.[a]
- He is the image of the invisible God.[b]
- He is the radiance of the glory of God and the exact imprint of His nature.[c]
- Whoever sees me [Jesus] sees Him who sent me.[d]
- Whoever has seen me [Jesus] has seen the Father.[e]

To continue with the metaphor that we have been using throughout this chapter, as sinners (a subject more thoroughly dealt with in the next chapter), we remain God's mirrors, but mirrors that have been thrown to the floor, broken and scattered into numerous shards and bits. Consequently, we reflect the glory and goodness of God poorly.

The restoration of the image of God, or proverbial collecting of the pieces and restoration of our mirror, is found only in the renewing power of the Gospel. Martin Luther says:

The Gospel has brought about the restoration of that image. Intellect and will indeed have remained, but both very much impaired. And so the Gospel brings it about that we are formed once more according to that familiar and indeed better image, because we are born again into eternal life or rather into the hope of eternal life by faith, that we may live in God and with God and be one with Him, as Christ says (John 17:21).[34]

This is precisely what Romans 8:29 means, "For those whom he foreknew he also predestined to be conformed to the image of his Son, in order that he might be the firstborn among many brothers." To be conformed to the image of Jesus means the Spirit causes the reflection of our life to be increasingly like Jesus Christ's. The renewal of the image of God in man is a process that God works in is lifelong sanctification by the Spirit. Importantly, this is not merely something passive that God does for us, but something that, by His grace through His Spirit, we have the honor of participating in as an act of mirroring Him.[f] Colossians 3:9-10 speaks of the "new self...renewed in knowledge after the image of its creator." In 2 Corinthians 3:18 Paul says, "We all, with unveiled face, beholding the glory of the Lord, are being transformed into the same image from one degree of glory to another. For this comes from the Lord who is the Spirit." Admittedly, as Christians we do sin, chase folly, and in our worst moments seem to be breaking our mirror while God is repairing it. Regardless, to image God requires ongoing humble repentance and a fiercely devoted steadfastness to change as God commands and with God pick up the pieces of our life shattered through sin.

As believers, we can work with God if we continually ask, "how can my words and deeds reflect the character of God to others?" This is what it means to glorify, or reflect, God. Because we were made to mirror God, He is glorified, and we are glad when His glory is reflected to others by us.

---

[a] 2 Cor. 4:4 [b] Col. 1:15 [c] Heb. 1:3 [d] John 12:45 [e] John 14:9 [f] Eph. 4:22-24; Col. 3:1-10

Amazingly, upon death, this life not only continues but is perfected, and the mirror of our life, along with all of creation, is fully restored and will reflect the light of the glory of God perfectly, beautifully, magnificently, unceasingly, and unendingly. Paul describes this mirroring we will experience to God's glory and our joy in the resurrected and perfected state: "Just as we have borne the image of the man of dust, we shall also bear the image of the man of heaven."[a] In addition, "our citizenship is in heaven, and from it we await a Savior, the Lord Jesus Christ, who will transform our lowly body to be like his glorious body, by the power that enables him even to subject all things to himself."[b]

QUESTIONS FOR PERSONAL JOURNALING AND/OR SMALL GROUP DISCUSSION

1. Do you believe that your life is lived in a healthy way with God and other people, or do you find yourself too relationally isolated?
2. As you reflect on the ways God has been good to you by creating you in His image, which are you most grateful for and why?
3. Since God made you for relationship with Him, how would you rate your current relationship with Him from 1 (nearly nonexistent) to 10 (warm and close)?
4. When you think of someone increasingly reflecting the character of Christ year after year, who comes to mind? How could you encourage them today?
5. How many mirrors do you have in your home, car, office, etc.? When you look into a mirror to see your reflection, remind yourself that you are God's mirror and He wants to see Himself in your life.
6. Which of God's unshared attributes are you most familiar with? Which of God's unshared attributes are you least familiar with?
7. Which of God's shared attributes do you believe God is growing your character in during this season of your life?
8. Can you think of someone you know personally who has an erroneous view of humanity? What could you do to lovingly discuss this issue with them to share a more biblical worldview?
9. Is there an aspect of your humanity that you tend to focus on too much (e.g. your mental learning)? Is there an aspect of your humanity that you tend to focus on too little (e.g. your physical health)?
10. Do you truly see everyone as equal, or are there honestly some people that you wrongly favor? Why?

---

[a] 1 Cor. 15:49 [b] Phil. 3:20–21

CHAPTER 5: FALL

"GOD JUDGES"

God made man upright, but they have sought out many schemes.
ECCLESIASTES 7:29

When I was a teenager in high school a friend of mine was given a beautiful, perfectly restored 1968 Chevy Camaro classic muscle car from his Father for a birthday present. I will never forget the first time I saw it as it sparkled in the sun. He opened the door to show off brand new, custom leather seats. Turning the key, the big block motor roared to life like a thunderstorm across a barren plain.

It was the nicest, baddest, loudest car I had ever seen up close. Then, we jumped in as he took us for a ride to learn that it was also the fastest.

I remember getting thrown back in my seat like I was on some high-speed, make-you-lose-your-lunch carnival ride. As the tires broke loose around every corner we took, I was glad that we had seat belts although I also grabbed the dash with two hands to stabilize myself.

We had a lot of fun nights with our friends in that car. I sat in the passenger seat when we would quickly crush people in drag races. We would also frequently slowly cruise the strip of beach on weekends where students gathered.

One day, as I was walking into our public high school, I noticed my friend getting out of a vehicle and heading into the school. It was a school bus, however, and not his car. I walked up to him and asked him why he was riding the beater bus when he had his beastly car.

"I wrecked it", he said somberly while looking at the ground.

He went on to explain that he was going too fast, hit a patch of gravel, hammered the gas instead of the brake, and drove it head first into a wall.

His car was now scrap metal. He pulled out a photo of what was once his car and, to be honest, I could not even recognize it. His father was furious. His car was beyond repair. His fun was over. He ruined the greatest gift he ever had.

Sound familiar?

Our world was like my buddy's car when God handed us the keys. We have wrecked it.

The Bible says that God made everyone and everything "very good."[a] This intended state of beauty and harmony in all things is described in the Old Testament as "shalom."[b] Everything is now very bad because something has gone very wrong as we have wrecked shalom.

Thankfully, unlike my buddy's dad who could not fix the wreck, our Heavenly Father is doing just that. This war to get back to "shalom" is not us versus God, but rather us and God versus an unseen enemy who is the cause of all misery. Ephesians 6:12 (NLT) says, "we are not fighting against flesh-and-blood enemies, but against evil rulers and authorities of the unseen world, against mighty powers in this dark world, and against evil spirits in the heavenly places." Our pains and problems started before this world, and exist beyond this world, according to the storyline of the Bible.

To explain what has gone wrong in the world, theologians like to talk about "original sin" and "the Fall" by talking about Adam and Eve in Genesis 3. The problem is that Adam and Eve did not commit the original sin. Their rebellion (and ours) was preceded by Satan and demons who, in fact, committed the original sin. Jesus told us that the Devil was a murderer and a liar from the beginning[c], who has been sinning from the beginning.[d] To make sense of what has gone wrong in the world, we need to start with a worldview based upon God's Word.

WHAT ARE THE FOUR LEGS OF A BIBLICAL WORLDVIEW?

Like a stool that is held up by four legs, a biblical worldview is held up by four truths. If one of more of these truths is missing, just like a stool, it falls over, toppling the person seated upon it. We'll now examine this idea as summarized from the book Win Your War that I wrote with my wife Grace detailing spiritual warfare.

1. The unseen realm

You cannot believe God's Word or understand God's world unless you embrace the supernatural. From beginning to end, the Bible is about an unseen realm as real as the visible world. Faith is required to believe in beings as real as we are who live in a world as real as ours and travel between these worlds, impacting and affecting human history and our daily lives. As a result, everything

---

[a] Gen. 1:31 [b] Isa. 2:2-4, 11:1-9, 32:14-20, 43:1-12, 60:1-22, 65:17-25; Joel 2:24-29, 3:17-18 [c] John 8:44; Gen. 1:1 [d] 1 John 3:8

FALL: GOD JUDGES

is spiritual, and nothing is secular. What happens in the invisible world affects what happens in the visible world and vice versa. Furthermore, everyone is both a physical being with a body that is seen and a spiritual being with a soul that is unseen. Spiritual warfare is like gravity—unseen. It exists whether or not you believe in it, and it affects you every moment of every day.

Christianity has largely downplayed, if not dismissed, this truth for hundreds of years. Other than Pentecostal and Charismatic Christians, many denominations and seminaries seeking to win the approval of worldly scholarship were too influenced by the rationalism, naturalism, and skepticism of modernity that corresponds in large part with the history of America to support the truly supernatural.

Rationalism disbelieved most anything that could not be seen through a telescope or microscope and believed only that which could be proven through the scientific method of testing and re-testing. Since miracles are by definition non-repeatable, one-time events, miracles became impossible to believe. This led to naturalism, a worldview that all is material, and nothing is spiritual. The result was skepticism about the spiritual, and eventually atheism and the denial of God altogether. Subsequently, there is little teaching about such things as the unseen realm, demons, miracles, and supernatural spiritual gifts in much Christian preaching and teaching. Beyond an obligatory nod to the big supernatural issues like Jesus' virgin conception and bodily resurrection, many Christians live as skeptics rather than seekers of the supernatural, something rather new in church history.[1][2][3][4][5][6][7]

Creeping into Bible interpretation, soon belief in such things as angels, demons, healing, speaking in tongues, and prophecy was looked down on as primitive and naïve. Surely humanity had evolved beyond such archaic views. Theologically, this is often referred to as cessationism, which is a worldly approach to the Bible that also ignores much of the supernatural record of church history, weakly arguing that the way God used to work is not the way God currently works as much of His supernatural work has ceased.[8]

Overreacting to cessationism is sensationalism as Christian teaching on the demonic and supernatural is combined with wild speculation not anchored to sound biblical principles. As a result, some Christians find talk of Satan and demons to be concerning as they have heard so much bad teaching.

There is a biblical option between the deficit of supernatural teaching in cessationism, and the deficit of Scriptural teaching in sensationalism. Thankfully there is a growing increase in credible academic work on the supernatural by scholars like Dr. Michael Heiser, whose work heavily influences what we will explore in the rest of this chapter and beyond.[9]

2. Binary thinking
Christians think in terms of black and white (binary thinking). Non-Christians think in terms of shades of gray. Biblical thinking is binary thinking.[10]

Biblical Christianity requires black-and-white thinking because it is dualistic. From beginning to end, the Bible is thoroughly categorical: Satan and God, demons and angels, sin and holiness, lies and truth, darkness and light, wolves and shepherds, non-Christians and Christians, damnation and salvation, Hell and Heaven. An exhaustive list could fill a book—but you get the point. The Bible makes clear distinctions and judgments between categories.

Mainstream culture is monistic. Monism does not allow black-and-white thinking. It refuses to allow any categories because that would require making distinctions, which ultimately ends in making value judgments. Instead of Satan and God, we have a "higher power." Instead of demons and angels, we have spirits or ghosts. Instead of sin and holiness, we have lifestyle choice. Instead of lies and truth, we have your truth and my truth. Instead of darkness and light we have shades of grey. Instead of wolves and shepherds, we have spiritual guides. Instead of non-Christians and Christians, we have everyone as God's child. Instead of Hell and Heaven, we have all people going to a better place when they die.

Monism is a religion. Although not always formal like Christianity, it is a religious worldview that rejects dualistic thinking and the Bible. In monism everything, including gender, is on a spectrum of equally valid options. This is a demonic deception. What God creates, Satan counterfeits. Satan creates nothing, but he does counterfeit, corrupt, and co-opt what God creates. Here are some examples:

God Creates	Satan Counterfeits
angels	demons
obedience	rebellion
truth	lies
Spirit-filled	demon-possessed
cleansing	defilement
humility	pride
forgiveness	bitterness
worship	idolatry
contentment	coveting
peace	fear
unity	division
shepherds	wolves
God-esteem	self-esteem
covenant with God	inner vow with self
spirit	flesh
freedom	slavery
revival	riot
life	death
church	world
Kingdom	Hell

FALL: GOD JUDGES

3. Group guilt

God holds both human and spirit beings responsible for their behavior. The devil and his demons tempt others to participate in their evil plots and plans, and when someone surrenders to Satan and does something evil, both the person and the demons are held responsible. Sadly, depending upon which Christian teachers you listen to, you will often find an imbalance. Some wrongly blame Satan for all of their wrongdoing and reduce human responsibility. Others wrongly blame people for all wrongdoing and overlook the role that the demonic realm plays in sinful human decision-making.

Genesis 3 is a case study and record of the first human sin. God judges the man first, holding him accountable for his sinful failure to lovingly lead and defend his family. The man is responsible for his sin and cannot point to God, Satan, or the woman to make himself a victim instead of a villain despite his efforts to do just that. God then judges the woman, holding her accountable for her sinful failure to follow God's command. She seeks to blame shift her sin to the devil, but God gives her consequences for her sin while not neglecting the role of the serpent. Lastly God judges the devil for his participation in the Fall, rendering a verdict of eventual defeat and destruction once he is crushed under the feet of Jesus.

Genesis 3 is a case study and the record of the first human sin. God confronts the man first, inviting him to confess that he ate of the tree. The man is responsible for his sin and cannot point to God, Satan, or the woman to make himself a victim instead of a villain despite his efforts to do just that. God then confronts the woman, holding her accountable for her sinful nature to follow God's command. God's first judgment falls on the Serpent, the ultimate opponent, for his deceptive questioning, rendering a verdict of eventual defeat and destruction once he is crushed under the feet of Jesus. Then God gives the woman consequences for her sin and then the man the consequences of his sin.

Who is responsible for the first sin? The man? The woman? The devil? The answer is yes. This is the principle of group guilt. Just as multiple people can be convicted and charged for involvement in the same crime, when sin occurs, numerous guilty persons are often involved. We will explore this more later in this chapter.

4. "Heaven down or Hell up"

There was a war in Heaven that came to the earth which we will explore later in this chapter. King Jesus has come down to the earth and will again come down one last time, bringing the Kingdom in His wake, to push the devil and his demons down to Hell forever. Every day on earth, we are living amidst a great battle that has been raging from long ago in Heaven. Each day, our decisions either invite Heaven down or pull Hell up into our lives.

Jesus' half-brother James used binary thinking, urging Christians not to pull Hell up into our lives through alternative lifestyle choices that are, "false to the truth… earthly, unspiritual, demonic…and…vile," but instead to invite Heaven down into our lives with the "wisdom from above."ª Paul exhorts, "Set your minds on things that are above, not on things that are on earth."ᵇ Jesus taught us to pray and then live Heaven down, not Hell up: "Your kingdom come, your will be done, on earth as it is in heaven."ᶜ When we see the Spirit fall on people in the Bible and to this day, this is living "Kingdom down" rather than culture up which is "Hell up". We are not fighting alone, and the battles we have on earth in the seen realm actually started in Heaven amidst the unseen realm with God's divine family.

WHO ARE GOD'S DIVINE AND HUMAN FAMILIES?

The Bible says that God is a Father and calls human beings (male and female) the "sons of God" denoting their joint and equal honorable position as full heirs of all that belongs to the Father.ᵈ
Most Christians know these facts well. What is far less known is that God also has a divine family in the unseen realm that is just as real as His human family in the seen realm.

Divine beings (angels and others) are also called the "sons of God". One scholarly source explains how the first readers of the Old Testament on divine beings would have understood what was written. Just as "sons of man" means human beings in Hebrew, so "sons of God" means divine beings, i.e., gods. In Canaanite religion and myth, the term "sons of God" or "sons of the gods" referred to the gods in general. They were the deities of the pantheon who convened to render decisions regarding the governance of the world. Ugaritic mythological texts, e.g., call this divine council "the assembly of the sons of God" (or "of 'El," the chief god).[11]

Here are some examples of where the Bible also calls the divine beings in the unseen realm "sons of God", which is the same language the Bible uses for human beings in the seen realm that together constitute the full family of God:

- Psalm 89:6 (NASB) – Who in the skies is comparable to the Lord? Who among the sons of the mighty is like the Lord...
- Job 1:6 – There was a day when the sons of God came to present themselves before the Lord, and Satan also came among them.
- Job 2:1 – There was a day when the sons of God came to present themselves before the Lord, and Satan also came among them to present himself before the Lord.
- Job 38:4-7 – "Where were you when I [God] laid the foundation of the earth? Tell me, if you have understanding. Who determined its measurements—surely you know! Or who stretched the line upon it? On what were its bases sunk, or who laid its cornerstone, when the morning stars sang together and all the sons of God shouted for joy?"

ª James 3:15-17 ᵇ Col. 3:2 ᶜ Matt. 6:10 ᵈ Ex. 4:22; Deuteronomy 14:1; Matt. 5:9; Rom. 8:14; Gal. 3:6-9, 23-29, 4:3-7

Importantly, the final verses in Job must refer to divine beings because they are present at the creation of our world which preceded human life. Therefore, this cannot refer to human beings.

For many, this understanding of God's one family in two realms might be rather new insight. Two reasons explain why many Christians know less than they should about God's divine family in the unseen realm.

One, Bible teachers have tended to simply refer to everyone in the unseen realm as angels. The Bible does speak of angels a lot – some 300 times in roughly 90 percent of the books of the Bible. There, we learn about "innumerable angels" and "a thousand thousands and ten thousand times ten thousand". Only two angels are named – Gabriel the messenger and Michael the warrior. There are also categories of angels like archangel and commander which denote senior leaders, and also kinds of angels such as cherubim and seraphim. Angels are also referred to as "stars" and "morning stars" because they are between us and the heavens spiritually like the stars are physically. Angel means messenger, and angels are most likely lower-level divine beings in God's divine family.

In addition to angels, however, there are also numerous other divine beings referred to throughout Scripture as "watcher", "holy one", "holy ones", "host of heaven", "Prince of the host", "Prince of Persia", "chief princes", "man clothed in linen" and a "lord". When God's divine family gathers together, they are referred to as the "divine council", "assembly of the holy ones", "the council of the holy ones", "hosts", "the seat of the gods", "the mount of assembly", "the court...in judgment", and "the heavenly host". It was the divine council that met with Jacob travelling down a ladder at Bethel (meaning house of God), and it was the divine council that Daniel, Isaiah, and John reported seeing gathered around Jesus on the throne in the unseen realm.

Two, there is a long-standing error within biblical scholarship interpreting the Old Testament word "elohim" as one of the names for God. The problem is that the word is not only used of God, but also numerous other divine beings which leads to the faulty conclusion that the Old Testament is polytheistic with many gods.

Dr. Michael Heiser explains, "The fact that biblical writers label a range of entities as 'elōhîm that they elsewhere take pains to distinguish as lesser than Yahweh tells us quite clearly that we ought not understand 'elōhîm as having to do with a unique set of attributes possessed by only one Being. A biblical writer would use 'elōhîm to label any entity that is not embodied by nature and is a member of the spiritual realm. This 'otherworldliness' is an attribute all residents of the spiritual world possess. Every member of the spiritual world can be thought of as 'elōhîm since the term tells us where an entity belongs in terms of its nature. The spiritual realm has rank and hierarchy: Yahweh is the Most High. Biblical writers distinguish Yahweh from other 'elōhîm by means of other descriptors exclusively attributed to him, not by means of the single word 'elōhîm..."[12]

A simple way of summarizing all of this is to say that any being in the divine realm is referred to in the Bible as an "elohim". That includes God, and other divine beings. Psalm 82:1 is one clear example of this principle, "God [elohim] has taken his place in the divine council; in the midst of the gods [elohim] he holds judgment."

The reason this matters is because there was a war in Heaven that continues on earth. Unless we understand the Great War, we cannot make sense of the bloodied battlefield of human history on our planet. Before there was a Fall on earth, there was a fall in Heaven.

WHAT WAS THE FALL IN GOD'S DIVINE FAMILY?

God is a King with a Kingdom, and His divine family members serve much like His military soldiers. If you've ever known a military family who loves one another but gets focused and intense when sent on a mission, then you have a good idea of God's spiritual family.[13]

For example, an angelic army defends Elisha, angels start a war on earth in the days of Daniel, the commander of the Lord's army visits Joshua, and at the end of the age an angel will show up on the earth brandishing a sharp sickle with which to strike down the nations.[a]

When we read the Bible, we receive God's revelation and perspective on the war we were born into. Throughout the Bible, spirit beings are deployed like soldiers to sustain and defend God's people.[b]

We need to be careful not to assume God is only at work when we see it. There is much we do not see. Faith is trusting that God sees what we do not see and is at work through His divine army warring for our well-being.

Much like a commanding military officer that seeks to incite a coup to overthrow a king and overtake a kingdom, one of the highest-ranking spirit beings, also called the "strong man" or "prince of demons,"[c] became filled with pride.[d] We now know him by various titles such as Satan, the devil, the evil one, the prince of the power of the air, the spirit of the world, Belial, the enemy, the adversary, the serpent, the dragon, the tempter, the god of this world, and the counterfeit spirit.[e] The Bible only refers to the devil with titles, never using his name. This seems to be a purposeful insult that his name never be spoken. It is akin to the omission of the name of the Pharaoh in Exodus, pointing us to the true heroes, the midwives Shiphrah and Puah.[f]

---

[a] 2 Kings 6:15-17; Dan. 10:12-21; Josh. 5:13-15; Rev. 14:19 [b] 1 Kings 19:5, 7; 2 Kings 6:17; Ps. 91:11 [c] Matt. 4:8-9; 9:34; 12:24, 29; Mark 3:22-27; Luke 4:6; 11:21-22; John 12:31; 14:30; 16:11; 1 John 5:19 [d] Isa. 14:11-23; Ezek. 28:12 [e] Rom. 16:20; 1 Cor. 5:5; 7:5; 2 Cor. 2:11; 11:14; 12:7; 1 Thess. 2:18; 2 Thess. 2:9; 1 Tim. 1:20, 5:15; Eph. 4:27, 6:11; 1 Tim. 3:6-7; 2 Tim. 2:26; Eph. 6:16; 2 Thess. 3:3; Eph. 2:2; 2 Cor. 6:15; Luke 10:19; 1 Tim. 5:14; 2 Cor. 11:3; Rev. 12:9; 1 Thess. 3:5; 2 Cor. 4:4; 11:4 [f] Ex. 1:15

FALL: GOD JUDGES

Rather than glorifying God, he wanted to be glorified as god. Rather than obeying God, he wanted to be obeyed as god. Rather than living dependently upon God, he wanted to live independently as his own god. Rather than building the Kingdom, he wanted to expand his own kingdom. The battlefield report from the unseen realm says, "Now war arose in heaven, Michael and his angels fighting against the dragon. And the dragon and his angels fought back, but he was defeated, and there was no longer any place for them in heaven. And the great dragon was thrown down, that ancient serpent, who is called the devil and Satan, the deceiver of the whole world—he was thrown down to the earth, and his angels were thrown down with him."[a]

God and the angels won that battle, but all humans, starting with our first parents, have our own little battles every day that feel like wars to us. After the great war in Heaven, continuing with the story of Scripture, the scene shifts to a new battlefield—earth. Jesus says, "I saw Satan fall like lightning from heaven."[b]

Opposing the ministry of God to forward the kingdom are demonic forces, fallen spirit beings who are at war. Paul wrote some of the most focused biblical passages on the war with the demonic realm. His goal was to equip local churches because they are on the front lines of the war. These are the terms Paul uses when describing the "rulers of this age" (1 Cor. 2:6, 8), the rulers "in heavenly places" (Eph. 3:10), and "the ruler of the authority of the air" (Eph. 2:2). Paul often interchanged these terms with others that are familiar to most Bible students:
- principalities (*archē*)
- powers/authorities (*exousia*)
- powers (*dynamis*)
- dominions/lords (*kyrios*)
- thrones (*thronos*)

It is important to note there is no possibility of salvation for sinful angels. There is only a possibility of salvation for sinful people. God could have treated us like the demons and simply cast every one of us into "the eternal fire prepared for the devil and his angels."[c] Clearly, "God did not spare angels when they sinned, but cast them into Hell and committed them to chains of gloomy darkness to be kept until the judgment."[d] Instead of this just fate in Hell, people are given the possibility of Heaven and forgiving grace through Jesus Christ.

As a result of the Fall, the descent into sin has continued unabated ever since. A respect for authority was replaced by rebellion. A clear conscience was replaced by guilt and shame. Blessing was replaced by physical, spiritual, and eternal punishment. Viewing God as a friend to walk with was replaced by viewing Him as an enemy to hide from. Trust was replaced by fear. Love was replaced by indifference and even hatred. Intimacy with God was replaced by separation from God. Freedom to obey God was replaced by enslavement to sin.

---

[a] Rev. 12:7-9 [b] Luke 10:18 [c] Matt. 25:41 [d] 2 Pet. 2:4

Honesty was replaced with lying and deceit. Self-sacrifice was replaced by self-centeredness. Peace was replaced by restlessness. Responsibility was replaced by blaming. Authenticity was replaced by hiding.

Theologian D. A. Carson says, "Consumed by our own self-focus, we desire to dominate or manipulate others: here is the beginning of fences, of rape, of greed, of malice, of nurtured bitterness, of war."[14]

We will explore our battles next as the fall of the divine family continued with the fall of the human family.

WHAT WAS THE FALL IN GOD'S HUMAN FAMILY?

The storyline of the Bible is wedding then war. Satan did not show up until a man and woman were married with a ministry call on their lives. The enemy's deceptive subversion of their trust relationship with God was also an attack on marriage, separating the husband and wife so he could then wreck their family and legacy. Spiritual warfare starts by attacking the relationship of a married couple.

Genesis 3 is one of the most important chapters in all of the Bible. It explains the source of and solution for sin and death. The scene is the beautiful and perfect garden made by God for our first parents to live in together.

Why did Satan come to the Garden of Eden? Likely because it was the place of God's divine council meetings. Throughout the Bible, God has chosen a connecting point on earth between the seen and unseen realms. Examples include the tabernacle, temple, and of course the body of Jesus Christ. The first such location chosen by God for divine council meetings was Eden. Heiser says, "Eden was God's home on earth. It was his residence. And where the King lives, his council meets."[15]

The meeting between Satan, Adam, and Eve was likely common and not the first time the couple had met there with a spirit being. This might explain why they were not startled or scared. Until sin entered the world and separation occurred, God's human and divine family members likely interacted with one another, particularly in the divine council meeting place of Eden. This also explains why an angel guarded Eden after our first parents were removed from the divine council upon sinning—God's loyal family removed His fallen family from their shared home.

The entrance of Satan the serpent[a] marks the beginning of chaos in creation. He is called "crafty", which is usually a positive description, "prudent" or "sensible".[b] But he uses his wisdom for evil. Satan began by tempting Eve to mistrust God's Word by changing its meaning, just as he did when likewise, later tempting Jesus. Rather than rebuking Satan, Eve entertained his lies and was

---

[a] Rev. 12:9; 20:2 [b] Prov. 12:16; 14:8; 22:3

FALL: GOD JUDGES

subsequently deceived by his crafty arguments.[a] Satan boldly contradicts God; he tempted them to grow up, trust their own perceptions, to be like God, defining good, right, true, beautiful, and real for themselves, which is the knowledge of good/evil. Satan invited humanity, starting with the husband and wife, to join him and his demons in self-centered independence, which amounts to a revolution against God – he was now continuing on earth the same battle he had lost in Heaven. Again, this attack was in the realm of the divine council meeting held in Eden where God and His two staff families—angelic and human—would meet. God intended from the beginning that His two families would work together in both the physical and spiritual realms and Satan sought to rule both realms. Sin has temporarily separated the two families until Jesus reunites them in His Kingdom.

The Lord had made a "grace garden" with one "law tree." Adam and Eve were free to eat of any tree with one exception. Satan's tactic was and is to misrepresent God as having us live in a "law garden" with many rules and restrictions. The truth is, God is a gracious Father, and when He says no, it is only for the sake of keeping His children from harm. Otherwise, we have great freedom. He is like a parent who fills the refrigerator with food and tells the kids not to eat the paint thinner on the shelf in the garage. To sin is to self-destruct, which explains human history.

WHY DOES ADAM'S SIN IMPLICATE EVERYONE?

The governance of God has the Father as the singular head, and the Son and Spirit joining Him in plural leadership. The government of home has the husband as the singular head, and the husband and wife in plural leadership.[b] Demonic attack is concentrated upon leaders because, since the war in Heaven, Satan is seeking to make himself the singular head in every sphere. Understanding singular headship and plural leadership helps us understand the satanic war in Eden and explains why Satan attacked the Father in heaven; Adam (as head of the human race on earth); Jesus (as the new head of the human race on earth); and Peter (as the human head of the early church).

Tragically Adam stood by silently while all of the coup attempts on earth occurred; he failed to lead his family in godliness. "She [Eve] also gave some to her husband [Adam] who was with her, and he ate."[c] Eve's sin was *commission*—doing the wrong thing; Adam's sin was *omission*—doing nothing.

This demonic pattern continues. Satan attacks marriage and family while passive, silent, non-relational, inactive men say and do nothing. Practically, this looks like a home in which Mom reads the Bible, prays, and goes to church with the kids while Dad sits on the other side of their teeter-totter not doing those things or leading his family spiritually. The pattern is crucial: though Eve sinned first,

---

[a] John 8:42–47; 2 Cor. 11:3; 1 Tim. 2:14 [b] 1 Cor. 11:3, Eph. 5:23 [c] Gen. 3:6

DOCTRINE

God held Adam firstly responsible because he was the singular head of his family. "The Lord God called to the man and said to him, 'Where are you?'"ᵃ The lesson from our first father is that if we do not head our home, Satan will gladly take our place.

Following the Fall, God cursed the parties involved as a penalty for their sin. Our first mother was given increased pain in childbirth and struggle with maintaining harmony with her hubby.ᵇ

Our first father's work became toil as the curse of sin extended to all of creation, including the ground he worked. For men this means struggles will mainly come in two forms: a career at work and a covenant with a wife.

As head, Adam was the representative and father of all mankind, and when he sinned and fell out of favor with God, so did every person who would ever live. The same is true on a smaller scale in a family where the decision of a father to bankrupt the family implicates every family member. One great demonic myth is that each of us is an isolated individual born into this world with a blank slate and able to determine our own destiny. The fact is that each of us is born on the wrong side of a war. When Adam sinned, he voted for every member of the human family.

- "Sin came into the world through one man, and death through sin, and so death spread to all men because all sinned."ᶜ
- "By a man came death...in Adam all die."ᵈ

You were born a rebel in the war against God. This rebellion is part of your nature, as according to the Bible we are sinners by nature from conception.ᵉ

According to Romans 5:12-21. Adam's sin affects us all in three ways:

1. There is inherited sin from the original sin of Adam that causes the rest of humanity to be born into a sinful state or condition. The corrupted sin nature that we inherit from Adam begins in our mother's womb.ᶠ This is what John Calvin referred to as "a hereditary depravity and corruption of our nature."[16]

2. There is imputed sin whereby Adam's sin and guilt are attributed, or reckoned, to us and our legal standing before and relationship with God is negated. Additionally, by the grace of God, the sinner's guilt and condemnation is imputed to Jesus Christ, who atones for sin on the cross and enables His righteousness to be imputed to the sinner as a Christian.

3. Adam's sin is imparted to us so that we are conceived in a fallen state and, apart from the enabling grace of God, are unable to respond to the Gospel or remedy our depravity. Simply put, we are each sinners both by nature and choice.ᵍ

ᵃ Gen. 3:9 ᵇ Gen. 3:16 and 4:17 use the same language for the conflict with Satan and sin ᶜ Rom. 5:12 ᵈ 1 Cor. 15:21-22 ᵉ Ps. 51:5; 58:3; Isa. 64:6; Rom. 3:23; 5:10; Eph. 2: ᶠ Ps. 51:5; 58:3 ᵍ Ps. 51:5; 58:3; Isa. 53:6; 64:6; Rom. 3:23, 1 John 1:8

FALL: GOD JUDGES

In 1 Corinthians 15, Paul called Jesus the "last Adam" because He is the remedy for sin and the redeemer of sinners, whereas the first Adam was the source of sin and the downfall of sinners. The first Adam turned from the Father in a garden; the last Adam turned to the Father in a garden. The first Adam was naked and ashamed; the last Adam was naked and bore our shame. The first Adam's sin brought us thorns; the last Adam wore a crown of thorns. The first Adam substituted himself for God; the last Adam was God substituting Himself for sinners. The first Adam sinned at a tree; the last Adam bore our sin on a tree. The first Adam died as a sinner; the last Adam died for sinners.

According to the Bible, we die in Adam but are born again in Christ: "For as in Adam all die, even so in Christ all shall be made alive".[a] In Adam there is condemnation, but in Christ there is salvation. In Adam we receive a sin nature, but in Christ we receive a new nature. In Adam we're cursed, but in Christ we're blessed. In Adam there is wrath and death, but in Christ there is love and life.

There are two teams in life; each of us takes the field with one of them, and the decisions made by the team captains affect the whole team, for better or worse. Not only does the captain win or lose; his whole team wins or loses along with him. One team has Adam as its captain. The other has Jesus as its captain. While there are many ways to categorize people in our society, the Bible has these two categories—those whose identity is in Adam and share in his defeat, and those whose identity is in Christ and share in His victory.

God cursed the serpent for what he had done before declaring his punishment on the humans, showing that the Serpent is the true enemy.[b] He was told he would be defeated one day by the woman's "seed," who is Jesus.[c] Theologians have long called the promise of Jesus in Genesis 3:15 the *protoevangelion* (first gospel), as God preaches the hope of salvation for the first time. His angel will preach it to the earth the last time before eternity is ushered in as God gets the first and last word on world history.[d] In the middle of history we join God and the angels by proclaiming the good news of Jesus Christ so that people transfer from Team Adam to Team Jesus.

WHAT IS SIN?

Sin is so nefarious, complex, and far-reaching that it is difficult to succinctly define. Cornelius Plantinga says:
The Bible presents sin by way of major concepts, principally lawlessness and faithlessness, expressed in an array of images: sin is the missing of a target, a wandering from the path, a straying from the fold. Sin is a hard heart and a stiff neck. Sin is blindness and deafness. It is both the overstepping of a line and the failure to reach it—both transgression and shortcoming. Sin is a beast crouching at

---

[a] 1 Cor. 15:22 [b] Eph. 6:12 [c] Gal. 3:16 (KJV) [d] Rev. 14:6

DOCTRINE

the door. In sin, people attack or evade or neglect their divine calling. These and other images suggest deviance: even when it is familiar, sin is never normal. Sin is disruption of created harmony and then resistance to divine restoration of that harmony. Above all, sin disrupts and resists the vital human relation to God.[17]

The Bible uses a constellation of images to explain sin as everything from rebellion to folly, self-abuse, madness, treason, death, hatred, spiritual adultery, missing the mark, wandering from the path, idolatry, insanity, irrationality, pride, selfishness, blindness, deafness, a hard heart, a stiff neck, delusion, unreasonableness, and self-worship. To help you understand sin, in general, and your sin, in particular, we will examine eight aspects of sin that the Old Testament teaches us.

1. Sin is first a relational breach. This is painfully clear in Genesis 2–3 where our first parents are separated from God and one another; hide from God and one another, fear God, blame one another, and seek to cover their sin and shame while living apart from God.
2. Sin is social destruction because shalom has been vandalized. This explains the litany of murder, perversion, drunkenness, the continual evil that precipitated the flood, and human attempts at an Edenic-like society without any regard for God that spring forth in Genesis 4–11.
3. Sin is a covenantal rebellion against God and his authority. This is witnessed perhaps most clearly in Exodus 32-34, where following God's liberation of His people, they dishonor, disregard, and disobey him by worshiping idols while God is giving them the Ten Commandments through their leader Moses.
4. Sin is a legal transgression causing guilt that necessitates punishment. Moses' worshipful song in Deuteronomy 32 recollects some of the most treasonous behavior of God's people and the price that had to be paid for justice to be maintained as one example.
5. Sin causes ritual uncleanness, pollution, and filth, marked by the use of words such as "filth," "defiled," "unclean," and "whore."[a] Importantly, this defilement happens both to sinners and victims; we defile ourselves by our own sin and are defiled by others when they sin against us.
6. Sin includes emotional pain such as shame and disgrace.[b] This is first seen in Genesis 3, where our first parents sin and then hide in shame and disgrace, whereas prior to their sin they "were not ashamed."[c]
7. Sin accumulates, piling up from one generation to the next.[d] Sin only worsens over time as people invent new ways to do evil more effectively.
8. Sin causes the finality of death.[e] In sinning, we unplug from God, who is the source of life, and exercise our dominion over creation until the dust of the

---

[a] Gen. 34:5; Lev. 19:31; 21:14; Num. 5:27; 1 Chron. 5:1; Ps. 106:39; Prov. 30:11–12; Lam. 4:14; Ezek.14:11 [b] E.g., Jer. 6:15; Ezek. 36:16 [c] Gen. 2:5
[d] E.g., Gen. 15:16; Lev. 18:24-28; Deut. 9:4-8 [e] E.g., Gen. 5; Deut. 30

FALL: GOD JUDGES

earth defeats us.[a]

The New Testament also speaks of sin in many ways, though four words are used most often.

1. The most common word for sin is the Greek word *hamartia*, which means wrongdoing, or missing the mark. It is the most general word used for sin and refers to the innumerable ways in which we fall short of what God intends for us and miss His will for our conduct.
2. The Greek word *paraptoma*, which means "to trespass", appears frequently. This word speaks of crossing a line of God's law, whether intentionally or unintentionally.
3. The Greek word *parabasis* speaks of sin as disobedience and transgression. By using this word, the Bible is referring to evil intent, whereby someone defiantly chooses to disobey God and thus sin, knowing full well what they are doing.
4. The Greek word *asebeias* speaks of sin in terms of ungodliness and godlessness. This word refers to sinners' active character of rebellion whereby they act as if there were no God and/or as if they were their own god and the highest authority in their life.

In summary, sin includes both omission, where we do not do what we ought, and commission, where we do what we ought not do. Sin includes our thoughts, words, deeds, and motives. Sin includes godlessness, which is ignoring God and living as if there were no God or as if we were a god. Sin is invariably idolatry, which is the replacing of God as preeminent with something or someone else—most often oneself.

Sin includes individuals, families, communities, cultures, nations, and the like as people partner together for the cause of sin. Sin includes entire ways of thinking and acting, such as racism and pornography. Sometimes a sin is also a legal crime, such as murder, and sometimes it is not, such as adultery. Sin can be done deliberately or in ignorance. The practice of a particular sin can occur once, regularly, or even frequently.

Sin includes breaking God's laws, breaching just human laws, defying godly authority such as parents and police, and violating one's own conscience as well as conviction wrought by God the Holy Spirit. Sin includes perversion, using good things for evil purposes. Sin includes pollution, infecting good things with evil. Lastly, sin is the turning of a good thing (e.g., sex, work, money, comfort) into an ultimate thing so that it is worshiped as a god in place of God and becomes a false god.

Sin is a trap we've all stepped in, "Who can say, 'I have made my heart pure; I am clean from my sin'?"[b] The answer is no one but Jesus Christ.

Some sinners seek to minimize their sin by comparing their sins to others' so that theirs appear minor and therefore somehow less sinful. Regarding degrees

---

[a] Gen. 3:17-19 [b] Prov. 20:9

of sin, on one hand, God sees people in the categories of perfection and imperfection[a] and considers any sin a violation of the entirety of His law.[b] One example is Jesus' teaching that people cannot excuse lust because it is not as bad as adultery.[c] Jesus doesn't say they are equal but that both are sin even though the Law of Moses only forbids adultery of the hands and not the heart. Legalists always look for creative ways to excuse their sin, but sinners must not compare themselves or their sin to others. They must rather compare themselves to Jesus and see all of their sin without diminishing any of it.

On the other hand, sins have degrees of consequence. The Bible speaks of the sin that leads to death[d], more severe judgment[e], stricter judgment for teachers[f], greater punishment[g], greater consequences for intentional sin than unintentional sin[h], greater punishment for child abusers[i], greater punishment for a man who does not feed his family than for an infidel[k], and twice the judgment for self-righteous religious people than for "sinners."[m]

This principle makes practical sense, seeing that, for example, it would be a sin for one man to lust after another man's wife, but the damage would be far greater if he actually seduced her and committed adultery with her. While shopping in the store, we would also prefer that someone covet our parked car rather than stealing it and forcing us to walk home. Sins are equally sinful, but their pains are not equally painful.

WHAT IS TOTAL DEPRAVITY?

Human depravity is an undeniable reality and explains why wars are fought, lawsuits are filed, arguments are had, doors are locked, and guns are loaded. Even atheists know humans are not as they should be. Psychological pioneer Sigmund Freud views our innermost self as a "hell." In "Civilization and Its Discontents", Freud writes:

Men are not gentle, friendly creatures wishing for love, who simply defend themselves if they are attacked, but that a powerful measure of desire for aggression has to be reckoned as part of their instinctual endowment. The result is that their neighbor is to them not only a possible helper or sexual object, but also a temptation to them to gratify their aggressiveness on him, to exploit his capacity for work without recompense, to use him sexually without his consent, to seize his possessions, to humiliate him, to cause him pain, to torture and to kill him. Homo homini lupus [man is a wolf]; who has the courage to dispute it in the face of all the evidence in his own life and in history?[18]

Despite the fact we are sinners, after the Fall we do retain the image of God.[n]

---

[a] Matt. 5:48 [b] James 2:10 [c] Matt. 5:27-28 [d] 1 John 5:16-18 [e] Luke 12:47-48 [f] James 3:1 [g] Matt. 11:20-24 [h] Lev. 4:1-35; 5:15-19; Num. 15:22-30; Ezek. 45:20; Luke 12:48 [i] Matt. 18:6 [k] 1 Tim. 5:8 [m] Matt. 10:15; 23:15 [n] Gen. 5:1-3; 9:6; 1 Cor. 11:7; James 3:9

FALL: GOD JUDGES

Included in this is a vestige of moral sense because of the conscience that God has given us as His image bearers.[a] Because people are made in God's image with a conscience, the Bible does speak of some non-Christians who, while not holy and living to God's glory, do some "good" things. Examples include Abimelech, Balaam, Rahab, Artaxerxes, and the Good Samaritan.[b]

There is a difference between total depravity that affects all of our being, and utter depravity where we would be like Satan and demons with no vestige of being made in God's good likeness. The existence of "good" non-Christians is evidence of God's common grace. Nonetheless, without saving grace, we sinners are unable to do anything that makes us pleasing in God's sight because it is not done in faith as an act of worship out of love for God. Doing something good is not the same as doing something for God.

While people are not utterly depraved and as evil as they could be, all people are totally depraved in that motive, word, deed, and thought is affected, stained, and marred by sin. This includes the mind, will, emotions, heart, conscience, and physical body.[c]

The totality of a person is pervasively affected by sin, and there is no aspect of their being not negatively impacted by sin. In this way, sin in our life is like sewage dropped into a glass of drinking water in that it infects and affects all of the water leaving none of it pure and clean.

Describing this pervasive depravity, J. C. Ryle said, "Sin...pervades and runs through every part of our moral constitution and every faculty of our minds. The understanding, the affections, the reasoning powers, the will, are all more or less infected."[19] Practically, we cannot fully trust any single aspect of our being (e.g., mind or emotions) because each is tainted and marred by sin and therefore not pure or objective. Subsequently, we need God's Spirit, God's Word, and God's people to help us see truly and live wisely.

As a result of our sin nature, in relation to God, we are by nature children of wrath[d], all sinners[e], and destined to death.[f] Speaking of our sin nature, A. W. Tozer says:

There is within the human heart a tough fibrous root of fallen life whose nature is to possess, always to possess. It covets "things" with a deep and fierce passion. The pronouns "my" and "mine" look innocent enough in print, but their constant and universal use is significant. They express the real nature of the old Adamic man better than a thousand volumes of theology could do. They are verbal symptoms of our deep disease. The roots of our hearts have grown down into things, and we dare not pull up one rootlet lest we die. Things have become necessary to us, a development never originally intended. God's gifts now take the place of God, and the whole course of nature is upset by the monstrous

---

[a] Rom. 2:14–15 [b] Gen. 20, Num. 22–24, Josh. 2, Ezra 7; Nehemiah 2, Luke 10:30–37 [c] Eph. 4:18, Rom. 6:16–17, Titus 3:3, Jer. 17:9, Titus 1:15, Rom. 8:10 [d] Eph. 2:3 [e] Rom. 5:12, 19 [f] 1 Cor. 15:21–22:43

substitution.[20]

Subsequently, God does not tempt us to sin, but instead the temptation arises from within our own sinful hearts. Jesus' own brother speaks of the source of sin within us:

Let no one say when he is tempted, "I am being tempted by God," for God cannot be tempted with evil, and he himself tempts no one. But each person is tempted when he is lured and enticed by his own desire. Then desire when it has conceived gives birth to sin, and sin when it is fully grown brings forth death.[a]

God wants more than just a change in our behavior, but a deeper change in our nature. God offers a new heart and nature, what the Bible calls regeneration or new birth, followed by ongoing Spirit-empowered sanctification into Christlikeness for victory over sin in our lives. God doesn't just make us better. God makes us new.

WHAT ARE SATAN'S SCHEMES AGAINST US TODAY?

Not only did Satan tempt the first Adam in a garden from which he was kicked into a desert, but he also tempted the Last Adam in a desert as Jesus picks up where Adam left off. In each of the Synoptic Gospels, Satan appears as the tempter of Jesus Christ.[b] From the opening to the closing pages of Scripture, Satan is presented as an enemy of God and God's people.

Sadly, it is not uncommon for people to make either too much or too little of Satan. C. S. Lewis says, "There are two equal and opposite errors into which our race can fall about the devils. One is to disbelieve in their existence. The other is to believe, and to feel an excessive and unhealthy interest in them."[21]

Foundational to our study of Satan is to recognize that he is in no way equal to God. His knowledge, presence, and power are limited because he is a divine being created by God and not the divine Creator.

The motivation for all of the Serpent's work is pride and self-glory instead of humility and God-glory.[c] Today, he has done a good job re-branding pride from a vice to a virtue under the guise of self-love, self-esteem, and self-actualization.

Regarding spiritual warfare as it is experienced on the personal level, 2 Corinthians 2:11 (NIV) says, "Satan might not outwit us. For we are not unaware of his schemes." Therefore, knowing Satan's tactics helps us in anticipating his work and living in victory rather than as victims.

Scheme 1: The World

The world is our external enemy that tempts us to sin against God. The world is an organized system in opposition and rebellion against God. In 1 John 2:16, the world is defined as corporate flesh working together in three ways.

---

[a] James 1:13-15; see also Prov. 27:19; Jer. 17:9; Mark 7:21-23; Luke 6:45 [b] Matt. 4:1-11; Mark 1:12-13; Luke 4:1-13 [c] Ezek. 28:2; James 4:6-7

FALL: GOD JUDGES

1. The world is the domain of the desires or lust of the flesh, sinful longings for physical pleasures in everything from gluttony to drunkenness, sexual sin, and chemical highs.
2. The world is devoted to the desires or lust of the eyes, sinful longings for coveted possessions manifested in everything from advertising and marketing to pornography.
3. The world is where pride in possessions is commended, resulting in coveting and stealing.

In response to the world, the Bible commands a threefold response.

1. We are not to love the world.[a] Because the world is our mission field, rather than our home, and the source of our temptation to sin, we must continually guard ourselves from falling in love with the world and the passions and pleasures it offers, not unlike the forbidden fruit that tempted our first parents.
2. We are not to let the world shape our values.[b] Because the world is where the devil and our desires converge, we must seek the conversion of the culture and not allow the culture to convert us.
3. Because Jesus died to the world, we should live crucified, or dead, to the world.[c] We are either alive to the sin of the world and dead to God, or dead to the temptation of the world and alive to God, which is true freedom.

While the world can tempt us, we are still the ones who choose to sin. Puritan Thomas Brooks says that our enemy will use the world to bait our hook with anything we desire.[22] He will give us sex, money, power, pleasure, fame, fortune, and relationships. Satan's goal is for us to take the bait without seeing the hook. When we see the bait, we need to remember the hook as the decision as to whether or not we bite is ours.

Scheme 2: The Flesh

The flesh is our internal enemy and a seed of corruption that lingers in us throughout this life to resist and rebel against God.[d] Flesh sometimes means a physical body, as when the Word became flesh in Jesus Christ.[e] But the Bible does not locate our sin in our physicality as ancient and contemporary Gnostics do. Sinful deeds of the flesh come from every part of our person.[f] Paul uses flesh to refer to our innate propensity to sin against God; he says that the flesh is the seat of our sinful passions, the realm of sinners, and the source of our evil desires.[g]

The Bible commands Christians to respond to the flesh in three ways.

1. Recognize that we are no longer under the flesh's bondage.[h] Jesus' death for our sin and His resurrection for our salvation

---

[a] 1 John 2:15 [b] Rom. 12:2 [c] Gal. 6:14 [d] Mark 7:21-23; Gal. 5:19-21; Col. 3:5-8; James 1:14-15 [e] John 1:14 [f] Gal. 5:19-21 [g] Rom. 7:18, 25 Gal. 5:16, 19; Eph. 2:3; Rom. 7:5; 8:8-9; Col. 3:5 [h] Romans 6

give us a new nature and a new power from God the Holy Spirit to say no to our flesh and yes to God.
2. Walk in conscious submission to the Holy Spirit as Jesus did on the earth.[a] The Holy Spirit is more powerful than any spirit tempting us, or any desire in us.
3. Put to death, or what the Puritan John Owen called "mortify," sinful desires.[b] Like an enemy combatant in war, the flesh must be killed before it kills us.

<u>Scheme 3: The Devil</u>

Satan's ultimate goal for believers is a compromised and fruitless life beset by heresy, sin, and ultimately death.[c] Demonic opposition is increasingly pronounced for those who serve God most faithfully. Puritan William Gurnall said, "Where God is on one side, you may be sure to find the devil on the other."[23] The Bible speaks of Satan's work as the ordinary and extraordinary demonic. Ordinary demonic work includes sexual sin, marriage between Christians and non-Christians, false religion with false teaching about a false Jesus, unforgiving bitterness, foolishness, drunkenness, idle gossiping, busybodying, lying, and idolatry.[d] Extraordinary demonic work includes torment, physical injury, counterfeit miracles, accusation, death, and false spirits.[e]

As God promised our first parents following their sin, the defeat of Satan and his works is possible only through the death, burial, and resurrection of Jesus Christ in our place for our sins. Hebrews 2:14–15 says, "Since therefore the children share in flesh and blood, he himself likewise partook of the same things, that through death he might destroy the one who has the power of death, that is, the devil, and deliver all those who through fear of death were subject to lifelong slavery."

WHAT ARE SOME SINFUL VIEWS OF SIN?

Because sin is a humanity-wide problem, speculation about the definition, source, and cause of sin arises from seemingly every conceivable explanation. A few examples can help us see sin more clearly, starting with our own.

In materialism that disbelieves in spiritual reality, "sin" is the result of electro-chemical imbalances leading to biological dysfunction. Therefore, the solution to evil and sin is solely medical and chemical improvement of the human body with no regard for the soul.

In evolutionism, "sin" is anything that hinders the perceived progress of the

---

[a] Gal. 5:16 [b] Rom. 8:13–16 [c] 1 Tim. 4:1–2, 1 John 3:7–10; John 8:44; 1 Pet. 5:8
[d] 1 Cor. 7:5; 2 Cor. 6:15; 1 Cor. 10:14–22; 1 Tim. 4:1–2; 2 Cor. 11:1–4; Eph. 4:17–32; Eph. 5:8–21;1 Tim. 5:11–15; John 8:44; 1 John 5:18–21
[e] Acts 5:16; Matt. 9:32–33, 12:22–23; Acts 8:4–8, 8:9–23, 16:16; 2 Thess. 2:9–10; Rev. 12:10; Prov. 8:36; John 8:44; 1 John 4:1–6

FALL: GOD JUDGES

human race rather than any offense against a personal God.

In psychologism, "sin" is blamed on low self-esteem, bad life experience, or excused by one's personality type. Subsequently, the answer to sinful behavior is not repentance and faith in God for help, but rather love and acceptance of oneself.

In humanism, "sin" is reduced to attitudes or actions that hurt other people. Because humanists see humanity as essentially good, the answer to evil behavior is better education and social conditioning to nurture our good nature.

In pantheism and panentheism, "sin" is being out of balance with the consciousness of the rest of the earth. Eastern practices like meditation and going into oneself, yoga to harmonize with all living things, animal rights, and environmentalism are prescribed as cures to heal everyone and everything.

There are also many errors that people who profess to be Christians believe about sin. As a result, their holiness, healthiness, and happiness sadly suffer.

Some see sin as only breaking the rules of God. Sin includes this, but sin is fundamentally violating the relationship with God and a personal betrayal of a loving Father. This error reduces faith to rule keeping rather than to loving relationship with God that underlies, empowers, and enables obedience. When we sin, we don't just break God's laws, we also break God's heart, "The LORD saw that the wickedness of man was great in the earth, and that every intention of the thoughts of his heart was only evil continually...and it grieved him to his heart."[a]

Some wrongly believe that since Jesus died for their sins, they need not fight for holiness and repent when they fail. Because Jesus died for our sins, we should honor Him by putting sins to death.

Some think that unless they confess every sin, they will wind up in Hell because not all of their sins will be forgiven. Because Jesus died for all of our sins, we can and should repent of all the sins we are aware of while realizing that our imperfection includes an imperfect sensitivity to our sins, causing us to be unaware of all our transgressions which Jesus paid for.

Some think that as long as they are nice and have a "good heart" God will not be displeased by their sin. God is concerned both with our inner life and our outer life. Moreover, since our life is simply the outworking of our heart, it is nonsensical to consider someone as having a good heart but bad actions.[b]

Some consider sin and fun synonymous and therefore sin in the name of having fun. Sin leads to death, killing everything it touches, particularly joy. Sin may appear to be fun initially, the distance it brings from God, the guilt it causes, and the damage it does to oneself and others are ultimately anything but fun. Sin poses as an attraction before becoming an affliction because it is deceptive and ultimately a lie.

Some wrongly believe that if no one is hurt then their sin does not really matter. But this is untrue on many accounts. Our sin is against God, it grieves Him

---

[a] Gen. 6:5-6 [b] E.g. Prov. 4:23

and distances us from Him. Sin hurts our church, family, friends, and those we are in community with, even if they are unaware of our sin, because our sin affects and changes us negatively. Lastly, our sin also hurts us because we were not made for sin, and to live in sin unrepentantly is to damage oneself. On this point, Plantinga says, "Sin hurts other people and grieves God, but it also corrodes us. Sin is a form of self-abuse."[24]

Some wrongly believe that sin is not a problem unless one is caught, so they persist in secret sin. Sin is never secret. God knows, the sinner knows, and those who know the sinner often know something is wrong even if they are unaware of exactly what.

Some think that if a sin is popular, then it is okay because a majority approves. Culture often labels a vice as a virtue. Abortion, for example, is presented not as murder but noble choice. When the Bible condemns being worldly it is often referring to the morality of the majority.[a]

Lastly, some think that sin and mistakes are synonymous, when they are in fact different things. A sin is a moral wrong, and a mistake is a morally neutral imperfection. Those who do not understand this distinction painfully try to live lives of perfectionism and are devastated at mistakes that do not trouble God and therefore should not trouble them. Parents that fail to recognize this distinction discipline their children not only for sins but also for mistakes. As an example, I once saw a very young child was drinking out of an open cup at a restaurant. Because her motor skills were not yet well developed, she accidentally spilled a bit of her milk. Rather than simply wiping it up since it was a morally neutral mistake, the parents yelled at the child as if she had sinned, though she had not. They disciplined her for being human, not sinful.

WHAT IS THE PROBLEM OF EVIL?

Evil can be very hard to understand. Where does it come from? Why does it exist? How does it relate to God?

Since the early days of the church Christians have referred to evil as a *privation* or a *defilement*. Evil is not so much a thing in itself but rather the corruption of the good, like cancer that preys on the host of a human body. The body can flourish without cancer, but cancer cannot flourish without the body. Similarly, good can exist without evil, but evil cannot exist without good. Before the evil sin of rebellion by angels, there was only good in God's Kingdom. Today, there is no evil in God's heavenly Kingdom, but rather only good. When God completes His redemption project, all in His Kingdom will be good without any evil of any sort.

---

[a] John 1:29; 3:6; Rom. 1:18-32; 1 Cor. 1:20-21, 27-28, 11:32; Gal. 3:22; 4:3; Eph. 2:2, 12; Col. 2:8, 20-33; 1 Pet. 2:11; 2 Pet. 1:4; 1 John 2:17; 3:6; 4:5

FALL: GOD JUDGES

Defining evil (the essence) and sin (the action) is very important. A helpful thinker on this point is Augustine. Prior to his conversion to Christianity, he was part of a cult called Manichaeism. That cult—like many Eastern religions, pantheism, panentheism, and the New Spirituality (or New Age)—considered God to be both good and evil. His mind changed when he was redeemed by Jesus, received the Spirit, and read the Scriptures.

Augustine's prayer in his book *Confessions* describes his own experience whereby God opened his eyes to his personal sin. Augustine prays:

But You, Lord, while he was speaking, turned me back towards myself, taking me from behind my own back where I had put myself all the time that I preferred not to see myself. And You set me there before my own face that I might see how vile I was, how twisted and unclean and spotted and ulcerous. I saw myself and was horrified, but there was no way to flee from myself...You were setting me face to face with myself, forcing me upon my own sight, that I might see my iniquity and loathe it. I had known it, but I had pretended not to see it, had deliberately looked the other way and let it go from my mind.[25]

Augustine rightly said that evil was a flaw, a lack or deficiency in something inherently good. For this reason, Zechariah 10:2 uses the four words nonsense, lies, false, and empty to explain sin in terms of privation. But evil is also actively destructive of the good. Jesus describes the devil as a murderer and a liar who comes to steal and kill and destroy.[a]

Regarding evil and sin, the Bible professes four essential truths. First, God is fully and continually all-powerful. Second, God is altogether good and there is no evil in Him whatsoever.[b] Third, evil and sin really do exist. Fourth, sinners are fully responsible for their sin.

For starters, we do need to make a distinction between moral evil and natural evil. Moral evil is the result of choices of a responsible agent, whether intentional or negligent. Natural evil is suffering that occurs without a moral agent involved (hurricanes, floods, earthquakes). Humans make no (or very few) actions causing natural evils.

Evil is felt very personally. We have all felt the pain of evil done to us, done by us, and done to those we love by us and others. When the pain of evil comes, we have two options. One: we can get frustrated with God as if He were the problem and not the solution. Two: we can bring our frustrations to God, trusting by faith that He is the solution and not the problem.

Surveying all of the evil, injustice, and suffering in the world, Habakkuk brought this question to God: "You who are of purer eyes than to see evil and cannot look at wrong, why do you idly look at traitors and remain silent when the wicked swallows up the man more righteous than he?"[c]

In more philosophical terms, Habakkuk is raising "the problem of evil". Here's

---

[a] John 8:44; 10:10 [b] Ps. 5:4; Isa. 59:2, 64:7; Zech. 8:17; 1 John 1:5 [c] Habakkuk 1:3

DOCTRINE

the question: If God is all-powerful, all-knowing, and all-good, why is there suffering and evil? This is one of the most practical, painful, and problematic questions that every generation asks about God. If this were a multiple-choice test, there are six possible answers.

1. There is no God. Atheism wrongly concludes that there is evil and suffering because there is no God to stop it. This is hopeless, which is why atheism leads to despair and even suicide.
2. God is not all-powerful. Finite Godism wrongly concludes that God is impotent and lacking the power to overcome evil and suffering. God is simply a loser and evil is a winner. This too is hopeless.
3. God is not all-knowing. Evolutionary Godism, or Open Theism, wrongly concludes that God does not know the future but is experiencing life as it comes, doing His best to learn, grow, and respond much like we do. This God might be a good friend for life's journey, but He is stuck rowing in the same boat we are. This is yet again hopeless.
4. God is not all-good. The Pantheism and Panentheism in many Eastern religions wrongly concludes that God is both good and evil and that both darkness and light come from and are expressions of God's character. If God is evil, then we are doomed as there is no one solely good outside of our broken world to mend it.
5. There is no suffering and evil. Subjectivism and Pluralism wrongly conclude that evil and the experience of suffering are not absolute but rather relative and therefore not always wrong or negative. This is of no help when your body or soul get shot and you need healing.
6. God is not done yet, so live by faith, not sight. Biblical Christianity concludes that God is all-powerful, all-knowing, and all-good and that our good God has a problem with evil. Therefore, suffering and evil are not the way that God is, the way that God made the world, or the way that the world will be when Jesus returns and establishes His Kingdom. God is at war with the devil and his dark kingdom. Jesus' followers partner with Him to overcome evil with good and crush the serpent. Until then, God reminds us that "the righteous shall live by his faith."[a]

Perhaps a classic preaching analogy will help. When a weaver uses a loom, the work looks very different from under the loom as compared to above the loom. When looking up from under the loom, one only sees knots and haphazard bits of yarn that seem out of place, random, and disorganized. Yet, when looking down upon the loom from the top, the picture is entirely different. From above, we can see that the weaver had a beautiful picture in mind, meticulously laboring to bring it to pass.

So, it is with God. As we look up, we do not see what He is doing. By getting spiritually above the loom of life through prayer, Scripture, and time with the

---

[a] Hab. 2:4

Spirit, we can begin to see, "...for those who love God all things work together for good, for those who are called according to his purpose."[a] The Bible promises us that one day, possibly not until we enter the Kingdom of God, evil will be bent for God's glory and our good. Until then evil is a problem that causes pain.

HOW DOES GOD'S SOVEREIGNTY RELATE TO SIN?

God is sovereign, powerful, and good. Evil exists and creatures bear moral responsibility for it. Philosophers have long sought to find a way to reconcile the character of God with the reality of sin. Gottfried Leibniz first coined the term theodicy in 1710 to describe this quest for understanding. Theologian J. I. Packer says that the word theodicy comes from the Greek *theos* ("God") and the root *dik-* ("just") and seeks to "justify the ways of God to man"...showing that God is in the right and is glorious and worthy of praise despite contrary appearances. Theodicy asks how we can believe that God is both good and sovereign in face of the world's evil—bad people; bad deeds, defying God and injuring people; harmful (bad) circumstances, events, experiences and states of mind, which waste, thwart, or destroy value, actual or potential, in and for humankind; in short, all facts, physical and moral, that prompt the feeling, "This ought not to be."[26]

Regarding theodicy, Christian philosopher C. Stephen Evans says:

Two of the more important theodicies are the "soul-making theodicy," which argues that God allows evil so as to make it possible for humans to develop certain desirable virtues, and the "free will theodicy," which argues that God had to allow for the possibility of evil if he wished to give humans (and angelic beings) free will. Theodicies are often distinguished from defenses, which argue that it is reasonable to believe that God has reasons for allowing evil even if we do not know what those reasons are.[27]

Specific forms of theodicy speculations vary wildly. Some teach a false universalism whereby everyone will be saved in the end. Others say that we will retain our freedom to sin even in our resurrected heavenly state, which leaves open the possibility of sin occurring again in the eternal state. Also, as J. I. Packer describes:

Some Calvinists envisage God permissively decreeing sin for the purpose of self-display in justly saving some from their sin and justly damning others for and in their sin. But none of this is biblically certain. The safest way in theodicy is to leave God's permission of sin and moral evil as a mystery, and to reason from the good achieved in redemption.[28]

Some say God ordains all sin, using it for his greater glory, but Scriptures like Jeremiah 32:26-35 make it clear that some sins are against His will in every sense. God says that His people have chosen to "provoke me to anger" by doing "nothing but evil in my sight from their youth." As a result, they have aroused

---
[a] Rom. 8:28

DOCTRINE

"anger and wrath". God goes on to say, "They have turned to me their back and not their face. And though I have taught them persistently, they have not listened to receive instruction. They set up their abominations in the house that is called by my name, to defile it. They built the high places of Baal...to offer up their sons and daughters to Molech, though I did not command them, nor did it enter into my mind, that they should do this abomination, to cause Judah to sin." God is emphatically clear that when grotesque evil occurs, including the slaughter of one's own child to a false demon "god", such sin is not anything that is in the will of the real God.

Others say God allows sin because He honors our free choice but stories like the judgments of Pharaoh and Jerusalem make it clear that there are limits to his patience. We can safely say that God is at war with sin and evil, overcoming it with good through His redemptive work as His promised Messiah crushes the Serpent.[a]

In regard to the coexistence of God and sin, humility is required, because we presently see and know only in part and because God has secrets He has chosen not to reveal to us.[b]

The Bible repeatedly declares that God is always, perfectly, and solely sovereign, powerful, and good. It is completely clear that God is angry because of sin and evil because creatures, not the Creator, are responsible for it. Sin never destroys His plan, never limits His power to act, and never stops Him from doing good in the worst evil. From the appearance of Satan in the garden onward, sin and evil are not dealt with in a systematic fashion but in such a way as to compel us to continued faith in God, trusting in His ultimate providence that one day the presence and power of sin will be no more. To assume that God cannot defeat evil (making him not sovereign and/or not powerful) or will not defeat evil (making Him not good) is to judge God before He judges evil, rendering the verdict prematurely. Since we are in the middle of history, until God is done with all of His work, we must not judge Him but rather trust Him until He is finished with sin and history as we know it.

In the meantime, evil is never outside the providential control of God. He is at work to do His good purposes in the context of evil. We see this in the story of Joseph in the final dozen chapters of Genesis. We read of Joseph's betrayal at the hands of his brothers, unjust suffering, and eventual rise to power because the Lord was with him, whereby many lives were saved. When he confronted his brothers, the providence of God at work in the life of Joseph crescendos: "As for you, you meant evil against me, but God meant it for good, to bring it about that many people should be kept alive, as they are today."[c]

Many years later, a descendant of Joseph named Jesus Christ suffered similarly. He too was betrayed by His "brothers," suffered the worst injustice in

---

[a] Gen. 3:15; Col. 2:15; Heb. 2:14-15; 1 John 3:8 [b] 1 Cor. 13:12; Deut. 29:29
[c] Gen. 50:20

FALL: GOD JUDGES

history, died in shame on a Roman cross, and, like Joseph, was thrown in a hole from which He emerged to sit at the right hand of a king ruling a kingdom. With Joseph and Jesus, God was vindicated as fully sovereign, good, and powerful despite human evil.

God also used the freely chosen evil of Judas, Herod, Pilate, Gentiles, and the Jews to accomplish His perfect purpose.[a] In the same way, God used the Chaldeans, a horribly evil nation, to punish the persistent sin of Judah and Jerusalem.[b] This does not mean that their evil is God's responsibility. People freely kill and destroy. In a cosmic irony, the God of all providence uses evil to judge evil. Even as His hand brings punishment to Israel and death to Jesus, He also brings redemption and resurrection into the context of judgment and death.

A day is coming when we will also rise with and to Jesus. On that day, our faith will be sight and we will see God fully vindicated. Until that day, our answer to the question of how God's sovereignty relates to sin is ultimately a prayerful, worshipful, humble, and continual meditation on Romans 8:28, which promises, "We know that for those who love God all things work together for good, for those who are called according to his purpose." That day is coming.

WHAT ARE SOME LOGS IN OUR EYES THAT CAUSE BLIND SPOTS TO SIN?

The truth is, we are all blind to our own blind spots. We can more easily see the sin of others than our own. So, we need to pay careful attention to the log in our own eye rather than the speck in someone else's. Here are some logs that cause blind spots to our sin:

1. We minimize a sin. This is often as simple as comparing one's sin to seemingly greater and more heinous sins so as to get off the hook of guilt.
2. We consider our sin as different from anyone else's because we have good reasons for our sin. Sometimes this goes so far as to say that because God in His grace used sin for something good, it was a good thing that the sin occurred. This is a horrendous evil because it uses God's grace, which works in spite of our sin, to portray our sin as a virtue and not a vice.
3. We rationalize sin as acceptable because of some extenuating circumstances. This includes wearing down our listeners by speaking passionately about our perspective on our motives and the conditions surrounding our sin in an effort to gain sympathy and excuse our sin.
4. We blame shift someone or something for our sin. This was the tactic of our first parents in the garden, where Eve blamed Satan, and Adam blamed Eve and blamed God for making Eve.
5. We create diversions from our sin by blaming someone else for

---

[a] Acts 2:23; 4:27-28 [b] Hab. 1

misunderstanding. Examples include saying, "I was just joking", "you misunderstood", and changing the subject from your sin to your feelings about the person who brought it up.
6. We partially confess only some of our sin in an effort to not deal with all of it and be able to move on from the subject quickly.
7. We commit what Paul calls "worldly grief,"[a] where we merely regret the consequences of our sin and not the sin itself.
8. We present ourselves as victims to sin, helplessly pitiful and unable to have done otherwise by naming someone (e.g., parent, Satan, past abuser) or something (e.g., genes, culture, personality) as responsible for our sin.
9. We practice mere confession. We acknowledge our sin, show remorse, and ask for forgiveness but never really change.
10. We present our sin as an unavoidable disease instead of an avoidable evil. Indeed, like an addiction or disease, sin affects our entire being; it is painful, tragic, and leads to death. Still, there are many ways in which sin is not like a disease; it is something we do rather than something we catch, and something we confess rather than treat.[29]

All of this matters because we are supposed to be loved as sinners, and to love fellow sinners. To love God and sinners, we must take their sin seriously, as God does. If we do not, we rob sinners, including ourselves, of the dignity God bestows on us as His image bearers capable of moral improvement. The bad news is we are sinful, the good news is we're made for more and by the grace of God's Spirit can become more like Christ. Indeed, as Plantinga says, "We ought to pay evildoers, including ourselves, the 'intolerable compliment' of taking them seriously as moral agents, of holding them accountable for their wrongdoing. This is a mark of our respect for their dignity and weight as human beings."[30]

HOW DOES GOD RESPOND TO SIN?

Who has betrayed you most painfully, hurt you most deeply, and disappointed you most shockingly? Every one of us knows what it is like to have someone we love shoot us in the soul.

Have you ever wondered what it must be like to have experienced that kind of evil from everyone all the time? As we study the doctrine of the Fall, it is incredibly important that we see things, as much as possible, from the vantage point of God who is the biggest victim in all of history. God has sinned against no one; everyone has sinned against Him. Theologian R. C. Sproul reminds us:

God voluntarily created us. He gave us the highest privilege of being His image bearers...We are not turtles. We are not fireflies. We are not caterpillars or coyotes. We are people. We are the image bearers of the holy and majestic King

---

[a] 2 Cor. 7:10

of the cosmos. We have not used the gift of life for the purpose God intended. Life on this planet has become the arena in which we daily carry out the work of cosmic treason...No traitor to any king or nation has even approached the wickedness of our treason before God...When we sin as the image bearers of God, we are saying to the whole creation, to all of nature under our dominion, to the birds of the air and the beasts of the field: "This is how God is. This is how your Creator behaves. Look in his mirror; look at us, and you will see the character of the Almighty." We say to the world, "God is covetous; God is ruthless; God is bitter; God is a murderer, a thief, a slanderer, an adulterer. God is all of these things that we are doing."[31]

What would you do if you were God and were treated as He has been by sinners, in general, and by our first parents, in particular? Would your first instinct be to act in grace toward sinners by pursuing them, speaking to them, teaching them, covering them, and promising them that the His Son would come to suffer and die at the hands of sinners for their salvation?[a] The stunning account of Genesis shows a God that no one would ever have invented, because He does what no one ever could have predicted.

Later in the storyline of the Bible, we learn that Jesus did come to save sinners, turning enemies into family.[b] He did this by becoming the one who succeeded where the first Adam failed.[c] He died in our place for our sins and rose for our salvation. The good news of the Bible is that we are more evil than we can fear, and God is more loving than we can hope.

We are all the Prodigal Son who hated his loving father, ran away from home, squandered the gifts he was given, and pursued sinful self-destruction. When we see the father running to embrace and bless his repentant son who came to his senses and came home to his father, we are encouraged to do that very same thing, experience that very same embrace, and receive that very same grace.

QUESTIONS FOR PERSONAL JOURNALING AND/OR SMALL GROUP DISCUSSION

1. Do you primarily see God as good and His laws to protect us? Or do you primarily see God as bad and making laws to restrict us?
2. Do you earnestly believe that God is altogether good and not the source of evil?
3. Are you prone to think too much or too little of Satan and demons?
4. In what areas of your life is pride an ongoing battle?
5. What definition(s) of sin are more helpful and insightful to you?
6. In what ways have you seen Satan at work in your life recently?
7. Is there any area of your life that you are experiencing victory over your

---

[a] 1 Cor. 15:45 [b] Matt. 1:21 [c] 1 Cor. 15:45

flesh? Is there any area of your life that you are experiencing defeat to your flesh?
8. What relationship(s) in your life have been most devastated by sin? What (if anything) can be done to mend those relationships?
9. Which sin have you committed in your life that has caused more harm than any other? Do you truly understand and believe that Jesus forgives you for this?
10. What bait is the most tempting on your hook? What sin or temptation to sin in your life do you need to take some time to talk with your Father about today?

CHAPTER 6: COVENANT

"GOD PURSUES"

The friendship of the Lord is for those who fear him, and he makes known to them his covenant.
PSALM 25:14

I met my wife Grace in high school. She was a pastor's daughter who was a Christian but was not walking closely with the Lord. I came from a Catholic family, and although my Catholic mom knew the Lord, I did not. I did not much understand that God was relational and wanted a relationship with me. So, I believed in some vague concept of God and tried to be a generally good person who stayed out of trouble but did not have a loving personal relationship with God.

When I met Grace, I absolutely adored her and soon our friendship was blooming. As a graduation present, Grace bought me a nice leather-bound Bible with my name embossed on the front. In college at a state university, I became a Christian reading that Bible and started my relationship with God, which started changing my relationship with Grace. The more I learned about how God loved me, pursued me, forgave me, and was present with me, the more I learned how I should treat Grace by following God's example to me.

Within a few years, Grace and I were engaged. To prepare for marriage, we met with our pastor who taught us that marriage was a covenant that reflected Jesus' covenant relationship with His bride, the Church. He taught us from Scripture that God's relationship with us was a covenant, and that we were supposed to invite God into our marriage so that it, too, would be a covenant relationship. Apart from the Bible, no one really thinks this way, but the concept

DOCTRINE

of covenant is revolutionary and more needed than ever in our world of broken relationships, marriages, and families.

COVENANT RELATIONSHIP WITH GOD

Immediately after the first sin of our first parents, God responds to His betraying enemies with grace that points to Jesus Christ. In Genesis 3, God pursued them, spoke to them, taught them, covered their shame, and sent them away so that they would not live forever apart from God, and promised that Jesus was coming to save sinners by defeating the dragon. All that was lost in the first Adam would be restored in the last Adam: "The first man Adam became a living being; the last Adam became a life-giving spirit."[a]

God's response to our sin was covenant—saving, glorious, loving covenant. This is because God is, by nature of being Trinitarian, covenantal. As the Father, Son, and Spirit are a covenantal community as one God, so too they are graciously covenantal with believers, despite the fact we start as sinful enemies and rebels.

God's choosing to enter into a loving covenant relationship with betraying sinners reveals seven things about God.

1. God is relational and invites us into loving relationship
2. God is gracious and gives us everything despite owing us nothing
3. God is sovereign and actively initiates covenant with us
4. God is Lord and solely establishes terms of the covenant
5. God is Holy and cuts covenants by having a sacrifice for sin
6. God is loving and pours out blessings to help us obey Him
7. God is just and has consequences, or curses, for those outside of covenant with Him

At the most basic level, a covenant is an agreement between parties.[b] Various covenants are made between people, between people and God, and between God and people. In the Old Testament, the word covenant appears hundreds of times and is used in a variety of ways. Personally, Job made a covenant with his eyes not to look at women lustfully.[c] Relationally, deep brotherly love is covenantal[d], as is marriage.[e] Nationally, the elders of Israel made a covenant with King David.[f] Benefits of covenants can include protection from an enemy[g], peace[h], financial blessing[i], and obtaining a homeland.[k]

When the Bible speaks of God's covenant with His people, it is explaining how our relationship with God is made by His provision and exists by His terms. Through covenant with God, we enjoy a relationship with Him that is akin to marriage and includes protection from Satan our enemy, peace with God though

---

[a] 1 Cor. 15:45 [b] Gen. 26:28; Dan. 11:6 [c] Job 31:1 [d] 1 Sam. 18:3 [e] Prov. 2:16-17; Mal. 2:14 [f] 2 Sam. 5:3 [g] Gen. 26:28-29; 31:50-52; 1 Kings 15:18-19 [h] Josh. 9:15-16 [i] 1 Kings 5:6-11 [k] Gen. 23:14-16

COVENANT: GOD PURSUES

we declared war on Him through sin, material provision in this life and the life to come, and a coming perfect Kingdom as our home where Jesus will forever rule over all as our gracious covenant King.

The word for covenant is berith in Hebrew and diatheke in Greek. A covenant is "a solemn commitment, guaranteeing promises or obligations undertaken by one or both parties, sealed with an oath".[1] When God enters into a covenantal relationship with humanity, God sovereignly institutes a life-and-death bond.[2] Or, to say it another way, a covenant is a life-and-death relationship with God on His terms.

As a bond, a covenant is a relationship that commits people to one another, God to His people, and people to God. Oaths, promises, and signs accompany the bond or commitment. This aspect of God's covenants reveals His loving grace and mercy because, although people deserve nothing but condemnation and suffering, God gives covenant and salvation.

By initiating covenants, God never enters into the relationship casually or informally. Covenant relationship signifies the life-and-death intensity of the bond. This intensity is seen in all three types of covenants: human to human[a], God to human[b], and human to God.[c]

The establishment of a covenant is called "cutting a covenant." It usually entails the slaughter of an animal. This symbolizes or represents the curse that the covenant maker calls down upon themselves if they should violate their covenant commitments. This aspect of God's covenants reveals His perfect holiness and justice.

In a covenant with God there is no bargaining, bartering, or contract negotiating regarding the terms of the covenant. Neither is God's covenant something we must earn by our good works. It is always a gracious provision from the loving Lord to His people. The sovereign Lord of heaven and earth dictates the terms of God's covenants. It is God's covenant in that it is conceived, devised, determined, established, confirmed, and dispensed by God Himself, who often says, "I will establish my covenant with you."[d][3] This aspect of God's covenants reveals His sovereign rule as Lord. God makes five major covenants in the Bible with the following[4]:

1. Noah and his family[e]
2. Abraham and his descendants[f]
3. Moses and the Israelites[g]
4. David and the kingdom of Israel[h]

---

[a] Gen. 21:27, 32; 2 Sam. 3:12, 13 [b] Abraham: Gen. 15:18; Moses: Ex. 24:8; Deut. 5:2; David: 2 Chron. 21:7; Ps. 89:3; the new covenant: Jer. 31:31; Ezek. 37:26 [c] 2 Kings 11:17; 23:3; 2 Chron. 29:10 [d] See Gen. 6:18, 9:9, 11, 17, 17:7, 19, 21; Ex. 6:4; Ezek. 16:60, 62; Heb. 8:8 [e] Gen. 6:18, 9:8-17 [f] Gen. 12:1-3, 15:18, 17:1-14, 22:16-18 [g] Ex. 3:4-10, 6:7, 19:5-6, 24:8 [h] 2 Sam. 7:8-19; Ps. 89:3

DOCTRINE

5. The new covenant of Jesus and the church[a]

For each of these covenants, it is helpful to highlight five special features:

1. The covenant mediator or head (the person with whom God makes the covenant) and their covenant role (whom the mediator represents)
2. The covenant blessings promised
3. The covenant conditions (or curses)
4. The covenant sign for celebration and remembrance
5. The covenant form that God's family takes as a result of the covenant

The purpose of these covenants was to address the problems sin unleashed in humanity and throughout all of creation. Across the Old Testament echo the promises and relationships in the covenants that will redeem God's people and restore God's sin-alienated creation to Himself. It is important to note that covenants themselves do not solve the problem, but they do point to Jesus who does.

GOD RESPONDS TO OUR EVIL WITH HIS COVENANT LOVE

Throughout the Old Testament, covenant love is referred to in various terms, but the main one is *khesed* especially in the Psalms. The word *khesed* in essence summarizes the entire history of God's covenantal relationship with Israel. *Khesed* is God's lovingkindness – the consistent, ever-faithful, relentless, constantly pursuing, lavish, extravagant, unrestrained, one-way love of God. It is often translated as covenant love, lovingkindness, mercy, steadfast love, loyal love, devotion, commitment, or reliability.

Khesed is typically translated "love" and sometimes as "mercy."[b] However, *khesed* has a much narrower definition than the English term love conveys. *Khesed* refers to a sort of love that has been promised and is owed—covenant love—as in Hosea 11:1: "When Israel was a child, I loved him, and out of Egypt I called my son."

Covenant love is the love God promised to His people, and which they, in turn, were to respond in kind, loving God with all their hearts, minds, and strength. *Khesed* does not suggest some kind of generic love of everyone. Rabbi Kamsler suggests that the best English word to use as a translation for *khesed* is loyalty, which refers to God's covenant loyalty because of His love for His people.[5] Perhaps the children's *Jesus Storybook Bible* says it best: "God loves us with a never-stopping, never giving up, unbreaking, always and forever love."[6]

Malachi 1:1-5 is a clear presentation of *khesed*. Malachi opens with the declaration of the word of Yahweh: "I have loved you." The people were not

---

[a] Matt. 16:17–19; 26:28; Luke 22:2 [b] Ps. 23:6

immediately convinced of this declaration; to them, because of their state of spiritual rebellion, it sounded good but was not convincing, because their life was hard. "How have you loved us?" they asked.

The prophet's response reminded them of their status as the chosen people of God: "Is not Esau Jacob's brother?" Yahweh says. "Yet I have loved Jacob but Esau I have hated." God, through Malachi, stressed that their existence as God's people was the clearest evidence of God's love. God chose the Israelites to be His kingdom of priests in the world. He gave them the Scriptures, temple, priesthood, prophets, covenants, and the Messiah. And His love for them was an everlasting love – even though they failed Him again and again, He still retained His covenant with them. Not only did God choose Israel ("Jacob"), but He also cared for the Israelites whenever they were in trouble. The simple fact was that God protected Israel down through the ages even though they were wicked like the nation of Edom ("Esau"), which He destroyed in His justice, is a supreme example of His *hesed*.

God lovingly living with His people is a theme throughout Scripture: "I will live among them and walk among them, and I will be their God and they will be my people."[a] The Bible's storyline begins with creation in harmony, unity, and peace, and it ends with a restored creation. In between these bookends is the drama of redemption. The covenants are major acts of this drama. Christ's work is intimately related to and fulfills each of the four covenants (with Noah, Abraham, Moses, and David) that God initiated in the Old Testament. New dimensions are brought to light when Christ's covenant is understood in the context of the previous covenants. God's activity and intention to redeem us and the covenants tell us about ourselves – our condition, our brokenness, our dignity, our role as images of God, our suffering, and our calling.

Regarding our calling, Christopher J. H. Wright says of God's covenant people (Israel and the church):

This people also has a mission, derived from the mission of God. Again the word is used to mean that this people exists for a purpose, or more precisely, have been brought into existence for the sake of the purposes of God. But, in their case, especially in the New Testament (though not absent from the Old Testament), the concept of mission as "sending and being sent" is an essential component in that overall orientation towards the goal of God's mission.[7]

Indeed, one way of walking through the story of God in Scripture is to see God sending His Son and His people into the world through covenants as an act of worship in relation to Himself and as an act of witness in relation to the nations.

---

[a] Lev. 26:12; Jer. 32:38; Ezek. 37:27

DOCTRINE

WHAT IS THE NOAHIC COVENANT?

God's calling of Noah to build the ark begins with the lengthy genealogy of Adam's descendants until the birth of Noah.[a] The primary theological point that every descendant of Adam was a sinner who lived and died without exception in a monotonous and unspectacular fashion, simply saying "and he died" repeatedly.

Peter, reflecting on God's patience but eventual justice in the days of Noah, sees a correlation with our own day.[b] As decades, centuries, and millennia pass in our rebellious world, it is easy to lose hope that things will ever be different. Will God ever change the world in a dramatic way and fix the mess? We may doubt at times, but we can take heart. God did not allow sin to go unpunished in Noah's time; He will not let it go unpunished in the future. He did not fail to rescue His people from judgment in Noah's day; He will not fail to rescue us in the future. Genesis 6:5-9 breaks from the cycle of mere sin and death:

The LORD saw that the wickedness of man was great in the earth, and that every intention of the thoughts of his heart was only evil continually. And the LORD was sorry that he had made man on the earth, and it grieved him to his heart. So the LORD said, "I will blot out man whom I have created from the face of the land, man and animals and creeping things and birds of the heavens, for I am sorry that I have made them." But Noah found favor in the eyes of the LORD. These are the generations of Noah. Noah was a righteous man, blameless in his generation. Noah walked with God.

It is easy to misread this passage and conclude that Noah was a good guy who earned God's favor through good works. Like everyone else through all history, he was saved by a faith response to God's freely given grace. Genesis 6:8 does not say that Noah began as a righteous man. Rather, he began as a sinner among sinners. His status with God was God's gracious gift, not a result of Noah's religious works. God's saving grace is a free gift. So, God worked, as He always does, by saving an ill-deserving sinner by grace alone, through faith alone, thereby enabling Noah to live a righteous life. Genesis 6:9 then explains the effects of God's grace to Noah: "Noah was a righteous man, blameless in his generation. Noah walked with God."

Indeed, Noah was a blameless and righteous man but only because he lived obediently by God's grace. By grace Noah, like Enoch, "walked with God,"[c] and, like Job, was, by grace, made "a blameless and upright man."[d] Noah was only this sort of man because God saved him by grace and empowered him to live a new life of obedience by that same grace. Noah's trusting obedience separated him from the others who refused God's gift of redemption and continued in their sins while he worked out God's grace in responsive righteousness.[8]

We see the same patterns at work in the blessings to obedient people of Israel

---

[a] Gen. 5:1-7:1 [b] 2 Pet. 3:3-7 [c] Gen. 5:22, 24 [d] Job 1:8; 2:3

and curses to those who disobey, a pattern Jesus repeats.[a] While God's saving grace is always apart from merit, His blessing grace comes to those who obey.[b]

After giving grace, God began speaking commands directly to Noah to obey. God informed Noah that he planned to end sin by killing all sinners through an enormous flood as judgment. Noah was then ordered to build an ark measuring some 1,400,000 cubic feet, shaped like a modern-day battleship and big enough to house some 522 modern-day railroad boxcars.

Noah obeyed God's commands and built the ark, likely with only the help of his sons. Hebrews 11:7 says that Noah did so in holy fear as a man of faith who believed that God would bring the flood even while others continued in sin without repentance. After Noah was spiritually saved by God's grace, built the ark according to God's instructions, and, in faith, loaded his family onboard with the animals as God commanded, God sent rain to also save them physically.[c] The rain continued for 40 days until it covered the land, drowning all the other sinners under God's righteous judgment. The only people spared in the flood were Noah and his family because, as Genesis 6:8 states, God gave them grace.

After the flood receded, the land appeared out of the water like the days of creation for Adam. The account of Noah echoes the account of Adam, with a sort of new creation and new humanity and new Fall. After the flood subsided and God dried the ground, Noah and his family exited the ark. Then Noah did a remarkable thing, "Noah built an altar to the LORD and took some of every clean animal and some of every clean bird and offered burnt offerings on the altar."[d] Noah, a righteous man, blameless among the people of his time, who walked faithfully with God, built the first altar in the Bible, making it out of the wood of the Ark which saved them from God's destruction. Noah, the righteous man, acting as a priest for all humans, took some of the precious, clean animals and offered them as a burnt offering to the God of judgment and grace. God was pleased with Noah's offering and responded to his intercession by promising never to curse the ground or destroy humanity, even though intentions of every human heart continue to be evil apart from God's saving grace. This is the first man who acts as a priest interceding for all humanity. He foreshadows the work of Jesus, the righteous Messiah, whose sacrifice would crush the Serpent, make atonement enabling salvation of all humans, and end the curse on the ground and as promised in Eden.[e]

God thus entered a covenant with Noah that extends to all people of the earth.[f] God promised that He would never again send a cataclysmic flood and that the seasons would continue by God's provision. In this covenant, we see that God's answer to human sin would be a covenant of grace, beginning with Noah. The sign of the covenant was the rainbow to remind God's people of His promise

---

[a] Deut. 28; Luke 11:28; John 13:17 [b] Ex. 12:12-36; Prov. 13:15; Isa. 66:2; Jas. 4:6; 1 Pet. 5:5 [c] Gen. 7:1–8:22 [d] Gen. 8:20 [e] Gen. 3:15 [f] Gen. 9:1–17

to never flood the earth again. Curiously, this symbol was created by God but has been counterfeited by Satan for ungodly social and political reasons. Through the covenant, God would restore His intentions to bless people.

The terms of the covenant for human beings include respect for the sanctity of human life and the freedom to eat animals as, at this point in history, meat was added to the human diet. These commands further build upon the teaching in Genesis 1, that while animal life is to be treated kindly, it is inferior to human life, which alone bears God's image. The effect of the covenant is the renewal of God's intentions in creation by distinguishing between those people, like Noah, in covenant with God from those who are not.

In Genesis 9:18-28, Noah responded to God's kindness by getting drunk and passing out naked in his tent like a redneck hillbilly on vacation. Noah's son Ham also walked into Noah's tent to gaze upon his father's nakedness. The text does not tell us much more than these bare details, but many people have inserted numerous speculations about what transpired. Whatever happened, one thing is sure: both Noah and his son sinned after they were saved from the flood.

With Noah, we have a sort of second Fall; God started over with Noah, who sinned like Adam. The point is simply that sin remains the human problem even after the flood. Furthermore, the Noahic covenant reveals that not only is ours a cursed earth but also a covenanted earth. The Noahic covenant is for both humanity and all of creation. God says, "Behold, I establish my covenant with you and your offspring after you, and with every living creature that is with you, the birds, the livestock, and every beast of the earth with you, as many as came out of the ark; it is for every beast of the earth."[a] Therefore, God's plan is to ultimately redeem all of creation along with His covenant people.

The flood is, in essence, a new start for creation and humanity despite the ongoing nature of sin. Noah and his family are blessed and called to fill the earth and exercise dominion over creation in a manner that echoes God's instructions to Adam and Eve. Additionally, the creation mandate is renewed with a special emphasis on respecting life and exercising creation care as responsible stewards of all that God has made.

We easily forget how much God's covenant with Noah enhances our lives. We grow so accustomed to the order of creation that we act as if it were something automatic, inherent in nature itself. But as scientists learn more about our world, we see more clearly that the universe is not self-sufficient. Nature is fragile, constantly teetering on the edge of disaster. Disruptions in the food chain, water pollution, atmospheric changes, and a host of other modern environmental concerns demonstrate dramatically that the earth needs the constant providential care of the Creator. The food we eat, air we breathe, ground we walk, cars we drive, books we read, buildings we erect, and everything else – all these good things in life are possible because God constantly upholds a safe place for humanity to multiply

---

[a] Gen. 9:9-10

and have dominion.

Summary of the Noahic Covenant
Covenant mediator	Noah
Covenant blessings	Spiritual salvation and promise to not flood the earth again
Covenant conditions	Not drinking animal blood and protecting the sanctity of human life
Covenant sign	The internal sign is faith, the external sign is the rainbow
Covenant community	Family

WHAT IS THE ABRAHAMIC COVENANT?

With the arrival of Abram in Genesis, the book shifts from the theme of God calling creation into existence in Genesis 1-11 and creation's catastrophic spiral down into deepest wickedness, to God calling people into covenant in chapters 12-50 to restart His program to redeem sinners.

God did not speak from the time of His covenant with Noah until He spoke to Abram to again initiate a covenant relationship.[a] When Abram was called by God to become the father of a new nation, the prototype of a life of faith, and one of the most important men in the Bible, he was simply yet another sinner living among the scattered nations. In this way, Abram starts where Noah started – a lost sinner like everybody else. We know very little about Abram before God called him other than his genealogy, his barren wife, and his temporary home in Haran after having been born in Ur of the Chaldeans.[b] Since Nehemiah 9:7 and Acts 7:2-3 seem to indicate that God called Abram in Ur of the Chaldeans, and the key city of the Chaldeans was Babylon, Abram may have even been called out of Babylon as a Babylonian who perhaps even sought to help build that great city that God judged, demonstrating the graciousness of God's grace.[c] It is amazing that Abram was seemingly just another sinner from a Godless family when, much like Noah, he too found gracious favor in the eyes of the Lord.[d]

God simply told Abram to leave his homeland and father to journey to a new land that God would show him. God then promised Abram that though his elderly wife was barren, he would be a father. He was promised a great nation blessed by God that would be a blessing to the nations of the earth through one of his offspring or seed. This refers back to the original "seed" promise of Jesus coming in Genesis 3:15. The noun is singular, meaning Jesus. It is also collective, referring to Israel, the carrier of promise.[e] Galatians 3:16 says, "Now the promises were made to Abraham and to his offspring. It does not say, 'And to offsprings,'

---

[a] Gen. 12:1-3 [b] Gen. 11:27-32 [c] E.g., Isa. 13:19, 48:14; Jer. 24:5, 25:12, 50:1; Ezek. 1:3, 12:13, 23:15 [d] Josh. 24:2 tells us that Abraham's father "served other gods." [e] Gen. 3:15; Matt. 1:1, 17

referring to many, but referring to one, 'And to your offspring,' who is Christ."

God promised that the nation of Israel would come through Abraham and, like Mary, be the "womb" through which Jesus Christ would be brought forth as the blessing to all nations, "The Scripture, foreseeing that God would justify the Gentiles by faith, preached the gospel beforehand to Abraham, saying, 'In you shall all the nations be blessed.'"[b] Abram was also told that his descendants would receive the Promised Land if he made a radical break with his past and left his home in faith.[c]

In faith, Abram believed and obeyed God, doing as God commanded at the age of 75. He took his wife, Sarai, their household, and his nephew Lot, who becomes a troublesome figure later in the story. God again appeared to Abram, who responded by worshiping God in faith by building an altar, something he does throughout the book after encountering God.[d]

By contrasting Abram with Babylon in the story that preceded his call, the Tower of Babel reveals the theme of God's grace. The Babylonians sought to be a great nation with a great name, glorifying and blessing themselves, protecting themselves from their enemies, and the centerpiece of world affairs.[e] But they pursued their aims apart from faith and apart from God. So, God called one of them, Abram, out into covenant with Himself and promised to give to Abram, by grace, all that the Babylonians had strived for. Therefore, God is showing that our hope cannot rest in the efforts of sinners to save, glorify, and bless themselves. Rather, our only hope is to be found in entering into gracious covenant relationship with God by faith.

Although God promised Abram a son through his wife and a nation in the Promised Land, Abram essentially gave both away.[f] Thankfully, God did intervene and, through inflicting diseases on Pharaoh and his household and causing Lot to choose land other than the Promised Land, God made good on His promises, in spite of His servant. The theological point is that while God's servants are imperfect, it is His sovereign covenant protection that saves them from themselves and makes His covenant promises become reality.

Genesis opens with God speaking and preparing creation for mankind by the power of His Word. Throughout Genesis, God has thus far spoken to Adam, Noah, and Abram. In Genesis 15:1, God again speaks to Abram in a vision. God poetically promised to be Abram's protector and provider. God promised that though Abram was childless and his wife, Sarai, was barren, they would have a son, and that through that son a nation would be born. Genesis 15:6 reports Abram's response to God's word with one of the most important verses in the Bible, "He believed the LORD, and he counted it to him as righteousness."

Abraham dared to believe God's unlikely promise of a son in his old age. This is the kind of total trust that God calls righteousness. That kind of trust in God's

---

[b] Gal. 3:8 [c] Gen. 12:7-8, 13:18 [d] Gen. 13:18, 22:9 [e] Gen. 11:1-9 [f] Gen. 12:10-13:18

Word, even when it makes no sense at all, receives the promise of God.

Genesis 15:6 becomes a central verse in the New Testament doctrine of faith, in general, and Paul's doctrine of justification by faith, in particular.[a] Additionally, Jesus' half-brother James quoted Genesis 15:6 to teach that true faith in God results in good works in life with God.[b]

God's covenant with Abram was confirmed with a sacrifice and the shedding of blood. This foreshadowed New Covenant salvation, which was confirmed with Jesus' sacrifice of His own life on the cross and the shedding of His blood.

God then promised Abram that though his descendants would inherit the Promised Land, it would not be in his lifetime but only after a future 400-year exile in Egypt, recorded in Exodus. God then chose His boundaries for the Promised Land, which also coincide with the Garden of Eden.[c]

Throughout God's dealings with Noah and Abraham, we witness a pattern of God speaking to them, calling them into covenant, establishing them as the head of a new humanity, promising to bless them, and inviting everyone to respond to Him in faith. We then see each falter in faith and sin against the Lord despite His patient kindness to them.

In Genesis 16 we see this pattern repeated in yet another mini-Fall of sorts. After the establishment of God's covenant in Genesis 15, Abram sought to take matters into his own hands by bearing a son with Sarai's Egyptian maidservant, Hagar. The faithless plot was conceived by Abram's wife, Sarai, who, like her first mother Eve, failed to trust the simple words of God and feared that God had not kept His promise to her.[d] Their actions were likely motivated at least in part because they had been waiting 10-plus years for God to give them the promised son, and Abram was now 86 years old, and his barren wife was 76 years old.

Following God's covenant with Abram in Genesis 15 and Abram's sexual sin with Hagar in Genesis 16, God institutes circumcision as the sign of the Abrahamic covenant in Genesis 17. Circumcision was performed either with a sharp knife or stone. Circumcision began in Genesis 17 with Abram, who was 99 years of age, as a sign of his covenant with God, like the rainbow was the sign of God's covenant with Noah. God spoke to Abram, and Abram responded to God's command in faith, falling down on his face to worship God. God then changed his name from Abram, meaning "exalted father," to Abraham, meaning "father of a multitude," as the time for God to fulfill His promise of a son for Abram was very near. God also expanded His covenant with Abraham to include Abraham's descendants.

God then told Abraham that his wife's name would also be changed from Sarai to Sarah, which means "princess". God also promised that, through Sarah the princess, kings would come with the ultimate fulfillment being the birth of Jesus Christ, who is the King of Kings promised to Sarah's great-grandson Judah.[e]

---

[a] Rom. 4:3; Gal. 3:6 [b] James 2:23-24 [c] Gen. 2:10-14 [d] Gen. 16:2 [e] Gen. 49:10

DOCTRINE

When God restated His Genesis 15 promise that He would give Abraham a son by Sarah, Abraham laughed at God in distrust that he and Sarah could conceive as God had promised.[a] Rather than giving up on Abraham, God graciously repeated His promise once again, even instructing Abraham to name him Isaac, which means "laughter," since God would get the last laugh.

Abraham immediately obeyed God "that very day".[b] Abraham was circumcised at the age of 99 along with every male in his household. He did this because God promised that any male who was not circumcised would be cut off altogether by God. Ever since, Jews have circumcised their sons on the eighth day, as that was the day chosen for their father Isaac.[c]

Scripture expands the concept of circumcision, the cutting away of the foreskin from the body, to the cutting away of sin from the heart.[d] Abraham's descendants expand from sons by physical birth to include those who are descendants by spiritual birth. Those with hearts circumcised by the Holy Spirit are truly Abraham's descendants, as they, like him, live in covenant relationship with God by faith in Jesus Christ.[e]

Genesis 21 ends with the serene portrait that Abraham's life has finally all come together under God's perfect covenantal blessing. Despite nearly losing his wife twice, Abraham still has Sarah. And despite waiting for 25 years, Abraham finally has his son Isaac. God is faithful.

Some time later, when Isaac was likely a young man, God tested Abraham. Perhaps the point of this test was not for God to see if Abraham had faith, but rather for Abraham to demonstrate the depth of his faith in front of his son Isaac so that he too would learn to walk in faith as his father had.

Echoing God's initial call to Abraham in Genesis 12, God commanded Abraham to "go" and sacrifice his son Isaac as a burnt offering.[f] This would have required that Abraham slaughter his son, dismember him, and burn his body. Obediently, Abraham awoke early the next morning without any noticeable hesitation and set out with his son to do as the Lord commanded. The Bible has no words adequate to describe Abraham's agony.

But just before Abraham killed his son, with the knife in the air above him, the angel of the Lord, who would later be incarnated as Jesus, called to Abraham from Heaven and commanded him not to harm his son. God then provided a substitute ram to be sacrificed. Moses recognized that this provision pointed ahead to a greater provision, noting "it is said to this day, 'On the mount of the Lord it shall be provided'". This dramatic event prefigured God's future messianic provision at the same mountain, Mount Moriah, also known as Mount Zion.[g]

The comparisons between this account and the death of Jesus are many:
• Isaac and Jesus were both sons of a promise that was given many years

---

[a] Gen. 17:17-18 [b] Gen. 17:22-27 [c] Gen. 17:12; Phil/ 3:4-5 [d] Deut. 10:16, 30:6; Jer. 4:4; Ezek. 44:7-9; Rom. 2:25-29; Col. 2:11 [e] Romans 4; Gal. 3:6-8 [f] Gen. 22:1-2 [g] Gen. 22:2, 14; 2 Chron. 3:1

COVENANT: GOD PURSUES

before their birth
- Isaac and Jesus were both born to women who could not have conceived apart from a miracle
- Isaac and Jesus were both firstborn sons
- Isaac and Jesus were both greatly loved by their father/Father
- Isaac and Jesus went to the top of Mount Moriah/Mount Zion
- Isaac carried the wood to his own sacrifice, just as Jesus carried His wooden cross to His crucifixion
- Isaac and Jesus each willingly laid down their lives to their father/Father
- Isaac's father and Jesus' Father both felt the agony watching the death of an innocent son
- Isaac was brought back from the dead figuratively and Jesus was brought back from the dead literally
- Isaac points us to Jesus, the Son, and Abraham to the Father in this prophetic portrait of their mutual agony as they partner together to provide substitutionary atonement for all people in this same area 2,000 years later

After having walked with God for many years and seeing God provide in very difficult situations, Abraham had apparently learned to trust God no matter what. This fact reveals that those in covenant with God can mature and grow in faith. Abraham's faith in God was so resolute that he believed that even if he killed his son that God, who gave him the son through a miracle, could give him back through yet another miracle.[a] After all, Abraham had also lost his wife on two occasions only to see God bring her back to him, and Abraham believed that God would do the same with Isaac because God is always good for his covenant promises.

Lastly, the promise of Jesus Christ is that He would come as the seed of Abraham and blessing to all nations of the earth. Revelation 7:9-10 reveals the fulfillment of this aspect of the Abrahamic covenant at the end of time around the throne of Jesus:

After this I looked, and behold, a great multitude that no one could number, from every nation, from all tribes and peoples and languages, standing before the throne and before the Lamb, clothed in white robes, with palm branches in their hands, and crying out with a loud voice, "Salvation belongs to our God who sits on the throne, and to the Lamb!"

<u>Summary of the Abrahamic Covenant</u>
Covenant mediator	Abraham
Covenant blessings	A son through whom would come Jesus Christ the Son of God
Covenant conditions	Obedience to God doing righteousness and justice
Covenant sign	The internal sign is faith, the external sign is circumcision

---

[a] Heb. 11:17-19

DOCTRINE

Covenant community   A family and nation that proceeded from that family

WHAT IS THE MOSAIC COVENANT?

Exodus powerfully demonstrates the faithfulness of God to His covenant promises to Abraham. Out of a barren elderly couple, a nation of perhaps a million was born over the course of 400 years. It is amazing that the entire Exodus event was revealed in advance to Abram directly from God Himself.[a] As promised, the people of God were enslaved for 430 years, then delivered by the judgments of God upon the Egyptians.

In the closing scenes of Genesis, Abraham's descendant Joseph is sold into slavery by his jealous older brothers. Despite slavery and imprisonment on false rape charges, God elevated Joseph to a position of power and prominence as the top advisor to Pharaoh, the great ruler of Egypt. Because of Joseph's exemplary service and wisdom from God, the entire nation of Egypt was spared the starvation of a famine, and the Hebrews were given privilege and dignity as resident workers in Egypt.

Exodus opens by noting that, in the years following Joseph's death, a new pharaoh rose to prominence and no longer remembered Joseph's service or the privilege given to His people. He enslaved God's people and treated them cruelly, attempting genocide out of fear of their numbers.[b] The Egyptian empire was the most powerful on earth for 1,300 years, twice as long as the famed Greek and Roman empires. But the Pharaoh was worshiped as a god and had no regard for the God of Israel.

In Exodus 3, God appears in Egypt by speaking directly to Moses, promising to deliver His covenant people from slavery. He reveals His tenderness in His powerful protection as He responds to the groaning of His people.[c] In Exodus 3:14, God reveals Himself by name, saying, "'I AM WHO I AM.' And he said, 'Say this to the people of Israel, "I AM has sent me to you."'" In Hebrew understanding, a name embodies the entire essence and identity of a person. So, in having a name, God revealed Himself as a person and gave sacred access to an understanding and experience of Him. The divine name Yahweh reveals His eternal self-existence. He is a relational being, unchangingly faithful and dependable, who desires the full trust of His people. As He states His name, He reminds Moses and the people of His promise of help for them in covenant faithfulness.

The Hebrews were so afraid of blaspheming God that they would not utter this sacred name, so the proper pronunciation was lost. They retained only the four sacred consonants, YHWH. When vowels were added to the original consonantal text, the vowels from the Hebrew Adonai were added to the consonants resulting

---

[a] Gen. 15:13-15 [b] Ex. 1:1-15:21 [c] Ex. 2:23-25; 3:7-10

in the name Jehovah which we are sure is not the way it is pronounced. While we really don't know exactly how the name should be pronounced, many scholars believe the most likely rendering is Yahweh. Jesus later takes this name "I am," designating Himself as that one who spoke to Moses in the burning bush, and He was nearly murdered for doing so.[a]

God acted decisively in judgment on Egypt, delivering His people through 10 plagues that culminated in the killing of the firstborn of Egypt. God passed over the houses of His people because they faithfully obeyed His instructions to paint the doorposts with blood of a slain lamb. Once delivered, they walked across the Red Sea on dry ground and turned to watch the pursuing Egyptians drown as the water returned to its place. In this we clearly see that life and death hinge on whether or not we trust and obey God.

In Exodus 19, God leads His people to the foot of Mount Sinai, just as He had promised to Moses in the burning bush.[b] But God's people were forbidden from ascending or even touching the mountain and entering into God's presence because of their sin. Any violation of this command would bring immediate death, as God needed His people to know that they cannot ascend to Him, but instead He initiates relationship and descends to them, as ultimately happened with the incarnation of Jesus Christ. They were then told to purify themselves for three days and prepare to receive the message God would give them through His mediators, the prophet Moses and the priest Aaron.

God began by reminding them of His faithfulness and His powerful redemption: "You yourselves have seen what I did to the Egyptians, and how I bore you on eagles' wings and brought you to myself."[c] Based on His grace and provision, God asked them for their faithful response: "Now therefore, if you will indeed obey my voice and keep my covenant..." His purpose is that they would "be my treasured possession among all peoples, for all the earth is mine, and you shall be to me a kingdom of priests and a holy nation."

God then gave His people the 10 Commandments to guide holy living. But instead of responding in faith, their fear drove them away from God,[d] beginning a pattern of moving away rather than drawing near and of disobedience, defilement, and spiritual adultery, culminating in judgment. Christopher J. H. Wright says:

As the people of YHWH they would have the historical task of bringing the knowledge of God to the nations, and bringing the nations to the means of atonement with God. The task of blessing the nations also put them in the role of priests in the midst of the nations. This dual movement is reflected in the prophetic visions of the law/light/justice and so on of YHWH going out to the nations from Israel/Zion, and the nations coming to YHWH/Israel/ Zion...The priesthood of the people of God is thus a missional function.[9]

---

[a] Ex. 3:14; cf. John 8:58 [b] Ex. 3:12 [c] Ex. 19:4-6 [d] Ex. 20:18-19

The conditions of enjoying the covenant centered on obeying all of God's laws, synthesized in the 10 Commandments, which are anchored in God alone being worshiped. On this point Wright says:

The priority of grace is a fundamental theological premise in approaching Old Testament law and ethics. Obedience to the law was based on, and was a response to, God's salvation. Exodus has eighteen chapters of redemption before a single chapter of law. The same is true in relation to Israel's mission among the nations. In whatever way Israel would be or become a blessing to the nations would be on the grounds of what God had done for them, not on the basis of their own superiority in any sense.[10]

The Law of Moses

The books of Moses, also called the books of the Law (Genesis through Deuteronomy), contain more than 600 commands with the 10 Commandments as the ethical center. The question of whether new-covenant Christians are under the Law of Moses is incredibly complicated, with everyday implications:[11] May believers eat bacon? May we charge interest on loaned money? Must we practice Sabbath? Some things are commonly agreed upon.

First, The New Testament declares the Mosaic Law "is holy and righteous and good."[a] Second, the Mosaic Law helps to show us our sin as we fall short.[b] Third, Jesus perfectly fulfilled all of the law for us.[c] Fourth, justification (being declared righteous before God) is wholly apart from us keeping the Mosaic Law.[d] Fifth, those who demand believers keep the whole law to be sanctified are wrong.[e] Sixth, the 10 Commandments express fundamentally important principles for the Christian life originally given in principle to Abraham. Seventh, not every old-covenant law is binding on Christians so that, for example, we should not sacrifice animals at church like once occurred in the Temple.

The difficulty is that we should not dismiss all the old-covenant laws (e.g., stealing and murdering), and we should not retain all the old-covenant laws (e.g., stoning adulterers). One proposed solution is to divide the law into three categories.

1. Ceremonial laws, referring to the priesthood, sacrifices, temple, cleanness, and so on, are now fulfilled in Jesus and therefore no longer binding. Nearly all of Hebrews is about this issue for Jews who struggled with the Old Testament laws once they were saved. These laws are no longer binding on us because Jesus is our priest, temple, sacrifice, cleanser, and so on.
2. Civil laws pertain to the governing of Israel as a nation ruled by God. Since we are no longer a theocracy, these laws, while insightful, are not directly

---

[a] Rom. 7:12; 1 Tim. 1:8 [b] Gal. 3:19-25 [c] Matt. 5:17-18 [d] Rom. 3:21, 27-28; 4:1-5; Gal. 2:16; 3:11; 5:4; Phil. 3:9 [e] Gal. 5

binding on us. Today, we are to obey our pagan government because God will work through it too.[a]

3. Moral laws refer to commands forbidding such things as rape, theft, and murder. These laws are still binding on us even though Jesus fulfilled their requirements through His sinless life. Nine of the 10 Commandments are repeated by Jesus, with the only possible exception being the Sabbath, as now Jesus is our rest.

Thus, according to this explanation, ceremonial and civil laws are no longer binding on us, but moral laws are.

Others see the solution in this statement: the whole Mosaic Law is valid until its purpose is accomplished in Christ.[b] Now that Jesus' work is complete, the Law of Moses is abolished, and we remain under the principles of the Abrahamic covenant. This seems to be supported by Paul's teaching that the law was added to God's promise to Abraham 430 years afterward because of sin.[c] It imprisoned the people of God until Jesus came. Paul summarizes, "So then, the law was our guardian until Christ came, in order that we might be justified by faith. But now that faith has come, we are no longer under a guardian."[d] Thus, we are to keep the Abrahamic commands to be loyal to God [e],trust His Word even when it makes no sense[f], keep the way of the LORD by doing righteousness and justice[g], and look for provision in Messiah.[h] Jesus summarized this permanent righteousness in the law of Christ: love God and neighbor as guided by the Spirit.[i]

The relationship between Moses and Jesus Christ is evidenced in a number of places and ways throughout the Scriptures. God said to Moses, "I will raise up for them a prophet like you from among their brothers. And I will put my words in his mouth, and he shall speak to them all that I command him."[k] Over a millennium later, in Acts 3:17-22, Peter quotes Deuteronomy 18:18 and applies its fulfillment to Jesus Christ; thus, Jesus' eventual coming was promised to Moses. Hebrews 3:1-6 adds that Jesus and Moses were faithful to the Father's leading, but that Jesus is worthy of greater honor because He is much greater than even Moses.

The Gospel of Jesus Christ is clearly and repeatedly foreshadowed throughout Exodus. It begins with God making a promise to elect a people as His own in the Abrahamic covenant. His people are then taken into slavery and ruled by a Godless and cruel lord (foreshadowing Satan and sin). Unable to save themselves, God Himself intervenes to redeem them from slavery and deliver them into freedom to worship Him alone by His miraculous hand (foreshadowing Jesus' death and resurrection to liberate us from our slavery to demonic pharaohs such as pride, drugs, alcohol, sex, and food). After taking His people out of Egypt, God's work with His people continues as He seeks to get Egypt out of His people (foreshadowing sanctification). Resisting God's continual attempt to lead His

---

[a] Romans 13:1-6 [b] See Rom. 10:4; Col. 2:17 [c] Gal. 3:16-4:7 [d] Gal. 3:24-25 [e] Gen. 12 [f] Gen. 15 [g] Gen. 18:18-19 [h] Gen. 22 [i] Matt. 22:36-40; Luke 10:27; Mark 12:30-31; Rom. 8, 13:8-10; 1 Cor. 9:20-21; Gal. 5:14; James 2:8 [k] Deut. 18:18

people as He desires, the people grumble against Moses and long to go back to Egypt (foreshadowing the believer's wrestling with their flesh).

Nonetheless, God's faithfulness persists, and He continues to lead His people by traveling with them in the pillar and cloud and loving providing for their needs, leading them on a journey to a land of rest and promise (foreshadowing Heaven).[a] God's interaction with His people is clearly that of a living God who defeats the demonic, speaks, acts, loves, declares His laws, judges sin, delivers from evil, redeems, provides, and is present with them like a Father over a family. The central picture of the Gospel in Exodus is one of covenantal redemption.

All of these great themes are included in the inauguration of Passover in Exodus. In the days leading up to His death, Jesus was a young man of perhaps 33. Jesus began speaking openly of His impending death, including at the Passover meal he ate with His friends as their Last Supper. There, Jesus broke with 15 centuries of protocol, showing that the Passover meal, which God's people had been eating annually, found its ultimate fulfillment in Him. The Passover memorialized the night in Egypt when, in faith, God's people covered the doorposts of their home with blood so that death would not come to the firstborn son but would rather pass over them.[b] Jesus, the firstborn Son of God, likewise had come to die and cover us with His blood so that God's just wrath would literally pass over us sinners as the essence of the new covenant[c] since Jesus is our Passover Lamb.[d]

Summary of the Mosaic Covenant
Covenant mediator	Moses
Covenant blessings	Redemption from bondage and the freedom to worship God
Covenant conditions	Obeying God's laws, including the 10 Commandments
Covenant sign	The internal sign is faith, the external sign is Passover
Covenant community	A holy nation and kingdom of priests to minister to the nations

WHAT IS THE DAVIDIC COVENANT?

Because God was faithful to His covenant with Noah, sinners continued to live and increase on the earth. Because God was faithful to His covenant with Abraham, His descendants became a nation. And because God was faithful to His covenant with Moses, the nation settled in their Promised Land, which set the stage of history for the establishing of a kingship to rule over the kingdom of Israel. In 2 Samuel 7:8-16, God chooses David to be the next covenant head:

Thus says the LORD of hosts...I will appoint a place for my people Israel and

---

[a] Ex. 40:34-38 [b] Ex. 6-12 [c] Luke 22:19-21 [d] 1 Cor. 5:7

will plant them, so that they may dwell in their own place and be disturbed no more...Moreover, the LORD declares to you that the LORD will make you a house. When your days are fulfilled and you lie down with your fathers, I will raise up your offspring after you, who shall come from your body, and I will establish his kingdom. He shall build a house for my name, and I will establish the throne of his kingdom forever...And your house and your kingdom shall be made sure forever before me. Your throne shall be established forever.

David was rightly overwhelmed by the gracious covenant promise that not only would a former shepherd boy be a king, but that from him would come a King whose Kingdom would endure forever, ruled by none other than the Son of God. David's humble response to God's covenantal grace is reported in 2 Samuel 7:18-19:

Then King David went in and sat before the LORD and said, "Who am I, O Lord GOD, and what is my house, that you have brought me thus far? And yet this was a small thing in your eyes, O Lord GOD. You have spoken also of your servant's house for a great while to come, and this is instruction for mankind, O Lord GOD!"

The Davidic covenant promise of an eternal kingdom was so treasured by God's people that they worshiped God in faith that He would be faithful to the covenant promises as He had been to Noah, Abraham, and Moses. One example is Psalm 89:3-4, "You have said, 'I have made a covenant with my chosen one; I have sworn to David my servant: "I will establish your offspring forever, and build your throne for all generations."'"

God poured a special measure of His grace on Israel in the days of David to lift His people to greater heights of dignity. He transformed the nation from a loose confederation of tribes into a strong empire. David, and many of his sons, accomplished much as they ruled over Israel.

Nevertheless, the Old Testament records a sad end for the house of David. The sin of David's sons caused God to remove the throne from Jerusalem. The nation and its king were taken into exile in Babylon. The prophets foretold that a descendant of David would restore the nation.

As we see the disarray of Israel's kingdom today, we have to wonder what happened to God's promises. Did God not assure David of an unending dynasty? Whatever came of the Kingdom blessings promised to Israel?

The New Testament answers these questions by identifying Jesus as the heir of David's throne. Matthew and Luke contain extensive genealogies to demonstrate that Jesus was the promised descendant of David.[a] Jesus was born in Bethlehem, the city of David, as God's providence brought pregnant Mary there to register for a governmental census.[b] As David's final heir, Jesus brings incomparable kingdom blessings to God's covenant people. He fulfills all the hopes of honor associated

---

[a] Matt. 1:2-16; Luke 3:23-37 [b] Luke 2:4-6

DOCTRINE

with the royal line in ways that go exceedingly beyond what David and his other sons accomplished.

The blessings of Christ's Kingdom encompass a vast array of benefits for God's covenant people. To gain a glimpse into what Christ does for us, we will focus on three blessings that came through the line of David during the Old Testament period. Then we will see how Christ brings these gifts to God's people in the New Testament age.

1. David's house was to provide **protection** against evil. David and his sons had the responsibility of safeguarding the nation. Even when the offensive conquest of the land subsided, the royal house had the responsibility of providing ongoing security. For this reason, the kings of Israel erected walls and maintained armies. Every responsible member of David's house devised ways to protect the people.

2. The royal line of Judah was to ensure **prosperity** for God's people. Within the walls of royal protection, Israel prospered. Righteousness prevailed when the king enforced the law. People could live and work without fear of criminals. Economic conditions improved as David's sons did their jobs properly. When kings ruled over the land in righteousness, the people prospered.

3. David's house was divinely ordained to ensure the special **presence** of God among the people. David spent his life preparing for the temple, a permanent edifice for the presence of God. Solomon constructed the temple and centered his kingdom on it. The kings of Judah always bore the responsibility of maintaining the proper functioning of the temple. Without the presence of God, all the efforts of royalty were in vain. There could be no protection or prosperity without the presence of God. The prayers, sacrifices, and songs associated with Israel's temple were the sources out of which all kingdom benefits flowed.

The kingdom blessings of divine protection, prosperity, and presence did not cease with the Old Testament. These ancient realities anticipated greater benefits to come in Christ. But we must remember that Jesus bestows these Kingdom blessings in two stages. He brought divine protection, prosperity, and presence at His first coming, which we now enjoy, and He will bring them at His second coming, which we are awaiting by faith for our full inheritance.

Samuel anointed David as king of Israel,[a] but it was many years before he began reigning on the throne.[b] In the meantime, David gathered followers who were loyal to him, influencing life in the kingdom ruled by the evil Saul until the day David began his reign on the throne. In a similar way after His resurrection and ascension, Jesus rose to the right hand of the Father as anointed King. From that place, He will one day return to earth as reigning king on the historic throne of David. In the meantime, He is gathering faithful followers who will continue the

---

[a] 1 Sam. 16 [b] 2 Sam. 5

COVENANT: GOD PURSUES

mission to bring people into the glory of the kingdom. From His exalted position, Jesus bestows Kingdom benefits on the people of God.

At this initial stage, Christ's blessings are primarily spiritual in nature. Jesus guaranteed His followers' protection: "No one will snatch them out of my hand."[a] As 1 John 4:4b says, "He who is in you is greater than he who is in the world." Neither human nor supernatural forces can rob us of our salvation in Christ. As our king, Jesus protects each one of His covenant people.

Christ also blesses His people with spiritual prosperity. Paul said we have been "blessed...in Christ with every spiritual blessing."[b] Jesus said He came "that they may have life and have it abundantly".[c] Christ guarantees spiritual prosperity to the people of His kingdom.

Finally, Christ provides the presence of God among His people. When Jesus ascended to heaven after His resurrection, He removed His physical presence, but sent the Spirit to comfort His followers with God's nearness: "I will not leave you as orphans; I will come to you."[d] For this reason, He could promise, "I am with you always, to the end of the age."[e]

The Kingdom blessings that we enjoy today are grand, but we must remember that they are primarily spiritual. Christ does not promise us protection from all physical evil in this stage of His Kingdom, "If they persecuted me, they will also persecute you."[f] Moreover, Christ's Kingship does not guarantee physical prosperity and health today. The trials of poverty and physical illnesses remain with many of us, as the book of 1 Peter continually communicates. Finally, Christ does not give us His physical presence at this time either. He is present in the Spirit, but we long to see Him and touch Him again. The church now cries out, "Come, Lord Jesus!"[g]

We have the firstfruits of the kingdom, which make us long for the fullness of the Kingdom.[h] While Christ guarantees us spiritual blessings today, His protection, prosperity, and presence will extend even to physical provisions when He returns. Within the new creation we will be protected against all forms of evil, physical and spiritual. The enemies of God will be utterly destroyed, and we will have nothing to fear:

"Then comes the end, when He delivers the kingdom to God the Father after destroying every rule and every authority and power. For He must reign until He has put all his enemies under his feet. The last enemy to be destroyed is death."[i]

In the fullness of Christ's Kingdom, we will receive glorified physical bodies. All illness and grief will be gone: "Death shall be no more, neither shall there be mourning, nor crying, nor pain anymore."[k] Finally, when Christ returns His physical presence will be among us. We will know Christ's presence both spiritually and physically. As John said, in the New Jerusalem he "saw no temple in the city, for

---

[a] John 10:28b [b] Eph. 1:3 [c] John 10:10 [d] John 14:18 [e] Matt. 28:20 [f] John 15:20b [g] Rev. 22:20 [h] Rom. 8:23; 1 Cor. 15:20-24 [i] 1 Cor. 15:24-26 [k] Rev. 21:4

its temple is the Lord God the Almighty and the Lamb."[a]

Thus, Christ inaugurates the fulfillment all the hopes of the Davidic covenant. He brings the blessings of God's kingdom to all who serve Him faithfully. David and his sons brought outpourings of tremendous benefits for God's people, but those Old Testament blessings fall short of the dignity for which we were designed and the fullness of God's covenantal grace. Christ alone brings full covenantal kingdom blessings in His second coming.

Indeed, the Davidic covenant is fulfilled today as the nations come to know Jesus Christ as King of Kings through evangelism and church planting. This explains why the great prayer of Psalm 72 that speaks of Jesus' kingdom includes this echo of the Abrahamic covenant in verse 17: "May his name endure forever, his fame continue as long as the sun! May people be blessed in him, all nations call him blessed!" It is amazing that God's covenant grace is nothing short of a global gift.

Summary of the Davidic Covenant
Covenant mediator   David
Covenant blessings   A kingdom that would bring forth King Jesus
Covenant conditions   The worship of God in the temple
Covenant sign   The internal sign is faith, the external sign is the throne
Covenant community   Kingdom

WHAT IS THE NEW COVENANT?

Our study of covenants now brings us to the ultimate covenant in all of Scripture, that covenant which is the fulfillment and extension of all prior covenants between God and His people, expanding the benefits to people from the nations of the earth. Jeremiah 31:31-34 promised the new covenant:

Behold, the days are coming, declares the LORD, when I will make a new covenant with the house of Israel and the house of Judah, not like the covenant that I made with their fathers on the day when I took them by the hand to bring them out of the land of Egypt, my covenant that they broke, though I was their husband, declares the LORD. But this is the covenant that I will make with the house of Israel after those days, declares the LORD: I will put my law within them, and I will write it on their hearts. And I will be their God, and they shall be my people. And no longer shall each one teach his neighbor and each his brother, saying, "Know the LORD," for they shall all know me, from the least of them to the greatest, declares the LORD. For I will forgive their iniquity, and I will remember their sin no more.

Many years after Jeremiah prophesied, as Passover approached, Jesus Christ sat down with His disciples to celebrate the Mosaic covenant by partaking of the

---
[a] Rev. 21:22

Passover meal. For over a millennium, God's covenant people had partaken of the Passover by following a strict order with sacred statements of promise interspersed throughout the meal. Keenly aware of the magnitude of the moment, Jesus did not speak the words tradition had dictated. Instead, Matthew 26:26-29 reports:

Now as they were eating, Jesus took bread, and after blessing it broke it and gave it to the disciples, and said, "Take, eat; this is my body." And he took a cup, and when he had given thanks he gave it to them, saying, "Drink of it, all of you, for this is my blood of the covenant, which is poured out for many for the forgiveness of sins. I tell you I will not drink again of this fruit of the vine until that day when I drink it new with you in my Father's kingdom.

Unlike previous covenants, the new covenant is God not merely giving us a human mediator but the second member of the Trinity Himself coming into human history as the man Jesus Christ. Rather than taking life as He did when He flooded the earth in the days of Noah or requiring sacrifices for sin in the Mosaic covenant, He offered Himself as the sacrificial substitute for sinners on the cross where He shed His blood in their place.

Commenting on one of the innumerable blessings enjoyed in the new covenant, 2 Corinthians 3:5-6 says:

Not that we are sufficient in ourselves to claim anything as coming from us, but our sufficiency is from God, who has made us competent to be ministers of a new covenant, not of the letter but of the Spirit. For the letter kills, but the Spirit gives life.

In the new covenant, God comes to be with each of His people as He did with Noah, Abraham, Moses, and David. He also places the Holy Spirit in them to make them into a temple where worship occurs. The Spirit makes them new creations as the dawning and firstfruits of the finality of the new creation that culminate with Jesus' second coming. The Spirit's work includes transfiguring us into Jesus' image bearers, as Moses was.

Perhaps the lengthiest treatment of the new covenant and its superiority to all preceding covenants is found in the book of Hebrews. In light of our study of covenants, the most helpful thing would be to simply read Hebrews 8:6-9:28.

In summary, Jesus is a better Noah who brings judgment of sin, salvation by grace to the family of God, and a new world free of sin and its effects. Jesus is a better Abraham, the blessing to the nations of the earth. Jesus is a better Moses as God's prophet who fulfilled the law for us, allows God's wrath to pass over us because of His shed blood, conquered our pharaoh of Satan, redeemed us from sin, and journeys with us toward home despite our sin and grumbling. And Jesus is a better David who is seated on a throne ruling as the King of Kings and is coming again to establish His eternal and global Kingdom of peace and prosperity.

When God speaks of His covenant relationship with His people throughout the Bible, the language is often that of marriage. God is like a groom. God's people are like a bride that He loves and is devoted to. In response, God desires that His people respond to His loving devotion with fidelity.

Some people wonder why God's people are forbidden to also worship other gods and participate in other religious and spiritual practices. The reason is simply because God sees such behavior as spiritual adultery. In the same way that a devoted husband does not want to have an open relationship with his wife where she can include others in intimate relations, so too God desires a faithfully devoted loving covenant relationship. For this reason, Christians need to be careful that they do not see God's requirements of fidelity as intolerant or narrow as the culture would decry. Instead, we need to look at our covenant with God in the most loving and serious of terms and be grateful that God wants our loving union to flourish by being fully devoted to one another.

THE DIFFERENCE BETWEEN COVENANT AND CONTRACT RELATIONSHIPS

In the early years of our marriage, we were in a covenant, but I was acting like we were in a contract which caused my wife to feel pressured to perform up to my unspoken expectations. A covenant and a contract are like a right and left hand – you need to know when to use one or the other. Covenants are for personal relationships, like marriage. Contracts are for professional relationships, like business. Here's a summary of the difference between contract relationships and covenant relationships.

Contract	vs	Covenant
Between 2 people		Between 3 people
I seek my will		We seek God's will
You serve me		We serve each other
Performance is recorded		No record of wrongs is kept
Failure is punished		Failure was punished at the cross
Win-lose		Win-win
A professional relationship		A personal relationship

This distinction between covenants and contract explains three kinds of people:
1. People who only understand contracts win at work with their professional relationships and lose at home with their personal relationships. One example is someone we knew who was very successful in the business world, but wearied their family with constant demands, expectations, and criticisms that made family dinner feel like a nightly performance review with a boss who was impossible to please.
2. People who only understand covenants win at home with their personal relationships but lose at work with their professional relationships. One example was a kind, gracious, trusting Christian man who started renovating a home for someone else without a contract and merely a handshake agreement since they both said they were Christians. Once he finished the

remodel, rather than paying, the homeowner bankrupted the trusting man because they did not have a contract to protect him.
3. People who understand both covenants and contracts win at home with their personal relationships and win at work with their professional relationships.

The governance of a covenant is singular headship and plural leadership. To be the head does not mean that the person is a bossy bully or domineering danger. To be the head means to bear additional responsibility which means that even if something is not the head's fault, out of love they make it their responsibility and get involved. This is exactly what our new covenant Head, Jesus Christ, did by coming to earth to take responsibility for human sin that was not His fault.

For the Christian, your relationship with God is covenantal and the Father is your singular head, exercising plural leadership with the Son and Spirit. For the Christian church, our relationship with God is also covenantal as Jesus is our covenant "head"[a] who leads with human and divine leaders (e.g. angels and other divine beings like the sons of God) in the church.[b] For the Christian family, their relationships are supposed to be covenantal as well with the father as the head[c] and father and mother to be honored and obeyed as plural leaders.[d]

Great problems arise when we fail to appropriately operate in contractual and covenantal relationships. Often, this includes forgetting that marriage and family are supposed to be covenant relationships. God reminds us of this in Malachi 2:10,13-14: "Have we not all one Father? Has not one God created us? Why then are we faithless to one another, profaning the covenant of our fathers?... And this second thing you do. You cover the Lord's altar with tears, with weeping and groaning because he no longer regards the offering or accepts it with favor from your hand. But you say, 'Why does he not?' Because the Lord was witness between you and the wife of your youth, to whom you have been faithless, though she is your companion and your wife by covenant."

From the beginning, families have suffered when heads like Adam do not engage in relationship with their family, love enough to speak into troubles, and take the initiative to do what is glorifying to God and good for their family. Many, if not most, of the social problems we face are because of the failure of people, starting with men, to understand the difference between contractual and covenantal relationships.

Perhaps a closing illustration will help. Before we had our five children, and our family had just a few young kids, I took our oldest daughter swimming in a pool one summer day. We were having fun throwing her into the air to splash down loudly over and over. We were alone in the pool, until three teenagers

---

[a] Eph. 1:22, 4:15, 5:23; Col. 1:18, 2:10, 2:19 [b] As one example, in Rev. 2-3 Jesus speaks to both the human leaders in the church as well as the divine leader or "angel" in each of the seven churches [c] 1 Cor. 11:3, 11:7; Eph. 5:23 [d] Gen. 28:7 Exodus 20:12; Deut. 5:16; Prov. 30:17; Matt. 15:4-6, 19:19, Mark 7:10, 10:19, Luke 18:20, Eph. 6:2

arrived – one girl wearing a small bikini with a boy on each arm. They jumped in the pool and each boy swam to opposite corners. The girl started in the middle of the pool flirting with each boy until she swam up to one boy and began aggressively making out with him. Some time later, she swam to the other boy and did the exact same thing. Startled, our daughter swam up to process what had happened with me. Whispering, she asked, "Daddy, did you see what that girl was doing with those boys?" I said, "Yes sweetheart, I'm sorry you had to see that. What are you thinking?" She said, "I just think it's really sad…that she doesn't have a better dad." That is loving covenantal thinking.

QUESTIONS FOR PERSONAL JOURNALING AND/OR SMALL GROUP DISCUSSION

1. What are the first five things that come to mind when you consider how God has blessed you?
2. In addition to God, who would you consider to be in covenant relationship with you?
3. Which of the five covenants do you know the most about? Which of the five covenants do you know the least about?
4. What would your life look like today if God did not intervene and enter into a covenant relationship with you?
5. What kind of sin were you, and your family before you, trapped in before God entered into covenant relationship with you?
6. What person or thing (e.g. an addiction) has been a cruel Pharaoh ruling over and harming you?
7. Why is it vital that we see Jesus as the center of all the Bible, and the center of all the covenants in the Bible?
8. Has God been faithful to you? Are you being faithful to God?

CHAPTER 7: INCARNATION

"GOD COMES"

And the Word became flesh and dwelt among us, and we have seen his glory, glory as of the only Son from the Father, full of grace and truth.
JOHN 1:14

Superheroes capture our imagination with their superhuman abilities. Wolverine can rapidly heal from injury. Invisible Woman can become invisible at will. Nitro can reform his own body after it explodes. Superman can fly. The Hulk has superhuman power. Aquaman can breathe underwater. Spiderman can climb walls. Wonder Woman can understand any language. Infinity is all-knowing. The Silver Surfer can manipulate gravity. Doomsday can resurrect from death. Kitty Pryde can pass through solid matter. And the Flash has superhuman speed.

Many children, and more than a few adults, have wondered what it would be like for a human being to have superhuman abilities. Yet Christian theology has something even more amazing because, unlike the superheroes, our Superhero truly lived, and his powers exceed those of comic book lore.

In Jesus, God enters the human realm. He turns water into wine and turns a boy's lunch into thousands of meals, walks on water, calms storms, heals the sick, raises the dead, commands the demonic, and conquers the grave.

J. I. Packer has described the incarnation as the "supreme mystery" associated with the gospel.[1] The incarnation is more of a miracle than the resurrection because in it somehow a holy God and sinful humanity are joined, yet without the presence of sin: "Nothing in fiction is so fantastic as is this truth of the incarnation."[2]

WHAT DOES INCARNATION MEAN?

Incarnation (from the Latin meaning "becoming flesh") is the word theologians use to explain how the second member of the Trinity entered into human history in flesh as the God-man Jesus Christ. One prominent theological journal explains:

The English word "incarnation" is based on the Latin Vulgate, "Et ver- bum caro factum est." The noun caro is from the root carn- ("flesh"). The Incarnation means that the eternal Son of God became "flesh," that is, He assumed an additional nature, namely, a human nature.[3]

The incarnation is expressly stated in John 1:14, "And the Word became flesh and dwelt among us, and we have seen his glory, glory as of the only Son from the Father, full of grace and truth." To better understand the incarnation, we must carefully consider the opening chapter of John's Gospel.

The Hebrew people, at the end of the first century, clung tightly to their proud religious heritage extending from Abraham to Isaac, Jacob, Moses, David, and a host of priests and prophets. At the center of their theology was a devotion to the Word of God. The sacred Scriptures of the Old Testament were penned in their native tongue by their Hebrew brothers with nothing less than the authority of God as his divine voice through appointed men. To the Hebrews, the Word of God was the presence and action of God breaking into human history with unparalleled power and authority. God's Word indicated action, an agent accomplishing the will of God. Some examples include God bringing things into existence by His word[a] and God's word being sent out to accomplish His purposes.[b] For the Hebrew, God's speech and action were one in the same.

Leon Morris provides insight into the Jewish concept of "the Word" from the Jewish Targums (Old Testament paraphrases), in which Jews replaced "God" for "the Word of God" out of reverence for His name. For example, where the Bible says, "Then Moses brought the people out of the camp to meet God,"[c] the Targum reads, "to meet the Word of God."[4]

The Jewish philosopher and historian Philo taught his misunderstanding of the "logos". Dualistic and much like early Gnostics, Philo taught that God is spirit and good, but that all matter is evil. Therefore, God could not have created or taken on the material lest He sin. He concluded that both God and matter are eternal and that an intermediary called the "logos" existed that permitted God to interact with the material world.

The Greek people living at the end of the first century also clung tightly to their proud heritage, a philosophical heritage extending from Heraclitus (540–480 BC), to Socrates (470–399 BC), Plato (428–348 BC), Aristotle (384–327 BC), Cicero (106–43 BC), and a host of other philosophers, poets, and playwrights. At the fountainhead of Greek philosophy was Heraclitus, who was known as the "weeping philosopher" and whose image could be found on the coins in Ephesus

---

[a] Gen. 1:3, 6, 9, 11, 14, 20, 24; Ps. 33:6 [b] Isa. 55:11 [c] Ex. 19:17

for several centuries following his death.

For Heraclitus, the creation of the world, the ordering of all life, and the immortality of the human soul were all made possible solely by the word (or logos) that was the invisible and intelligent force behind all that we see in this world. Also, it was the word through which all things were interrelated and brought into harmony, such as life and death, good and evil, darkness and light, and the gods and people. He went so far as to say that truth could be known and wisdom, the great aim of Greek existence, found not by a knowledge of many things but instead by a deep and clear awareness of one thing—the word, or logos.

Jesus Christ was born of a virgin as the one true God who became a man, living at a time and place in which the Hebrew and Greek worlds collided. John sought to be a faithful missionary to the Greeks and to remain loyal to the Hebrew Old Testament Scriptures, by seeking to present the gospel of Jesus Christ faithfully to the larger world dominated by Greek philosophy and language. In this context, John wrote his biography of Jesus in the Greek language, and he began with the concept of "the word," a common ground in the presuppositions of both Hebrew theology and Greek philosophy. Logos is from the Greek meaning "word," or "reason." As we have seen, it was used by the ancient Greeks to convey the idea that the world was governed by a universal intelligence. However, John used logos differently from other writers, that is, to refer to the second person of the Trinity, Jesus Christ.

John begins with a declaration that both Hebrews and Greeks would have agreed with, that before the creation of the world and time, the Word existed eternally. He then scandalizes both groups by stating that Jesus is the Word and was with the one and only God and, in fact, was Himself God and was face-to-face with God the Father from eternity.[a] This thundering declaration would have been stunning to both Jews and Greeks who had vigorously argued that a man could never become a god, though they may never have considered that God had become a man, as John's eyewitness testimony revealed.

John then explains that the Word is not merely the invisible force of the Greeks or the agent of God's action for the Hebrews, but a person through whom all things were created[b], and a person in whom is life and light for mankind.[c] This light that exposes sin and reveals God has come into the darkness of this sinful, cursed, and dying world. The darkness opposed His light but was unable to understand or overcome Him.[d]

It is important to note that John was fully monotheistic in his understanding of God.[5] He would have understood the magnitude of what he was saying, and, as a result, he very clearly outlined his position. John was acutely aware of and intentional in his revolutionary teaching regarding five aspects of this Logos.

1. The Logos is eternal.[e] According to Ron Rhodes, "'In the beginning' (Gk. en

---

[a] John 1:1–2 [b] John 1:3; cf. Col. 1:16 [c] John 1:4 [d] John 1:5; cf. 1 John 1:5–10; 2:8–11 [e] John 1:1–2

archei) refers to a point in eternity past beyond which it is impossible for us to go. Moreover, the verb was ('in the beginning was the Word') is an imperfect tense in the Greek, indicating continued existence."[6]

2. The Logos has always been with God, face-to-face with the Father as an equal in relationship.[a]
3. The Logos is a person distinct from, yet equal to, God.[b] The Greek preposition pros (translated "with" in 1 John 1:1 and 1:2) implies two distinct persons. Therefore, while the Father and the Logos are not the same, they do belong together as one.
4. The Logos is the creator[c] and therefore eternal, self-existent, and all-powerful.
5. The Logos became flesh.[d] In refutation to the Gnostics and dualistic teachings of Philo, John clearly taught that matter is not inherently evil, and that God does involve Himself with the material. It is also noteworthy that Jesus came to dwell among His people in a way that is similar to the tabernacle that God had the Israelites build as His sanctuary so that He might dwell in their midst.[e] Implicitly, we are told that the Logos that was present in the sanctuary became physically present in the space-and-time world. As George Eldon Ladd observes, the Logos became flesh to reveal to humans five things: life[f], light[g], grace[h], truth[i], glory[k], and even God Himself.[7]

How John uses the word Logos elsewhere in his writings is also insightful. First John 1:1 indicates that John and others heard, saw, and touched the Logos, "which was from the beginning." Again, this is a clear reference to Jesus Christ. Revelation 19:12–13 also pictures Christ as the conquering warrior, the Logos of God.

In summary, the Logos is one of the strongest arguments for the deity of Jesus as the personal, eternally existing Creator of the universe, distinct from yet equal with God the Father, who became incarnate (or came in the flesh) to demonstrate His glory in grace and truth to reveal life and light to men.

HOW DID PEOPLE KNOW GOD WAS COMING?

Because God is sovereign over the future, He alone is capable of giving prophetic insight into the future. In great mercy, He did this for His people in the Old Testament. He detailed for them who was coming to save them, how He would come, where He would come, when He would come, and why He would come, so that they would anticipate the incarnation and salvation of Jesus Christ.

After Adam and Eve sinned, God prophesied to them that the Messiah (Jesus) would be born of a woman; He makes no reference to a father. This notable

---

[a] John 1:1–2 [b] John 1:1–2 [c] John 1:3 [d] John 1:14 [e] Ex. 25:8 [f] John 1:4 [g] 1 John 1:4–5 [h] John 1:14 [i] Ibid. [k] Ibid.

omission makes one wonder and points toward his virgin birth. This prophecy was given by God Himself and was the first time the Gospel was preached: "I will put enmity between you [the Serpent] and the woman, and between your offspring and her offspring; he shall bruise your head, and you shall bruise his heel."[a]

Around 700 BC, Isaiah prophesied exactly how Jesus would come into human history: "Therefore the Lord himself will give you a sign. Behold, the virgin shall conceive and bear a son, and shall call his name Immanuel."[b] The promise that Jesus' mother would be a virgin who conceived by a miracle did, in fact, come true.[c] Jesus' mother, Mary, was a Godly young woman and chaste virgin who conceived by the miraculous power of God the Holy Spirit.

Furthermore, Jesus, a name that means "he saves his people from their sins," came as "Immanuel," which means, "God is with us." God became a man at the incarnation of Jesus. Matthew 1:22–23 reveals that Isaiah's prophecy came true: "All this took place to fulfill what the Lord had spoken by the prophet: 'Behold, the virgin shall conceive and bear a son, and they shall call his name Immanuel' (which means, God with us)."

Some contend that the prophecy in Isaiah does not refer to a virgin. They argue that the Hebrew word *almah* (which is used in Isaiah 7:14) typically means "young woman," not "virgin," whereas the Hebrew word *bethulah* typically means "virgin." However, there are many reasons why the verse should be read as referring to a virgin.

The word does mean a "marriageable girl" or "young woman." But that would also mean that she was a virgin because in that day, young women were virgins. Fathers and the community protected these young women. Anyone engaged in sexual relations outside marriage were subject to possible death under the law. If there was any question about her virginity, a woman was subject to physical inspection, which we see in Deuteronomy 22:14–22.

Additionally, the word *almah* is used elsewhere in the Old Testament to refer specifically to a young virgin woman. One clear example is Rebekah, who is described as "very attractive in appearance, a maiden [*bethulah*] whom no man had ever known."[d] Further in the chapter we read that Rebekah was a "virgin [*almah*]."[e] While the two words are virtually synonymous, apparently *bethulah* required a bit more clarification that the woman was a virgin whereas almah did not. Furthermore, two centuries before Jesus was born, we find that the Jews understood exactly what almah means: the Septuagint, the Jewish translation of the Hebrew Bible into Greek, translates almah as *parthenos*, which unambiguously means "virgin". Lastly, in the New Testament, Isaiah 7:14 is clearly interpreted as a prophetic promise about the birth of Jesus to Mary, who was both a young woman and a virgin.

Concerning Jesus' birthplace, in roughly 700 BC, Micah prophesied that Jesus would be born in the town of Bethlehem, saying, "But you, O Bethlehem

---

[a] Gen. 3:15 [b] Isa. 7:14 [c] E.g., Matt. 1:18–23 [d] Gen. 24:16 [e] Gen. 24:43

DOCTRINE

Ephrathah, who are too little to be among the clans of Judah, from you shall come forth for me one who is to be ruler in Israel, whose coming forth is from of old, from ancient days."[a] D. A. Carson says that this verse reveals that the incarnation of Jesus was the entrance of the eternal God: "The Hebrew behind from ancient means from 'the remotest times,' 'from time immemorial'...when used with reference to some historical event; when it is used of God, who existed before creation, 'everlasting' is an appropriate translation (e.g. Ps. 90:2)."[8]

This prophecy was fulfilled in Luke 2:1–7. Caesar Augustus had called for a census to be taken, which required that every family register in their hometown. Jesus' adoptive father, Joseph, was thus required to return to Bethlehem because he was a descendant of the family line of David. In God's providence, this census was required right when Mary was pregnant; she journeyed with her husband from their home in Nazareth to Bethlehem so that Jesus was born in Bethlehem in fulfillment of Micah's prophecy.

As to the timing of Jesus' incarnation, in 400 BC Malachi prophesied, "Behold, I send my messenger, and he will prepare the way before me. And the Lord whom you seek will suddenly come to his temple; and the messenger of the covenant in whom you delight, behold, he is coming, says the LORD of hosts."[b] The messenger of whom Malachi spoke was John the Baptizer, who prepared the way for Jesus' incarnation to bring the new covenant, and the Lord he speaks of is the Lord Jesus Christ. It is important that we are told that Jesus would come to "his temple." Since the temple was destroyed in AD 70 and has not existed since, this places the incarnation of Jesus Christ prior to AD 70. Practically, this means that our Jewish friends who are still awaiting the coming of their Messiah missed Him; they wait in vain because He has already come to His temple and brought the new covenant of salvation.[c]

Lastly, Isaiah prophesies in 700 BC about why Jesus would become incarnate—He is God's arm of salvation reaching down to save sinners.[d] Isaiah also says that Jesus would come from humble circumstances and suffer great sorrow and grief by men in order to deal with the human sin problem through His death, burial in a rich man's tomb, and resurrection.[e] The purpose of Jesus' incarnation was fulfilled when, just as promised, He suffered and died in the place of sinners, though He Himself was sinless, was buried in a rich man's tomb, and rose from death to make righteous the unrighteous.[f]

Besides these explicit prophecies predicting Jesus' incarnation, on many occasions the Old Testament speaks of God anthropomorphically, or in human terms. Old Testament scholar Roy Zuck says:

Deuteronomy refers to God's hand (2:15; 3:24; 4:34; 7:19; 11:2; 26:8; 33:11; 34:12) and arm (4:34; 5:15; 7:19; 11:2; 26:8) as expressions of His

---

[a] Mic. 5:2 [b] Mal. 3:1 [c] Luke 2:25–27 [d] Isa. 53:1–12 [e] Isa. 52:13–53:12 [f] Matt. 27:38, 57–60; Luke 23–24; Acts 2:25–32

INCARNATION: GOD COMES

power. His eyes (11:12; 12:28; 13:18; 32:10) represent His omniscience and constant attention, while His face (5:4; 31:18; 33:20; 34:10) and mouth suggest His communication of His glory and word. In fact the "mouth" of Yahweh is a metonymy for His word as propositional revelation (1:26, 43; 8:3; 9:23; 17:6, 10–11; 19:15; 21:17; 34:4). In startlingly human terms Yahweh is said to write (10:4), to walk (23:14), and to ride (33:26).[9]

Jacob Neusner is the most respected scholar of Judaism, and his book "The Incarnation of God" examines the notion of divine incarnation as it emerges in rabbinic literature.[10] Neusner is so aware of the force of the anthropomorphisms in Hebrew Scripture that he actually calls them incarnational.[11] He defines incarnational as "the representation of God in the flesh, as corporeal, consubstantial in emotion and virtue with human beings, and sharing in the modes and means of action carried out by mortals."[12] Neusner goes on to say:

God's physical traits and attributes are represented as identical to those of a human being. That is why the character of the divinity may accurately be represented as incarnational: God in the flesh, God represented as a person consubstantial in indicative physical traits with the human being.[13]

He argues that some earlier rabbis held to a doctrine of incarnation; he is fully aware of the theological connections this has for Christianity, despite the fact that he is Jewish, because he sees that the biblical evidence of the Old Testament leads to the incarnation.

In summary, people knew of Jesus' incarnation in advance because God prophetically revealed to them who would come, where He would come, when He would come, and why He would come.

HOW DID GOD COME INTO HUMAN HISTORY?

Before we examine how the incarnation occurred, we will note some important truths about this doctrine, for the sake of precision.

First, the incarnation is not an idea borrowed from pagan mythology. In mythology there are stories such as Zeus begetting Hercules, and Apollo begetting Ion and Pythagoras. As a result, some have speculated that Christians stole the virgin birth story from such myths. This speculation must be rejected on three grounds. (1) Some such myths came after the prophecy of Isaiah 7:14 and therefore could not have been the origination of the story. (2) The myths speak of gods having sex with women, which is not what the virgin birth account entails. (3) The myths do not involve actual human beings like Mary and Jesus but rather fictional characters similar to our modern-day superheroes in the comics.

A contemporary account of the "virgin birth" of Augustus was told in the days when Jesus was born.

"When Atia had come in the middle of the night to the solemn service of Apollo, she had her litter set down in the temple and fell asleep, while the rest of the matrons also slept. On a sudden a serpent glided up to her and shortly

went away. When she awoke, she purified herself, as if after the embraces of her husband, and at once there appeared on her body a mark in colors like a serpent, and she could never get rid of it; so that presently she ceased ever to go to the public baths. In the tenth month after that Augustus was born and was therefore regarded as the son of Apollo."[14]

Even the briefest glance shows how different this account is from God's miraculous working in the womb of Mary to beget the God-man, Jesus, who is Emanuel the Messiah.

Second, the Mormon teaching that God the Father had physical, flesh-and-bone sexual relations with Mary, thereby enabling her to conceive Jesus, is horrendously incorrect.

Third, the incarnation does not teach that a man became God. From the time the Serpent told our parents, "You will be like God"[a], there has been an ongoing demonic false teaching that we can be gods (e.g., Mormonism) or part of God (e.g., pantheism, panentheism, and New Ageism). Simply, the incarnation teaches the exact opposite, namely that God became a man.

Fourth, the second member of the Trinity did not come into existence at the incarnation of Jesus Christ. Rather, the eternal Son of God became the God-man Jesus Christ. Theologian Martyn Lloyd-Jones says it this way:

"The doctrine of the incarnation at once tells us that that is not what happened. A person, we repeat, did not come into being there. This person was the eternal Person, the second Person in the Trinity. When a husband and a wife come together and a child is born a new person, a new personality, comes into being. That did not happen in the incarnation."[15]

Fifth, while it is true in one sense that God did become a man, we must be careful to note that the second divine person in the Trinity became a man and that the entire Trinity did not incarnate as a human being. Lloyd-Jones explains:

"But to me it seems always to be wise not to say that God became man. That is a loose statement which we had better not use. We often do say that, but believing as we do in the Persons of the Trinity, what we should say is that the second Person in the Trinity was made flesh and appeared as man. If we merely say, 'God became man', then we may be saying something that is quite wrong, and if people believe something wrong as the result of our statement, we cannot really blame them. We must be particular and we must be specific and we should always be careful what we say...Jesus Christ has not been changed into a man; it is this eternal Person who has come in the flesh. That is the right way to put it."[16]

Therefore, by incarnation we mean that the eternal second person of the Trinity entered into history as the man Jesus Christ.

The incarnation of Jesus Christ is recorded in detail in the first two chapters of both Matthew's and Luke's Gospels. There we read that the angel Gabriel was sent as a messenger from God to the town of Nazareth to a young virgin named

---

[a] Gen. 3:5

Mary who was betrothed to a man named Joseph. The angel announced:

"Do not be afraid, Mary, for you have found favor with God. And behold, you will conceive in your womb and bear a son, and you shall call his name Jesus. He will be great and will be called the Son of the Most High. And the Lord God will give to him the throne of his father David, and he will reign over the house of Jacob forever, and of his kingdom there will be no end." And Mary said to the angel, "How will this be, since I am a virgin?" And the angel answered her, "The Holy Spirit will come upon you, and the power of the Most High will overshadow you; therefore the child to be born will be called holy—the Son of God...For nothing will be impossible with God." And Mary said, "Behold, I am the servant of the Lord; let it be to me according to your word." And the angel departed from her.[a]

Further, the Bible reveals the birth of Jesus as the pattern for our new birth—both are miracles of God the Holy Spirit to be received by faith. Belief in Jesus' incarnation is an essential truth that Christians have always held. One scholar says, "Apart from the Ebionites...and a few Gnostic sects, no body of Christians in early times is known to have existed who did not accept as part of their faith the birth of Jesus from the Virgin Mary."[17] Another writes, "Everything that we know of the dogmatics of the early part of the second century agrees with the belief that at that period the virginity of Mary was a part of the formulated Christian belief."[18] Furthermore, the church father Ignatius, who was trained by the disciple John, testified to this fact, speaking of the "virginity of Mary."[19] Lastly, J. Gresham Machen summarized the evidence for that fact, saying, "There is good ground, we think, to hold that the reason why the Christian Church came to believe in the birth of Jesus without a human father was simply that He was a matter of fact so born."[20]

WAS JESUS FULLY GOD?

Jesus is nearly universally recognized as a great moral example, insightful teacher, defender of the poor and marginalized, humble servant to the needy, and unprecedented champion of overturning injustice with nonviolence. However, the divinity of Jesus Christ is most frequently and heatedly debated. Simply stated, the question as to whether Jesus Christ is fully God is the issue that divides Christianity from all other religions and spiritualities. For example, the Jehovah's Witnesses Watchtower Society says, "Jesus never claimed to be God."[21] Bahá'í's say that Jesus was a manifestation of God and a prophet but inferior to Muhammad and Bahá'u'lláh. Buddhism teaches that Jesus was not God but rather an enlightened man like the Buddha. Christian Science founder Mary Baker Eddy flatly states, "Jesus Christ is not God." Conversely, we believe that there are numerous

---

[a] Luke 1:30–38

incontrovertible reasons to believe that Jesus Christ was and is fully God. God the Father said Jesus was God. The Bible is clear that the Father declares the Son to be God. In Hebrews 1:8 the Father speaks of the Son as God, saying, "But of the Son he says, 'Your throne, O God, is forever and ever.'" When Jesus is brought forth out of the water at his baptism, God the Father says, "This is my beloved Son, with whom I am well pleased."[a]

At Jesus' transfiguration, "a voice from the cloud said, 'This is my beloved Son, with whom I am well pleased; listen to him.'"[b] Indeed, there can be no greater testimony to the deity of Jesus Christ than that of God the Father.

Demons said Jesus was God. Even demons called Jesus "the Holy One of God"[c] and "the Son of God."[d] Mark 1:34 says that Jesus "would not permit the demons to speak, because they knew him." Again, Luke 4:41 says Jesus "would not allow them [the demons] to speak, because they knew that he was the Christ."

Jesus said He was God. Jesus' claim to be God is without precedent or peer, as no founder of any major world religion has ever said He was God. Yet, Jesus clearly, repeatedly, and emphatically said He was God in a variety of ways. If this claim were untrue, He would have been guilty of violating the first commandment and, as a blasphemer, would have deserved death. This is why the people who disbelieved His claim kept seeking to put him to death. The eventual murder of Jesus for claiming to be God is recorded in Matthew 26:63–65, which says:

"But Jesus remained silent. And the high priest said to him, 'I adjure you by the living God, tell us if you are the Christ, the Son of God.' Jesus said to him, 'You have said so. But I tell you, from now on you will see the Son of Man seated at the right hand of Power and coming on the clouds of heaven.' Then the high priest tore his robes and said, 'He has uttered blasphemy. What further witnesses do we need? You have now heard his blasphemy.'"

By declaring that He came down from heaven, Jesus revealed that He was eternally God in heaven before His incarnation on the earth.[e] By saying He was the only way to heaven, Jesus claimed to be both God and savior.[f] Jesus refused to be considered merely a good moral instructor and instead claimed to be "God alone."[g]

Those who heard Jesus say these kinds of things wanted to kill Jesus because he was "making himself equal with God."[h] On this point, Billy Graham says, "Jesus was not just another great religious teacher, nor was he only another in a long line of individuals seeking after spiritual truth. He was, instead, truth itself. He was God incarnate."[22]

Jesus' claims to be God were clearly heard and understood by his enemies, and Jesus never recanted.[i] John 8:58–59 reports that Jesus said, "'Truly, truly, I say to you, before Abraham was, I am.' So they picked up stones to throw at him,

---

[a] Matt. 3:17 [b] Matt. 17:5 [c] Mark 1:24; Luke 4:33–34 [d] Luke 4:40–41 [e] John 6:38, 41–46 [f] John 14:6 [g] Mark 10:17–18 [h] John 5:18 [i] Mark 14:61–64

INCARNATION: GOD COMES

but Jesus hid himself and went out of the temple." In John 10:30-33, Jesus also said:

"'I and the Father are one.' The Jews picked up stones again to stone him. Jesus answered them, 'I have shown you many good works from the Father; for which of them are you going to stone me?' The Jews answered him, 'It is not for a good work that we are going to stone you but for blasphemy, because you, being a man, make yourself God.'"

On this point, New York's Judge Gaynor once said of Jesus' trial at the end of His earthly life, "It is plain from each of the gospel narratives, that the alleged crime for which Jesus was tried and convicted was blasphemy."[23] The Bible plainly says Jesus is God. Without question, the New Testament often refers to Jesus Christ as God, and a few examples will illustrate this truth clearly. Matthew refers to Jesus as "'Immanuel' (which means, God with us)."[a] Thomas calls Jesus, "My Lord and my God!"[b] Romans 9:5 speaks of "the Christ who is God over all, blessed forever. Amen." Titus 2:13 refers to "our great God and Savior Jesus Christ" and Titus 3:4 calls Jesus, "God our Savior." First John 5:20 says that Jesus Christ "is the true God." Lastly, 2 Peter 3:18 speaks of "our Lord and Savior Jesus Christ."

Jesus is given the names of God. When picking a title for himself, Jesus was apparently most fond of "Son of Man."[c] He spoke of Himself by this term roughly 80 times between all four Gospels. He applied the title from the prophet Daniel, who penned it some 600 years before Jesus' birth.[d] In Daniel's vision, the Son of Man comes to the Ancient of Days, the Lord Himself. But He comes from the clouds, from heaven, not from the earth. This indicates that He isn't a human. He is given messianic dominion and authority, something no angel can obtain and is reserved for God. The Old Testament sees this divine person sitting alongside the Lord as an equal. This second person of the Trinity was promised to receive the messianic mission to redeem the world, to defeat every enemy and liberate people. As God, He is exalted over all peoples, nations, cultures, and religions to be worshiped as the eternal King. Jesus is the one who claimed He would be the Son of Man coming with the clouds as God.

Many other names for God are also attributed to Jesus Christ. Jesus claimed to be the "Son of God" on many occasions.[e] In so doing, He was claiming to be equal to and of the same substance as God the Father. Those who heard Him use this title rightly understood that it was a divine title: "This was why the Jews were seeking all the more to kill him, because not only was he breaking the Sabbath, but he was even calling God his own Father, making himself equal with God."[f]

The New Testament refers to Jesus Christ as "Lord" several hundred times.[g] That term is the equivalent of the Old Testament term "Jehovah," which is one of

---

[a] Matt. 1:23 [b] John 20:28 [c] Matt. 24:30; 26:64; Mark 13:26; 14:62-64; Luke 21:27; 22:69 [d] Dan. 7:13. Also see Psalm 110 [e] E.g., John 5:17-29 [f] John 5:18 [g] E.g., Rom. 10:9, 13; 1 Cor. 2:8; Heb. 1:10

DOCTRINE

the highest titles the Bible ascribes to God. Thus, this title is ascribed to Jesus Christ as God and Lord.

In Revelation 22:13, Jesus says, "I am the Alpha and the Omega, the first and the last, the beginning and the end." With these titles, He is obviously referring to Himself as eternal God. Bible commentator Grant Osborne says:

"The titles refer to the sovereignty of God and Christ over history. They control the beginning of creation and its end, and therefore they control every aspect of history in between. Since this is the only passage to contain all three titles, it has the greatest emphasis of them all on the all-embracing power of Christ over human history."[24]

Jesus' miracles confirm His claim to be God. The nearly 40 miracles that Jesus performed throughout the New Testament demonstrate God is with Jesus. Just as miracles confirmed the authority and anointing of the ancient prophets and Jesus' apostles, the miracles of the Messiah are God's way of giving His stamp of approval to the claims of Jesus.[a] They point to Him as the person through whom God is doing his work. For example, when Jesus gave sight to the blind man, the people would have been reminded of Psalm 146:8: "The LORD opens the eyes of the blind." The fact of Jesus' miracles is so well established that even his enemies conceded it.[b]

The Jewish Talmud charged that Jesus "practiced magic."[25] Celsus, a strong opponent of Christianity, later repeated that claim.[26] The noted Jewish historian Josephus also reported that Jesus was "a doer of wonderful works."[27] In John 10:36–39, Jesus speaks of these works:

"Do you say of him whom the Father consecrated and sent into the world, 'You are blaspheming,' because I said, 'I am the Son of God'? If I am not doing the works of my Father, then do not believe me; but if I do them, even though you do not believe me, believe the works, that you may know and understand that the Father is in me and I am in the Father." Again they sought to arrest him, but he escaped from their hands.

Jesus' claim to deity includes declaring Himself to be without any sin in thought, word, deed, or motive and therefore morally perfect. In John 8:46, Jesus openly invites His enemies to recall any sin He ever committed saying, "Which one of you convicts me of sin?" Those who testify to the sinlessness of Jesus are those who knew Him most intimately, such as His friends Peter[c] and John[d], His half-brother James[e], and even His former enemy Paul.[f] Additionally, even Judas, who betrayed Jesus, admitted that Jesus was without sin[g], along with the ruler Pontius Pilate, who oversaw the murder of Jesus[h], the soldier who participated in the murder of Jesus[i], and the guilty sinner who was crucified at Jesus' side.[k]

---

[a] John 10:36-38 [b] John 3:2; 5:36; 10:25, 32, 37-38; Acts 2:22; 10:38 [c] Acts 3:14; 1 Pet. 1:19; 2:22; 3:18 [d] John said that anyone who claims to be without sin is a liar (1 John 1:8) and that Jesus was without sin (1 John 3:5) [e] James 5:6 [f] 2 Cor. 5:21 [g] Matt. 27:3-4 [g] Luke 23:22 [i] Luke 23:47 [k] Luke 23:41

INCARNATION: GOD COMES

Furthermore, not only was Jesus God and without sin, He also forgave sin.[a] The Bible is clear that our sin is ultimately committed against God[b] and that God alone can forgive sin.[c] Thus, Luke 5:20-21 reveals Jesus doing the work of God:

And when he [Jesus] saw their faith, he said, "Man, your sins are forgiven you." And the scribes and the Pharisees began to question, saying, "Who is this who speaks blasphemies? Who can forgive sins but God alone?"

Lastly, Jesus also claimed the power to raise the dead[d], judge our eternal destiny[e], and grant eternal life.[f]

People worshiped Jesus as God. The Bible is emphatically clear that only God is to be worshiped.[g] To worship anyone other than God is both idolatry and blasphemy—two sins that the Bible abhors from beginning to end with the strongest condemnations. Jesus Himself repeats the command to worship God only when the Devil tempts Jesus to worship him. Therefore, the fact that Jesus accepted worship as God is one of the strongest arguments that Jesus Christ was and is fully God.

Jesus repeatedly invited people to pray to Him as God.[h] As a result of His teaching, both men like Stephen[i] and women like the Canaanite[k] did pray to Jesus as God.

Jesus also said that He is to be worshiped along with the Father: "All may honor the Son, just as they honor the Father. Whoever does not honor the Son does not honor the Father who sent him."[m] Upon His triumphal entry into Jerusalem when children worshiped him, Jesus quoted Psalm 8:2 in reference to Himself as God to be worshiped:

"When the chief priests and the scribes saw the wonderful things that he did, and the children crying out in the temple, 'Hosanna to the Son of David!' they were indignant, and they said to him, 'Do you hear what these are saying?' And Jesus said to them, 'Yes; have you never read, "Out of the mouth of infants and nursing babies you have prepared praise"?'"[n]

Commenting on this event, Craig Blomberg says:

"Jesus' response, again using the introductory rebuke 'Have you never read?' tacitly applauds their acclamation in light of Ps 8:2 (LXX [Septuagint] 8:3, which is quoted verbatim). There the children are praising Yahweh, so Jesus again accepts worship that is reserved for God alone."[28]

Also, after being healed by Jesus, a man worshiped Jesus, and Jesus accepted his worship.[o] Lastly, Philippians 2:10-11 envisions a day in which everyone bends their knee in subjection to Jesus and lifts their voice in worship of Jesus as Lord.

Taken together, all of this evidence reveals that Jesus was and is God. Or, as Colossians 2:9 says perfectly, "in him the whole fullness of deity dwells bodily."

---

[a] E.g., Luke 7:48 [b] Ps. 51:4 [c] Ps. 130:4; Isa. 43:25; Jer. 31:34 [d] John 6:39-44 [e] John 5:22-23 [f] John 10:28 [g] Deut. 6:13; 10:20; Matt. 4:10; Acts 10:25-26 [h] John 14:13-14; 15:7 [i] Acts 7:59-60 [k] Matt. 15:25 [m] John 5:23 [n] Matt. 21:15-16 [o] John 9:38

DOCTRINE

WAS JESUS FULLY HUMAN?

The Bible affirms the humanity of Jesus Christ in a variety of ways. Jesus had a human name—Jesus (meaning "Yahweh saves") Christ (meaning "anointed one")—and a human genealogy.[a] He was born of a woman[b], had brothers and sisters[c], and was racially Jewish.[d] Jesus grew physically, spiritually, mentally, and socially[e], learned[f], experienced fatigue[g], slept[h], grew hungry[i], and thirsty[k], worked as a craftsman[m], had male and female friends He loved[n], gave encouraging compliments[o], loved children[p], celebrated holidays[q], went to parties[r], loved his mom[s], prayed[t], worshiped[u], and obeyed God the Father.[v]

Furthermore, not only did Jesus have a physical body[w], but He also suffered and died "in the flesh."[x] In addition to His body, Jesus also had a human spirit.[y] Jesus was emotional as well, for the Bible notes that Jesus experienced grief[z], had compassion[aa], was stressed[bb], was astonished[cc], was happy[dd], told jokes[ee], and even wept.[ff]

Taken together, these are clearly the ways we speak of human beings and reveal that Jesus was, as Jesus and other Scriptures state, a man.[gg] The importance of this fact is found in 1 John 4:2–3:

"By this you know the Spirit of God: every spirit that confesses that Jesus Christ has come in the flesh is from God, and every spirit that does not confess Jesus is not from God. This is the spirit of the antichrist, which you heard was coming and now is in the world already."

The belief in the full humanity of Jesus Christ was the dominant position of the early Christian church. The church father Athanasius expressed the church's opinion well:

"Peter writes in his letter, 'Christ therefore suffered in the flesh for our sakes' [1 Pet. 4:1]. So when it is said that he hungered and thirsted and toiled and was ignorant and slept and cried out and made requests and fled and was born and turned away from the cup—in general, did all the things which belonged to the flesh — let...all things of this sort be asserted as 'for our sakes in the flesh,' for this is precisely the reason the apostle himself said, 'Christ therefore suffered' not in

---

[a] Matt. 1:1–17; Luke 3:23–38 [b] Matt. 1:18–25; Luke 2:7; Gal. 4:4 [c] Matt. 13:55 [d] John 4:9 [e] Luke 2:42, 52; 3:23 [f] Matt. 4:12; Mark 11:13–14; Luke 2:40, 52 [g] Matt. 8:24; Mark 4:38; Luke 8:23–24; John 4:7 [h] Mark 4:36–41 [i] Matt. 4:2; Mark 11:12; Luke 4:2 [k] John 4:7; 19:18 [m] Mark 6:3 [n] John 11:3–5 [o] Mark 12:41–44 [p] Matt. 19:13–15 [q] Luke 2:41 [r] Matt. 11:19 [s] John 19:26–27 [t] Matt. 14:23; Mark 1:35; 14:32–42; John 17 [u] Luke 4:16 [v] John 5:30; 6:38; 8:28–29, 54; 10:17–18 [w] Rom. 8:3; Phil. 2:7–8; Heb. 2:14; 1 John 4:2–3 [x] Rom. 8:3; Eph. 2:15–16; Col. 1:21–22; Heb. 2:14; 10:19–20; 1 Pet. 2:24 [y] John 12:27; 13:21; 19:30 [z] Matt. 23:37; Luke 19:41 [aa] Matt. 9:36; Mark 1:41; Luke 7:13 [bb] John 13:21 [cc] Mark 6:6; Luke 7:9 [dd] Luke 10:21–24; John 15:11; 17:13; Heb. 12:2, 22 [ee] Matt. 7:6; 23:24; Mark 4:21 [ff] John 11:34–35 [gg] John 8:40; Acts 17:31; 1 Tim. 2:5

the Godhead but 'for our sakes in the flesh,' in order that the passions might be recognized to be natural properties not of the Logos but of the flesh."[29]

HOW COULD GOD BECOME A MAN?

In AD 451, the Council of Chalcedon met to wrestle with the confusion that surrounded the divinity and humanity of Jesus. They issued the Chalcedonian Creed, which cleared up many heresies that wrongly defined the humanity and divinity of Jesus. In sum, the creed declared that Jesus Christ is one person with two natures (human and divine) who is both fully God and fully man.

Theologically, the term for the union of both natures in Jesus Christ is hypostatic union, which is taken from the Greek word hypostasis for "person." Summarizing the hypostatic union, three facts are noted: (1) Christ has two distinct natures: humanity and deity; (2) there is no mixture or intermingling of the two natures; (3) although He has two natures, Christ is one person. The Chalcedonian summary of the incarnation is the position held by all of Christendom, including Orthodox, Catholic, and Protestant Christians.

In keeping with the biblical position of Chalcedon, we must retain both the full divinity and full humanity of Jesus Christ. To accomplish this, we must conclude that when Jesus became a man, He did not change His identity as God but rather changed His role. According to the church father Augustine, "Christ added to himself which he was not, he did not lose what he was."[30]

Jesus, who was fully equal with God in every way, who was the very form of God, did not see that as something to keep in His grip, but emptied Himself of that equal status and role to take the status and role of humanity.[a]

He, who was and is God, took the likeness of humanity. God became the "image of God" for the sake of our salvation.[b]

Theologians capture this humble emptying Himself of the divine equality, the divine lifestyle, with the phrase *he laid aside the exercise of his incommunicable divine attributes*. Some theologians would say that Jesus retained all of His divine attributes while on the earth but did not avail Himself to them to instead limit Himself to what humans can do. Other theologians would say that Jesus did not retain all of His divine attributes while on the earth but rather humbly set them aside during his incarnation. Either way, what this means is that Jesus did not continually use the attributes unique to deity such as His omniscience, or omnipresence, or immortality while on the earth. So, Jesus in his humble state does not know the date of the Second Coming[c], is not present when Lazarus dies[d], and dies.[e] He did supernatural works like knowing that Lazarus was dead[f], raising the dead[g], healing diseases and casting out demons[h] by the power of the Holy Spirit.[i]

---

[a] Phil. 2:6-7 [b] Gen. 1:27; 2 Cor. 4:4 [c] Matt. 24:36 [d] John 11:6, 21, 32 [e] Matt. 27:50; Phil. 2:8 [f] John 12:1-14 [g] John 11:39-41; Mark 5:35-43 [h] Matt. 4:23-24; 8:16-33 [i] Matt. 12:28

An analogy of this emptying would be a general manager of a resort who brings his family for a vacation week. He puts his general manager access key with all its power, rights and privilege in his pocket and uses a guest access key. For the duration of the week, he is fully the general manager, but lives authentically as a guest.

The key Scripture describing that God came as the man Jesus Christ because of humility and a willingness to be our suffering servant is Philippians 2:5–11, which says:

"Have this mind among yourselves, which is yours in Christ Jesus, who, though he was in the form of God, did not count equality with God a thing to be grasped, but emptied himself, by taking the form of a servant, being born in the likeness of men. And being found in human form, he humbled himself by becoming obedient to the point of death, even death on a cross. Therefore God has highly exalted him and bestowed on him the name that is above every name, so that at the name of Jesus every knee should bow, in heaven and on earth and under the earth, and every tongue confess that Jesus Christ is Lord, to the glory of God the Father."

This amazing section of Scripture reveals to us that the second member of the Trinity came into human history as the man Jesus Christ. In doing so, Jesus exemplified perfect and unparalleled humility. In His incarnation, the Creator entered His creation to reveal God to us, identify with us, and live and die for us as our humble servant.

By saying that Jesus "emptied himself," Paul means that Jesus set aside His rights as God and the rightful continual use of his incommunicable divine attributes. The eternal Son of God chose to become human and live by the power of the Holy Spirit. This does not mean that Jesus in any way ceased to be fully God, but rather that He chose not to avail Himself of His divine rights and those attributes unique to deity while on the earth. Thus, He lived as we must live—by the enabling power of God the Holy Spirit. We want to be clear: Jesus remained fully man and fully God during His incarnation, and He maintained all of his divine personhood and attributes though He humbly emptied Himself of use of those unique to deity.

Jesus did not lose His divine attributes; He simply chose not to use them but rather live as a perfectly Spirit-filled human on mission of Messiah. In becoming a human being, Jesus did not lose anything but rather added humanity to His divinity.[31] Therefore, Jesus Christ retained all of His divine attributes. He did not, however, avail Himself of the continual use of His divine attributes. Perhaps this was for two primary reasons.

One, on occasion Jesus would reveal His divinity as God. Matthew 9:35 says, "Jesus went throughout all the cities and villages, teaching in their synagogues and proclaiming the gospel of the kingdom and healing every disease and every affliction." In Mark 4, some sailors on a boat with Jesus were exhausted from rowing all night until Jesus awoke and commanded the storm to stop, which it did. Those present, "were filled with great fear and said to one another, 'Who then is this, that even the wind and the sea obey him?'" (v. 41). In John 2:11 Jesus turned water into wine, and we read, "This, the first of his signs, Jesus did at Cana in Galilee, and manifested his glory. And his disciples believed in him." In summary, sometimes Jesus performed miracles to reveal the kingdom of God and Himself as King.

Two, Jesus would use His divine characteristics to benefit others but not Himself. For example, we read in Mark 2:5–7 "Jesus...said to the paralytic, 'Son, your sins are forgiven.' Now some of the scribes were sitting there, questioning in their hearts, 'Why does this man speak like that? He is blaspheming! Who can forgive sins but God alone?'" Ultimately, we sin against God; therefore, only God has the authority to truly, completely, and eternally forgive our sin. When Jesus forgave sin, the religious critics who heard Him were correct; He was doing divine work reserved for God alone to benefit a needy sinner.

In summary, while on the earth, Jesus did retain His divine attributes, but He did not continually avail Himself to the use of His divine attributes. Furthermore, Jesus did not use His divine characteristics (e.g., all-knowing, all-powerful, all-present) in a way to benefit Himself. When suffering, Jesus suffered as we do; when learning, Jesus learned as we do; and when tempted, Jesus faced temptation as we do. In no way did Jesus cheat to make His life easier by using divine attributes that we do not possess.

In this regard, Jesus was not like Clark Kent. Superman had special powers that other people did not have, but he lived in disguise as Clark Kent, pretending to be like the rest of us when, in fact, he was not. Jesus is not like that. Jesus was not pretending to be a humble, homeless, hated peasant who was faking His suffering, learning, and tempting. When the Bible said Jesus was hungry, tired, wept, bled, and died, it was in His full humanity without an ounce of fakery. Hebrews 2:17–18 talks about this when it says,

"He had to be made like his brothers in every respect, so that he might become a merciful and faithful high priest in the service of God, to make propitiation for the sins of the people. For because he himself has suffered when tempted, he is able to help those who are being tempted."

Nonetheless, Jesus' life was lived as fully human in that He lived it by the power of the Holy Spirit.[32]

WHAT ARE SOME PROMINENT FALSE TEACHINGS ABOUT THE DOCTRINE OF THE INCARNATION?

Regarding the full divinity and humanity of Jesus Christ, theologian J. I. Packer has said:

The really staggering Christian claim is that Jesus of Nazareth was God made man—that the second person of the Godhead became the "second man" (1 Cor. 15:47), determining human destiny, the second representative head of the race, and that He took humanity without loss of deity, so that Jesus of Nazareth was as truly and fully divine as He was human. Here are two mysteries for the price of one—the plurality of persons within the unity of God, and the union of Godhead and manhood in the person of Jesus.[33]

There are two general ways in which various thinking has erred regarding the humanity and divinity of Jesus. The first is to deny the full divinity of Jesus in favor of His humanity; the second is to deny the full humanity of Jesus in favor of His divinity.

The denial of the full divinity of Jesus has been done by heretics such as the Ebionites, dynamic monarchianists, Socinians, Servetusites, Nestorians, modalists, monarchianists, Sabellianists, Unitarians, Social Gospel proponents, "death of God" theologians, liberal "Christians," Arians, Jehovah's Witnesses, Mormons, functionalists, Adoptionists, Kenotics, Apollinarians, and more recently by the popular book and film "The Da Vinci Code".

The denial of the full humanity of Jesus has been done by heretics such as Marcionites, Docetists, Gnostics, modal monarchianists, Apollinarian Paulicians, monophysitists, New Agers, and Eutychians. Perhaps the people who most commonly prefer Jesus' divinity over his humanity in our present age are Protestant Christian fundamentalists. They are so committed to preserving the divinity of Jesus that they tend to portray His humanity as essentially overwhelmed by His divinity so that He was largely not tempted to sin, if indeed tempted at all.

In addition, the Bultmannian school (after Rudolf Bultmann) has separated the "Christ of faith" from the "Jesus of history." Subsequently, Jesus is more like an ancient Greek god. Some evangelical Christians make a similar error by removing Jesus' life and teachings from history in the world and relegating Him to the subjective realm of religious experience so that Jesus becomes little more than a figurative object for devotion and experience only in our heart.

Lastly, it is falsely believed that the Christian concept of incarnation is commonly held across many ideologies, if not even borrowed from them. Humanist mystic Aldous Huxley famously asserted that "the doctrine that God can be incarnated in human form is found in most of the principal historic expositions of the Perennial Philosophy."[34] In response, Geoffrey Parrinder has shown that Huxley's claim is grossly overstated.[35] Nonetheless, it is true that there is a long history of religious beliefs claiming that a god or goddess came to the earth in physical form. These are considered in the broadest sense to be incarnational teachings, although none of them is the same as Christian incarnation.[36] In no other story does the god come to earth to live a whole life in true humanity and service or to die voluntarily for the sins of humans.

In many idolatrous religions, a deity is said to be present in or physically manifested as an object, which then comes to eventually be worshiped as the deity itself. Some idolatrous religions (e.g., Sikhism, Bahá'', Hinduism) refer to incarnations as avatars, which literally means "descent." Christian apologist Timothy C. Tennent notes three ways in which such avatars are different from what Christians believe about the incarnation of Jesus Christ.[37] (1) Avatars are repeated endlessly throughout each cycle of history, whereas the incarnation is a unique, singular act in history. Jesus will not return for another incarnated life cycle or be replaced by another person housing His spirit. (2) An avatar comes forth because of accumulated karma and is therefore not a free act of God, like the determination of the Father to send Jesus into history before time began. (3) An avatar is a mixture and blending of the divine and human, whereas Jesus is not a blending of a god and a man but rather God becoming man.

Therefore, because Jesus is the only God and his incarnation alone is altogether unique, it is a grievous error in any way to portray his earthly life as similar to avatars and the like that are postulated by other religions.

In another book I (Mark) wrote called *Christians Might be Crazy* we discovered numerous false views of Jesus through more than 900,000 phone calls and focus groups in four U.S. cities.[38] Many participants were curious about or highly committed to alternative theories about Jesus. One woman said that Jesus studied under Indian mystics for some 30 years. Another called Him a lightworker. Many guys thought He was a magician like David Copperfield or Criss Angel. One guy asserted that Jesus was not a zombie but a lich. A few people even called Jesus an alien, à la the History Channel series "Ancient Aliens." Like Tony said, "That's my favorite series. What I love about that show is that they base it off of actual facts. They have proof that blows my mind when it comes to religion."

Is it possible Jesus was a mystic, lightworker, magician, lich, or alien? Perhaps—but is it probable? Is the evidence for those profiles more complete than the ancient eyewitness testimony of Scripture? Would low-budget specials on the History Channel or Discovery Channel hold up to the same scrutiny as the New Testament has faced for 2,000 years?

It is simply false that, at some point long after Jesus, Christians selected from among competing ideas to create a storyline that would consolidate their own power. Church leaders did convene in councils including Laodicea (AD 363), Hippo (AD 393), and Carthage (AD 397). But they simply recognized writings already known and trusted by Christians everywhere as inspired Scripture for hundreds of years, in the case of the New Testament, and thousands of years, in the case of the Old Testament. The fact that these councils convened nearly four centuries after Jesus attests to the wide consensus that existed until heretics arose in that era.

HOW IS JESUS' INCARNATION A SOURCE OF GREAT COMFORT?

There are two categories of reason why Jesus' incarnation is a source of great comfort. The first is that, in the incarnation, Jesus is like us. The second is that, in the incarnation, Jesus is unlike us.

How Jesus Is Like Us
As the man Jesus Christ, the second member of the Trinity has lovingly and humbly identified with the frailty of our humanity by enduring temptation, distress,

weakness, pain, and sorrow. He did so by coming as our priest.

In the Old Testament, the priest would humbly stand between God and people as a mediator of sorts. He would bring the hopes, dreams, fears, and sins of the people before God as their advocate and intercessor. He would hear their confession of sin and pray for them.

Furthermore, offering sacrifices was central to his role, to show that sin was very real and deserved death, while asking God for gracious forgiveness. Then he would speak God's blessing on the people. All the functions of the priest are ultimately fulfilled in Jesus.

The book of the Bible that deals most thoroughly with the priestly role of Jesus is Hebrews. In Hebrews, we are told that Jesus is our "high priest."[a] As our priest, Jesus has offered a sacrifice to pay the penalty for our sin. Not only is Jesus a priest superior to the Old Testament priests, but His sacrifice is also superior to theirs—He gave his own life and shed His own blood for our sin.[b]

Hebrews reveals that Jesus' ministry as our priest did not end with His return to heaven. Rather, Jesus is alive today and ministers to us as our high priest who intercedes for us before God the Father.[c] Practically, this means that Jesus actually knows us, loves us, pays attention to our lives, and cares for us. At this very moment, Jesus is bringing Christians' hurts, suffering, needs, and sins to the Father in a prayerful and loving way as our priest.

Jesus' priestly intercession makes both our prayer and worship possible. We pray and worship the Father through Jesus our priest by the indwelling power of God the Holy Spirit, who has made our bodies the new temples in which He lives on the earth.

When we understand Jesus as our priest, we are able to know that He loves us affectionately, tenderly, and personally. Furthermore, Jesus' desire for us is nothing but good, and His ministry results in nothing less than life-changing intimacy with God the Father. Jesus makes new life and obedience possible by His loving, compassionate, and patient service to us as a faithful priest.

In his role as priest, Jesus is different from all other man-made religions and their false portraits of God. Virtually every religion sees God in a harsh way. Jesus is the only God who gets off His throne to humbly serve us and give us grace and mercy.

Perhaps the most insightful text of Scripture on the importance of the priestly ministry of Jesus is Hebrews 4:15–16, which says:

"For we do not have a high priest who is unable to sympathize with our weaknesses, but one who in every respect has been tempted as we are, yet without sin. Let us then with confidence draw near to the throne of grace, that we may receive mercy and find grace to help in time of need."

Thus, Jesus is sympathetic to our temptations, weakness, suffering, sickness,

---

[a] Heb. 3:1; 4:14 [b] Heb. 9:26 [c] Heb. 7:25

disappointment, pain, confusion, loneliness, betrayal, brokenness, mourning, and sadness. Jesus does not refrain from entering our sick, fallen, and crooked world. Instead, He humbly came into this world to feel what we feel and face what we face, while remaining sinless. Subsequently, Jesus can both sympathize with and deliver us. Practically, this means that in our time of need, we can run to Jesus, our sympathetic priest, who lives to serve us and give us grace and mercy for anything that life brings.

How Jesus Is Unlike Us

In addition to being fully God, a primary way in which Jesus is unlike us is that He alone is without sin.[a] While the Bible is clear that Jesus never sinned, the question of whether He had a sin nature as we do has been a point of historical division between various Christian traditions.

The Eastern church says yes. They focus on Romans 8:3 (that the Father sent his own Son "in the likeness of sinful flesh and for sin"), Hebrews 2:17 (Therefore he had to be made like his brothers in every respect), and Hebrews 4:15 (which says he was one "who in every respect has been tempted as we are"). They then argue that this could not be if Jesus did not have any of the sinful thoughts or desires like the ones we wrestle with all the time. It is then argued that, although Jesus had a sin nature, He overcame it and showed us the perfect obedience that we can follow to live holy lives. The Western church says no. They focus on Hebrews 7:26-27: We "have such a high priest, holy, innocent, unstained, separated from sinners, and exalted above the heavens. He has no need, like those high priests, to offer sacrifices daily, first for his own sins." It is argued that if Jesus had a sin nature, He could not fit this description. Furthermore, if He had sinful character, then He would be a sinner.

We are inclined to agree with the Western church and see the "likeness of sinful flesh" in Romans as a point of similarity rather than a point of character whereby Jesus had a sin nature. Subsequently, as the "last Adam"[b], Jesus was like the first Adam prior to the fall—without a sin nature—and therefore had a completely free will to choose obedience out of love for God the Father.

Because Jesus is like us in that He was tempted, yet unlike us in that he never did sin, He can help us when we are tempted and show us how to escape sinful situations.

Hebrews 2:17-18 says:

"Therefore he had to be made like his brothers in every respect, so that he might become a merciful and faithful high priest in the service of God, to make propitiation for the sins of the people. For because he himself has suffered when tempted, he is able to help those who are being tempted."

In conclusion, Jesus alone can mediate between God and us because He

---

[a] 2 Cor. 5:21; Heb. 9:14; 1 Pet. 2:22, 1 John 3:5 [b] 1 Cor. 15:45

alone is fully God and fully man and thereby able to perfectly represent both God and man. Regarding the vital importance of both Jesus' humanity and divinity, theologian Jonathan Edwards says:

"First, I would consider Christ's taking upon him our nature to put himself in a capacity to purchase redemption for us. This was absolutely necessary, for though Christ, as God, was infinitely sufficient for the work, yet to his being in an immediate capacity for it, it was needful that he should not only be God, but man. If Christ had remained only in the divine nature, he could not have purchased our salvation; not from any imperfection of the divine nature, but by reason of its absolute and infinite perfection; for Christ, merely as God, was not capable either of obedience or suffering."[39]

In other words, to redeem man, Christ first had to become a man. This is precisely what the Bible teaches: "For there is one God, and there is one mediator between God and men, the man Christ Jesus."[a] This verse reveals the threefold reasoning as to why Jesus' incarnation is of such great comfort. (1) There is one God for all peoples, times, and places. (2) There is one mediator between sinful humanity and the one sinless God. This mediator remedies the sin problem that divides people and God so that there can be salvation and reconciliation. (3) Christ Jesus alone can mediate between God and man because he alone is the God-man.

HOW IS JESUS' INCARNATION OUR EXAMPLE FOR MINISTRY AND MISSION?

In most religions, the holiest people are those who are most separated from culture and sinners. They live as monks or nuns in remote areas or behind walls away from average people. Conversely, Jesus Christ came into the mess of human history and spent time in relationship with believers and unbelievers alike. Subsequently, religious people who separated themselves from sinners and cultures were prone to denounce Jesus for the kind of company He kept.[b]

Jesus' incarnation is our missional model. Roughly 40 times in John's Gospel, Jesus declares that the Father sent him. Indeed, the incarnation is the sending of the second member of the Trinity into human history as a missionary. This is what Jesus meant when he taught that Christians would be sent as missionaries like Him into cultures by the power of the Holy Spirit: "'As the Father has sent me, even so I am sending you.' And when he had said this, he breathed on them and said to them, 'Receive the Holy Spirit.'"[c]

From the missional life of Jesus, we learn five great missional truths for our own life. First, an incarnational missional life is contextual and crosses cultural barriers. Just as Jesus left heaven to enter into culture on the earth, Jesus' people are to do the same and not merely remain in community with people of their own gender,

---

[a] 1 Tim. 2:5 [b] Matt. 11:19 [c] John 20:21–22

race, income level, nationality, and the like.

Despite being contextual, a missional life does not condone or partake in the sinful worldly aspects of a culture, just as Jesus never sinned. Nonetheless, Jesus dressed, spoke, and ate according to Jewish culture, participated in their holidays, and observed their customs, so Jesus' people are also to live as missionaries in whatever culture God has sent them. Thus, in a very real sense, every Christian is a missionary whether they minister across the street or across the globe.

Second, an incarnational missional life is evangelistic. Just as Jesus did not merely come only to do good works for the needy but primarily to save lost people, Jesus' people are likewise to pursue lost people for evangelistic friendships.[a]

Third, an incarnational missional life is humble. Just as Jesus willingly left His state in glory to live a humble life and work a humble job, a missional life is one not lived solely for personal glory and upward mobility but rather values the gospel above all else. Subsequently, an incarnational approach to life often means that we make less money and live simpler lives than we could because we value Gospel ministry above what worldly standards measure as success.

Fourth, an incarnational missional life is one devoted to the church. Jesus came to found, build, and head the church—his metaphorical body to continue his evangelistic plan for the world; therefore, Jesus' people are to give themselves to the church. This includes service and generosity as Jesus demonstrated[b] so that not only can local churches grow, but more churches can be planted, more people reached, and more nations impacted by the Gospel of Jesus Christ.

Fifth, an incarnational missional life is global. While Jesus mainly confined His ministry to Israel, He did minister to a Samaritan woman who then evangelized to her people, and the deaf man of Decapolis.[c] Additionally, the announcement of Jesus' birth by both the angels and Simeon was to be good news for all nations.[d] This is because Jesus came to take away the sins of the world[e] and establish the church as a mission center for the nations[f] from which He would send out believers to be the salt and light of the nations.[g] Jesus also prophesied that most of His worshipers would be from nations other than Israel[h] because His love is for the entire world.[i]

Indeed, the world is our mission field, and Jesus is our model incarnational missionary who went before us and now goes with us as we continue in His work by His Spirit as His church for His glory to our joy.[k]

---

[a] Luke 19:10 [b] 2 Cor. 8–9 [c] Matt. 15:21–28; 8:5–13; Mark 5:1–20, 7:31–37; John 4:1–42 [d] Luke 2:10, 32 [e] John 1:29 [f] Mark 11:17 [g] Matt. 5:13–14 [h] Matt. 21:43; Luke 13:28–29 [i] John 1:9, 29, 3:16–17, 19, 4:42, 6:33, 12:47, 16:8, 17:21 [k] Matt. 28:18-20

DOCTRINE

WHAT IS THE SECRET TO JESUS' SUCCESS?

The life of Jesus Christ, without peer, has left the greatest footprint in world history. When someone's life towers above everyone else, we study them to learn the secret to their success.

In the Old Testament, things such as a divine ladder, a cloud by day and a pillar of fire by night, a tabernacle, and then a temple that housed God's presence closed the distance between the holy God and the unholy people. All of this prefigured the coming of Jesus Christ as the connecting point between God in Heaven and people on earth. 1 Timothy 2:5 describes the fulfillment this way, "There is one God, and there is one mediator between God and men, the man Christ Jesus." In Jesus Christ, God humbled Himself for the special task of reconciling people to Himself.

The holiest person is also the humblest person. The Creator entered the creation, the eternal God stepped into human history, the omnipresent God walked from place to place—all to reveal God and redeem people.

If Jesus did not use His divine attributes to live His life and leave His legacy, how did He do it? Can you access the same life-giving, destiny-altering, God-revealing power for your life?

If we look to the ancient church creeds (doctrines) that are very helpful for many things, there is one thing missing—how Jesus lived His life. Notice how each creed moves from the birth of Jesus to the death of Jesus and omits the entirety of His life. The Apostles' Creed (fourth century AD) says Jesus was "born of the Virgin Mary; suffered under Pontius Pilate, was crucified..." The Nicene Creed (fourth century AD) says Jesus "was incarnate by the Holy Ghost of the Virgin Mary, and was made man, and was crucified also for us under Pontius Pilate..."

What is missing? Jesus' earthly life. If we do not know how Jesus lived His life on earth, how are we supposed to know how to live our life on earth?

Regarding the relationship between Jesus and the Holy Spirit, Martyn Lloyd-Jones says:

"What, then, does all this mean? It means that there was no change in His deity, but that He took human nature to Himself, and chose to live in this world as a man. He humbled Himself in that way. He deliberately put limits upon Himself. Now we cannot go further. We do not know how He did it. We cannot understand it, in a sense. But we believe this: in order that He might live this life as a man, while He was here on earth, He did not exercise certain qualities of His Godhead. That was why...He needed to be given the gift of the Holy Spirit without measure".[40]

Abraham Kuyper writes of the importance of the relationship between Jesus and the Holy Spirit:

This ought to be carefully noticed, especially since the Church has never sufficiently confessed the influence of the Holy Spirit exerted upon the work of Christ. The general impression is that the work of the Holy Spirit begins when the work of the Mediator on earth is finished, as tho [sic] until that time the Holy Spirit celebrated His divine day of rest. Yet the Scripture teaches us again and again that Christ performed His mediatorial work controlled and impelled by the Holy Spirit.[41]

In the book *Spirit-Filled Jesus*, I (Mark) write in detail about the personal relationship between Jesus Christ and the Holy Spirit and how we can live by His power as Jesus did. The empowerment of Jesus by God the Holy Spirit is repeatedly stressed in the Gospel of Luke, which precedes Acts in showing the Spirit-filled life of Christ and then Christians as the two-part history of our faith. Here are a few examples:

1. Jesus was conceived by the Holy Spirit and given the title "Christ," which means anointed by the Holy Spirit.[a]
2. Jesus' relative Elizabeth was "filled with the Holy Spirit" when greeting Jesus' pregnant mother Mary, and her husband Zechariah went on to prophesy in the Spirit that their son John was appointed by God to prepare the way for Jesus.[b]
3. An angel revealed to Mary that she would give birth to Jesus because "the Holy Spirit will come upon you."[c]
4. Once born, Jesus was dedicated to the Lord in the temple according to the demands of the law by Simeon; "the Holy Spirit was upon [Simeon]" and the Holy Spirit had revealed to him that he would not die until seeing Jesus Christ.[d]
5. Simeon was "in the Spirit" when he prophesied about Jesus' ministry to Jews and Gentiles.[e]
6. John prophesied in the Spirit that one day Jesus would baptize people with the Holy Spirit.[f]
7. The Holy Spirit descended upon Jesus at His own baptism.[g] Matthew adds the interesting statement that the Spirit rested on Jesus, as if to suggest that the remainder of His life and ministry on the earth would be done under the anointing and power of the Holy Spirit.[h]
8. Jesus was "full of the Holy Spirit."[i]
9. Jesus was "led by the Spirit."[k]
10. Jesus came "in the power of the Spirit."[m]
11. After reading Isaiah 61:1–2, "The Spirit of the Lord GOD is upon me," Jesus declared, "Today this Scripture has been fulfilled in your hearing."[n]
12. Jesus "rejoiced in the Holy Spirit."[o]

---

[a] Luke 1-2 [b] Luke 1:41-43, 67, 76 [c] Luke 1:35-37 [d] Luke 2:25-27 [e] Luke 2:27-34 [f] Matt. 3:11; Mar. 1:8; Luke 3:16; John 1:34 [g] Matt. 3:16; John 1:32-33 [h] Matt. 3:16 [i] Luke 4:1-2 [k] Luke 4:1-2 [m] Luke 4:14 [n] Luke 4:14-21 [o] Luke 10:21

Gerald Hawthorne, who has written one of the most compelling books on the subject of Jesus' relationship with the Holy Spirit, says, "[Jesus] is the supreme example for them of what is possible in a human life because of his total dependence upon the Spirit of God."[42]

How did Jesus Christ live His life and leave His legacy? By the Spirit.

It is common for Christians to speak about having a personal relationship with Jesus Christ. We absolutely encourage this.

Jesus, however, lived His life by a personal relationship with the Holy Spirit. Our Helper was also Jesus Helper.

As God's person, the Holy Spirit is fully God and the third member of the Trinity.

As God's presence, the Holy Spirit is God with us.

As God's power, the Holy Spirit empowered the life of Jesus Christ and also empowers the life of believers to live by His power.

If Jesus were living your life, what would He be doing and how would He be doing it? By the Spirit. That's the key that unlocks the rest of your life. We don't want you to live your life for Christ. We want Christ to live His life through you!

QUESTIONS FOR PERSONAL JOURNALING AND/OR SMALL GROUP DISCUSSION

1. If there was one miracle or event you could have been present to witness in the life of Jesus Christ on earth, what would it be?
2. Do you consider Jesus to merely be a good man, or actually the only God-man?
3. If you were God, would you have left the glory and pleasure of Heaven to come down to this earth and suffer like Jesus did?
4. Have you ever considered that, in a very real sense, Jesus was adopted by Joseph since they were not biologically related? How does this encourage Christians to be involved in such things as foster care and adoption?
5. If Jesus were walking around on the earth today and said He was God, what do you think the reaction would be?
6. If someone asked you to give your best reason why you believe that Jesus is God, what would your answer be?
7. What is your favorite miracle of Jesus that the Bible records? Why?
8. If Jesus were not truly God and invited people to worship Him and pray to Him, could He actually have been a good man at all? Would that not make Him a con man?
9. Do you more easily connect with the humanity or divinity of Jesus Christ?
10. Do you have a personal relationship with the Holy Spirit? If not, spend some time in prayer today inviting the Holy Spirit to make you more like Jesus.
11. How is Jesus the supreme example of what it means to truly be Spirit-filled?

INCARNATION: GOD COMES

12. What is the one thing that Jesus said or did during his earthly ministry that you find most amazing?
13. What people has God put in your life that you need to talk to about Jesus in hopes that they become Christians?

CHAPTER 8: CROSS

"GOD DIES"

God shows his love for us in that while we were still sinners, Christ died for us.
ROMANS 5:8

What kind of suffering are you experiencing in your life lately? Relationally, is there a conflict with someone you care about, or even a breaking of a relationship you value? Financially, are you struggling to make ends meet? Emotionally, do you find yourself anxious and overwhelmed, grieved and saddened, or angry and hurt? Spiritually, does it feel like you are under attack or that God is distant in this season? Politically, are you beat down by the constant attacks over every issue with no end or hope in sight? Physically, are you battling some injury or ailment or just feeling worn down and tired?

Imagine, for a moment, how wonderful it will be in the eternal Kingdom of Heaven when all your relationships there are reconciled, you have no financial needs, you are fully emotionally healed, God is close continually, politics are over forever as God alone rules and reigns over all, and you are in perfect health once and forever! How amazing will that be? For Christians, the hope of leaving this fallen world that is falling apart to go to a new and perfect forever Home is our great goal.

For Jesus, the opposite is true. While ruling and reigning in Heaven, Jesus was experiencing our dream and left it all to enter our nightmare. Everything we want to get off of us is what Jesus put onto Himself by entering this world. Like a firefighter running into a burning building that everyone else is running out of, Jesus chose to put Himself in harm's way to pull us out of harm's way. He did not have to do this, and in doing it He showed us what love really is.

Not only did Jesus suffer throughout His life, He suffered death in the most painful, shameful, and damnable ways.

CRUCIFIXION

The Bible gives few details about crucifixion. This is likely because the original audience had witnessed them often and knew all too well what it was. However, since few people in the modern era have personally witnessed a crucifixion, it is important for us to examine it in detail so as to fully appreciate the suffering of Jesus Christ.

Imagine a long wooden stake being run through a person's midsection, and that stake then being driven into the ground, with the impaled person left to die slowly over the course of many days. It is believed that this kind of barbarous torture may in fact be the earliest form of crucifixion, occurring as early as the ninth century BC.[1]

In the sixth century BC, the Persians commonly practiced crucifixion, especially King Darius I, who crucified three thousand Babylonians in 518 BC. In 332 BC, Alexander the Great crucified two thousand people whom he conquered in Tyre. The transition from impalement to crucifixion occurred under Alexander, as he was a master of terror and dread. In 71 BC the former gladiator Spartacus and 120,000 prisoners fell in battle to the Romans, which resulted in six thousand men being crucified along the shoulder of the highway for 120 miles.

The Romans perfected crucifixion; they reserved it as the most painful mode of execution for the most despised people, such as slaves, the poor, and Roman citizens guilty of the worst high treason. The crucifixion methods varied with the sadism of the soldiers. They tried to outdo one another and experimented with various forms of torture. They grew and learned in ways to prolong the pain and agony.

The Romans are believed to be the first to crucify on an actual cross. The Tau was a capital T cross and the Latin was a lowercase t cross. Both had the stipe (the vertical post) and patibulum (the crossbar). The stipe was probably permanent while each man carried his own patibulum.

As a young boy, Jesus may have viewed crucifixions in Judea, because there was a Jewish uprising against the Romans that resulted in a mass crucifixion of about two thousand Jews in AD 4 at the time of the death of Herod.

The pain of crucifixion is so horrendous that a word was invented to explain it—excruciating—which literally means "from the cross." The victim was affixed to the cross with either ropes or nails. The pain of crucifixion is due in part to the fact that it is a prolonged and agonizing death by asphyxiation. Crucified people could hang on the cross for anywhere from three to four hours or for as long as nine days, passing in and out of consciousness as their lungs struggled to breathe while laboring under the weight of their body.

In an effort to end the torment, it was not uncommon for those being crucified to slump on the cross to empty their lungs of air and thereby hasten their death. Further, there are debated archaeological reports that suggest sometimes seats were placed underneath the buttocks of those being crucified to prevent slumping, thereby ensuring a lengthy and most painful death.

None of this was done in dignified privacy, but rather in open, public places. It would be like nailing a bloodied, naked man above the front entrance to your local mall. Crowds would gather around the victims to mock them as they sweated in the sun, bled, and became incontinent from the pain.

Once dead, some victims were not given a decent burial but rather left on the cross for vultures to pick apart from above while dogs chewed on the bones that fell to the ground, even occasionally taking a hand or foot home as a chew toy, according to ancient reports.[2] Whatever remained of the victim would eventually be thrown in the garbage and taken to the dump unless the family buried it. Furthermore, the wooden crosses and nails were considered more valuable than the bodies of the deceased, and those resources were kept and reused.

As a general rule, it was men who were crucified. Occasionally a man was crucified at eye level so that passersby could look him directly in the eye as he died and cuss him out and spit on him in mockery. In the rare event of a woman's crucifixion, she was made to face the cross. Not even such a barbarous culture was willing to watch the face of a woman in such excruciating agony.

The ancient Jewish historian Josephus called crucifixion "the most wretched of deaths."[3] The ancient Roman philosopher Cicero asked that decent Roman citizens not even speak of the cross because it was too disgraceful a subject for the ears of decent people.[4] The Jews also considered crucifixion the most horrific mode of death, as Deuteronomy 21:22–23 says: "If a man has committed a crime punishable by death and he is put to death, and you hang him on a tree, his body shall not remain all night on the tree, but you shall bury him the same day, for a hanged man is cursed by God."

The Roman emperor Nero was so cruel to Christians that he had some of them crucified. Their number included Peter, who, it is said, was crucified upside down at his own request because he did not feel worthy of dying exactly as Jesus did. Roman crucifixion continued until Emperor Constantine reportedly saw the vision of a cross and the next day won a historic battle and overtook the Western Roman Empire. Following his victory, Christianity was no longer outlawed but instead became a state-sponsored religion. Historians have debated whether he experienced a true conversion or simply practiced political expediency. Either way, he abolished crucifixion around AD 300.

In light of all this, perhaps most peculiar is the fact that the symbol for Jesus, which has become the most famous symbol in all of history, is the cross. The church father Tertullian (155–230 AD) tells us of the early practice of believers' making the sign of the cross over their bodies with their hand and adorning their necks and homes with crosses to celebrate the brutal death of Jesus. In so doing, the early Christians turned a symbol of terror and intimidation into a symbol of salvation and hope.

HOW CAN JESUS' CRUCIFIXION BE GOOD NEWS?

When someone tells us that they have good news to share, we expect them to tell us that they got married, are pregnant, earned a promotion at work, or got a clean bill of health from a doctor after a medical scare. Perhaps the last thing we'd expect to hear in the context of good news is to hear that someone who loved us was murdered. Among the scandals of the cross is the fact that Christians have called it their gospel, or good news, and celebrate it every year on Good Friday. To understand the good news of Jesus' death we must first examine how he died. Then we can examine why he died.

In the days leading up to his death, Jesus was a young man in his early thirties. He was in good health due to his job as a craftsmen and his constant walking of many miles as an itinerant minister. Jesus began speaking openly of his impending death, including at the Passover meal he ate with his friends as the Last Supper. There, he broke with fifteen centuries of protocol. In so doing, he showed that the Passover meal, which God's people had been eating annually, found its ultimate fulfillment in him. The Passover memorialized the night in Egypt when in faith God's people covered the doorposts of their home with blood so that death would not come to the firstborn son in their home but would rather pass them over.[a] Jesus, the firstborn Son of God, likewise had come to die and cover us with his blood so that God's just wrath would literally pass over us sinners as the essence of the new covenant.[b]

During the Last Supper, Satan entered one of Jesus' disciples, Judas, who had been stealing money from Jesus' ministry fund for some time and had agreed to hand him over to the authorities to be crucified. After Judas left the meal to lead the soldiers to Jesus, Jesus went to the garden of Gethsemane, where he spent a sleepless night in the agony of prayer. Meanwhile, his disciples failed to intercede for him in prayer and instead kept falling asleep. At this point, Jesus was fully aware of his impending crucifixion and was so distressed that, as the Bible records, he sweat drops of blood, a physical condition that doctors report is rare because it requires an elevated level of stress that few people ever experience.

After an exhausting, sleepless night of distress, Judas arrived with the soldiers and betrayed Jesus with a kiss. Jesus was then arrested. He was forced to walk through a series of false trials where contradicting false witnesses were brought forward to offer false testimony. Despite the absence of any evidence supporting the false charges, Jesus was sentenced to be murdered. He was eventually blindfolded as a mob of cowardly men beat him mercilessly. He was then stripped in great shame, and the Bible simply says that they had him scourged.

---

[a] Exodus 6-12 [b] Luke 22:19-21

CROSS: GOD DIES

Scourging itself was such a painful event that many people died from it without even making it to their cross. Jesus' hands would have been chained above his head to expose his back and legs to an executioner's whip called a cat-o'-nine tails or a flagrum. Two men, one on each side, took turns whipping the victim. The whip was a series of long leather straps. At the end of some of the straps were heavy balls of metal intended to tenderize the body of a victim, like a chef tenderizes a steak by beating it. Some of the straps had hooks made of glass, metal, or bone that would have sunk deeply into the shoulders, back, buttocks, and legs of the victim. Once the hooks had lodged into the tenderized flesh, the executioner would rip the skin, muscle, tendons, and even bones off the victim. The victim's skin and muscles would hang off the body like ribbons as the hooks dissected the skin to the nerve layers. The damage could go so deep that even the lungs were bruised, which made breathing difficult. Some doctors have compared the damage of flogging to the results of a shotgun blast.[5] The victim would bleed profusely and would often go into shock, due to severe blood loss and insufficient blood flow near and through the heart.

Jesus' bare back and shoulders, though bloodied and traumatized, were then forced to carry his roughly hewn wooden cross to his place of crucifixion. If Jesus carried the entire cross, it would have weighed a few hundred pounds, and many think it is more likely he carried just the crossbar (patibulum), which would have been about one hundred pounds.

Despite his young age and good health, Jesus was so physically devastated from his sleepless night, miles of walking, severe beating, and scourging that he collapsed under the weight of the cross, unable to carry it alone. Doctors have said that the trauma from the heavy crossbar crushing his chest into the ground could have caused a bruised heart, similar to the chest trauma caused by a car accident without a seatbelt where the driver is violently thrown against the steering wheel.[a] Understandably unable to continue carrying his cross on the roughly one-mile journey to his execution, a man named Simon of Cyrene was appointed to carry Jesus' cross. Upon arriving at his place of crucifixion, they pulled Jesus' beard out—an act of ultimate disrespect in ancient cultures—spat on him, and mocked him in front of his family and friends.

Jesus the carpenter, who had driven many nails into wood with his own hands, then had five-to seven-inch rough metal spikes driven into the most sensitive nerve centers on the human body, through his hands and feet. Jesus was nailed to his wooden cross. His body would have twitched involuntarily, writhing in agony.

In further mockery, a sign was posted above Jesus that said, "Jesus of Nazareth, the King of the Jews."[b] A painting later discovered from a second-century Roman graffito further shows the disrespect of Jesus at his crucifixion. The painting depicts the head of a jackass being crucified, with a man standing

---

[a] Ibid. [b] John 19:19

alongside it with his arms raised. The caption reads, "Alexamenos worships his god."

At this point during a crucifixion, the victims labored to breathe as their bodies went into shock. Naked and embarrassed, the victims would often use their remaining strength to seek revenge on the crowd of mockers who had gathered to jeer them. They would curse at their tormentors while urinating and spitting on them. Some victims would become so overwhelmed with pain that they would become incontinent and a pool of sweat, blood, urine, and feces would gather at the base of their cross.

Jesus' crucifixion was a hideously grotesque scene. Hundreds of years in advance, the prophet Isaiah saw it this way:

He was despised and rejected by men; a man of sorrows, and acquainted with grief; and as one from whom men hide their faces he was despised, and we esteemed him not. Surely he has borne our griefs and carried our sorrows; yet we esteemed him stricken, smitten by God, and afflicted.[a]

Crucifixion usually kills by asphyxiation in addition to other factors—the heart is deeply stressed, the body is traumatized, the muscles are devastated, and the blood loss is severe. Doctors have thought that Jesus likely had a chest contusion and possibly a bruised heart from falling with the cross on top of him, which caused an aneurysm.[6] Subsequently, Jesus' heart would have been unable to pump enough blood and his lungs would have filled up with carbon monoxide. Jesus not only lived through all of this, but he even spoke lucidly and clearly with enough volume to be heard by those present.

From the cross he announced forgiveness for those who crucified him, assured the criminal crucified next to him that they would be together in paradise, commended his mother to John, cried of forsakenness showing his spiritual death and separation from the Father, and expressed his agonized thirst.[7]

At last Jesus said in a loud voice of triumph, "It is finished."[b] At this moment, the atonement for sin was made and the holiness, righteousness, justice, and wrath of the triune God were satisfied in the crucifixion of Jesus Christ.

Jesus then said, "Father, into your hands I commit my spirit!"[c] Jesus reserved his final breath from the cross to shout his triumphant victory to the world by confirming that he had been restored to God the Father after atoning for human sin.

The Bible then simply records that Jesus breathed his last and died.

Jesus hung on the cross for at least six hours—from the third hour to the ninth hour, when the darkness ended.[d] How long thereafter that he breathed his last and died is not clear in Scripture. What is more clear is the fact that if a victim remained alive on the cross for too long so that it interfered with another event like a major holiday, it was customary to break the victim's legs, disabling him from

---

[a] Isa. 53:3-4 [b] John 19:30 [c] Luke 23:46 [d] Mark 15:25,33

CROSS: GOD DIES

pushing himself up on his cross to fill his lungs with air and thereby prolong his life. However, in accordance with the promise of Scripture, Jesus died quickly enough that his legs were not broken.[a]

Furthermore, to ensure Jesus was dead, a professional executioner ran a spear through his side, which punctured his heart sac, and water and blood flowed from his side. This is further evidence that Jesus died of a heart attack; the sac around the heart filled with water until the pressure caused Jesus' heart to stop beating. Thus, Jesus possibly died with both a literal and metaphorical broken heart.

For many years, the most sacred place on earth had been the temple, where the presence of God dwelled behind a thick curtain. Only one person each year, the high priest, was allowed to pass by that curtain and enter the presence of God on one day, the Day of Atonement. At the death of Jesus, however, the temple curtain was torn from top to bottom, signifying that God had opened his presence to the world through the cross of Jesus.

The most succinct summary of the gospel in Scripture provides insight into this theological meaning: "that Christ died for our sins in accordance with the Scriptures, that he was buried, that he was raised on the third day in accordance with the Scriptures."[b] In this packed section of Scripture, Paul appoints the death, burial, and resurrection of Jesus as the most important event in all of history and the verification of the truthfulness of all Scripture.

He then explains why this is good news with the simple word "for," showing that Jesus died "for our sins." The word "for" can mean either "for the benefit of" or "because of." Jesus did not die "for the benefit of" our sins. He did not help them at all! Rather, he died "because of" our sins. So it was our sins but his death. From the beginning of sacred Scripture[c] to the end[d], the penalty for sin is death. Therefore, if we sin, we should die. But it is Jesus, the sinless one, who dies in our place "for our sins." The good news of the gospel is that Jesus died to take to himself the penalty for our sin. In theological terms, this means that Jesus' death was substitutionary, or vicarious, and in our place solely for our benefit and without benefit for himself. Therefore, we find the cross of Jesus to be the crux of good news because it was there that Jesus atoned for our sin according to the promises of Scripture.

Jesus' work for us on the cross is called atonement (at-one-ment); Jesus our God became a man to restore a relationship between God and humanity. The concept of Jesus' dying in our place to pay our penalty for our sins has been expressed in theological shorthand as penal substitution. Scripture repeatedly and clearly declares that Jesus died as our substitute paying our penalty "for" our sins.[e]

One theologian has called the cross the great jewel of the Christian faith, and like every great jewel it has many precious facets that are each worthy of

---

[a] Ps. 34:20; John 19:36 [b] 1 Cor. 15:3b-4 [c] Gen. 2:17 [d] Rev. 21:8 [e] Isa. 53:5, 12; Rom. 4:25; 5:8; Gal. 3:13; 1 Pet. 3:18; 1 John 2:2

examining for their brilliance and beauty.[8]

Therefore, you will be well served to see each side of this jewel shining together for the glory of God in complementary, not contradictory, fashion. Most poor teaching about the cross results from someone denying, ignoring, or overemphasizing one of these facets at the expense of the others, often due to an overreaction to someone else's overreaction.

Many of these facets were foreshadowed in the Old Testament, specifically by the annual celebration of the Day of Atonement (Yom Kippur) according to the regulations of the book of Leviticus. The Day of Atonement was the most important day of the year and was often referred to simply as "the day." It was intended to deal with the sin problem between humanity and God. Of the many prophetic elements on this special day, one stands out. On that day, two healthy goats without defect were chosen; they were therefore fit to represent sinless perfection.

The first goat was a propitiating sin offering. The high priest slaughtered this innocent goat, which acted as a substitute for the sinners who rightly deserved a violently bloody death for their many sins. He then sprinkled some of its blood on the mercy seat on top of the Ark of the Covenant inside the Most Holy Place. The goat was no longer innocent when it took the guilt of sin; it was a sin offering for the people.[a] Subsequently, its blood represented life given as payment for sin. The dwelling place of God was thus cleansed of the defilement that resulted from all of the transgressions and sins of the people of Israel, and God's just and holy wrath was satisfied.

Then the high priest, acting as the representative and mediator between the sinful people and their holy God, would take the second goat and lay his hands on the animal while confessing the sins of the people. This goat, called the scapegoat, would then be sent away to run free into the wilderness away from the sinners, symbolically expiating our sins by taking them away.

These great images of the priest, slaughter, and scapegoat are all given by God to help us more fully comprehend Jesus' work for us on the cross, which we will now examine in depth.

HOW DOES GOD SATISFY HIMSELF THROUGH THE CROSS?

New-covenant Sacrifice

Today, most people don't raise or butcher the animals they eat. We pay someone else to do those things and buy our groceries at the store. We don't like to see blood or death, and when we do many people feel nauseous. In the ancient world, and in many places on the earth today, people lived on farms where they ate the crops they grew and animals they raised for food. As a result, they were a lot more familiar with blood and death.

---

[a] Lev. 16:15

One scholar says that blood is mentioned some 362 times in the Old Testament and some ninety-two times in the New Testament and even more often than the cross or death of Jesus; thus, it is the most common means by which the Scriptures refer to the death of Jesus.

Throughout Scripture, blood is inextricably connected with sin for two primary reasons. First, shed blood reminds us that sin results in death. Second, God is sickened by sin, which causes death, a connection first made in Genesis 2:17 and repeated throughout the Bible. So, when God sees blood, it points to the sickening reality of sin and death. Leviticus 17:11 says it this way: "For the life of the flesh is in the blood, and I have given it for you on the altar to make atonement for your souls, for it is the blood that makes atonement by the life." Blood is sacred, epitomizing the life of the sacrificial victim given as substitute for the sinner's death. Practically every sacrifice included the sprinkling or smearing of blood on an altar, thus teaching that atonement involves the substitution of life for life.

The Old Testament often used the theme of blood to prepare people for the coming of Jesus to die for our sins. In fact, it was God who shed the first blood in human history in response to sin. In Genesis 3 when our first parents, Adam and Eve, committed the original human sin, it was God who slaughtered an animal to make clothes to cover their nakedness. From then on, blood sacrifices were the standard way to worship God.[a]

One of the bloodiest books of the Bible is Exodus. The people were given two choices. (1) They could repent of sin and place their faith in God, demonstrated by slaughtering an animal and covering the doorposts of their home in blood. If this was done, then God promised to pass over (hence the related feast of Passover) their house and not kill the firstborn son in the home but rather accept the substitution of the life of the sacrificial animal. (2) They could fail to repent of their sin and not place their faith in God and see death come to their home. On that night in Egypt, much blood was shed and death came to every home as either the blood of a substitute animal was shed for the sinners, or the firstborn son in each home was put to death by God.

One of the major functions of the Old Testament temple was the slaughtering of animals, as seen by the stream of blood that often flowed out of the temple. Blood is in fact a major aspect of Old Testament religion. There were some eleven different sacrifices that fit into one of four groupings (burnt, peace, sin, or guilt) and sacrifices were made both in the morning and evening, all of which involved blood.

Despite all of this bloodshed, the Old Testament sacrificial system was never meant to be something sufficient in itself. When Israel misunderstood the purpose of the sacrifices, putting their faith in the sacrifices themselves, there were major problems. The first problem was that the bloodshed of a substituted animal did

---

[a] Gen. 8:20; 12:7–8; 13:4, 8; Job 1:5; 42:7–9

DOCTRINE

not forgive human sin.ᵃ The second problem was that it enabled hypocrisy; people could undergo external rituals such as offering a sacrifice without having truly repented of sin and trusted in God internally.ᵇ The third problem was that it was only preparatory, prophesying the death of God's promised Messiah, and therefore incomplete until the coming of Jesus, who made the better new covenant possible.ᶜ

This theme of blood, like every theme of Scripture, finds its fulfillment in the coming of Jesus Christ into human history. Early in Jesus' life, his cousin John saw Jesus coming and declared, "Behold, the Lamb of God, who takes away the sin of the world!"ᵈ This, of course, would be accomplished when Jesus was slaughtered on the cross where his blood flowed freely.

The results of Jesus' shed blood are staggering. Hebrews 9:22 says, "Indeed, under the law almost everything is purified with blood, and without the shedding of blood there is no forgiveness of sins." Also 1 Peter 1:18–19 says, "You were ransomed from the futile ways inherited from your forefathers, not with perishable things such as silver or gold, but with the precious blood of Christ, like that of a lamb without blemish or spot."

In the Bible the word covenant appears more than three hundred times and is therefore essential to our rightly understanding how God relates to us. Both the Old and New Testaments speak of the new covenant.ᵉ The Bible tells us that a new epoch in human history has arrived with the coming of God into human history as the man Jesus Christ. In the new covenant, all of the prophecies, promises, foreshadowing, and longing of the old covenant are fulfilled. In the new covenant it is Jesus Christ who serves as our covenant head.ᶠ Jesus went to the cross to shed his blood in our place for our sins so that we can have a new covenant relationship with him.

Today, in the new covenant, we no longer need a priest because we have Jesus, who is our Great High Priest.ᵍ We no longer need to offer blood sacrifices because Jesus is our sacrifice for sin.ʰ We no longer need to visit the temple to be near to God because Jesus is our temple.ⁱ We no longer need to celebrate the Passover because Jesus is our passover.ᵏ Finally, we no longer need to live in habitual sin because through Jesus we have been made holy and have been given new life.ᵐ

Propitiation

In our day of camera phones and the Internet, we get to see more evil, and injustice, than any other generation that has lived on the earth. When something

---

ᵃ Ps. 51:16; Mic. 6:6–8; Heb. 10:4 ᵇ 1 Sam. 15:22; Prov. 15:8; Hos. 6:6 ᶜ Heb. 7:22; 8:5-7,13 ᵈ John 1:29 ᵉ E.g., Jer. 31:31–34; Matt. 26:28; Luke 22:20; Rom. 11:27; 1 Cor. 11:25; 2 Cor. 3:6; Heb. 7:22; 8:8–13; 9:15; 12:24 ᶠ Eph. 1:10, 22; 4:15; 5:23; Col. 1:18; 2:10, 19 ᵍ Heb. 2:17; 4:14-15 ʰ John 1:29 ⁱ Rev. 21:22 ᵏ 1 Cor. 5:7 ᵐ Heb. 9:26; 10:10

CROSS: GOD DIES

is posted showing the clear abuse of another human being, the immediate global response is anger that demands justice. Because we were made by God with a conscience, when God's eternal laws that rule over us all, we cry out for justice appealing to a fixed standard of right and wrong whether we know God or not.

When is the last time that you felt this kind of moral outrage at evil? What category of evil most quickly makes you angry and want justice?

The more we know what is going on in this world, the angrier and more frustrated we become. Imagine, for a moment, what it must be like to be God? Every moment of every day God sees, hears, knows, and feels all of the evil and injustice occurring constantly across our entire planet. God getting angry at evil is not a bad thing; in fact God gets angry at evil precisely because He is good.

The Bible is filled with examples of God getting angry at sinners and of His anger as hostile, burning, and furious.[a] Because God is holy, good, and just, He not only feels angry about sin but also deals with it in ways that are holy, good, and just. Because God is perfect, his anger is perfect and as such is aroused slowly[b], sometimes turned away[c], often delayed[d], and frequently held back.[e]

God's anger is not limited to the Old Testament. Even Jesus got angry, furious, and enraged.[f] Also, Revelation 19 reveals Jesus coming again as a warrior riding on a white horse to slaughter evildoers until their blood runs through the streets like a river.

Furthermore, God feels angry because God hates sin.[g] Sadly, it is commonly said among Christians that "God hates the sin but loves the sinner." This comes not from divinely inspired Scripture but instead from the Hindu Gandhi who coined the phrase "Love the sinner but hate the sin" in his 1929 autobiography.

The Bible clearly says that God both loves and hates some sinners.[h] People commonly protest that God cannot hate anyone because he is love. But the Bible speaks of God's anger, wrath, and fury more than his love, grace, and mercy. Furthermore, our God is the one who loves the sinner enough to die for them while they were still enemies John 3:16; Romans 5:10-11) and the one whose anger abides on those who reject His sacrificed Son (John 3:36).

Additionally, God's anger at sin and hatred of sinners causes him to pour out His wrath on unrepentant sinners. This doctrine is not as popular among professing Christians in our day as it was in past times, but the fact remains that in the Old Testament alone nearly twenty words are used for God's wrath, which is spoken of roughly six hundred times. The wrath of God also appears roughly twenty-five times in the New Testament.[i]

God's wrath is both active and passive. When people think of God's wrath, they generally think of God's active wrath, where people are swiftly punished for their sin with something like a lightning bolt from heaven. God can and does enact

---

[a] Lev. 26:27-30; Num. 11:1; Deut. 29:24 [b] Ex. 34:6-8 [c] Deut. 13:17 [d] Isa. 48:9 [e] Ps. 78:38 [f] Mark 3:5 [g] Prov. 6:16-19; Zech. 8:17 [h] Ps. 5:5; 11:4-5; Hos. 9:15; Rom. 9:13 cf. Mal. 1:2-3 [i] John 3:36; Eph. 5:6; Col. 3;6; 1 Thess. 1:9-10

his active wrath upon occasion.[a] Still, He seems to also frequently work through His subtler passive wrath. Passive wrath occurs when God simply hands us over to our evil desires and allows us to do whatever we want.[b]

The truth is that everyone but the sinless Jesus merits the active wrath of God. None of us deserves love, grace, or mercy from God. Demons and sinful people who fail to repent will have God's wrath burning against them forever.[c] The place of God's unending active wrath is hell.

However, God's active wrath is diverted from some people because of the mercy of God. This is made possible because on the cross Jesus substituted himself in our place for our sins and appeased God's righteous wrath. Two sections of Scripture in particular speak to this matter pointedly:

1. Since, therefore, we have now been justified by his blood, much more shall we be saved by him [Jesus] from the wrath of God.[d]
2. You turned to God from idols to serve the living and true God, and to wait for his Son from heaven, whom he raised from the dead, Jesus who delivers us from the wrath to come.[e]

Scripture also has a single word to designate how Jesus diverts the active wrath of our rightfully angry God from us so that we are loved and not hated. That word is propitiation, which summarizes more than six hundred related words and events that explain it. The American Heritage Dictionary defines propitiation as something that appeases or conciliates an offended power, especially a sacrificial offering to a god. Propitiate is the only English word that carries the idea of pacifying wrath by taking care of the penalty for the offense that caused the wrath.

Because so many Christians are not familiar with this word, various Bible translations use different words in an effort to capture its meaning. For example, the New International and New Revised translations use "sacrifice of atonement," and the New Living Translation uses "sacrifice for sin" in such places as Romans 3:23–25, Hebrews 2:17, 1 John 2:2, and 1 John 4:10. But this obscures the appeasing of wrath facet of the original *hilaskomai* word group.

The Revised Standard Version and The New English Bible deny appeasing of wrath by using "expiation" instead of "propitiation." These latter two translations change the entire meaning of the verse, because propitiation deals with the penalty for sin whereas expiation deals with the cleansing from sin. The English Standard Version, New American Standard, Christian Standard Bible are translations which have retained "propitiation". This term includes the other facets of meaning of *hilaskomai*: mercy seat, the place where atonement was made and God revealed, and expiation, the removal of sin. There are four primary occurrences of the word propitiation in the New Testament:

---

[a] Gen. 38; 1 Cor. 11:28-29 [b] Rom. 1:18,24,26 [c] Deut. 32:21022; John 3:36; Eph. 5:6; 2 Pet. 2:4; Rev. 14:9-11 [d] Rom. 5:9 [e] 1 Thess. 1:9-10

CROSS: GOD DIES

1. For all have sinned and fall short of the glory of God, and are justified by his grace as a gift, through the redemption that is in Christ Jesus, whom God put forward as a propitiation by his blood, to be received by faith. This was to show God's righteousness.[a]
2. Therefore he [Jesus] had to be made like his brothers in every respect, so that he might become a merciful and faithful high priest in the service of God, to make propitiation for the sins of the people.[b]
3. He is the propitiation for our sins, and not for ours only but also for the sins of the whole world.[c]
4. In this is love, not that we have loved God but that he loved us and sent his Son to be the propitiation for our sins.[d]

These magnificent passages teach us that the Father and the Son partnered together, both agonizing, to perform the substitutionary sacrifice to appease the wrath of the Father and the Son. Revelation 6:15-16 says:

Then the kings of the earth and the great ones and the generals and the rich and the powerful, and everyone, slave[a] and free, hid themselves in the caves and among the rocks of the mountains, calling to the mountains and rocks, "Fall on us and hide us from the face of him who is seated on the throne, and from the wrath of the Lamb."

Furthermore, God's wrath will remain on those who reject this propitiatory offering. John 3:36, says, "Whoever believes in the Son has eternal life; whoever does not obey the Son shall not see life, but the wrath of God remains on him." Romans 5:9 says, "Since, therefore, we have now been justified by his blood, much more shall we be saved by him from the wrath of God." And, Ephesians 5:6 says, "Let no one deceive you with empty words, for because of these things the wrath of God comes upon the sons of disobedience."

At the cross, justice and mercy kiss; Jesus substituted himself for sinners and suffered and died in their place to forgive them, love them, and embrace them, not in spite of their sins, but because their sins were propitiated and diverted from them to Jesus. Jesus did this not by demanding our blood but rather by giving his own.

Justification

When something wrong is done to us, be it illegal or immoral, the conscience God placed within us cries out for justice. If someone stole our car, we want the police to find it so we can have it back. If someone breaks into our home and steals our belongings, we want the insurance company to compensate us. If someone tells some awful lies about us on social media, we want them to delete what they have said. However, when we are the villain and not the victim, the person who did wrong rather than the person wronged, we tend to want grace for

---

[a] Rom. 3:23-25 [b] Heb. 2:17 [c] 1 John 2:2 [d] 1 John 4:10

DOCTRINE

ourselves instead of justice. The same is true of how many people relate to God. We want God to give justice to our enemies, but grace to us even though we have acted as His enemies. Through the cross of Jesus Christ, God made a way for Him to receive justice and us to receive grace.

Like us, God deserves justice. Because of our sinful condition and ensuing sinful actions, though, our impending day in God's proverbial courtroom seems utterly hopeless for anything other than a guilty verdict and a sentence to eternity in the torments of hell. In light of our obvious guilt, if God were to declare us anything but guilty, he would cease to be a just and good God. God himself says that he "will not acquit the wicked."[a]

Guilty sinners would likely prefer that God simply overlook their offenses against him. To do so, however, would by definition render God unjust, unholy, and unrighteous, which is impossible because he is always just, holy, and righteous.

Clearly, God does not owe us anything. If we were to spend forever in the torments of hell as guilty and condemned sinners, we would have simply gotten what we deserved. Pondering this same point, Job asks, "But how can a man be in the right before God?"[b]

Thankfully, God is merciful, gracious, slow to anger, loving, faithful, and willing to forgive.[c] Thus, the dilemma is this: how could God justify us and remain just?

The answer is the doctrine of justification: guilty sinners can be declared righteous before God, that is forgiven of sin before God and accepted as His children by by grace alone through faith alone because of the person and work of Jesus Christ alone. Justification is mentioned more than two hundred times in various ways throughout the New Testament alone.

The penalty of sin is death. God warned Adam in the garden that "in the day that you eat of it you shall surely die."[d] Paul confirms this: "they know God's decree that those who practice such things deserve to die."[e] The amazing truth is that God himself, the second person of the Trinity, paid our debt of death in our place.

Additionally, not only did Jesus take all our sins (past, present, and future) on the cross, but he also gave to us his perfect righteousness as a faultless and sinless person.[f] This is why Paul says that Jesus alone is our righteousness.[g] Therefore, justification through the work of Jesus Christ in our place for our sins on the cross is only possible by grace from Jesus Christ alone, through faith in Jesus Christ alone, because of Jesus Christ alone.

There is absolutely nothing we can do to contribute to our justification. When Jesus said, "It is finished" on the cross, he was declaring that all that needed to be done for our justification was completed in him. For this reason, Titus 3:7 speaks of "being justified by his grace." Furthermore, Romans 5:16–17 says:

---

[a] Ex. 23:7 [b] Job 9:2 [c] Ex. 34:6-7 [d] Gen. 2:17 [e] Rom. 1:32 [f] 2 Cor. 5:21 [g] 1 Cor. 1:30

CROSS: GOD DIES

The free gift is not like the result of that one man's [Adam's] sin. For the judgment following one trespass brought condemnation, but the free gift following many trespasses brought justification. For if, because of one man's trespass, death reigned through that one man, much more will those who receive the abundance of grace and the free gift of righteousness reign in life through the one man Jesus Christ.

To be justified means to trust only in the person and work of Jesus and no one and nothing else as the object of our faith, righteousness, and justification before God.[a]

Gift Righteousness

On the day I was working on this chapter, I went in to get my haircut. The barber started talking a lot about the girlfriend he lives with, all the marijuana they smoke and alcohol they drink, and other nefarious hobbies. About halfway into my haircut, he asked what I did for a job.

Whenever this happens, there is an awkward silence as I know that my answer will be the equivalent of throwing a cold glass of water on the face of a person taking a nap. So, I took a deep breath and said, "I am a Christian pastor."

His countenance suddenly changed, it was obvious he felt bad for all the bad behavior he was bragging about, and he changed the conversation to tell me about all the good things he had done in his life. Like a defense attorney for his own life, he presented the case for his goodness while I just sat there quietly getting my hair cut. His closing statement was, "I believe in God and I try to live a good life as a good person."

He is not alone. We all want to be perceived as good people.

Why?

Because we were created for righteousness, people continue to yearn for righteousness. However, we sinfully pursue it through self-righteousness.[b] Self-righteousness exists in both irreligious and religious forms.

Irreligious self-righteousness includes the attempts to justify one's decency through everything from social causes to political involvement and being a good steward of the planet. Religious self-righteousness is the pursuit of personal righteousness through our own attempts to live by God's laws in addition to our own rules.

Regarding such vain attempts at self-righteousness, Jesus said, "Unless your righteousness exceeds that of the scribes and Pharisees, you will never enter the kingdom of heaven."[c] No one has been more religiously devoted than the Pharisees who, for example, actually tithed out of their spice rack in an effort to be certain that they gave God a tenth of literally all they had. Still, our attempts at self-righteousness are simply repugnant to God.[d]

---

[a] Acts 13:38; Rom. 4:3-5; 5:1 [b] Rom. 10:3 [c] Matt. 5:20 [d] Isa. 64:6

On the cross what Martin Luther liked to call the "great exchange" occurred. Jesus took our sin and gave us his righteousness. Second Corinthians 5:21 says, "For our sake he [God] made him [Jesus] to be sin who knew no sin, so that in him we might become the righteousness of God." Unlike the self-righteousness of religion, gift righteousness is not something we bring to God to impress him, but rather something that God does in us and we receive as a gift by personal faith in him alone. It gives us a new identity as child of God, a new nature through new birth, a new power which is the indwelling Holy Spirit of God, and a new community, the church. The goal and final outcome of his working will be the full Christ like righteousness of the people of God individually and as a Spirit unified community.

The greatest things we have in life tend not to be things earned by us, but instead gifts given to us. Examples would include the love of a spouse or friend, or birth of a child or grandchild.

The gifted righteousness of Jesus is imparted to us at the time of faith, simultaneous with our justification. Not only does God give us family status, but he also gives us new power and a new heart through the indwelling Holy Spirit. This is what theologians call regeneration. Therefore, we not only have a new status of family member by virtue of being justified, but we also have a new heart from which new desires for holiness flow and a new power through God the Holy Spirit to live like, for, and with Jesus.

Finally, in saying that righteousness comes from Jesus alone and by virtue of none of our good works, we are not advocating a kind of lawless Christianity where we are permitted to live in unrepentant and ongoing sin, unconcerned about whether we are living righteously. Rather, we are saying that only by understanding the righteousness of Jesus Christ in us can we live holy lives out of his righteousness as our new status as Christians.

Ransom

For most people, the worst thing each month is sitting down to pay all the bills. To see in total all the debt we have accrued is, frankly, discouraging. Compounded interest, late fees, and other financial penalties feel like an ongoing avalanche that we are constantly shoveling out from under. Even if we try our best to keep it, it seems like there is always something we missed that damages our all-important credit score which is altogether frustrating.

Most people are well aware of their financial debt to lenders. What most people are not nearly as aware of is their financial debt to the Lord.

God made us to love, honor, and obey him in thought, word, and deed. Every time we fail to do that perfectly, we accrue a debt to God. Every person has sinned against God, and hell is the eternal prison for spiritual debtors who have stolen from God by living sinful lives. Like all debtors, we need a plan if we hope to pay this debt off.

First, we need a mediator to stand between us and God to establish our total debt and come up with a resolution that God the Father, to whom we are indebted, will find acceptable. The Bible repeatedly speaks of Jesus as our only mediator: "For there is one God, and there is one mediator between God and men, the man Christ Jesus."[a] Our spiritual debt is to God, and there is only one possible mediator between God and us to work out the dangerous mess we are in.

Second, we need a redeemer willing to intercede for us and pay our debt to God the Father. A redeemer is a person who pays the debt of someone else. Paul speaks of "our great God and Savior Jesus Christ, who gave himself for us to redeem us from all lawlessness and to purify for himself a people for his own possession who are zealous for good works."[b] He also says that "Christ redeemed us from the curse of the law by becoming a curse for us—for it is written, 'Cursed is everyone who is hanged on a tree [Deut. 21:23].'"[c] Because our sins are against God, only God can forgive our debt of sin. Jesus is God who paid our debt on the cross in order to forgive our sin.[d]

Third, we need a ransom, which is a repayment sufficient enough to erase our debt to God the Father. The problem, though, is that our sins are against a completely holy and perfect God and therefore require a perfect payment. Since all human beings are sinful, we cannot be a ransom for another. There is no way that any other sinful human can ever repay God for our spiritual debt. Psalm 49:7-8 says it this way: "Truly no man can ransom another, or give to God the price of his life, for the ransom of their life is costly and can never suffice." Referring to himself in Mark 10:45, Jesus said, "For even the Son of Man came not to be served but to serve, and to give his life as a ransom for many." Paul also speaks of "the man Christ Jesus, who gave himself as a ransom."[e]

Consider, for a moment, how happy you would be if someone paid off all of your past and current debts in full with no cost to you? Additionally, imagine how much happier you would be if they also said that they would also pay off any debts you were to have in the future no matter what! Spiritually speaking, this is precisely what happened when Jesus Christ died on the cross to pay your past, present, and future debt to God in full!

HOW DOES GOD REDEEM US THROUGH THE CROSS?

Redemption

My wife Grace and I really enjoy watching suspenseful action movies. Our favorites are the ones where the bad guys capture some defenseless folks, holding them captive until some good guys show up to shoot the bad guys and set the captives free. The leader of the good guys is always the fearless and selfless hero and the storyline for this entire genre of movies is borrowed from the Bible where

---

[a] 1 Tim. 2:5; see also Heb. 9:15; 12:24 [b] Titus 2:13-14 [c] Gal. 3:13 [d] Matt. 26:63-65; Mark 2:5; John 6:41-58; 8:46, 58-59; 10:30-33; 11:25; 14:6, 8-9; 16:28 [e] 1 Tim. 2:5-6

Jesus takes down Satan and sets us free.

To use a very biblical word, sinners are captives or slaves held in bondage. Second Peter 2:19b explains it this way: "For whatever overcomes a person, to that he is enslaved." Like a prisoner locked in a cell who cannot escape, so sinners too are locked in a prison of sin and cannot get free. This includes self-selected slavery, such as addictions and sin patterns that are habitual.

In the book of Exodus, God's people were enslaved to a king named Pharaoh who ruled over the most powerful nation on the earth, Egypt. He was worshiped as a god and brutally mistreated the people whom he enslaved. God raised up a man named Moses to speak on his behalf to the pharaoh, demanding that the slaves be set free in order to live new lives in worship to the real God. God graciously, but authoritatively, called him to righteousness. Pharaoh became hardhearted under God's provocation, just as God said he would, and he refused to release the people from their brutal slavery. As a result, God sent a succession of plagues as judgments and warnings upon the pharaoh, kindly giving him many opportunities to repent and do what God demanded.

The pharaoh repeatedly refused to repent of his ways and release the people, so God sent a terrible series of judgments upon the entire nation. The wrath of God was eventually poured out on the firstborn son of every household, each killed in one night. As we have noted, the only households spared from death to their firstborn son were those families who, in faith, took a young, healthy lamb without blemish or defect and slaughtered it as a substitute and then took its blood and covered the doorposts around the entry to their home with it. As a result, the wrath of God passed over them and was diverted because of the lamb.

Like the people in Moses' day, we sinners are completely unable to free ourselves from slavery. As slaves we need to be redeemed from our slavery. Redemption is synonymous with being liberated, freed, or rescued from bondage and slavery to a person or thing. The word and its derivatives (e.g., redeemer, redeem) appear roughly 150 times in the English Bible, with only roughly twenty occurrences in the New Testament.

Sadly, it has been commonly taught by some Christian theologians since the early days of the church (e.g., Origen) that the concept of redemption was adopted from the pagan slave market where a price was paid to free a slave. This led to wild speculation that Jesus died to pay off Satan, which is preposterous because Jesus owes Satan nothing.

The prototype for redemption is not the pagan slave market but rather the Exodus. There, God liberated his people but in no way paid off the satanic pharaoh. God simply crushed him. Exodus 6:6 is one of many Bible verses that present the exodus as the prototype of redemption: "Say therefore to the people of Israel, 'I am the LORD, and I will bring you out from under the burdens of the Egyptians, and I will deliver you from slavery to them, and I will redeem you with

CROSS: GOD DIES

an outstretched arm and with great acts of judgment.'"[a]

The theme of God the Redeemer echoes throughout the Old Testament.[b] Even before Jesus' birth it was prophesied that he was God coming into human history to redeem sinners from slavery.[c] At the birth of Jesus, it was prophesied that he is God the Redeemer.[d] Paul often spoke of Jesus as our redeemer: "Jesus Christ . . . gave himself for us to redeem us" and "Redemption . . . is in Christ Jesus."[e] Many more examples of Jesus being offered as the redeemer of slaves are scattered throughout the New Testament.[f]

When Jesus was crucified and his blood was shed, he suffered and died in our place for our sins so that we could be redeemed.[g] Jesus has redeemed us from and to many things. Jesus has redeemed us from the curse of the law[h], Satan and demons[i], our sinful flesh[k], and sin.[m] Furthermore, Jesus has redeemed us to eternal life with God[n], the return of Jesus[o], and a glorified resurrection body.[p]

FOR WHOM DID JESUS CHRIST DIE?

Unlimited Limited Atonement

Every Christmas, families gather to open presents. To prepare for the gift opening, someone has to go through and read all the tags to determine who gets each present. If the wrong person gets the gift, the person whom it was intended for runs the risk of missing out on what was intended for them by the gift giver.

What is true of Christmas presents is also true of the greatest gift ever given – the salvation of Jesus Christ. Who gets this present, and does not get this present, is vital to understand correctly.

The question, for whom did Jesus Christ die? has generated some of the most heated and varied answers in church history. To help you understand the different answers to this question, we offer the following chart:

	Heresy of "Christian" Universalism	Heresy of Contemporary Pelagianism	Unlimited Atonement	Limited Atonement	Unlimited Limited Atonement
View of Sin	We are born sinful but guilty for our sins, not Adam's.	We are born sinless like Adam but follow his bad example.	We are born sinful but guilty for our sins, not Adam's.	We are born sinners guilty in Adam.	We are born sinners guilty in Adam.

---

[a] See also Ex. 15:1–18; Deut. 7:8; 15:15; 2 Sam. 7:23; 1 Chron. 17:21; Isa. 51:10; Mic. 6:4 [b] Ps. 78:35; Isa. 44:24; 47:4; 48:17; 63:16; Jer. 50:34; Hos. 7:13; 13:14. [c] Luke 1:68; 2:38 [d] Ibid. [e] Rom. 3:24; Titus 2:13–14; see also 1 Cor. 1:30; Gal. 3:13–14; 4:4–5; Eph. 1:7 [f] 1 Cor. 1:30; Gal. 3:13–14; 4:4–5; Eph. 1:7 [g] 1 Pet. 1:18–19 [h] Gal. 3:13 [i] Col. 1:13–14 [k] Rom. 6:6–12 [m] Gal. 6:14–15 [n] Ps. 49:15 [o] Job 19:25 [p] Rom. 8:23

DOCTRINE

	Heresy of "Christian" Universalism	**Heresy of Contemporary Pelagianism**	**Unlimited Atonement**	**Limited Atonement**	**Unlimited Limited Atonement**
Who Jesus Died For	Jesus took all the sin and pain of the world onto himself.	Jesus lived and died only as an example for sinners.	Jesus died to provide payment for the sin of all people.	Jesus died to achieve full atonement for the elect.	Jesus died to provide payment for all, but only in a saving way for the elect.
How Atonement is Applied	God's powerful love in Jesus will overcome all sin.	Anyone can follow the example of Jesus by living a good life.	God will apply the payment to those who believe in Christ.	God designed the atonement precisely for the elect.	While God desires the salvation of all, He applies the payment to the elect, those whom He chose for salvation.
Heaven & Hell	Everyone will be saved and will go to heaven. There is no eternal Hell.	Those who live a Christlike life will be saved and go to heaven. Those who reject goodness will go to Hell.	All who accept the gift go to heaven. Everyone else gets to follow their free will and choose to go to Hell.	God does not need to save anyone from Hell, but chooses to save some.	God does not need to save anyone from Hell, but chooses to save some.

The first two conclusions (universalism and Pelagianism) are unbiblical and therefore unacceptable. Universalism erroneously contradicts the clear teachings of Scripture on human sinfulness and hell.[a] Pelagius denied human sinfulness and taught that people begin their life morally good (like Adam), and through the decision of their own will can live a holy life that would obligate God to take them to heaven upon death. Pelagius was condemned as a heretic at the Council of Carthage in AD 418.

We are left with three options for Christians regarding the question of who Jesus died for. All three positions are within the bounds of evangelical orthodoxy.

First, some Christians believe that Jesus died for the sins of all people. This position is commonly referred to as Arminianism (after James Arminius), Wesleyanism (after John Wesley), or unlimited atonement. Arminians appeal to those Scriptures that speak of Jesus dying for all people[b], the whole world[c],

---

[a] E.g., Dan. 12:2; Matt. 5:29–30; 10:28; 18:9; 23:23; 25:46 [b] 2 Cor. 5:14–15; 1 Tim. 2:1–6; 4:10; Titus 2:11 [c] John 1:29; 3:16–17; 1 John 2:2; 4:14; Rev. 5:9

CROSS: GOD DIES

everyone[a], and not wanting anyone to perish.[b] Arminians then teach that to be saved, one must make the decision to accept Jesus' atoning death and become a follower of Jesus. Furthermore, it is said that anyone can make that choice either by inherent free will (Arminians) or by God's universal enabling, so-called prevenient, or first, grace (Wesleyans). Subsequently, election is understood as God choosing those he foreknew would choose him, and since people choose to be saved, they can also lose their salvation.

Second, some Christians believe that Jesus died only for the sins of the elect. Election means that before the foundation of the world, God chose certain individuals to be recipients of eternal life solely on the basis of his gracious purpose apart from any human merit or action. He calls them effectually, doing whatever is necessary to bring them to repentance and faith.[c]

This position is commonly referred to as five-point Calvinism (after John Calvin), Reformed theology, or limited atonement, which is also sometimes called particular redemption. These Calvinists commonly appeal to those Scriptures that speak of Jesus' dying only for some people but not all people[d], his sheep[e], his church[f], the elect[g], his people[h], his friends[i], and all Christians.[k] They disagree with unlimited atonement, pointing out that if Jesus died for everyone, then everyone would be saved, which is the heresy of universalism. They also teach that people are so sinful that they cannot choose God, and so God regenerates people before their conversion and ensures they will be preserved until the end because salvation cannot be lost.

One vital point of debate is the intent of Jesus when he died on the cross. Did Jesus intend to provide payment for all sins of all people, opening the doorway to salvation for all? That would be unlimited atonement, or what the Wesleyans and the Arminians believe. Do we accept it at face value when Paul said that Christ Jesus "gave himself as a ransom for all" in 1 Timothy 2:6? Or did Jesus die to complete the purchase of our pardon on the cross? That is limited atonement, or what five-point Calvinists believe. Do we accept it at face value when Jesus said, "It is finished" in John 19:30?

At first glance, unlimited and limited atonement appear to be in opposition. But that dilemma is resolved by noting two things. First, the two categories are not mutually exclusive; since Jesus died for the sins of everyone, this means that he also died for the sins of the elect. Second, Jesus' death for all people does not accomplish the same thing as his death for the elect. This point is complicated but is in fact taught in Scripture. For example, 1 Timothy 4:10 makes a distinction between Jesus' dying as the savior of all people in a general way and the Christian elect in a particular way, saying, "For to this end we toil and strive,

---

[a] Isa. 53:6; Heb. 2:9 [b] 1 Tim. 2:4; 2 Pet. 3:9 [c] Isa. 55:11; John 6:44; Rom. 8:30; 11:29; 1 Cor. 1:23-29; 2 Tim. 1:9 [d] Matt. 1:21; 20:28; 26:28; Rom. 5:12-19 [e] John 10:11, 15, 26-27 [f] Acts 20:28; Eph. 5:25 [g] Rom. 8:32-35 [h] Matt. 1:21 [i] John 15:3 [k] 2 Cor. 5:15; Titus 2:14

because we have our hope set on the living God, who is the Savior of all people, especially of those who believe."

Additionally, 2 Peter 2:1 speaks of people for whom Jesus died as not being saved from heresy and damnation by Jesus: "False prophets also arose among the people, just as there will be false teachers among you, who will secretly bring in destructive heresies, even denying the Master who bought them, bringing upon themselves swift destruction." Simply, by dying for everyone, Jesus purchased everyone as his possession, and he then applies his forgiveness to the elect—those in Christ—by grace and applies his wrath to the non-elect—those who reject Christ. Objectively, Jesus' death was sufficient to save anyone, and, subjectively, only efficient to save those who repent of their sin and trust in him. This position is called unlimited limited atonement, or modified Calvinism, and arguably is the position that John Calvin himself held as a very able Bible teacher.[a] Christ died for the purpose of securing the sure and certain salvation of his own, His elect.

This is the intentionality the five-point Calvinists rightly stress. Christ died for all people. This is the universality the Arminians rightly stress. If the five-point Calvinist is right and no payment has been made for the non-elect, then how can God genuinely love the world and desire the salvation of all people? There is a genuine open door for salvation for anyone who believes in Jesus, and this makes the rejection of Jesus completely inexcusable. Jesus' death reconciles "all things" to God.[b] God will overcome all rebellion through Jesus' blood. In this sense, all those in hell will stand reconciled to God but not in a saving way, as the universalists falsely teach. In hell unrepentant and unforgiven sinners are no longer rebels, and their sinful disregard for God has been crushed and ended.[c]

HOW DOES GOD TRIUMPH THROUGH THE CROSS?

Christus Victor

From video games to blockbuster movies and bigger than life sporting events, people never grow weary of heroes who rise up to lead their team to victory. Something in us wants to see someone step onto the field of battle to defeat a foe so that everyone on their side of the fight wins.

Scripture clearly says that there is a very real war between Jesus and the angels and Satan and the demons; sinners have been taken as captives in war.[d] Jesus himself confirmed this fact at the beginning of his earthly ministry when he said he had come to set captives free.[e] Jesus said this because there is no way that Satan would release us from his captivity and no way that we could liberate ourselves. Therefore, Jesus came as our triumphant warrior and liberator.

---

[a] E.g., see his commentaries on Romans 5, Galatians 5, Colossians 1, and Hebrews [b] Col. 1:18–20 [c] On this point, Dr. Bruce Ware has been very helpful to both of us as we studied this doctrine together [d] Col. 1:13; 2 Tim. 2:25-26 [e] Luke 4:18

CROSS: GOD DIES

The first promise of Jesus as our victor over Satan came to our first parents. In Genesis 3:15, God preached the first good news (or gospel) of Jesus to our sinful first mother, Eve. God promised that Jesus would be born of a woman and would grow to be a man who would battle with Satan and stomp his head, defeat him, even as the serpent strike his heel killing him, and liberate people from their captivity to Satan, sin, death, and hell through Messiah's substitutionary death.

Leading up to the cross, Satan entered one of Jesus' own disciples, Judas Iscariot, and conspired with him to betray Jesus and hand him over to be crucified. Through the cross, Satan and his demons thought that they had finally defeated Jesus. However, crucifying Jesus was the biggest mistake the Devil ever made. Had he understood what was happening, he would never have killed Jesus.[a]

An essential portion of Scripture on the victory of Jesus over Satan, sin, and death is Colossians 2:13-15:

You, who were dead in your trespasses and the uncircumcision of your flesh, God made alive together with him, having forgiven us all our trespasses, by canceling the record of debt that stood against us with its legal demands. This he set aside, nailing it to the cross. He disarmed the rulers and authorities and put them to open shame, by triumphing over them in him.

Thus, the authority of the Devil and his demons has already ended. Matthew 28:18 makes it very clear that Jesus has all authority now, which means that Satan has no authority over Christians. As a result, we can now live in accordance with Colossians 1:10-14 and "walk in a manner worthy of the Lord, fully pleasing to him, bearing fruit in every good work and increasing in the knowledge of God...He has delivered us from the domain of darkness and transferred us to the kingdom of his beloved Son, in whom we have redemption, the forgiveness of sins." The Bible uses the word grace to explain the victory Jesus achieved for us on the cross because there is no logical reason that God would love us and die in our place to liberate us from captivity to Satan, sin, and death, other than his wonderful nature.

Expiation

Consider, for a moment, all of the time and energy you put into cleaning yourself and the things in your life. For starts you bath your body, brush your teeth, wash your windows, clean your dishes, vacuum your house, wash your clothes, change your sheets, and detail your car. If you are a germ freak, the list is much longer. What is true physically is also true spiritually as our souls also need to be cleansed.

The typical gospel presentation is that we are all sinners and that if we confess our sins to Jesus, He will forgive our sins through his sinless life, substitutionary death, and bodily resurrection. This is clearly true according to Scripture.

---

[a] 1 Cor. 2:6-9

DOCTRINE

However, this gospel only addresses the sins that you have committed (as a sinner) and neglects to deal with the sins that have been committed against you (as a victim).

Throughout the Bible, some dozen words are used frequently to speak of sin in terms of staining our soul, defiling us, and causing us to be filthy or unclean.[a] The effect of sin, particularly sins committed against us, is that we feel dirty. The Bible mentions a number of causes for our defilement, such as any sin at all, as well as involvement with false religions and/or the occult[b], violence[c], and sexual sin.[d]

Thus, souls are stained and defiled by the filth of sins that people commit and that are committed against them. In Scripture, places[e], objects (such as the marriage bed)[f], and people are defiled by sin. Subsequently, the Old Testament and the Gospels are filled with people who were ritually unclean and not to be touched or associated with. The commandments for ceremonial washings and such foreshadow the cleansing power of the death of Jesus.

The predictable result of defilement is shame, including the fear of being found out and known, and our deep, dark secret getting revealed. This pattern was firmly established with our first parents, who covered themselves in shame and hid from God and one another after they sinned. Shame exists where there is sin, and so feeling ashamed, particularly when we sin, is natural and healthy. Therefore, shame is not bad, but unless the underlying sin that causes the shame is properly dealt with through the gospel, then the shame will remain, with devastating implications.

Jesus forgave our sins at the cross and cleanses us from all sins that we have committed and that have been committed against us. Through the cross, Jesus Christ has taken our sin away forever, as was foreshadowed by the scapegoat on the Day of Atonement. This goat was sent away to run free into the wilderness, symbolically taking the people's sins with it. Theologically, we call this the doctrine of expiation, whereby our sin is expiated or taken away so that we are made clean through Jesus, who is our scapegoat.

The Bible uses words such as atonement, cleansing, and purifying fountain that washes away our defilement and shame to explain that our identity must be marked only by what Jesus Christ has done for us and no longer by what has been done by or to us. The Bible clearly teaches that dirty sinners can be cleansed.

- For on this day shall atonement be made for you to cleanse you. You shall be clean before the LORD from all your sins.[g]
- I will cleanse them from all the guilt of their sin against me, and I will forgive all the guilt of their sin and rebellion against me.[h]
- On that day there shall be a fountain opened...to cleanse them from sin and uncleanness.[i]

---

[a] E.g., Ps. 106:39; Prov. 30:11–12; Mark 7:20 [b] Lev. 19:31; Ezek. 14:11 [c] E.g., Lam. 4:14 [d] Gen. 34:5; Lev. 21:14; Num. 5:27; 1 Chron. 5:1 [e] Lev. 18:24–30; Num. 35:34 [f] Heb. 13:4 [g] Lev. 16:30 [h] Jer. 33:8 [i] Zech. 13:1

Jesus not only went to the cross to die for our sin, but also to scorn our shame. As Hebrews 12:1-2 says, "Let us run with endurance the race that is set before us, looking to Jesus, the founder and perfecter of our faith, who for the joy that was set before him endured the cross, despising the shame, and is seated at the right hand of the throne of God."

As a result, we can walk in the light with others who love us in authentic community. On this point, 1 John 1:7-9 says:

If we walk in the light, as he is in the light, we have fellowship with one another, and the blood of Jesus his Son cleanses us from all sin. If we say we have no sin, we deceive ourselves, and the truth is not in us. If we confess our sins, he is faithful and just to forgive us our sins and to cleanse us from all unrighteousness.

Jesus does "cleanse us from all unrighteousness." This means that because of Jesus' cross we can be cleansed and made pure. The beauty of this truth of the expiating or cleansing work of Jesus is poetically shown in symbolic acts throughout Scripture, including ceremonial washings[a], baptism[b], and the wearing of white in eternity as a continual reminder of the expiating work of Jesus.[c]

HOW DOES GOD INSPIRE US THROUGH THE CROSS?

Christus Exemplar

When I was a little boy, my grandpa was a diesel mechanic and my dad was a construction worker. I remember they both wore steel toed work boots, carried a lunch box and thermos, and wore overalls and jeans respectively. As a little boy, I looked up to them and so I followed their example. I had my own jeans and boots I wore, and thermos and lunch box that I would bring when I would ride in their trucks to help them with projects. The truth is, we all have people we look up to as role models and examples. Since Jesus Christ is perfect, it makes sense that He would be our perfect role model to follow.

Jesus died for our sins, thereby enabling us to experience new life. Jesus lived as our example showing us what it means to live a truly holy human life.

Throughout Jesus' life he repeatedly stated that the purpose of His life on earth was to glorify God the Father, or to make the Father's character visible. Jesus' glorifying God the Father included dying on the cross.[d] Practically, this means that there is joy not only in our comfort and success, but also in our suffering and hardship, just as there was for Jesus.[e]

At the cross of Jesus, we learn that to be like Jesus means that we pick up our cross and follow him as he commanded.[f] Practically, this means that we glorify God by allowing hardship, pain, and loss to make us more and more like Jesus and give us a more credible witness for Jesus. As Christians we should neither run

---

[a] Ex. 19:10 [b] Acts 22:16 [c] Rev. 19:7-8 [d] John 12:23, 27-28; 13:30-32; 17:1 [e] Heb. 12:1-6 [f] Matt. 16:24

to suffering as the early Christian ascetics did, nor run from it as some modern Christians do. Instead, we receive suffering when it comes as an opportunity for God to do something good in us and through us. We rejoice not in the pain but rather in what it can accomplish for the gospel so that something as costly as suffering is not wasted but used for God's glory, our joy, and others' good.

In order to suffer well—that is, in a way that is purposeful for the progress of the gospel both in and through us—we must continually remember Jesus' cross. Peter says:

What credit is it if, when you sin and are beaten for it, you endure? But if when you do good and suffer for it you endure, this is a gracious thing in the sight of God. For to this you have been called, because Christ also suffered for you, leaving you an example, so that you might follow in his steps. He committed no sin, neither was deceit found in his mouth. When he was reviled, he did not revile in return; when he suffered, he did not threaten, but continued entrusting himself to him who judges justly. He himself bore our sins in his body on the tree, that we might die to sin and live to righteousness. By his wounds you have been healed.[a]

WHAT DOES THE DOCTRINE OF THE CROSS REVEAL ABOUT GOD'S LOVE?

When all is said and done, a lot more is said than done. People talk a lot about their love and concern for others. Social media is flooded with hashtags and likes for good causes. Yet, little action ever happens. As an elderly man, John was a bit sick of this trend to say a lot but do a little. After seeing Jesus not just say He loved us, but dying and rising to show He loved us, John wrote in 1 John 3:18, "let us not love in word or talk but in deed and in truth." Some of the time, love is what you say. Most of the time, love is what you do.

On the cross, Jesus revealed to us the love of God. The following verses state how the love of God is most clearly revealed at the cross of Jesus:

- For God so loved the world, that he gave his only Son, that whoever believes in him should not perish but have eternal life.[b]
- Greater love has no one than this, that someone lays down his life for his friends.[c]
- But God shows his love for us in that while we were still sinners, Christ died for us.[d]
- In this the love of God was made manifest among us, that God sent his only Son into the world, so that we might live through him. In this is love, not that we have loved God but that he loved us and sent his Son to be the propitiation for our sins.[e]

At the cross we see that the love of God is not merely sentimental but also

---

[a] 1 Pet. 2:20-24 [b] John 3:16 [c] John 15:13 [d] Rom. 5:8 [e] 1 John 4:9-10

CROSS: GOD DIES

efficacious. When people speak of love, they usually mean an emotional love that feels affectionate but may not do anything to help the beloved. Thankfully, God does not merely feel loving toward us; His love actually compels Him to act on our behalf so that we can be changed by His love.

God has lovingly worked out a way for our friendship with Him to be reconciled. Through the cross, Jesus took away our sin so that we could be reconciled to God.[a] Thankfully, God not only graciously takes away our sin, but mercifully extends Himself to us, knowing that we desperately need Him.[b]

The cross is something done by you. You murdered God incarnate. The cross is something done for you. God loves you and died to forgive you.

Through the cross and empty tomb of Jesus Christ, there are at least nine ways that God has loved you by Jesus taking your place and putting you in His place.

1. Jesus died so you can live!
2. Jesus paid the ultimate price for your debt to God!
3. Jesus was cursed so you could be blessed!
4. Jesus became unrighteous so you could become righteous!
5. Jesus endured God's wrath so you could experience God's grace!
6. Jesus was rejected by the Father so you could be reconciled to the Father!
7. Jesus was shamed to that you could be unashamed!
8. Jesus became unclean to make you clean!
9. Jesus was hated so you could be loved!

QUESTIONS FOR PERSONAL JOURNALING AND/OR SMALL GROUP DISCUSSION

1. Was there anything new from this chapter that most impactful to you personally? What? Why?
2. What would it have been like for you to be standing with John and Mary at the feet of Jesus on the cross?
3. Do you completely and confidently believe that, because of your faith in Jesus Christ, all of your sin and debt to God is paid in full?
4. Do you truly believe that Jesus has made you completely clean from all that you have done and all that others have done to you?
5. How does understanding Jesus' sacrifice on the cross help deepen your understanding of God's love for you?
6. What self-destructive patterns in your life has Jesus died to set you free from by dying so that you could put them to death?
7. How does Jesus' example help you know how to love and forgive those who have sinned against you? Who do you need to forgive as God has forgiven you through the cross?

---

[a] Isa. 59:2; Hos. 5:6 [b] 1 Tim. 1:15–16; Titus 3:4–5

8. Who do you know that needs to hear more about what Jesus has done for them to either help them become a Christian, or help them grow as a Christian?
9. What are some ways you can follow Jesus' example by serving someone else in love?
10. What do you think it will be like in the Kingdom of God when you see the nail scars in Jesus' hands as He wipes every tear from your eyes and welcomes you to heal from the past?

CHAPTER 9: RESURRECTION

"GOD SAVES"

Jesus said... "I am the resurrection and the life. Whoever believes in me, though he die, yet shall he live, and everyone who lives and believes in me shall never die."
JOHN 11:25–26

When I was a little boy, one of my favorite people was my Grandpa George. He was a big man with a big heart and a big laugh who liked to tell big stories. A former diesel mechanic, his wardrobe mainly consisted of overalls. He had quite a sweet tooth, and I remember eating a lot of caramel apples with him and always getting a sucker out of the glove box of his Buick whenever we rode in his car.

When I was 10 years old, my parents showed up early to my Cub Scouts meeting. It was obvious that my mom had been crying and that something was wrong. Pulling me aside, my mom privately told me that her dad, my grandpa, had died.

There are many days of my childhood that I don't remember. This day, however, is one I will never forget. At first, I was in shock. I never even considered that one day my grandpa would die and that we would no longer have fun together on woodworking projects in his garage or go out to breakfast together ever again. To make matters worse, he died suddenly of a heart attack, and we did not get to say goodbye.

Grandpa George's funeral is the first one I remember ever attending. As a child, I remember feeling very confused and unsure how I was supposed to act and react. Making matters worse, the funeral was open casket, so the last sight of my grandpa was of his cold, lifeless, dead body. My cousin was worried that grandpa would need some money in Heaven, so he climbed up and stuffed a dollar into his suit coat pocket.

As we sat down to listen to the religious leader officiating the service, I only remember one thing that he said because it angered me. After speaking kindly about Grandpa George, he said that there is a natural order to the world with seasons of life and death for everyone and everything, and that death is natural and normal. To me, nothing about seeing my dead grandpa seemed natural or normal. Death felt to me to be unnatural and abnormal – a cold enemy and not a warm friend.

At that funeral something in my heart and mind changed. I felt that religion and religious leaders did not really know what they were talking about and so I had no real interest in either for many years. My mom took me to church and put me in a Catholic school for a few years, but I was indifferent. It was not until I was in college that I started to wrestle with life's three big questions:

1. Origins: Where do we come from?
2. Purpose: Why are we here?
3. Destiny: Where are we going?

Wrestling with these questions in philosophy classes at a state university, I stumbled upon Jesus and started to investigate Him and what He had to say about life's big three questions. I was encouraged to hear the Apostle Paul call death our "enemy". After reading the Bible some, along with Christian philosophers, I came to one simple conclusion. If Jesus is dead, then Christianity is dead. If Jesus is alive, then Christianity is alive. Paul himself declared as much in 1 Corinthians 15:17: "If Christ has not been raised, your faith is futile and you are still in your sins."

Apart from the resurrection of Jesus Christ, there is no savior, no salvation, no forgiveness of sin, and no hope of resurrected eternal life. Apart from the resurrection, Jesus is reduced to yet another good but dead man and therefore is of no considerable help to us in this life or at its end. Plainly stated, without the resurrection of Jesus, the few billion people today who worship Jesus as God are gullible; their hope for a resurrection life after this life is the hope of silly fools who trust in a dead man to give them life. Subsequently, the doctrine of Jesus' resurrection is, without question, profoundly significant and worthy of the most careful consideration and examination as we come from God, are here for God, and will die to stand before God.

WHAT IS RESURRECTION?

Defining what resurrection does and does not mean is incredibly important. Resurrection does not mean revivification. Revivification occurs when someone who dies comes back to life only to die again; revivification happens throughout

RESURRECTION: GOD SAVES

Scripture.[a] Unlike revivification, resurrection teaches that someone dies and returns to physical life forever, or what the Bible calls eternal life[b], patterned after Jesus' death and resurrection.[c]

Resurrection does not mean there is a second chance for salvation after death, as both reincarnation and postmortem salvation wrongly purport. *Reincarnation* is the belief that the human soul individually migrates from one body to another through a succession of lives in pursuit of complete purification where the soul is finally joined to the ultimate reality of the divine. *Postmortem salvation* teaches that God pursues people beyond the boundary of death to be sure they have had a real opportunity to respond to the Gospel. Hebrews 9:27 refutes both errors: "it is appointed for man to die once, and after that comes judgment."

Resurrection does not mean that everyone, believers and unbelievers alike, avoid hellish punishment in the end. Universalism wrongly teaches that everyone is eventually saved and goes to Heaven. Annihilationism wrongly teaches that at some point following death, unbelievers simply cease to exist rather than going to an eternal hell. Instead, Daniel 12:2 declares that both believers and unbelievers will rise, and some will go to everlasting Heaven and others to everlasting hell, which refutes both errors: "Many of those who sleep in the dust of the earth shall awake, some to everlasting life, and some to shame and everlasting contempt."

Resurrection does not mean what is called "soul sleep," where both the body and the spirit lie at rest until the resurrection, as is taught by some Seventh-Day Adventists. When the New Testament speaks of believers as "asleep," it does so as a metaphor to distinguish the death of believers from the death of unbelievers. The Dictionary of Biblical Imagery says:

The Bible also uses sleep as a metaphor for the death of the righteous. "Christ has indeed been raised from the dead, the firstfruits of those who have fallen asleep".[d] In Christ, death is nothing more than a nap from which the righteous will awaken to endless day.[1] This is why Paul speaks of his death as gain, because it means his soul goes to be with Jesus: "For to me to live is Christ, and to die is gain."[e]

Neither does resurrection simply mean life after death. This is because life after death does not initially include the physical body; rather, the body lies in the ground while the spiritual soul goes to be with God. Paul speaks of believers being "away from the body and at home with the Lord."[f]

The Bible teaches that we are both a material body and an immaterial soul. Upon death, these two parts are separated. Our body goes into the ground and, as believers, our soul goes to be with God. For unbelievers, their soul goes to a place called by such names in the Bible as a "prison"[g] and "Hades."[h] That place is a place of just suffering for unbelievers until they stand before Jesus and are

---

[a] E.g., 2 Kings 4:18-37; Matt. 9:18-26, 27:52-53; Mark 5:22-43; Luke 8:40-56; John 11:1-44; Acts 9:36-42, 20:9-12 [b] E.g., John 5:24 [c] 1 Cor. 15 [d] 1 Cor. 15:20 [e] Phil. 1:21 [f] 2 Cor. 5:8 [g] 1 Pet. 3:19 [h] Luke 16:19-31

DOCTRINE

sentenced to the conscious eternal torments of hell.[a]

Resurrection refers to the eventual reuniting of our body and soul. In his impressive 700-page tome *The Resurrection of the Son of God*, notable New Testament scholar N. T. Wright provides a most helpful definition of resurrection, which he repeats throughout the book as one of his main points. Wright proposes that in the first century, resurrection did not mean "life after death" in the sense of "the life that follows immediately after bodily death."[2] According to Wright:

"Here there is no difference between pagans, Jews and Christians. They all understood the Greek word *anastasis* and its cognates, and the other related terms we shall meet, to mean...new life after a period of being dead. Pagans denied this possibility; some Jews affirmed it as a long-term future hope; virtually all Christians claimed that it had happened to Jesus and would happen to them in the future."[3]

In other words, resurrection was a way of "speaking of a new life after 'life after death' in the popular sense, a fresh living embodiment following a period of death-as-a-state."[4] According to Wright, the meaning of resurrection as "life after 'life after death'" cannot be overemphasized. This is due in large part to the fact that much modern writing continues to use "resurrection" as a synonym for "life after death." In contrast, belief in "resurrection" for the ancients meant belief in what Wright calls a "two-step story"[5]:

"Resurrection itself would be preceded...by an interim period of death-as-a-state. Where we find a single-step story—death-as-event being followed at once by a final state, for instance of disembodied bliss—the texts are not talking about resurrection. Resurrection involves a definite content (some sort of re-embodiment) and a definite narrative shape (a two-step story, not a single-step one). This meaning is constant throughout the ancient world."[6]

Wright reiterates what resurrection is and what it is not:

"'Resurrection' denoted a new embodied life which would follow whatever 'life after death' there might be. 'Resurrection' was, by definition, not the existence into which someone might (or might not) go immediately upon death; it was not a disembodied 'heavenly' life; it was a further stage, out beyond all that. It was not a re-description or redefinition of death. It was death's reversal."[7]

While we correctly say believers go to Heaven when they die, that is to be with Jesus, we must add that our eternal home is on the New Earth as whole persons in a resurrected body.

WHAT WERE ANCIENT NON-CHRISTIAN VIEWS OF THE AFTERLIFE?

It is commonly purported by some that the entire idea of a bodily resurrection was in fact not a novel idea, but one borrowed from other ancient philosophies

---

[a] Rev. 20:13-14

and spiritualities. Wright has done a painstakingly exhaustive and revolutionary study of ancient beliefs regarding resurrection that is incredibly helpful. Most books on the resurrection of Jesus begin by studying the Gospel narratives and then work outwardly from this vantage point to an analysis of the appropriate pagan and Jewish sources found in antiquity. Wright takes the exact opposite approach. He begins with a study on resurrection (or, better, the lack thereof) in ancient paganism and then narrows the scope of his investigation tighter and tighter, concluding with a study of the resurrection as recorded by the writers of the canonical Gospels. Wright concludes, "In so far as the ancient non-Jewish world had a Bible, its Old Testament was Homer. And in so far as Homer has anything to say about resurrection, he is quite blunt: it doesn't happen."[8]

The idea of resurrection is denied in ancient paganism from Homer all the way to the Athenian dramatist Aeschylus, who wrote, "Once a man has died, and the dust has soaked up his blood, there is no resurrection."[9] Wright provides a helpful summary: "Christianity was born into a world where its central claim was known to be false. Many believed that the dead were non-existent; outside Judaism, nobody believed in resurrection."[10]

One of the most influential writers in antiquity was Plato. Wright summarizes Plato's views on the soul and body as follows:

"The soul is the non-material aspect of a human being, and is the aspect that really matters. Bodily life is full of delusion and danger; the soul is to be cultivated in the present both for its own sake and because its future happiness will depend upon such cultivation. The soul, being immortal, existed before the body, and will continue to exist after the body is gone."[11]

This dualistic view promoted a tendency to see the body as a prison of the soul that made death something to be desired. According to Wright, "in Greek philosophy, care for and cure of the soul became a central preoccupation."[12] Furthermore, "neither in Plato nor in the major alternatives just mentioned [e.g., Aristotle] do we find any suggestion that resurrection, the return to bodily life of the dead person, was either desirable or possible."[13]

This view is also evident in the writings of Cicero:

"Cicero is quite clear, and completely in the mainstream of Greco-Roman thought: the body is a prison-house. A necessary one for the moment; but nobody in their right mind, having got rid of it, would want it or something like it back again. At no point in the spectrum of options about life after death did the ancient pagan world envisage that the denials of Homer, Aeschylus and the rest would be overthrown. Resurrection was not an option. Those who followed Plato or Cicero did not want a body again; those who followed Homer knew they would not get one."[14]

After surveying several other ancient pagan writers and philosophers, Wright concludes: "Nobody in the pagan world of Jesus' day and thereafter actually claimed that somebody had been truly dead and had then come to be truly, and bodily, alive once more."[15]

Death, in ancient paganism, was a one-way street. According to Wright:

"The road to the underworld ran only one way. Throughout the ancient world, from its 'bible' of Homer and Plato, through its practices (funerals, memorial feasts), its stories (plays, novels, legends), its symbols (graves, amulets, grave-goods) and its grand theories, we can trace a good deal of variety about the road to Hades, and about what one might find upon arrival. As with all one-way streets, there is bound to be someone who attempts to drive in the opposite direction. One hears of a Protesilaus, an Alcestis or a Nero redivivus, once or twice in a thousand years. But the road was well policed. Would-be traffic violators (Sisyphus, Eurydice and the like) were turned back or punished. And even they occurred in what everybody knew to be myth."[16]

Wright notes: "We cannot stress too strongly that from Homer onwards the language of 'resurrection' was not used to denote 'life after death' in general, or any of the phenomena supposed to occur within such a life. The great majority of the ancients believed in life after death; many of them developed...complex and fascinating beliefs about it and practices in relation to it; but, other than within Judaism and Christianity, they did not believe in resurrection."[17]

Furthermore, not even Judaism believed in the resurrection of an individual from death in the middle of history. Rather, their understanding was that their entire nation alone would rise from death together at the end of history. William Lane Craig's lengthy studies of the resurrection of Jesus Christ culminated in the publishing of two scholarly books on the issue.[18] Craig asserts:

"Jewish belief always concerned a resurrection at the end of the world, not a resurrection in the middle of history...The resurrection to glory and immortality did not occur until after God had terminated world history. This traditional Jewish conception was the prepossession of Jesus' own disciples.[a] The notion of a genuine resurrection occurring prior to God's bringing about the world's end would have been foreign to them...Jewish belief always concerned a general resurrection of the people, not the resurrection of an isolated individual."[19]

Finally, noted historian and professor Edwin Yamauchi has spoken to this matter with great clarity based upon his lifetime of scholarly research.[20] Yamauchi has said that there is no possibility that the idea of a resurrection was borrowed because there is no definitive evidence for the teaching of a deity resurrection in any of the mystery religions prior to the second century.[21] In fact, it seems that other religions and spiritualities stole the idea of a resurrection from Christians! For example, the resurrection of Adonis is not spoken of until the second to fourth centuries.[22] Attis, the consort of Cybele, is not referred to as a resurrected god until after 150 AD.[23]

Some have postulated that the taurobolium ritual of Attis and Mithra, the Persian god, is the source of the biblical doctrine of the resurrection. In this ritual, the initiate was put in a pit, and a bull was slaughtered on a grating over him,

---

[a] Mark 9:9–13; John 11:24

drenching him with blood. However, the earliest this ritual is mentioned is 160 AD, and the belief that it led to rebirth is not mentioned until the fourth century. In fact, Princeton scholar Bruce Metzger has argued that the taurobolium was said to have the power to confer eternal life only after it encountered Christianity.[24]

The myths of pagans are admittedly fictitious events centered on the annual death and rebirth of vegetation and harvest cycles. Conversely, the resurrection of Jesus Christ is put forth as a historical fact in a place, at a time, with eyewitnesses and numerable lines of compelling evidence. Furthermore, not only is the theory that Christianity borrowed the concept of resurrection untrue, but it also completely ignores the historical facts of the empty tomb and post-resurrection appearances of Jesus Christ.

WHAT IS THE BIBLICAL EVIDENCE FOR JESUS' RESURRECTION?

The biblical evidence for Jesus' resurrection is compelling and can be briefly summarized in 10 points. Each of these points is consistent, and together they reveal that the Bible is emphatically and repeatedly clear on the fact of Jesus' resurrection.

1. Jesus' resurrection was prophesied in advance. Roughly 700 years before the birth of Jesus, the prophet Isaiah promised that Jesus would be born into humble circumstances to live a simple life, die a brutal death, and then rise to take away our sin.[a]
2. Jesus predicted His resurrection. On numerous occasions, Jesus plainly promised that He would die and rise three days later.[b]
3. Jesus died. Before Jesus died, He underwent a sleepless night of trials and beatings that left Him exhausted. He was then scourged—a punishment so horrendous that many men died from it before even making it to their crucifixion. Jesus was crucified, and a professional executioner declared Him dead. To ensure Jesus was dead, a spear was thrust through His side and a mixture of blood and water poured out of His side because the spear burst His heart sac.[c] Jesus' dead body was wrapped in upwards of 100 pounds of linens and spices, which, even if He was able to somehow survive the beatings, floggings, crucifixion, and a pierced heart, would have killed Him by asphyxiation. Even if through all of this Jesus somehow survived (which would in itself be a miracle), He could not have endured three days without food, water, or medical attention in a cold tomb carved out of rock. In summary, Jesus died.
4. Jesus was buried in a tomb that was easy to find. Some 700 years before Jesus was even born, God promised through Isaiah that Jesus would be

---

[a] Isa. 53:8-12 [b] Matt. 12:38–40; Mark 8:31, 9:31, 10:33–34; John 2:18–22 [c] John 19:34–35

DOCTRINE

assigned a grave "with a rich man in his death."[a] This was incredibly unlikely, because Jesus was a very poor man who could not have afforded an expensive burial plot. Following Jesus' death, though, a wealthy and well-known man named Joseph of Arimathea gifted his expensive tomb for the burial of Jesus.[b] As a result, the place of Jesus' burial was easy to confirm. Joseph, who owned the tomb, governmental leaders and their soldiers who were assigned to guard the tomb, and the disciples and women who visited the tomb and found it empty all knew exactly where Jesus' dead body was laid to rest. Had Jesus truly not risen from death, it would have been very easy to prove it by opening the tomb and presenting Jesus' dead body as evidence.

5. Jesus appeared physically, not just spiritually, alive three days after His death. Following Jesus' resurrection, many people touched His physical body: His disciples clung to his feet[c], Mary clung to him[d], and Thomas the doubter put his hand into the open spear hole in Jesus' side.[e] Jesus also appeared to His disciples after His resurrection, but they were uncertain if He had truly physically risen from death. Still, Jesus was emphatic about His bodily resurrection and went out of His way to prove it:

> "As they were talking about these things, Jesus himself stood among them, and said to them, 'Peace to you!' But they were startled and frightened and thought they saw a spirit. And he said to them, 'Why are you troubled, and why do doubts arise in your hearts? See my hands and my feet, that it is I myself. Touch me, and see. For a spirit does not have flesh and bones as you see that I have.' And when he had said this, he showed them his hands and his feet. And while they still disbelieved for joy and were marveling, he said to them, 'Have you anything here to eat?' They gave him a piece of broiled fish, and he took it and ate before them."[f]

Furthermore, Jesus appeared physically alive over the course of 40 days[g] to crowds as large as 500 people at a time.[h] It is also significant to note that no credible historical evidence from that period exists to validate any alternative explanation for Jesus' resurrection other than His literal bodily resurrection.[25]

6. Jesus' resurrected body was the same as His pre-resurrection body. His disciples recognized Him as the same person who had been crucified[i] and Mary Magdalene recognized Him by the sound of His voice.[k] While Jesus' resurrection body was the same, it was transformed. This explains why Jesus was not always immediately recognized after His resurrection[m] and seemed to appear and reappear mysteriously.[n] As James Orr noted,

---

[a] Isa. 53:9 [b] Matt. 27:57-60 [c] Matt. 28:9 [d] John 20:17 [e] John 20:20-28 [f] Luke 24:36-43 [g] Acts 1:3 [h] 1 Cor. 15:6 [i] Luke 24:31; cf. John 21:7,12 [k] John 20:16 [m] John 20:14, 15, 21:4; Luke 24:15-16 [n] John 20:19; Luke 24:31,36

RESURRECTION: GOD SAVES

"[In] the narratives...it is implied that there was something strange – something unfamiliar or mysterious – in His aspect, which prevented His immediate recognition...which held them in awe."[26] Paul explains this phenomenon in the lengthiest treatment of the nature of a resurrection body in all of Scripture[a]: "It is sown a natural body; it is raised a spiritual body. If there is a natural body, there is also a spiritual body."[b] This "spiritual body" refers to a resurrected body that has been perfected to its glorious state by the power of the Holy Spirit.

7. Jesus' resurrection was recorded as Scripture shortly after it occurred. Mark's Gospel account of the days leading up to Jesus' crucifixion mentions the high priest without naming Him.[c] It can logically be inferred that Mark did not mention the high priest by name because he expected his readers to know who he was speaking of. Since Caiaphas was high priest from AD 18–37, the latest possible date for the tradition is AD 37.[27] This date is so close to the death of Jesus that there would not have been sufficient time for a "legend" of His resurrection to have developed. This proves that the biblical record of Jesus' resurrection was penned while the eyewitnesses were still alive to verify the facts. Thus, His resurrection is not a mythical legend that developed long after the time of Jesus. In fact, John Rodgers, former dean of Trinity Episcopal School for Ministry, says, "This is the sort of data that historians of antiquity drool over."[28]

8. Jesus' resurrection was celebrated in the earliest church creeds. In 1 Corinthians 15:3-4, Paul says, "Christ died for our sins in accordance with the Scriptures, that he was buried, that he was raised on the third day in accordance with the Scriptures." This statement is widely accepted as the earliest church creed, which began circulating as early as AD 30-36, shortly after Jesus' resurrection. Considering the early age of this creed, there was not sufficient time between the crucifixion and the creed for any legend about Jesus' resurrection to accrue. In addition, the witnesses mentioned were still alive and available to be questioned about the facts surrounding the resurrection. The early date of this creed also proves that the church did not corrupt the truth about Jesus with fables and folklores. Rather, the early church simply clung to the plain and incontrovertible facts of Jesus' death, burial, and resurrection.

9. Jesus' resurrection convinced His family to worship him as God. James, Jesus' half-brother, was originally opposed to the claims of deity by his brother.[d] A transformation occurred in James, though, after he saw his brother resurrected from death.[e] James went on to pastor the church in Jerusalem and authored the New Testament epistle bearing his name.[f] He was also actively involved in shaping the early church, which suffered and

---

[a] 1 Cor. 15 [b] 1 Cor. 15:44 [c] Mark 14:53, 54, 60, 61, 63 [d] John 7:5 [e] 1 Cor. 15:7 [f] James 1:1

died to proclaim to everyone that Jesus is the one true God.[a] Also, Jesus' mother Mary was part of the early church that prayed to and worshiped her son as God[b], as was Jesus' other brother Jude, who wrote a book of the New Testament bearing his name.[c] While it is not impossible to imagine Jesus convincing some people that He was God if He were not, it is impossible to conceive of Jesus convincing His own mother and brothers to suffer persecution in this life and risk the torments of Hell in eternal life for worshiping Him as the one true God unless He truly was.

10. Jesus' resurrection was confirmed by his most bitter enemies, such as Paul. Paul was a devout Jewish Pharisee who routinely persecuted and killed Christians.[d] After an encounter with the risen Christ, Paul was converted and became the most dynamic defender and expander of the church.[e] Had Jesus not truly risen from death, it is absurd to assume that Paul would ever have worshiped Him as God, particularly when Paul rightly believed that worshiping a false God would send one into the eternal flames of Hell. Simply, Paul hated Jesus and would never have changed his religious practice unless Jesus had risen from death to prove him wrong. Furthermore, Paul insisted that Jesus had risen in almost all of his letters that are saved for us in the New Testament.

WHAT IS THE CIRCUMSTANTIAL EVIDENCE FOR JESUS' RESURRECTION?

Effects have causes. Jesus' resurrection is no exception, as is evident by eight effects caused by it. Together, they are compelling circumstantial evidence for Jesus' resurrection. Further, for those wanting to deny Jesus' resurrection, the burden of proof remains on them to account for these multiple effects with a reasonable cause. Craig explains, "Anyone who denies this explanation is rationally obligated to produce a more plausible cause of Jesus' resurrection and to explain how it happened."[29] He goes on to assert, "The conclusion that God raised Him up is virtually inescapable. Only a sterile, academic skepticism resists this inevitable inference."[30]

1. Jesus' disciples were transformed. Prior to the resurrection, His disciples were timid and fearful, even hiding when Jesus appeared to them.[f] Following the resurrection, however, they were all transformed into bold witnesses to what they had seen and heard, even to the point of dying in shame and poverty for their convictions, including Peter.

    Regarding the apostles' eyewitness testimony to Jesus' resurrection, Simon Greenleaf, professor of law at Harvard University and a world renowned scholar on the rules of legal evidence, said that it was "impossible that they

---

[a] Acts 12:17; 15:12-21; 21:18; Gal. 2:9 [b] Acts 1:14 [c] Acts 1:14; Jude 1
[d] Phil. 3:4-6; Acts 7:54-60 [e] Acts 9 [f] John 20:19

could have persisted in affirming the truths they have narrated, had not Jesus actually risen from the dead, and had they not known this fact as certainly as they knew any other fact."[31]

2. Jesus' disciples remained loyal to Jesus as their victorious Messiah. Modern-day "messiahs" include, for example, politicians who propose to save and deliver us from a terrible fate such as terrorism, poverty, or unreasonable taxation. Supporters flock around their messiah in hopes that he will deliver on his promise to make their dreams come true. However, when a messiah fails to deliver as promised, his followers either abandon both the cause and the messiah, or they retain the cause and abandon the messiah to instead pursue another messiah. Either way, a failed messiah is a forgotten messiah.

   However, Jesus' disciples did not abandon their cause of forgiven sin and life with God or their devotion to Jesus as their victorious Messiah. Furthermore, their devotion to both their cause and Messiah grew in numbers and passionate devotion. They endured widespread persecution and even martyrdom, which would have been unthinkable had Jesus merely died and failed to rise as He promised He would. On this point, the historian Kenneth Scott Latourette has said:

   "It was the conviction of the resurrection of Jesus which lifted his followers out of the despair into which his death had cast them and which led to the perpetuation of the movement begun by him. But for their profound belief that the crucified had risen from the dead and that they had seen him and talked with him, the death of Jesus and even Jesus himself would probably have been all but forgotten."[32]

3. The disciples had exemplary character. To claim that the disciples preached obvious lies and deluded people into dying for the world's greatest farce, one would have to first find credible evidence to challenge the character of the disciples. Also, these men were devout Jews who knew that if they worshiped a false god and encouraged others to do the same, they would be sentenced by God to the fires of eternal Hell for violating the first two commandments. Lastly, does not such egregious lying conflict with the character of men and women who gave their lives to feeding the poor, caring for widows and orphans, and helping the hurting and needy?

4. Worship changed. The early church stopped worshiping on Saturday, as Jews had for thousands of years, and suddenly began worshiping on Sunday in memory of Jesus' Sunday resurrection.[a] The Sabbath was so sacred to the Jews that they would not have ceased to obey one of the Ten Commandments unless Jesus had resurrected in fulfillment of their Old Testament Scriptures. Yet, by the end of the first century, Sunday was called "the Lord's Day."[b]

---

[a] Acts 20:7; 1 Cor. 16:1 [b] Rev. 1:10

Not only did the day of worship change after the resurrection of Jesus, but so did the object of worship. Considering that one of the Ten Commandments also forbids the worship of false gods, it is impossible to conceive of devout Jews simply worshiping Jesus as the one true God without the proof of Jesus' resurrection.

According to even non-Christian historians, multitudes began worshiping Jesus as the one true God after His resurrection. For example, Lucian of Samosata was a non-Christian Assyrian-Roman satirist who, around AD 170, wrote:

> "The Christians, you know, worship a man to this day – the distinguished personage who introduced their novel rites, and was crucified on that account...You see, these misguided creatures start with the general conviction that they are immortal for all time, which explains their contempt of death and voluntary self-devotion which are so common among them; and then it was impressed on them by their original lawgiver that they are all brothers, from the moment that they are converted, and deny the gods of Greece, and worship the crucified sage, and live after his laws."[33]

Additionally, the early church rejected the observances of the law because they saw it as having been fulfilled in Jesus; thus, the law was no longer binding upon them in the same way as it had been for some 1500 years since Sinai. This was a cataclysmic shift in belief that was only considered possible because a new epoch had been ushered in by the resurrection of Jesus.

Lastly, God's people welcomed the sacraments of baptism and communion into their worship of Jesus as God. In baptism they remembered Jesus' resurrection in their place for their salvation and anticipated their personal future resurrection. In communion, the early Christians remembered Jesus' death in their place for their sins.

5. Women discovered the empty tomb. The women who discovered the tomb were mentioned by name, were well known in the early church, and could have easily been questioned to confirm their findings if they were untrue.[a] Moreover, since the testimony of women was not respected in that culture, it would have been more likely for men to report discovering the empty tomb if the account was fictitious and an attempt were being made to concoct a credible lie about Jesus' resurrection. Therefore, the fact that women are said to have been the first to arrive at Jesus' empty tomb is confirmation that the account of Scripture is factual, not contrived.

6. The entirety of early church preaching was centered on the historical fact of Jesus' resurrection. If the empty tomb were not a widely accepted fact, the disciples would have reasoned with the skeptics of their day to defend the

---

[a] Mark 15:40, 47; 16:1

central issue of their faith. Instead, we see the debate occurring not about whether the tomb was empty, but why it was empty.[34] Also, nowhere in the preaching of the early church was the empty tomb explicitly defended, for the simple reason that it was widely known as an agreed-upon fact. Furthermore, a reading of the book of Acts shows that on virtually every occasion that preaching and teaching occurred, the resurrection of Jesus from death was the central truth being communicated because it had changed human history and could not be ignored. Jesus' resurrection appears in 12 of the 28 chapters in Acts, which records the history of the early church.

7. Jesus' tomb was not enshrined. Craig says, "It was customary in Judaism for the tomb of a prophet or holy man to be preserved or venerated as a shrine. This was so because the bones of the prophet lay in the tomb and imparted to the site its religious values. If the remains were not there, then the grave would lose its significance as a shrine."[35]

    Of the four major world religions based upon a founder as opposed to a system of ideas, only Christianity claims that the tomb of its founder is empty. Judaism looks back to Abraham, who died almost 4,000 years ago, and still cares for his grave as a holy site at Hebron. Thousands visit Buddha's tomb in India every year. Islam founder Mohammed died on June 8, AD 632, and his tomb in Medina is visited by millions of people every year.

    Additionally, Yamauchi has discovered evidence that the tombs of at least 50 prophets or other religious figures were enshrined as places of worship and veneration in Palestine around the same time as Jesus' death.[36] Yet, according to James D. G. Dunn, there is "absolutely no trace" of any veneration at Jesus' tomb.[37] The obvious reason for this lack of veneration is that Jesus was not buried but instead resurrected.

8. Christianity exploded on the earth and a few billion people today claim to be Christians. On the same day, in the same place, and in the same way, two other men died, one on Jesus' left and one on His right. Despite the similarities, we do not know the names of these men, and billions of people do not worship them as God. Why? Because they remained dead and Jesus alone rose from death and ascended into Heaven, leaving the Christian church in His wake. On this point, C.F.D. Moule of Cambridge University says, "The birth and rapid rise of the Christian Church...remain an unsolved enigma for any historian who refuses to take seriously the only explanation offered by the Church itself."[38]

WHAT IS THE HISTORICAL EVIDENCE FOR JESUS' RESURRECTION?

Because Jesus' death is a historical fact, the corroborating evidence of non-Christian sources in addition to the Bible, helps to confirm the resurrection of Jesus Christ. The following testimony of Romans, Greeks, and Jews is helpful because

DOCTRINE

these men are simply telling the facts without any religious devotion to them.

Josephus (AD 37–100)

Josephus was a Jewish historian born just a few years after Jesus died. His most celebrated passage, called the "Testimonium Flavianum," says:

"Now there was about this time Jesus, a wise man, if it be lawful to call him a man; for he was a doer of wonderful works, a teacher of such men as receive the truth with pleasure. He drew over to him both many of the Jews and many of the Gentiles. He was [the] Christ. And when Pilate, at the suggestion of the principal men among us, had condemned him to the cross, those that loved him at the first did not forsake him; for he appeared to them alive again the third day, as the divine prophets had foretold these and ten thousand other wonderful things concerning him. And the tribe of Christians, so named from him, are not extinct at this day."[39]

Suetonius (AD 70–160)

Suetonius was a Roman historian and annalist of the Imperial House. In his biography of Nero (Nero ruled AD 54–68), Suetonius mentions the persecution of Christians by indirectly referring to the resurrection: "Punishment was inflicted on the Christians, a class of men given to a new and mischievous superstition [the resurrection]."[40]

Pliny the Younger (AD 61 or 62–113)

Pliny the Younger wrote a letter to the emperor Trajan around AD 111 describing early Christian worship gatherings that met early on Sunday mornings in memory of Jesus' resurrection day:

"I have never been present at an examination of Christians. Consequently, I do not know the nature of the extent of the punishments usually meted out to them, nor the grounds for starting an investigation and how far it should be pressed... They also declared that the sum total of their guilt or error amounted to no more than this: they had met regularly before dawn on a fixed day [Sunday in remembrance of Jesus' resurrection] to chant verses alternately amongst themselves in honor of Christ as if to a god."[41]

The Jewish Explanation

The earliest attempt to provide an alternative explanation for the resurrection of Jesus did not deny that the tomb was empty.[a] Instead, Jewish opponents claimed that the body had been stolen, thus admitting the fact of the empty tomb. But this explanation is untenable for the following reasons. (1) The tomb was closed with an enormous rock and sealed by the government, and there is no explanation for how the rock was moved while being guarded by armed Roman soldiers. (2) If the

---

[a] Matt. 28:13–15

body had been stolen, a large ransom could have been offered to the thieves, and they could have been coerced to produce the body. Or if it had been taken by the disciples, then the torture and death they suffered should have been sufficient to return the body. (3) Even if the body was stolen, how are we to account for the fact that Jesus appeared to multiple crowds of people, proving that he was alive? In conclusion, the theft of the body is unlikely and still fails to account for it returning back to life.

Summarily, the historical testimony of those who were not Christians stands in agreement with Scripture that Jesus died and rose because those are the historical facts.

WHAT ARE THE PRIMARY ANCIENT OBJECTIONS TO JESUS' RESURRECTION?

Jesus did not die on the cross but merely swooned.

Some have argued that Jesus did not in fact die on the cross but rather swooned or basically passed out and therefore appeared dead. Regarding this claim, theologian John Stott has asked if we are to believe that after the rigors and pains of trial, mockery, flogging and crucifixion He could survive 36 hours in a stone sepulcher with neither warmth nor food nor medical care? That He could then rally sufficiently to perform the superhuman feat of shifting the boulder which secured the mouth of the tomb, and this without disturbing the Roman guard? That then, weak and sickly and hungry, He could appear to the disciples in such a way as to give them the impression that He had vanquished death? That He could go on to claim that He had died and risen, could send them into all the world and promise to be with them unto the end of time? That He could live somewhere in hiding for 40 days, making occasional surprise appearances, and then finally disappear without explanations? Such credulity is more incredible than Thomas' unbelief.[42]

Also, as we've noted, crucifixion is essentially death by asphyxiation, because the prisoner grows too tired to lift himself up and fill his lungs with air. This explains why the Romans would often break a prisoner's legs, thus preventing him from continuing to fill his lungs with air. Since the professional executioners did not break Jesus' legs, these professional executioners must have been convinced of His death. The only way Jesus could have deceived the executioners would have been to stop breathing, which in itself would have killed Him.

Lastly, John 19:34–35 tells us that the Roman soldier thrust a spear into Jesus' heart to confirm His death. The water that poured out was probably from the sac surrounding His heart, and the blood most likely came from the right side of His heart. Even if He had been alive, this would have killed Him.[43]

Jesus did not rise and His body was stolen.

The original explanation given for the empty tomb by those Jews who did not choose to worship Jesus as God was that the tomb was indeed empty, but not because of a resurrection but because of a theft of Jesus' dead body.[a] For this to be true, a number of impossibilities would have had to occur. (1) Despite the fact that it would have cost them their lives, all the guards positioned at the tomb would have had to fall asleep at the same time. (2) Each of the guards would have had to not only fall asleep but also remain asleep and not be awakened by the breaking of the Roman seal on the tomb, the rolling away of the enormous stone which blocked the entrance, or the carrying off of the dead body. (3) Even if Jesus' body was stolen, there is no way to account for its returning to vibrant and triumphant life.

The issue of motive is also a key factor in refuting this hypothesis. What benefit would there be for the disciples to risk their lives to steal a corpse and die for a lie as a result? What motive would there be for the Jews, Romans, or anyone else to steal the body? And, if the body were truly stolen, could not a bounty have been offered and someone enticed to provide the body in exchange for a handsome cash reward?

A twin brother, or a look-alike, died in Jesus' place.

It has been suggested by some people that Jesus was not the one crucified but rather a brother or other man who looked like Him. However, there is not a shred of evidence to prove that someone who looked like Jesus existed at that time. Additionally, Jesus' mother was present at His crucifixion, and the likelihood of fooling His mother is minimal. Also, the physical wounds He suffered during the crucifixion were visible on Jesus' resurrection body and carefully inspected by the disciple Thomas, who was very doubtful that Jesus had risen until he touched scars from the crucifixion evident on Jesus' body.[b] In addition, the tomb was empty, and the burial cloths were left behind.

Jesus' followers hallucinated His resurrection.

Some people have suggested that the disciples did not actually see Jesus risen from death but rather hallucinated, or projected, their desires for his resurrection into a hallucination. One example is John Dominic Crossan, co-chairman of the Jesus Seminar. He told Time Magazine that after the crucifixion, Jesus' corpse was probably laid in a shallow grave, barely covered with dirt, and eaten by wild dogs. The subsequent story of Jesus' resurrection, he says, was merely the result of "wishful thinking."[44]

Similarly, fellow Jesus Seminar member John Shelby Spong, an Episcopal bishop, denies the resurrection and believes Jesus' body was thrown in a common grave along with other crucifixion victims. Subsequently, he says the "Easter moment" happened to Peter, not to Jesus. Peter saw Jesus alive in "the heart of God" and began to open the eyes of the other disciples to this reality.[45] Spong

---

[a] Matt. 28:11–15 [b] John 20:24-28

writes, "That was the dawn of Easter in human history. It would be fair to say that in that moment Simon felt resurrected."[46]

This thesis is unbelievable for five reasons. (1) A hallucination is a private, not public, experience. Yet Paul clearly states that Jesus appeared to more than 500 people at one time.[a] (2) Jesus appeared in a variety of times at a variety of locations, whereas hallucinations are generally restricted to individual times and places. (3) Certain types of people tend to be more prone to hallucination than others. Yet Jesus appeared to a great variety of personalities, including His brothers and mother. (4) After 40 days, Jesus' appearances suddenly stopped for everyone simultaneously. Hallucinations tend to continue over longer periods of time and do not stop abruptly. (5) A hallucination is a projection of a thought that preexists in the mind. However, the Jews had a conception of resurrection that applied to the raising of all people at the end of history[b], not the raising of any particular individual in the middle of history.[47] Therefore, it is inconceivable that the witnesses to the resurrection could have hallucinated Jesus' resurrection.

In considering the objections to the resurrection of Jesus Christ, C. S. Lewis's charge of "chronological snobbery" begins to make sense.[48] Each of the objections is predicated upon the assumption that people in Jesus' day were less intelligent and more gullible than we are today. However, it can be argued persuasively that in their world with fewer hospitals, medicines, and hospices to care for dying people, they were more personally aware of the finality of death than we moderns are. Additionally, as we have already surveyed, they did not even believe in resurrection, and because of the influence of Greek dualism upon them, which considered the body an unwanted husk to be discarded so the soul could truly live, the entire idea of resurrection was undesirable. Taken together, it is apparent that such chronological snobbery reveals more about the character of those moderns who appeal to it than those ancients who are dismissed by it.

WHAT HAS THE RESURRECTION ACCOMPLISHED FOR CHRISTIANS?

Those who come into God's family will be joined to Jesus in His death and resurrection life.[c] This is what John calls being born again[d] and Peter calls new birth.[e] This is what theologians call regernation, which means we have a new heart, godly desires at the core of our being, the indwelling Holy Spirit, and live with resurrection power.

Jesus' resurrection reveals Him as our Messiah King. In the Davidic covenant[f], God the Father promised that his Son, Jesus Christ, would be raised up from David's lineage to rule over an everlasting kingdom. Paul reveals that this was fulfilled at the resurrection of Jesus: "Concerning his Son, who was descended from David according to the flesh and was declared to be the Son of God in

---

[a] 1 Cor. 15:1–6 [b] E.g., Dan. 12:2 [c] Rom. 6:3-5 [d] John 3:1-16 [e] 1 Pet. 1:3,23 [f] 2 Sam. 7:7-16

power according to the Spirit of holiness by his resurrection from the dead, Jesus Christ our Lord."[a] Now that the risen Christ has been installed as our Messiah King, we can rest assured that one day Jesus will return to establish His throne on the earth and rule over His Kingdom, which extends to all of creation.

Furthermore, following Jesus' resurrection, an angel declared, "He is not here, for he has risen, as he said."[b] Therefore, the resurrection is proof that Jesus' teaching was and is truth that we can trust. Practically, Jesus' resurrection gives us confidence in His other promises that we are waiting to see fulfilled, such as His returning one day to judge sinners[c] and reward saints.[d] The Bible often speaks of our being united with Christ by His resurrection[e], being raised with Christ[f], and enjoying the same powerful Holy Spirit that raised Christ.[g] In so doing, the Bible is stressing the innumerable blessings and benefits conferred on believers because of Jesus' resurrection.

Paul stresses the fact that, through Jesus' death and resurrection, we have forgiveness of sins.[h] Because of Jesus, those with faith in Him can live with the great joy of knowing that all their sins – past, present, and future – have been forgiven once and for all by Jesus Christ. Furthermore, as the power of Jesus' resurrection works itself out in our sanctification, we grow in holiness, learning to live in victory over sin, until one day, upon our own resurrection, we will live forever, free from the presence, power, and practice of all sin. Elsewhere, Jesus' resurrection is spoken of as the source of our justification, thereby enabling us, though sinners, to be declared righteous in the sight of God. Paul explicitly states that Jesus was "raised for our justification".[i]

Regarding our future, Jesus' resurrection is the precedent and pattern of our own: "Christ has been raised from the dead, the firstfruits of those who have fallen asleep."[k] As His body was resurrected in complete health, so too will we rise and never experience pain, injury, or death ever again. This is because, through the resurrection, Jesus has put death to death. Additionally, Wright makes the insightful observation that "the message of the resurrection is that this present world matters."[49] Because Jesus rose from death physically, we learn that God, through Christ, intends to reclaim and restore all that he made in creation and saw corrupted through the Fall. Our eternity will be spent in a world much like the one enjoyed by our first parents in Eden, because the earth has been reclaimed and restored by God through Jesus' resurrection.

The full effects of Jesus' resurrection will be seen one day, following Jesus' return. The time between Jesus' resurrection and our resurrection is a lengthy season of love, grace, and mercy as news of the Gospel goes forth, inviting sinners to repent of sin and enjoy the present and future salvation of Jesus Christ. Paul preached just this fact and the urgent need for sinners to repent:

---

[a] Rom. 1:3-4 [b] Matt. 28:6 [c] John 3:16, 18, 36, 5:25-29 [d] John 14:3 [e] Rom. 6:5 [f] Col. 2:12; 3:1 [g] 1 Cor. 6:14; 2 Cor. 5:15 [h] 1 Cor. 15:3-58 [i] Rom. 4:25 [k] 1 Cor. 15:20

"The times of ignorance God overlooked, but now he commands all people everywhere to repent, because he has fixed a day on which he will judge the world in righteousness by a man whom he has appointed; and of this he has given assurance to all by raising him from the dead."[a] In closing, no one can remain neutral regarding Jesus' resurrection. The claim is too staggering, the event is too earthshaking, the implications are too significant, and the matter is too serious. We must each either receive or reject it as truth for us, and to remain indifferent or undecided is to reject it.

WHAT IS THE HOPE OF JESUS' RESURRECTION?

Many years after the death of my Grandpa George, history repeated itself. My wife Grace got a call shortly after Christmas that her dad was dying. We were out of state on vacation at the time and hurried to the hospital to say our goodbyes.

Our five children had a lot of questions about the death of their grandpa Gib, most of them the same ones I had with my Grandpa George. In the days surrounding his death, we had some amazing and hopeful conversations.

Grandpa Gib was a pastor who loved Jesus and spent most of his life ministering to hurting people. So, we gave them the hope of the resurrection of Jesus Christ. First, we told them that, after dying, Grandpa Gib had everything not only get better but become perfect because "to live is Christ, and to die is gain."[b] Second, we told them that Grandpa Gib was hanging out with Jesus Christ, his favorite Person because to be "away from the body" is to be "at home with the Lord."[c] Third, we told them that my Grandpa George and their Grandpa Gib were probably hanging out as friends having fun. Fourth, we told them that one day there would be a huge family reunion when Jesus returns to give us perfect health in a resurrected body to live forever in a world filled with peace, joy, and sunshine together since "in fact Christ has been raised from the dead, the firstfruits of those who have fallen asleep. For as by a man came death, by a man has come also the resurrection of the dead. For as in Adam all die, so also in Christ shall all be made alive."[d]

The Bible says that believers should grieve, but not like unbelievers who have no hope because our hope is in the risen Christ Jesus![e] So, we grieved as a family, thanked God for the memories with our grandpas, and had fun imagining what eternity will be like at the family reunion. One of the kids asked if they could play whiffle ball with the grandpas. Another asked if the grandpas could take them swimming and buy them ice cream. Since none was a sin, I told them that sounded like a good thing to look forward to. We explained that, after resurrection, we would all be happy living in a Kingdom made up by brothers and sisters from

---

[a] Acts 17:30-31 [b] Phil. 1:21 [c] 2 Cor. 5:8 [d] 1 Cor. 15:20-22 [e] 1 Thess. 4:13

DOCTRINE

across the nations enjoying sunshine every day.

Hilariously, one of the kids said, "So heaven is basically like Disneyland in California!" We chuckled, thought about it for a moment, and said yes but only it's better. King Jesus is better than Mickey Mouse, the church is a better bride than Minnie Mouse, the Kingdom of Heaven is better than the magical Kingdom, and there's no entrance fee as Jesus picks up the tab for everyone forever. Since that time, every time we go to Disneyland, we joke that we are practicing for Heaven.

QUESTIONS FOR PERSONAL JOURNALING AND/OR SMALL GROUP DISCUSSION

1. If someone asked you about your belief in Jesus' resurrection, what would your answer be?
2. When you think of Heaven, do you mainly think of life without a body or life with a resurrected body? Why or why not?
3. Do you believe that the concept of Jesus' resurrection was unique or borrowed from previous non-Christian beliefs?
4. Do you believe there is any way that Jesus could have survived all that He endured without dying? Why or why not?
5. Do you believe that Jesus Christ died and rose from death? What is the most compelling line of reasoning for your position?
6. Can you think of any reason that the disciples would talk about and suffer for Jesus' resurrection if it were, in fact, a big hoax?
7. Have you ever been baptized to associate yourself with the risen Jesus? Why or why not?
8. What difference does it make when people are suffering and dying to believe that Jesus conquered death and, because of Him, so can other people?
9. Have you ever known a Christian who was preparing to die? How did their belief in Jesus' resurrection change their view of death?
10. Is there someone you would most like to rise from death and spend time with? Who?

CHAPTER 10: CHURCH

"GOD ACTS"

Christ loved the church and gave himself up for her.
EPHESIANS 5:25

On the day that Jesus died, He was crucified with two other men. All three suffered the same fate in the same way on the same day. The other men, we know nothing about. Like countless other criminals, their names are not famous, and no movement or tribute of any sort or kind has arisen in their wake.

In stark contrast, no movement of any sort or kind is as stunning as the Christian Church. From one unmarried, poor, rural peasant who died in his early thirties, a few thousand years later, Christianity is the most diverse, long-lasting, far reaching, global movement of any kind in world history with a few billion people on planet earth who confess devotion to Jesus Christ.

Napoleon Bonaparte even admitted that Jesus greatly surpassed his own conquests saying, "I know men; and I tell you that Jesus Christ is not a man. Superficial minds see a resemblance between Christ and the founders of empires, and the gods of other religions. That resemblance does not exist. There is between Christianity and whatever other religions the distance of infinity...His religion is a revelation from an intelligence which certainly is not that of man...Alexander, Caesar, Charlemagne, and myself founded empires; but upon what foundation did we rest the creations of our genius? Upon force! But Jesus Christ founded His upon love; and at this hour millions of men would die for Him."[1]

The story of the Christian Church is among the most amazing in history. It proves the power of the presence of the Holy Spirit among God's people to continue the message and ministry of Christ through Christians.

HOW DID JESUS PREPARE HIS PEOPLE FOR THE COMING OF THE CHURCH?

Before a product hits the market, politician hits the campaign trail, or movie hits the screen, a great deal of advance marketing is done to let people know and prepare for what is coming. The hope is to increase awareness and excitement that translates to action.

Before His death and resurrection Jesus did something similar announcing His plan for His Church, "I will build my church, and the gates of hell shall not prevail against it."[a] Jesus' imagery is one of spiritual warfare. Satan has held people captive and surrounded them with bars to hold them in their cell. The bars are things like lies, temptations, addictions, and deceptions that keep them in bondage. The Church is to be the equivalent of a spiritual military force coming in to kick down gates and set captives free.

This offensive, on-mission kind of Church is possible only by the power of the Holy Spirit. The only way to battle the unholy spirits at work in the world is by the power of the Holy Spirit at work in the Church. In the days leading up to His death, Jesus also said, "it is to your advantage that I go away, for if I do not go away, the Helper will not come to you. But if I go, I will send him to you…When the Spirit of truth comes, he will guide you into all the truth, for he will not speak on his own authority, but whatever he hears he will speak, and he will declare to you the things that are to come. He will glorify me, for he will take what is mine and declare it to you."[b]

Following His resurrection, just prior to His ascension back into heaven, Jesus promised the first Christians, "You will receive power when the Holy Spirit has come upon you, and you will be my witnesses in Jerusalem and in all Judea and Samaria, and to the end of the earth."[c] Jesus' promise has come true and remained true every day since. The Church has exploded on the earth from 120 people in one nation with one language to a few billion people in a few thousand languages in countless nations. What accounts for the power of the church is not it's amazing leadership, political strength, or favorable press? The only thing that can explain the power of the Church is the presence of the Spirit.

Before dying, rising, and returning to His throne over all, Jesus anticipated a question that would arise after He departed. God is holy in Heaven, and we are sinful on earth. When Jesus came down, He bridged an infinite gap that no one and nothing else could fill. However, when He returned to Heaven, would we be orphaned without God's presence, and abandoned by a God like a father who walked out on his family? Jesus promised the family of God called the Church, "I will ask the Father, and he will give you another Helper, to be with you forever, even the Spirit of truth…You know him, for he dwells with you and will be in you.

---

[a] Matt.16:18 [b] John 16:7-14 [c] Acts 1:8 [d] John 14:16-17; 25-26

I will not leave you as orphans; I will come to you...These things I have spoken to you while I am still with you. But the Helper, the Holy Spirit, whom the Father will send in my name, he will teach you all things and bring to your remembrance all that I have said to you."[d]

WHAT IS THE RELATIONSHIP BETWEEN THE HOLY SPIRIT AND THE CHURCH?

Not only did Jesus come from Heaven to earth on a global rescue mission, He sent the Holy Spirit to fill the Church with His power to proclaim His message and continue His mission. From Pentecost to the present, the driving power force behind this global rescue force unleashed from Heaven is God the Holy Spirit through the Christian Church.

The historian of Christ and one of the first Christians is the medical doctor, Luke. The Gospel of Luke was written to tell the history of the Spirit-filled Christ and Acts to tell the history of the Spirit-filled Christians. This insight is crucial in the same way that understanding a prequel movie is vital to fully appreciating the sequel.

Luke's work is important because the Christian Church is more than philosophy or spirituality, as our faith rests upon historical facts like Jesus' resurrection from death and the Spirit falling on the Church in power. Sir William Ramsay, a world-famous archaeologist who taught at Oxford and Aberdeen, was knighted for his service to scholarship, made an honorary member of almost every historical and archaeological association, and was awarded the Victorian Medal of the Royal Geographical Society. He began examining the writings of Dr. Luke in the New Testament with the express intent of disproving them as actual and factual history. In the end, Ramsay concluded, "Luke is a historian of the first rank...This author should be placed along with the very greatest of historians."[2] Dr. William Lane Craig concludes, "Given Luke's care and demonstrated reliability as well as his contact with eyewitnesses within the first generation after the events, this author is trustworthy."[3]

Luke opens Acts saying, "'In the first book [Luke], O Theophilus, I have dealt with all that Jesus began to do and teach, until the day when he was taken up, after he had given commands through the Holy Spirit to the apostles whom he had chosen. He presented himself alive to them after his suffering by many proofs, appearing to them during forty days and speaking about the kingdom of God. And while staying with them he ordered them not to depart from Jerusalem, but to wait for the promise of the Father...you will be baptized with the Holy Spirit not many days from now...you will receive power when the Holy Spirit has come upon you, and you will be my witnesses in Jerusalem and in all Judea and Samaria, and to the end of the earth.' And when he had said these things, as they were looking on, he was lifted up, and a cloud took him out of their sight."

The book of Acts is often called the Acts of the Apostles, but a better title might be the Acts of the Holy Spirit. Jesus was clear that the continuation of His message

and ministry were impossible without the same Spirit who empowered Him. In this, we learn three tantamount truths:
1. God works for you. This is Jesus' life, death, burial, and resurrection for you to become a Christian.
2. God works in you. This is Jesus' life through the Holy Spirit in you growing you as a Christian to be more and more like Christ.
3. God works through you. This is Jesus' life through the Holy Spirit working through you as a member of the Church to help others become Christians.

HOW DID THE NEW COVENANT CHURCH BEGIN?

The fulfillment of Jesus' promise that the Holy Spirit would come in power once He ascended back into Heaven is historically reported by Luke in Acts 2:1-7, 14-18, "When the day of Pentecost arrived, they were all together in one place. And suddenly there came from heaven a sound like a mighty rushing wind, and it filled the entire house where they were sitting. And divided tongues as of fire appeared to them and rested on each one of them. And they were all filled with the Holy Spirit and began to speak in other tongues as the Spirit gave them utterance. Now there were dwelling in Jerusalem Jews, devout men from every nation under heaven. And at this sound the multitude came together, and they were bewildered, because each one was hearing them speak in his own language...But Peter, standing with the eleven, lifted up his voice and addressed them...But this is what was uttered through the prophet Joel: 'And in the last days it shall be, God declares, that I will pour out my Spirit on all flesh...I will pour out my Spirit, and they shall prophesy. And I will show wonders in the heavens above and signs on the earth below...'"

God and His family of divine beings who were present for Creation[a] were also present for the Church. This is because the Church is the place between the cultures on earth and God's Kingdom of Heaven, connected by the Spirit who brings the seen and unseen realms together.

Dr. Michael Heiser has done a great deal of groundbreaking scholarly research on the unseen realm in the Bible. Regarding the Church on the day of Pentecost, he says, "The first two points of the description that deserve attention are the 'violent rushing wind' and the 'divided tongues like fire.' Both are images in the Old Testament associated with God's presence—the disciples are being commissioned by God in his council like the prophets of old." He goes on to say, "The whirlwind is familiar from divine encounters of Elijah (2 Kgs 2:1, 11) and Job (Job 38:1; 40:6). Ezekiel's divine commissioning likewise has the enthroned Yahweh coming with great wind (Ezek 1:4). The whirlwind motif is often accompanied by storm imagery, which can also include fire (Isa 30:30). Having 'wind' as an element in describing God's presence makes sense given that the

---
[a] Job 38:3-7

Hebrew word translated 'wind' can also be rendered 'spirit/Spirit' (ruach)." And, he concludes by explaining, "Ezekiel's commissioning is particularly instructive since not only does Yahweh come to him with a wind, but with the wind there is 'fire flashing' (Ezek. 1:4). Burning fire is a familiar element of divine-council throne-room scenes (e.g., Isa 6:4, 6; Dan 7:9). It is especially prominent in the appearances at Sinai (Exod 3:2; 19:18; 20:18; Isa 4:5). Fire in the Old Testament was an identifier of the presence of God, a visible manifestation of Yahweh's glory and essence. It was also a way of describing divine beings in God's service (Judges 13:20; Psalm 104:4)."[4]

The new covenant church of Jesus Christ began with the pouring out of the Spirit of God on the day of Pentecost. What happened that day "came from Heaven" as the unseen realm flooded and invaded the seen realm and included "a sound like a mighty rushing wind" (Spirit of God) as "tongues as of fire appeared to them and rested on each one of them. And they were all filled with the Holy Spirit."

God intended that His two families—human and divine—live and work together as one united family with the unseen and seen realms united. Sin caused humanity to rebel against God and side with Satan and demons, separating us from God and angels. Everything changed with Jesus defeating the demonic realm on the cross, reclaiming us as His people, and reconnecting human beings and divine beings as God's one family. At Pentecost, the two realms and two families were reunited once again, as the divine council was present at Pentecost with the first Christians.

The wind and fire in Acts 2 signified to readers informed by divine council scenes that the gathered followers of Jesus were being commissioned by divine encounter. They were being chosen to preach the good news of Jesus' work. The fire connects them to the throne room. The tongues are emblematic of their speaking ministry.[a]

The Church in one realm is created by the Kingdom in the other realm. The Church serves as the outpost for the Kingdom, exists to witness to the Kingdom, and is the beginning of the unveiling of God's Kingdom across all creation. Starting at Pentecost, God intended that both His families would work together through the Church until they were together as one united forever family upon Jesus' Second Coming.

The union of God's divine and human families in the unseen realm of the invisible Church and the seen realm of the visible Church includes divine leaders in addition to human leaders in local churches. We see this fact in Revelation 2-3 where each of the seven local churches is said to have an "angel" and is told, "he who has an ear, let him hear what the Spirit says to the churches." There is a lot more going on in a local church than we see with our eye, and a lot more supernatural activity than we are aware of in the unseen realm. Just because we

---

[a] Ibid.

DOCTRINE

don't see what is happening does not mean that God is not acting. All of this is overseen by Jesus who is the Head over the Church, ruling over the seen realm from the unseen realm.

WHAT IS JESUS' RELATIONSHIP TO THE CHURCH?

Jesus' incarnation was in many ways a mission trip led and empowered by God the Holy Spirit.[a] Jesus' cross-cultural transition from Heaven was starker than any missionary has ever experienced. Jesus came down from Heaven to live in this sinful culture. He participated in it fully by using a language, participating in various holidays, eating food, enjoying drink, attending parties, living under Godless government, enduring religious critics, experiencing demonic attack, and befriending people. Jesus identified with its real brokenness to bring a better redemption. Still, Jesus did not condone sin, nor did He Himself ever sin. Finally, Jesus sent and sends the Christian Church on His exact same mission to be missionaries in culture as he was.

In fact, the term "Christian" only appears three times in the New Testament. It was originally a pejorative term, mocking believers for trying to be a little Jesus. Since that is actually our hope, believers adopted the negative name as a positive goal, and we've been called Christians ever since. To be a Christian is to, by God's grace through the Spirit's power, seek to be a little bit of Jesus in this world. Therefore, the key is to learn about Jesus so we can follow Him on mission into the world.

In John's Gospel alone, Jesus told us no less than 39 times that He was a missionary from Heaven who came to minister incarnationally in an earthly culture.[b] In His magnificent high priestly prayer[c], Jesus prayed that we would become neither syncretistic liberals who sin by going too far into culture by rebelling against God, nor separatist fundamentalists who sin by not going far enough into culture by becoming religious. There is always a tendency to become the younger brother who was unrighteous or the older brother who was self-righteous as Jesus taught in the Parable of the Prodigal and also prayed against.

Jesus commands us to live in the world like a boat in water. The boat should be in the water, but there are real problems when the water gets into the boat. Jesus' commands for us to be missionaries in culture as He was could not be clearer. In John 17:18, Jesus said, "As you sent me into the world, so I have sent them into the world." In John 20:21, Jesus said, "As the Father has sent me, even so I am sending you."

The Gospels give us the story of the Spirit-empowered ministry of Jesus Christ

---

[a] Luke 1:35, 67-79, 2:11, 25-38, 3:22, 4:14, 4:18; cf. Isa. 61:1-2 [b] John 3:34, 4:34, 5:23, 24, 30, 36, 37, 38, 6:29, 38, 39, 44, 57, 7:16, 28, 29, 33, 8:16, 18, 26, 29, 42, 9:4, 10:36, 11:42, 12:44, 45, 49, 13:20, 14:24, 15:21, 16:5, 17:3, 8, 18, 21, 23, 25, 20:21 [c] John 17:15-18

so we would know who He is. Acts gives us the story of the Spirit-empowered ministry of Jesus' people, the Church, who worship Jesus as God and continue His mission so we would know who we are. As the church, we follow the example of Jesus by being Spirit-filled and Spirit-led, which defines the mission of the Church. This is why Luke is careful to show that the Holy Spirit descended on both Jesus and the church, empowering the church to continue the mission of Jesus in the world.[a]

As we take the Gospel to the world, churches, as communities of Jesus followers, will come together. It is essential that we never forget that Jesus and Jesus alone is:

- The head of the Church.[b] He is supreme. He is prominent. He is preeminent.
- The apostle who plants a church.[c] There is no church that comes into existence apart from Him. Those who are caught up in the hard work of church planting must always remember that Jesus is the apostle. While we can start an organization, only He can plant a church.
- The leader who builds the Church.[d] Ministry leaders go to work with Him, but unless He shows up, a church will not be built.
- The Chief Shepherd who rules the Church.[e] The Bible is clear that all the other pastors and leaders in churches are supposed to work under His leadership following His teaching and extending His mission.
- Present with the Church.[f] Jesus is the one who says, "I am with you always." In His exaltation, and through the Spirit, He is with us[g] and we are in Him.[h]
- The judge of the Church.[i] Since churches belong to Jesus, He has the authority to judge them, scatter them, close them, or whatever else He wants for whatever reasons He decides.

Jesus Himself said that He is the vine, and we are the branches.[k] What Jesus meant is that there is no Christian life for the Church apart from Him. There are many branches that we know as denominations, networks, and traditions of Christian churches. Assemblies of God, Evangelical Free, Lutheran, Presbyterian, Baptist, Foursquare, and independent churches are each one of many branches. What keeps every church alive, healthy, growing, and fruitful is an ongoing rootedness in and connectedness to the living Jesus Christ. Seeing things as Jesus does allows us to celebrate the fruitfulness in both our branch as well as the branches of other churches, since we are all the same proverbial tree.

WHAT ARE THE CHARACTERISTICS OF THE CHURCH?

The assumption that Christians innately know what the Church is has a long history. The early church debated many things, such as the Trinity and the

---

[a] Luke 3:21-22; Acts 2:1-4 [b] Eph. 1:22, 4:15, 5:23 [c] Heb. 3:1 [d] Matt. 16:18 [e] 1 Pet. 5:4 [f] Matt. 28:18-20 [g] Col. 1:27 [h] John 17:21; Rom. 8:1; 1 Cor. 1:30; 2 Cor. 5:17; Phil. 3:9 [i] Rev. 2:5 [k] John 15:1-8

relationship between the humanity and divinity of Jesus Christ. However, one issue it did not debate was what constitutes the Church. After Cyprian, bishop of Carthage, wrote "The Unity of the Church" in AD 251 until Wycliffe wrote "The Church" in 1378, there was no significant monograph on the Church.[5]

Everything changed in the sixteenth century when the Reformation forced Protestants and Roman Catholics alike to actually define church. This led to numerous definitions and debates, which continue to this day with no widespread agreement. For example, the Evangelical Dictionary of Theology says: "The Arnoldists emphasized poverty and identification with the masses; the Waldenses stressed literal obedience to Jesus' teachings and emphasized evangelical preaching. Roman Catholics claimed that the only true church was that over which the pope was supreme as successor of the apostle Peter. The Reformers Martin Luther and John Calvin, following John Wycliffe, distinguished between the visible and invisible church, claiming that the invisible church consists of the elect only. Thus, an individual, including the pope, might be a part of the visible church but not a part of the invisible and true church."[6]

Part of the confusion is that the Greek word *ekklēsia*, which is translated "church," has a wide range of meaning.[7] Originally, it sometimes designated any public assembly, including a full-blown riot.[a] In the Septuagint (the Greek translation of the Hebrew Old Testament), the word is translated *qāhāl*, which designates the assembly of God's people.[b] So, in the New Testament, *ekklēsia* may signify the assembly of the Israelites.[c]

Most of the uses of the word *ekklēsia* in the New Testament designate the Christian church as both the local church[d] and the universal Church.[e]

The English word church derives from the Greek word *kyriakon*, which means "the Lord's."[f] Later it came to mean the Lord's house, a church building which is not the original biblical emphasis. The church is a family, and every family needs a house to live in. But the important thing is the family and not the house. Wayne Grudem helpfully summarizes the uses of a church:

"A 'house church' is called a 'church' in Romans 16:5 ('greet also the church in their house') and 1 Corinthians 16:19 ('Aquila and Prisca, together with the church in their house, send you hearty greetings in the Lord'). The church in an entire city is also called 'a church' (1 Cor. 1:2, 2 Cor. 1:1 and 1 Thess. 1:1). The church in a region is referred to as a 'church' in Acts 9:31: 'So the church throughout all Judea and Galilee and Samaria had peace and was built up.' Finally, the church throughout the entire world can be referred to as 'the church.' Paul says, 'Christ loved the church and gave himself up for her' (Eph. 5:25) and says, 'God has appointed in the church first apostles, second prophets, third teachers...' (1 Cor.

---

[a] Acts 19:32, 39, 41 [b] Deut. 10:4; 23:2-3; 31:30; Ps. 22:23 [c] Acts 7:38; Heb. 2:12 [d] Matt. 18:17; Acts 15:41; Rom. 16:16; 1 Cor. 4:17, 7:17, 14:33; Col. 4:15 [e] Matt. 16:18; Acts 20:28; 1 Cor. 12:28,15:9; Eph. 1:22 [f] 1 Cor. 11:20; Rev. 1:10

12:28) ...We may conclude that the group of God's people considered at any level from local to universal may rightly be called 'a church.'"[8]

Various Christian traditions are prone to define the Church—or their church—in an unhealthy and reductionistic manner, focusing on one primary metaphor at the expense of the full breadth of New Testament teaching. As a result, they become imbalanced in some way and, therefore, unhealthy. For example, the corporate Church is referred to as the bride of Christ. The result of overemphasizing this metaphor is the effeminate nature of much of evangelical preaching and singing and partial explanation why grown men are the least likely people to attend church.[9]

There are innumerable erroneous definitions and assumptions about what the Church is. The Church is not where two or more or gathered, as that is actually the minimal number of witnesses required to convict someone for a sin.[a] The Church is not a holy building in which spiritual meetings take place even though, like other families, the Church family often does have a physical home. The Church is not a Eucharistic society through which God dispenses grace by means of the sacraments and a duly authorized and empowered hierarchy of bishops and priests operating in unbroken succession from the apostles. The Church is not the moral police force of a society seeking mere behavioral change through legislation. The Church is not a weekly social club where people gather to do spiritual things that they find pleasing.

Thankfully, what the Church is can be found in Scripture. The book of Acts is the historical account of the early church. There, we see the New Testament church birthed through the Spirit-filled preaching of Peter's sermon at the holiday of Pentecost. Summarizing the church as described in Acts 2:42–47, we get a biblical definition of Church as God meant it to be:

The local church is a community of regenerated believers who confess Jesus Christ as Lord. In obedience to Scripture, they organize under qualified leaders, gather regularly for preaching and worship, observe the biblical sacraments of baptism and Communion, are unified by the Spirit, correct works of the flesh for holiness, and scatter to fulfill the Great Commandment and the Great Commission as missionaries to the world for God's glory and their joy.

Throughout the centuries, church leaders have characterized the church according to four marks:

1. The Church is unified by the confession and shared life of Christ through the Spirit.
2. The Church is holy by its Christlike character, not just by what it doesn't do through religiously obeying rules, but by actually living out new life modeled after Jesus by the Holy Spirit's power.
3. The Church is catholic (universal); the Church and its Gospel have no limits in time or space because Jesus is Lord of all people, not just a people.

---

[a] Deut. 19:15; Matt. 18:15-20

DOCTRINE

    4. The Church is apostolic as it lives under apostolic authority, following the faith and life of the apostles given to us in the Bible.

In addition to these marks, the Reformers added the marks of:

    5. Pure preaching of the Word centered on Christ
    6. Right administration of the sacraments of baptism and communion
    7. Discipline or correction of works of the flesh to be replaced by the fruit of the Spirit

While good, we believe that even these seven marks are not quite sufficient to capture the thoroughness of the biblical definition of the Church. They omit both the Great Commandment to love God and neighbor and the Great Commission to take the Gospel to the whole world. If we follow the definition of "church" summarized from Acts 2, we can identify eight key characteristics of the local church. Understanding them will provide standards for planning for and evaluating health in every church.

    1. The church is made up of believers born again of the Spirit.[a] The Spirit dwells in them and has given them new hearts that love Jesus and a new nature that desires holiness. A church is a fellowship of true disciples who are devoted to the apostles' teaching and the fellowship, to the breaking of bread and the prayers[b], and to attending meetings together and fellowshipping in their homes with glad and generous hearts as the family of God.[c]

        There are unbelievers and outsiders who participate in the activity of the church and have an important place in the extended community.[d] Likewise, children are welcomed into the church to be loved and served so that they would become Christians with saving faith and later become church members. But the church itself, the body of Christ, is made up of confessing believers who are justified by faith and made new by the Spirit. The church is a community manifesting the supernatural life of the triune God.

    2. The church is organized under qualified and competent Spirit-led leadership. In Acts 2 we see them exercising their unique role of teaching the whole church.[e] They led the congregation in wise decision-making about a potentially divisive problem.[f] They sent Peter and John to Samaria to confirm the authenticity of the evangelistic outbreak there.[g] We also see the appointment of leaders.[h] In the next chapter, they practice their leadership in a doctrinal dispute with the party of the Pharisees in Jerusalem. The Bible also describes leaders in the church with a myriad of terms, including ministry teams led by both men and women.[i]

    3. The church regularly gathers for Bible preaching and worship. The church is under the apostolic authority of Scripture. In Acts, people eagerly devoted

---

[a] Acts 2:36–41 [b] Acts 2:42 [c] Acts 2:46 [d] 1 Cor. 14:22–25 [e] Acts 2:42 [f] Acts 6:1–6
[g] Acts 8:14 [h] Acts 14:23 [i] Acts 6:1–6; Phil. 1:1; 1 Tim. 3:1–13

themselves to the teaching of the apostles[a], not because they had to but because their regenerated hearts wanted to. They had received the Spirit, seen remarkable miracles, and witnessed an evangelistic event that was history-altering. But they refused a simple experience-based Christianity. As disciples, they were keenly aware of their need to continually increase in their understanding of Scripture, and so they studied not just for information but also for transformation in all of their life. Therefore, the Church studies Scripture to show submission to the apostolic authority of the Word of God.

Importantly, not only is the church to gather to hear the preaching of Scripture, but it also is to respond to God's truth and grace with worship. In the earliest days of the New Testament church, we witness a worshiping community where believers praised God and had favor with all people.[b] Worship is a response to the revelation of the Lord for who He is, what He has done, and what He will do. It consists of: (1) adoration and proclamation of the greatness of the Lord and His mighty works;[c] (2) action, which is serving Him by living out His character in gracious service to others in obedience to the commands of Scripture; and (3) participation in the divine life and mission.[d] It is both *proskuneo*, to fall down and kiss Jesus' feet in an expression of one's allegiance to and adoration for God[e], and *latreia* or *leitourgeo*, which is ministering, or doing work and service in the world in the name of Jesus.[f]

4. The church is where the biblical sacraments of baptism and communion are performed regularly as visible symbols of the Gospel in the life of the church.
5. The church is unified by the Spirit by confessing Christ as Lord and sharing life together. The unified life of the Trinity itself is manifested among God's people who live in loving unity together as the church. This unity comes in several concrete aspects.
    - Theological unity. The leaders and members of the church must agree on what they will and will not fight over. Every local church must clarify what it considers to be primary, closed-handed doctrines. We would urge as primary for every church doctrine such as the Trinity as the only God and object of worship, the Scriptures as God's perfect Word, Jesus as fully God and man born of a virgin to live without sin before dying for our sins and physically rising for our salvation, and salvation by grace alone through faith alone in Christ alone. There are also secondary, open-handed doctrines, such as musical style, mode of communion, schooling options for children, view of certain

---

[a] Acts 2:42 [b] Acts 2:47 [c] Acts 2:11 [d] John 17:21; 1 John 4:12–15 [e] Matt. 2:11; 4:9; 8:2; 28:9; Rev. 19:10 [f] Rom. 1:9; 12:1; Rev. 7:15

supernatural gifts, or belief in the rapture, which permit a range of beliefs providing they fall within the limits of biblical truth and are held with a humble and teachable spirit.

- Relational unity does not necessarily mean that everyone likes one another, but it does mean that people love one another and demonstrate it by being cordial, respectful, friendly, and kind in their interpersonal interactions. To like someone is dependent upon their conduct. To love someone is dependent upon God's character. For this reason, we can love people we aren't enjoying by considering their viewpoint, finding ways to bless them, and valuing our relationship.
- Philosophical unity characterizes ministry methods and style. These are house rules or ministry philosophy about how the church does things, and they are in many ways the cause of a particular and primary cultural style in a church. This includes everything from one service to multiple services, owning versus renting a building, what people wear to church gatherings, style of worship music, service order, etc.
- Missional unity concerns the objective of the church. Ideally, the goal of every Christian in the church should be to biblically glorify God in all they say and do, with the hope of seeing the nations meet God and also live to glorify Him. No church ever achieves this goal perfectly, but the goal is constant progress.
- Organizational unity is based on how things are done in the church, such as job descriptions, performance reviews, and financial policies, so that the church can be a unified good steward of the resources God has entrusted to its oversight.

6. The church teaches people how to obey all that Christ commands. This is the discipline of discipleship. The heart of discipline is Christlikeness. Leaders use Scripture to teach, correct, train, and equip Christians to be a holy people who continually grow in Christlikeness by the Spirit's power. When believers sin, they are supposed to confess and repent. If someone should fail to repent, fellow Christians in relationship with them should lovingly enact godly, gentle correction in hopes of bringing the sinner to repentance and a reconciled relationship with God and His people.[a]

7. The church obeys the Great Commandment to love, which is also the fruit of the Spirit. God's people should live together in intentional relational community to seek the well-being of one another in every way – physical, mental, spiritual, material, and emotional. This does not mean that everyone is required to be best friends with everyone else, but it does mean that people take care of each other like extended family. The people who make up the church gather regularly[b] for such things as worship, learning, the

---

[a] Matt. 18:15-20; 1 Cor. 5:1-5; Gal. 6:1; 2 Tim. 2:24-26; Titus 3:10 [b] Acts 20:7; 1 Cor. 5:4; 11:17-20; 14:23-26; Heb.10:25

sacraments, and encouragement. But even when not gathered, the church is still the church. There is a Spirit-bond of belonging and mission that unites the believers wherever they are, in the same way that a family is still a family even when Dad is at work, Mom is at the store, and the kids are at school.

Not only does Scripture command Christians and churches to love, but it also tells us whom we are to love. First, we are to love God.[a] Second, we are to love our family.[b] Third, we are to conduct ourselves in such an honoring and respectful way that our church leaders find it a joy to pastor us, which is a practical way of loving them.[c] Fourth, we are to love fellow Christians.[d] Fifth, we are to love our neighbors even if our neighbor is a difficult person.[e] Sixth, we are to love strangers.[f] Seventh, we are to love even our enemies.[g]

8. The church obeys the Great Commission to evangelize and make disciples. The church is an evangelistic community where the Gospel of Jesus is constantly made visible through its proclamation of the Gospel, the witness of the members' lives, and its Spirit-empowered life of love. From the first day, "the Lord added to their number day by day those who were being saved"[h] because they took Jesus' command seriously: "You will receive power when the Holy Spirit has come upon you, and you will be my witnesses in Jerusalem and in all Judea and Samaria, and to the end of the earth."[i]

The Church is to be an evangelistic people on mission in the world, passionate to see lost people meet Jesus Christ as Savior, God, and Lord. Any church submitting to the Holy Spirit and obedient to Scripture wants fewer divorces, addictions, thefts, and abuses and knows the only way to see that happen is to make more disciples. The message of the church is that God forgives, makes new, and makes life worth living! The church loves people and is continually and painfully aware of the devastation that is wrought in this life and in the life to come for those who are not reconciled to God. Therefore, while not imposing religion on anyone, the Church of Jesus Christ is to constantly be lovingly, humbly and persuasively proposing reconciliation with God to everyone.[k]

As local churches implement these characteristics of the Church, it is vital that the distinction between principle and method be retained. These eight characteristics give us timeless biblical principles that are unchanging regardless of culture. Nevertheless, they also require church leaders to use timely biblical methods that are changing depending upon culture. This is the essence of what it

---

[a] Matt. 6:24; 22:39 [b] Eph. 5:25; 6:1-4; Titus 2:4 [c] 1 Tim. 5:17; Heb. 13:17
[d] 1 John 3:14 [e] Matt. 22:39; Luke 10:30-37; Rom. 13:9-10; Gal. 5:14; James 2:8
[f] Heb. 13:2 [g] Matt. 5:43-45; Luke 6:32 [h] Acts 2:47 [i] Acts 1:8 [k] Acts 13:43, 17:4, 17, 18:4, 19:4, 26, 26:1-28, 28:23-24; 2 Cor. 5:11, 20; Col. 1:28-29

means to be a missional church that contextualizes its ministry. Paul demonstrated this by not changing his doctrine or principles but often changing his methods, depending upon his audience. Paul explains missional contextualization in 1 Corinthians 9:19–23:

"For though I am free from all, I have made myself a servant to all, that I might win more of them. To the Jews I became as a Jew, in order to win Jews. To those under the law I became as one under the law (though not being myself under the law) that I might win those under the law. To those outside the law I became as one outside the law (not being outside the law of God but under the law of Christ) that I might win those outside the law. To the weak I became weak, that I might win the weak. I have become all things to all people, that by all means I might save some. I do it all for the sake of the gospel, that I may share with them in its blessings."

Practically, this means, for example, that it is fine for churches to meet in different kinds of buildings or outside under a tree, have services that take an hour or a whole day, and sing different songs with different instrumentation (if any), as is most fitting for each one's specific cultural context. Different churches prefer a variety of Bible translations, songs to sing, and programs to have. These are distinctions in the family of God but should not be divisions between the family of God. The only place where everyone agrees on everything is usually a cult, and, in the church, the love for God and commitment to closed-handed truths is the basis of our unity.

We have both given our lives to serving the Church. We know the Church is imperfect and led by imperfect people like us. But we are thoroughly convinced that the Gospel of Jesus Christ through the ministry of the Church is the hope of the world. And as these eight characteristics of a church are pursued by grace, we trust that the glory of God the Father will be made visible through lives changed by Jesus Christ through the ministry of the Holy Spirit.

WHAT ARE THE EXPRESSIONS OF THE CHURCH?

The Bible uses a number of images to help us understand what is meant by the church. Each of these images helps us understand an aspect of the Church. Furthermore, each image helps various people and people in various cultures best understand and love the Church.

1. The church is an assembly or gathering, meaning a beloved people called out from the world to meet with God.[a]
2. The Church is God's people who are in special relationship with Him now and forever.[b]
3. The Church is the Family of Abraham, born again of the Spirit and part of a great legacy of faith.[c]

---

[a] Acts 5:11, Rom. 16:5 [b] Acts 15:14; Rom. 9:25-26 [c] Gal. 3:29, 6:16; Rom. 9:11-24

CHURCH: GOD ACTS

4. The church is the temple of God's presence, the place where God uniquely chooses to be present with His people.[a]
5. The Church is the priesthood of believers set apart for ministry to glorify God by doing good for others.[b]
6. The church is a branch of Jesus the Vine, so that the power of His life-giving Spirit flows through us to bear much fruit that nourishes others.[c]
7. The church is a body with many parts, which explains how we have unity and diversity when we work together.[d]
8. The church is a community of the Spirit, spiritually reborn and sustained by the power and presence of the person of the Spirit.[e]
9. The church is a flock with a Shepherd who protects them from wolves, feeds them, and leads them.[f]
10. The church is a field planted by God to bring a harvest of righteousness to the earth.[g]
11. The Church is the bride of Christ deeply beloved and faithfully served by Jesus the groom.[h]
12. The Church is God's Family adopted by the same Father and saved by the same Big Brother.[i]

Part of the confusion about the Church is exactly what is meant by the word. Christian theologians have long differentiated between the three aspects of what is meant when we use the term "church".

One, the Church is both universal and local. Sometimes we distinguish between these two as the Church and the churches. The universal Church is all God's people in all times and places. Someone becomes a member of the universal Church by virtue of being a Christian. Local churches are smaller gatherings of the universal Church where Christians assemble as God's people. In fact, the word for church in the Greek New Testament (*ekklesia*) means "gathering," "meeting," or "assembly. Most of the New Testament is written to local churches in places like Corinth, Galatia, and Rome, often naming these locations in the opening of the letters written to the local churches.

Two, the Church is both visible and invisible. Right now, there are departed saints in God's presence along with divine beings who are worshipping God as the Church. For example, in the book of Revelation, John sees into the unseen realm and witnesses angelic beings along with departed human beings gathered around Jesus' throne as the Church in the invisible unseen realm. In addition, there are Christians scattered all over the world that can be seen gathering together as the Church. In addition, there are people in the local churches who are not Christians, as well as Christians who are not in the local churches. Thankfully, God sees and knows all unlike us and "The Lord knows those who are his..."[k]

---

[a] 1 Cor. 3:16-17; 2 Cor. 6:16-18 [b] 1 Peter 2:9; Rev. 1:6 [c] John 15:1-17
[d] Rom. 12:3-8; 1 Cor. 12:12-31 [e] Eph. 4:1-16; 1 Cor. 12:13 [f] John 10:1-21 [g] 1 Cor. 3:6-9 [h] Eph. 5:25; Rev. 19:7 [i] 1 Tim. 3:15; Gal. 6:10 [k] 2 Tim. 2:19

DOCTRINE

Three, the church is both gathered and scattered. Just as a family is still a family whether they are all at home together for dinner, or each scattered in different directions, so it is with God's family the Church. We are the Church whether we are together or not, because wherever we go, we are still indwelt by the same Spirit, born again into God's Family by the same Son, and adopted by the same Father.

This multi-faceted view of the Church and local churches helps us understand it at both the most global and personal levels.

WHY IS PREACHING IMPORTANT FOR THE CHURCH?

God created the world through preaching. No less than ten times does Genesis 1 say, "God said". We then read seven times, "God saw" as creation was preached into existence by the sheer power of God's Word. The Church and local churches come into existence the same way – by the Word of God being unleashed through preaching to bring something out of nothing.

In Genesis 3, we see that Satan soon showed up to preach a counterfeit message. He continues this to this day in everything from cults to entertainment and false teaching in everything from school classrooms to product advertising.

The Old Testament is a parade of prophets who were preachers of repentance from sin and faith in God. The Old Testament ends with the promise of John the Baptist coming as the preacher to prepare the way for Jesus, "Behold, I send my messenger, and he will prepare the way before me. And the Lord whom you seek will suddenly come to his temple; and the messenger of the covenant in whom you delight, behold, he is coming, says the LORD of hosts."[a] Roughly 400 years later, "John the Baptist came preaching in the wilderness of Judea, 'Repent, for the kingdom of heaven is at hand.' For this is he who was spoken of by the prophet Isaiah [40:3] when he said, 'The voice of one crying in the wilderness: 'Prepare the way of the Lord; make his paths straight.'"[b]

Jesus' ministry included feeding the hungry, healing the sick, loving the outcast, and befriending the sinner, as well as bringing people to repentance and forgiveness. But we must never forget that Jesus' ministry began with and centered on preaching,
From that time Jesus began to preach, saying, "Repent, for the kingdom of heaven is at hand."[c]

When Jesus sent the Twelve on their short-term mission, he told them to preach the message of the Kingdom.[d] Peter's sermon was the very first activity of the Church after the Spirit came upon them.[e] The rest of Acts records the preaching and teaching ministry of the leaders of the church. Thus, preaching the Gospel in its transforming fullness is a priority ministry of the Church. God's mission is

---

[a] Mal. 3:1 [b] Matt. 3:1-3 [c] Matt. 4:17 [d] Matt. 10:7 [e] Acts 2:14-36

accompanied by various other ministries that support, supplement, and sustain the preaching of God's Word in truth with passion.

The Bible has good advice on how to make better decisions in books like Proverbs and other wisdom literature. The Bible also has commands for good deeds like caring for widows, orphans, and bringing justice to the oppressed. But the good advice and good deeds in the Bible are not the most important message – that is reserved for the Good News of what God has done for us in Christ.[a] The Good News alone has the power to save and bring people to maturity.[b] Unlike other forms of communication, preaching comes with the power of the Spirit[c] and the answer to prayer.[d] Preaching brings faith for hearers[e] and is spiritual food to nourish people to health.[f]

Paul warned that times would come when people would not tolerate preaching.[g] God's people have always viewed preaching as something to be done when the church gathers. Preaching is proclaiming with authority and passion the truth of God's Word. In preaching, the authority of God's Word is upheld, and God's people are collectively led and taught according to the Scriptures. The willingness of Christians to sit under preaching is an act of worship, as they are humbly submitting to Scripture. Preaching is among the most essential ministries of a church because the authoritative preaching of Scripture informs and leads God's people in the rest of the church's ministries. The Bible tells us to simply "preach the word" but does not tell us exactly how this is to be done, thereby leaving some creative freedom for preachers.[h]

A healthy church will always have Bible preaching. The preaching will be (1) biblical, focusing on what Scripture says; (2) theological, teaching what Scripture means; (3) memorable, practically speaking to the lives and culture of people; (4) transformational, leading to repentance, response, and spiritual maturity; (5) missional, explaining why this matters for the mission of God and the salvation of lost people; (6) Christological, showing how Jesus is the hero-savior; (7) apologetical, answering the likely objections of the hearers to remove as many barriers as possible to believing the Bible.

Faithful Gospel proclamation, which began with God in Genesis, is to continue by faithful Gospel preachers until the Gospel is consummated in the return of Jesus, to whom all biblical preaching points.

WHAT IS BAPTISM?

Baptism and Communion are visible presentations of the Gospel performed regularly by the Church. Churches in every age and culture perform these special ceremonies to celebrate the transforming reality of the gospel. Christians call

---

[a] 1 Thess. 2:13; 1 Pet. 1:12, 23-25; 2 Pet. 1:19-21 [b] 1 Thess. 1:5 [c] 1 Cor. 1:17-2:7; 2 Cor. 1:12, 2:17, 4:2; 1 Thess. 2:5 [d] Eph. 6:18-20; Col. 4:3 [e] 1 Cor. 2:4-5 [f] 1 Pet. 2:2 [g] 2 Tim. 4:3-4 [h] 2 Tim. 4:2

them sacraments because they are visible symbols of invisible spiritual realities. We believe in the supernatural real presence of Jesus in these services, which are occasions of grace he ordained for His Church when the Word is spoken and made visible.

While some faithful Christians would disagree with us, we believe that water baptism is for those Christians who have already received Spirit baptism, when the Spirit makes them part of the Church. We also believe in the ongoing, empowering filling of the Spirit, which many call the baptism with the Spirit.[a] In water baptism, Christians are immersed in water, which identifies them with the death and burial of Jesus in their place for their sins. Coming up out of the water identifies them with the resurrection of Jesus for their salvation and new life empowered by the Holy Spirit. Altogether, baptism identifies a Christian with Jesus, the universal Church, and the local church.

When we speak of baptism, we must remember that we are talking about more than a simple rite that people undergo. As a sacrament, it is a symbol of something far bigger. Baptism is an aspect of the whole person's acts of repentance and faith, an external expression of an internal transformation. Being baptized in the name of the Father, the Son, and the Holy Spirit expresses the believer's death to sin, burial of the old life, and resurrection to a new Kingdom life in Christ Jesus.

Jesus and the apostles commanded that all Christians be baptized as an initial act of discipleship.[b] In the book of Acts and in the early church, baptism is administered upon conversion.[c] Practically speaking, we think it is best that believers be baptized immediately upon credible profession of faith in Jesus.

While virtually every Christian tradition practices baptism, there are deep disagreements on what baptism means, who should be baptized, if you must be baptized to be saved, and how baptism should be administered. We will answer these questions briefly.

1. Do I need to be baptized to be a Christian?

Salvation is a gift given to people whose faith rests in the grace of God to forgive their sins through the death and resurrection of Jesus.[d] For example, when the Philippian jailer asked what was required of him to be saved, Paul did not mention baptism but rather simply said "Believe in the Lord Jesus..."[e] Likewise, the thief who died on the cross next to Jesus was promised by our Lord that "...today you will be with me in paradise" though he had not been baptized.[f] Saved people should get baptized in the same way that a married person should wear a wedding ring. But the absence of either sign pointing to a covenant relationship does not negate that relationship. An unbaptized Christian who does not wear a wedding ring is still in relationship with God and their spouse even though the

---

[a] Rom. 6:1-10; 1 Cor. 12:12-13; 1 Pet. 3:2. See also 1 Cor. 10:1-4; Gal. 3:27; Col. 2:12; Titus 3:5-6 [b] Matt. 28:19; Acts 2:38 [c] Acts 2:38-41, 8:12, 36-38, 9:18, 10:47-48, 16:15, 33, 18:8, 19:5 [d] Eph. 2:8-9 [e] Acts 16:31 [f] Luke 23:43

outward sign of the inward commitment is not present.

2. How should baptism be conducted?

We believe that Christians should be baptized like Christ, by immersion, for a number of reasons. First, the Greek word used for baptism in the New Testament means to plunge, dip, or immerse in water. In secular, ancient Greek this word was used, for example, to explain such things as the sinking of a ship which had been submerged in water. Curiously, even the great theologians John Calvin and Martin Luther who practiced and strenuously advocated the baptism of newborn infants agree.

Second, John the Baptizer immersed people in water.[a] John also selected the Jordan River as the place for conducting his baptisms because there was "plenty of water".[b]

Third, when Jesus was baptized, He was immersed in water.[c]

Fourth, Philip baptized the Ethiopian eunuch by immersion in water.[d]

Fifth, baptism is the remembrance of Jesus' burial and resurrection and therefore is best conducted with immersion.[e]

Sixth, when someone who was not racially Jewish would convert to Judaism in both the Old Testament and present day, they underwent a Jewish Proselyte Baptism to show cleansing from sin. The mode of this baptism was (and is) by immersion.

3. Who should be baptized?

When Jesus was a baby, He was dedicated to the Lord by His parents. When He was older, He was then baptized by immersion in water. We believe that Christians should follow this pattern of Christ for numerous reasons.

First, John the Baptizer required that people repent of sin before they could be baptized.[f]

Second, every baptism in the New Testament is preceded by repentance of sin and faith in Jesus.[g]

Third, baptism is reserved solely for those people who have put on Christ.[h]

Fourth, baptism shows the burial and resurrection of Jesus.[i]

Fifth, the Bible does record occurrences where entire households were baptized.[k] And the Bible also records that each member of these households believed in Jesus and was saved.[m] Therefore, any member of any household who repents of sin and trusts in Jesus alone for salvation should be baptized.

Sixth, both Jesus[n] and His apostles[o] commanded that believing Christians be

---

[a] Mark 1:5 [b] John 3:23 [c] Mark 1:10 [d] Acts 8:34-39 [e] Rom. 6:1-10, Col. 2:12 [f] Matt. 3:2,6, Mark 1:4, Luke 3:3 [g] Acts 2:38-41, 2:41, 8:12, 9:18-19, 10:44-48, 16:14-15 cf:40, 16:29-36, 18:8, 19:1-7, 22:16 [h] Gal. 3:27 [i] Rom. 6:1-10, Col. 2:12 [k] Acts 10:33 & 44-48 cf. 11:14, 16:15, 16:23; I Cor. 1:16 [m] John 4:53; Acts 18:8; I Cor. 16:15 [n] Matt. 28:19 [o] Acts 2:38

DOCTRINE

baptized. Therefore, only believing Christians should be baptized.

WHAT IS COMMUNION?

The second sacrament that constitutes the Christian church has several names. When calling it Communion, we emphasize the fellowship we have with God the Father and each other through Jesus. Calling it the Lord's Table emphasizes that we follow the example Jesus set at the Last Supper Passover meal He ate with his disciples. The name Eucharist (meaning thanksgiving) emphasizes thanksgiving and the joyful celebration of God's work for us, in us, through us, and in spite of us.

The real issue is not the name but the fourfold meaning of the sacrament itself. It is a dramatic presentation that (1) retells visibly our inclusion in the New Covenant community of the Spirit (2) reminds us in a powerful manner of the death of Jesus Christ in our place for our sins; (3) calls Christians to put our sin to death in light of the fact that Jesus died for our sins and compels us to examine ourselves and repent of sin before partaking; (4) shows the unity of God's people around the person and work of Jesus; and (5) anticipates our participation in the marriage supper of the Lamb when His kingdom comes in its fullness.

Practically speaking, Communion is to be considered as participation in a family meal around a table rather than as a sacrifice upon an altar. Furthermore, it should be an occasion when God's loving grace impacts us intensely so that the Gospel takes a deeper and deeper root in our lives. Understood biblically, grace is unmerited favor or God's goodwill[a], His helpful enablement for life and service[b], and a transformational power from the Spirit that brings blessing to us.[c] Each of these aspects of God's grace is inextricably connected to the partaking of Communion.

In some ways, Communion is about a community of union around the person and work of Jesus Christ. Thousands of times throughout the Bible we read of people eating and feasting together, in addition to even more instances of eating and drinking. In some regards, all of human history can be viewed as a series of five meals.

Meal #1 – Forbidden Fruit without God (Genesis 3)
In Genesis 3, the counterfeit communion of Satan was offered to Adam and Eve. All the trouble in our world started with a meal where our first parents literally dined with the devil.

Meal #2 – Unblemished Lamb Passover (Exodus 12)
In Exodus 12, God's people invited Him into their home at the Passover Meal. The family would gather to confess their sin and offer an unblemished lamb as a

---

[a] John 1:16, 17; Eph. 2:8 [b] Rom. 12:6; 1 Cor. 15:10; 2 Cor. 9:8 [c] Rom. 6:1, 14–17; 2 Cor. 6:1ff.; Eph. 1:7, 2:5–8

substitute to die for their sins. Then, they would eat the meal together and paint the doorway of their home with the blood of the lamb to as a witness to the world of their worship at home. This meal with God foreshadowed Jesus, who is our Passover Lamb, who causes the wrath of God to pass over us.[a]

Meal #3 – Bread and wine Last Supper (Luke 22)
In Luke 22, Jesus sat down to eat the Passover Meal with His disciples just before going to the cross to fulfill all that the meal symbolized and foreshadowed. Breaking with tradition since the first Passover meal, He said that the bread and wine were symbols pointing to His broken body and shed blood.

Meal #4 – Communion meal in the early church (1 Corinthians 10-11)
In 1 Corinthians 10:14-22 and 11:17-34, we read about the table fellowship of early Christians who would gather in homes to eat together as God's family. We also read how some people treated it more like a pagan feast with gluttony, selfishness, and drunkenness, which elicited God's judgment.

Meal #5 – Wedding supper of the Lamb (Revelation 19)
In Revelation 19:6-9, we learn that all the trouble that began in history when we ate without God is resolved when we sit down as the church to eat a meal with God. This shows us that sitting down to eat a meal is how we get friendship and family and explains why God has this sacrament for His people in the church as practice for Family Dinners together forever in the Father's House.

Regarding Communion, the more you interact with Christians from different traditions and denominations the more you realize that there are four basic views about the sacrament.
1. Catholics teach transubstantiation where the elements of bread and wine become the body and blood of Christ, in essence, while remaining the bread and wine in attribute, so that the Mass is like an Old Testament event complete with a priest in a holy building offering a sacrifice for sinners. This explains why this sacrament is the centerpiece of the Catholic church service.
2. Theologian Ulrich Zwingli was a Swiss Reformer who taught that Communion was a memorial meal to remember the sacrifice of Jesus. Churches including many Baptists, independent and Bible Churches, as well as Charismatic and Protestant churches hold versions of this teaching. Many take Communion less frequently to purge it from the sacramental connotations of the Catholic Mass, which centers every service on the Eucharistic meal.
3. German Reformer Martin Luther taught the real bodily presence of Jesus in,

---
[a] 1 Cor. 5:7

with, and under the bread and wine. He believed Jesus' words, "this is my body...this is my blood" meant people physically eat Christ's body and drink His blood in Communion. Thus, it is a means of God's grace. To this day, Lutherans would share in this view, which explains why their services are generally preaching-centered but include Communion in every service.
4. French Reformer John Calvin taught the spiritual presence of Christ in the meal so that His body and blood are presented spiritually to those who partake in faith. Word and Sacrament come together in the worship services of the gathered local church. Eating the meal together in glory to God and gladness with each other stimulates praise for God and love for other people.

The sacraments are great gifts that help the Church stay Gospel-centered. In preaching, the Gospel is spoken. In sacrament, the Gospel is seen. In correction, the Gospel is safeguarded.

WHAT IS THE CHURCH'S GOSPEL?

The New Testament church was birthed with Peter's preaching of the Gospel in Acts 2. This Gospel is the means by which God's power is exercised both for and through the Church. The Gospel pattern of Acts 2, as well as of other Scriptures, breaks down into three aspects:
1. God's work for us, or what God has revealed He's done for us in Christ
2. God's work in us, or how the Holy Spirit changes our desires and response to God's work for us in Christ
3. God's work through us, or how God's work for and in us results in fruitful good works by the grace of God's Spirit to continue the ministry of Christ[10]

God's work for us: Revelation
Peter begins by affirming that Jesus fulfills the promises of a divine Messiah, God come among us, with miracles, signs, and wonders, showing that He is both Lord and Messiah (vv. 22, 36). Next, Peter declares that Jesus died on the cross according to God's prophetic purpose (v. 23). Then he proceeds to emphasize the reality that God bodily raised Jesus from death in fulfillment of Old Testament prophecy (vv. 24–32). Peter concludes with the final acts of God exalting Jesus above all the demonic powers to the right hand of the Father and pouring out the Spirit in fulfillment of Old Testament prophecy (vv. 33–35). This revelation is of God's work for us in the life, death, burial, resurrection, and exaltation of Jesus Christ, who poured out the Spirit on His church.

God's work in us: Response
The first thing we are to do in response to God's revelation is repent based upon the work of God in us (vv. 36–38). Repentance is the Spirit-empowered acknowledgment of sin that results in a change of mind about who and what is

lord in our life, what is important, and what is good and bad.[a] This is followed by a change of behavior flowing out of an internal change of values. The second response is to accept the revealed message about Jesus by Spirit-empowered faith (v. 41). Faith means taking God at His word and trusting our life and eternity to the truth of His revelation. All of this is seen in the act of baptism, which is the visible expression of our connection with the death, burial, and resurrection of Jesus through repentance and faith (vv. 38, 41). This whole person response of repentance and faith manifested in devotion to Him and His body is the result of God's work in us.

God's work through us: Results

Peter immediately announces the gift of forgiveness of our sins, which is the result of the propitiatory death of Jesus (v. 38). This gift flows into justification, or the imputed righteousness of Jesus. Peter goes on to the second gift: The Holy Spirit and the new heart and new life of Christ (v. 38). This regeneration, or the imparted righteousness of Jesus, is for living a new life as a Christian with, like, for, to, and by the living Jesus. The third gift is membership in the body of Christ, the new community of the Spirit called the church. This community is a supernatural community where God's power and generosity are seen from miracles and supernatural signs to the sharing of possessions among the community members and giving to all in need (vv. 41–47). The fourth gift is participation in the mission of the church to join God's mission to rescue the world from sin and condemnation through the gospel (v. 47). All of this is the result of God's work through us by the power of the Spirit.

Tragically, many Christians have lost the understanding of the new life of the Spirit. They do not preach or live the regeneration of believers. Rather than living out a joy-filled life flowing from their deepest desire to be like Jesus, they settle for being sinners saved by grace, obligated to do all they can to keep the law of God by duty rather than by delight. Christians don't have to read the Bible, pray, or worship. Christians GET TO read the Bible, pray, and worship, which is exactly what their new nature empowered by the Spirit has as its deepest desires!

Subsequently, they have not fully enjoyed the double gift of imputed righteousness, which accompanies our justification[b], and the imparted righteousness of the indwelling Spirit, which accompanies our new heart and regeneration.[c] On the cross, God did a work for us by saving us through the death of Jesus in our place for our sins; with His resurrection, He conquered death, bringing us the power of His life.[d] We then see at Pentecost that God does a work in us through the Holy Spirit in our hearts for regeneration. Together, both our eternity and every step along the way can be filled with hope, joy, purpose, and passion if we see the relationship between the cross and Pentecost. The regenerating work of the Holy Spirit in the heart is the source of the Christian life

---

[a] Acts 26:20 [b] Rom. 5:18 [c] Rom. 5:19 [d] Eph. 1:19-20; 1 Pet. 1:3

DOCTRINE

and Christian church and the powerful result of the Gospel doing its redemptive work.

WHAT IS CHURCH HURT?

In talking about the Church, we know many people, starting with Christians, who have had a painful experience with the Church. The result is often a gnawing sense of guilt that they should be connected to a local body of believers, but some level of anxiety triggered by past troubles which keeps them at arm's length. As pastors and ministry leaders, we have to admit that not only have we experienced church hurt from others, but that we have also created church hurt for others. Like any family, our church family can be complicated and messy.

Christ is perfect, Christians and our churches most certainly are not. The New Testament is painfully honest about this fact, and it was written to correct churches that had problems. For starters, in Revelation 2-3 we see Jesus as Head of the Church speaking to seven kinds of churches.

1. *The fundamentalist church: Ephesus*
   The fundamentalist church is typified by Ephesus. Jesus walked among this church spiritually, and the people were encouraged for serving faithfully, enduring hardship, having sound doctrine, and rejecting false teaching. Conversely, Jesus told them if they did not repent of their unloving and non-relational Christianity, He would shut down their church.

2. *The persecuted church: Smyrna*
   The persecuted church is typified by Smyrna. This city was the center for emperor worship. Those Christians who refused to do so were marginalized or even martyred. Jesus had no rebuke for this church and told them that, though they were financially poor, they were spiritually rich and would be rewarded generously in the Kingdom for suffering in a Godless culture.

3. *The heretical church: Pergamum*
   The heretical church is typified by Pergamum. Jesus encouraged them that they had not completely abandoned their faith despite suffering both physically and spiritually. In their city, Satan sought to establish the headquarters of his demonic counterfeit kingdom and the place "where Satan's throne is" (Rev. 2:13). However, they were rebuked for allowing false-teaching wolves into their church who encouraged sexual sin and syncretism (living culture up instead of Kingdom down).

4. *The liberal church: Thyatira*
   The liberal church is typified by Thyatira. This church was encouraged for its social justice work of helping those in need, being kind and relational, and having a growing ministry. On the other hand, it was rebuked for also tolerating sin (especially sexual sin) and demonic false teaching from a false prophet and false prophetess, which brought suffering upon the church. The liberal church has some good deeds for the community but has a lot of bad

deeds in personal morality and spirituality that opens the door to demonic deception.

5. *The dead church: Sardis*
   The dead church is typified by Sardis. Jesus had nothing good to say about this church, as it was Godless, dead, and no longer experiencing the life of the Spirit. Jesus said the people looked alive on the outside but were spiritually dead, and they must repent quickly or experience the death of their church and be sentenced to Hell for eternity. Sadly, there are a lot of dead churches that are still open on Sunday but not open to the Spirit.

6. *The faithful church: Philadelphia*
   The faithful church is typified by Philadelphia, a wealthy city known for its wine and its chief deity Dionysius, the demon god of wine and debauchery. Despite enormous cultural and spiritual pressure to indulge in every excess, the church did not give in to the demonic seduction to sin. Jesus only had good things to say to this church, as the people had endured hardship and been publicly slandered yet remained godly and patient.

7. *The lukewarm church: Laodicea*
   The lukewarm church is typified by Laodicea. This was an arrogant and affluent city built on a high place. They literally and figuratively looked down on everyone else. Jesus had nothing good to say about this church, which was little more than a comfortable place for rich people to gather. Jesus said their doors were basically locked and that even He had not been welcomed into their Godless country club.

There are churches on the spectrum from amazing to abysmal. There are Christians in every church who are on that same spectrum. Which kind of church do you attend? Which kind of Christian are you? If we are going to be honest about churches, we need to also be honest about ourselves as Christians.

Adding to the problem of church hurt is the fact that what God creates, Satan counterfeits. One church, for example, was told, "the work of Satan...counterfeit power and signs and miracles. He will use every kind of evil deception..."[a] If Satan sought to undermine and overthrow God's Kingdom in Heaven, and tried again with Jesus' ministry through Judas, we should assume that he also has a plan to attack our local churches. The Bible warns us over and over against these counterfeits:

1. False Apostles – 2 Corinthians 11:13-15; Revelation 2:2-5
2. False Prophets – Ezekiel 13:8-9; Matthew 7:15
3. False Teachers – 2 Peter 2:1-9
4. False Doctrines – 1 Timothy 4:1-2; Galatians 1:8, 3:1
5. False Brothers – 2 Corinthians 11:26; Galatians 2:4
6. False Elders – Acts 20:17-38

---

[a] 2 Thess. 2:9-10 (NLT)

The truth is, sometimes, the people or teachings in a church that hurt us were not even Christian. Just like Judas was in Jesus' ministry, but was not a believer, Satan uses this same tactic to cause as much harm as possible and have people confused thinking that it was done by God or God's people. The result is division, which is demonic, that undermines unity, which is Godly. Writing to the church about people sent by Satan into the church to cause division, Paul closes his letter to the Roman church warning, "watch out for those who cause divisions and create obstacles contrary to the doctrine that you have been taught; avoid them. For such persons do not serve our Lord Christ...I want you to be wise as to what is good and innocent as to what is evil. The God of peace will soon crush Satan under your feet. The grace of our Lord Jesus Christ be with you."[a]

What Satan hopes to do to you through church hurt is threefold.

One, he wants you to allow your hurt to become bitterness through unforgiveness. Since forgiveness invites Heaven down into your life, and bitterness pulls Hell up into your life, Satan hopes that you will become bitter against God, other Christians, and the church so that he can then recruit you in his war against God just as he did the angels, who are now demons. He will even seek to convince you that your war against the church is for the Lord, which is part of his demonic deception.

Jesus' heart for and commitment to the Church should compel us to love and serve the Church. In Ephesians 5:25 Paul says, "Christ loved the church and gave himself up for her." The context in which Paul speaks is marriage, and without overstating the analogy, he is saying that the Church is like Jesus' bride, whom He loves and serves despite all her faults and flaws. Those who ignore the Church, criticize the Church, despise the Church, or even harm the Church must seriously question whether they truly love Jesus and are His followers, since true Christians love and serve the Church because Jesus does. To love Jesus and hate or even attack the Church is like telling a husband that you want to be his close friend even though you hate his wife and will occasionally assault her.

Two, he wants to isolate you so that you are no longer close with fellow Christians. The reason justifying this isolation is that since you were hurt, you cannot heal, and relationships with Christians cannot be healthy. When the Bible first said it was not good for us to be alone, that was before sin even entered the world, and in a fallen world, to be alone is to be in harm's way. Jesus is a Shepherd who wants you to be part of a flock, and Satan is a wolf who want you to wander off from a flock so he can destroy you.

Being a Christian means being a Jesus follower, a disciple. His call to "follow me" means joining a group of disciples who, together, are the people of God. The New Testament uses collective metaphors to describe the church of Christ.

---

[a] Rom. 16:17-20

CHURCH: GOD ACTS

They include flock, temple, body, and family or household.[a] Each of the images communicates the same big idea that God's people are to remain together. Sheep die individually but live as a flock, fed and protected by a shepherd; a building falls down if too many bricks are removed; limbs die if removed from the body; a family is destroyed if its members do not live in love together.

Three, the demonic counterfeit of a covenant with God is an inner vow with self. Rather than entering into a covenant relationship with God's family the Church, Satan wants you to make an inner vow with yourself that you will never again trust or participate in God's family ever again. He will even bring along other hurt people with the same bitterness and inner vow to justify and reinforce your decisions which cause your destructions.

We love God. We love you. And we love the Church. Every Christian has varying degrees and kinds of church hurt. The New Testament letters written to churches include incredible religious legalism where people are attacking each other like wild dogs in Galatia, and rebellious licentiousness where people are getting drunk at communion and sleeping with even family members in Corinth. The New Testament was written to local churches that were hospitals filled with sick people needing a lot of help and nothing has changed in our day.

Despite all the pains and problems in the churches, the New Testament tells us how to make it better. Over and over, the phrase "one another" is used in some form or fashion. These commands in the Bible cannot be obeyed unless you are part of a local church family as they were written to churches to be read in churches and obeyed by people in those churches:

<u>Romans</u>
12:5	Belong to one another
12:10	Be devoted to one another
12:10	Honor one another
12:16	Live in harmony with one another
12:18	Live at peace with one another
15:7	Accept one another

<u>1 Corinthians</u>
1:10	Agree with one another
4:6	Don't take pride over against one another
10:24	Look out for one another
12:25	Have equal concern for one another
16:20	Greet one another with a holy kiss

---

[a] John 10:11–16; Acts 20:28–29; 1 Pet. 5:2–3. 1 Cor. 3:16–17; Eph. 2:21. Rom. 12:4–5; 1 Cor. 10:17, 12:12–30; Eph. 4:15–16; Gal. 6:10; Eph. 2:19; 1 Pet. 4:17. Eph. 2:19–22; 1 Tim. 3:15; 1 Pet. 2:5

Galatians
5:13	Serve one another
5:15	Don't devour one another
5:26	Don't envy one another
5:26	Don't provoke one another
6:1	Carry one another's burdens

Ephesians
4:2	Bear with one another
4:25	Speak truthfully with one another
4:32	Be kind to one another
4:32	Be compassionate to one another
4:32	Forgive one another
5:19	Speak to one another with psalms, hymns and spiritual songs
5:21	Submit to one another

Philippians
2:4	Look to the interests of one another

Colossians
3:9	Don't lie to one another
3:13	Bear with one another
3:13	Forgive one another
3:16	Teach one another
3:16	Admonish one another

1 Thessalonians
4:9	Love one another
4:18	Encourage one another
5:11	Encourage one another
5:11	Build up one another
5:13	Live in peace with one another
5:15	Be kind to one another

Hebrews
10:24	Spur on one another
10:25	Meet with one another
10:25	Encourage one another
13:1	Love one another

James
5:9	Don't grumble against one another
5:16	Confess your sins to one another

5:16	Pray for one another

<u>1 Peter</u>
1:22	Love one another
3:8	Live in harmony with one another
4:9	Offer hospitality to one another
5:14	Greet one another with a kiss of love

<u>1 John</u>
1:7	Have fellowship with one another
3:11	Love one another
3:16	Lay down your lives for one another
3:23	Love one another
4:7	Love one another

<u>2 John</u>
5	Love one another

The Church needs you, and you need the Church. We would encourage you to forgive whatever church hurt you have, find a group of Godly people you can trust to do life with you, and commit yourself to that local church like a family with all of its faults and flaws but love and serve because that's what family is all about. There's no such thing as a perfect family or church family, but both become better if we become part of the solution rather than just pointing out the problems.

Lastly, Christians in the Church are told, "let us consider how to stir up one another to love and good works, not neglecting to meet together, as is the habit of some, but encouraging one another, and all the more as you see the Day drawing near."[a] Being together is how we stir one another up to be more loving and helpful. Think of it like a fire. When the logs are stacked together, they radiate heat and life to one another to burn brighter and longer. When those same logs are separated and scattered, they quickly stop burning, grow dim, and eventually smolder out altogether. Christians are like those logs.

QUESTIONS FOR PERSONAL JOURNALING AND/OR SMALL GROUP DISCUSSION

1. What is your most memorable church experience?
2. What areas is your church strong in that you can thank God for? What areas in your local church are weak and could benefit from your prayer and help?
3. What are some of the most influential church leaders and sermons that God has used to bless you?
4. Is there anything more you could be doing to encourage unity in your local

church?
5. Which non-Christians do you need to be praying for and inviting to church?
6. What do you most appreciate about your Christian friends from other teams, tribes, and traditions?
7. What top three changes have you seen in your life by the power of the Holy Spirit?
8. Have you been baptized? Why or why not?

CHAPTER 11: WORSHIP

"GOD TRANSFORMS"

Christ loved the church and gave himself up for her.
EPHESIANS 5:25

Like most who have been on an international mission trip, I will never forget my first time worshipping with brothers and sisters in Christ in another nation. There were two experiences in particular that were life-changing, and they are common for people who have been on a similar trip.

First, the worship of God transcends culture, language, and every other difference between God's people. When the Spirit of God is present with the people of God, our joint heavenly citizenship overrides our earthly distinctions. Even if the language you speak is different, worshipping with God's people feels like a lovingly unified family reunion.

Second, after spending some time with Christians from another culture, you are blessed with fresh eyes to see your own culture. I was in India, and we traveled far outside of the city into a rural area. The evidence of Hinduism and the worship of demon-gods was everywhere. Alongside the road were small shrines where prayers and animal sacrifices were offered to appease the local demons. In various villages, people were gathered together to dance and shout to their false gods, with some in a trance-like state as it seemed they were controlled by demonic spirits. As we passed the ocean, the beach was filled with people who had painted themselves in bold colors and were worshipping and vainly throwing themselves into the water to cleanse themselves from evil which tormented them.

Eventually, we arrived at a thatched roof hut built where pastors traveled to, many on foot, from great distances for a few days of Bible training. I taught through a translator, and many of their questions revolved around what to do with the witch doctors who lived in the villages and would cause great harm and even bring death through curses. The overt worship of demonic false gods was incredibly obvious.

During one of the breaks, I visited with a pastor and his wife who spoke English. They kindly asked me if I had ever been to India, and how my trip was going. I asked if they had been to America. They had visited once, and when I asked them if they planned on returning, she got an odd look on her face. I asked her what she was thinking, and she politely declined to share. I told her I really wanted to hear her impression of my country, and she kindly told me she would never return to America because of all the idolatry she witnessed.

I was stunned. She went on to explain that our stadiums reminded her of great temples where we worship athletes and musicians as gods. Restaurants reminded her of Paul's words to not make our stomach our god. Large shopping malls reminded her of Jesus' words to not worship money or worry about what we wear. Strip clubs reminded her of the pagan temples in ancient cities like Corinth where sex was part of worship. She opened my eyes to a new perspective on my culture. Every culture worships, and most do not worship the Father through the Son by the Spirit. What we consider art, entertainment, politics, culture, sport, and leisure is often the worship of someone or something other than the God of the Bible.

When our culture is considered through the lens of worship and idolatry, primitive ancient paganism seems far less primitive or ancient. Everyone everywhere is continually worshiping, and idolatry is, sadly, seen more easily when we examine other cultures rather than our own. This is because we often have too narrow of an understanding of worship and do not see that idolatry empowers our sin. Worship is love in action. Worship is making sacrifices so that we can outpour our resources (e.g. time, money, emotion, energy) to someone or something that we prioritize above all else. The question, therefore, is not whether or not someone worships, but instead who or what they worship and how they worship.

Harold Best writes, "We were created continuously outpouring—we were created in that condition, at that instant, imago Dei. We did not graduate into being in the image of God; we were, by divine fiat, already in the image of God at the instant the Spirit breathed into our dust. Hence we were created continuously outpouring."[1]

WHAT IS WORSHIP?

The purpose of a mirror is to reflect an image. When we look in the mirror, we expect the mirror to image, or reflect, who we are. In the same way, God made people as His mirrors on the earth, "God created man in his own image, in the image of God he created him; male and female he created them."[a] We worship God by mirroring Him.

Jesus never sinned because He was always worshipping. When we look at Jesus, we see perfectly and continually the character of God the Father reflected in His life. When we see Jesus' love, forgiveness, rebuke, and the like, we are witnessing the perfect reflection of God the Father. Paul says, "He is the image of the invisible God", and Jesus said, "Whoever has seen me has seen the Father."[b]

Since Jesus lived by the power of the Holy Spirit, the only way that we worship God by reflecting His character is to also live by the power of the Holy Spirit. The person without the Spirit can be a good neighbor, kind person, and helpful friend but they simply cannot worship God. For the Christian, however, we can live like Moses. He entered into God's presence, and the glory of God literally reflected off of him as he imaged God, "Now the Lord is the Spirit, and where the Spirit of the Lord is, there is freedom. And we all, with unveiled face, beholding the glory of the Lord, are being transformed into the same image from one degree of glory to another. For this comes from the Lord who is the Spirit."[c]

When we understand what it means that God made us to reflect His image through the Holy Spirit, the issue of our identity is settled. Once we know who we are, then we know what to do. This frees us from living out of an identity that has been created for us by others, or even by ourselves, and instead live solely out of the identity God has created for us. This frees us to stop living for our identity, and instead start living from our identity. This frees us from the trap of thinking that what we do determines who we are and allows us to live in the liberating truth that who we are determines what we do. Once we know who we are in Christ, then we know what to do in life.

Sadly, many if not most people, do not really and truly know who they are. This is even true of Christians who believe the Bible and love Jesus. This epidemic identity crisis started in Eden when the Serpent told our first parents that they could be "like God" by living according to their own plans and creating for themselves an identity apart from God. Our first parents, and every one of us since, has bought this lie and forgotten that we do not need to do anything to create our identity to become "like God". Why? Because God has already graciously created us in His "likeness". Thankfully, in the opening pages of Scripture, God graciously tells us not only who He is, but also who we are and how our relationship with Him is to be one in which we reflect Him. This truth transforms how we see ourselves and how we live our lives.

Mirroring explains much, if not most, of the fascination with celebrities and the power of media and social media. One of the medical and psychological experts who appears often on radio and television is Dr. Drew Pinksy, often referred to simply as "Dr. Drew". He writes and speaks about addiction and health, as well

---

[a] Gen. 1:27 [b] Col. 1:15; John 14:9 [c] 2 Cor. 3:17-18

as cultural and political trends. My wife Grace and I have appeared as guests on his television show to discuss marriage and sexuality. I also flew to Los Angeles to cohost his nationally syndicated radio show Loveline. During breaks, we discussed his book *The Mirror Effect: How Celebrity Narcissism is Seducing America*. I do not believe he considers himself a Christian, but his insight after a lifetime of surveying human behavior echoed the Bible.

In summary, Dr. Drew says that celebrities model behavior that others then mirror, which explains celebrity culture, product endorsements, and social media influencers. Since people were made to mirror, people who do not know God treat other people like gods and goddesses. We follow them on social media and like and repost whatever they post. We believe what they believe, say what they say, buy what they buy, eat what they eat, drink what they drink, wear what they wear, do what they do, and have sex how they have sex. Celebrities lead fashion, politics, and entertainment and their followers are really worshippers by modeling what others mirror. Two tragedies ensue.

One, the mirror effect destroys the celebrity. Once a celebrity does something that was previously considered dangerous, scandalous, or unique and everyone else then does the same, it is no longer noteworthy. To stay relevant, a celebrity must continually increase their reckless behavior, and open up their life to become some form of reality show, until they self-destruct. Making this even more dangerous is the competition from other celebrities building competing platforms and trolls who want to tear down the celebrities that work together to demonize the person that others idolize. This explains why we see so many famous people ruin, and even end, their lives.

Two, this mirror effect destroys the followers of the celebrity. As the celebrity who models begins to self-destruct, their followers mirroring them do the same. This is why, for example, we have teenage girls following celebrities, watching their sex tapes, and then making their own version with boys at school, and passing it around school so that everyone is watching them, talking about them, and ultimately mirroring them as they become the local celebrity modeling for fellow students what to mirror.

We become like who or what we worship. When anyone but God is the model for us to mirror, the result is misery for everybody. Even good people make bad gods. The only way to worship that ends in life and not death, freedom and not slavery, Heaven and not Hell is to worship God as a Christian.

WHAT IS CHRISTIAN WORSHIP?

The worship of God is a mega-theme of the entire Bible. In the remainder of this chapter, we will provide an overview of worship and how this includes the priorities we hold, money we spend, and activities we choose. To begin with, we will look at two key New Testament Scriptures about worship that help serve as a frame in which a life of worship is painted for God's glory and our joy.

WORSHIP: GOD TRANSFORMS

Romans 11:36-12:1 says, "To him be the glory forever. Amen. I appeal to you therefore, brothers, by the mercies of God, to present your bodies as a living sacrifice, holy and acceptable to God, which is your spiritual *worship*."

First, worship is who/what we live for. The language of "glory" speaks of who/what weighs heaviest on your heart and in your life as your priority. Who/what is in the glory position lives at the center of your life and your life revolves around them/it. This can be God, another person, your job, success, beauty, status, hobby, comfort, pet, etc.

Second, worship is how we live. When the Bible speaks of worship, it often does so in terms of sacrifice. Since we have limited time, energy, thoughts, money, and emotion, we must decide where to spend it. Who/what you make the biggest sacrifices for is how you worship who/what you hold in the glory position. For example, the lazy person lives for comfort, the addict lives for pleasure, and the people pleaser lives for approval.

As a Christian, it is possible to belong to God and get sidetracked from living as a worshipper of God. We've all done it. Sometimes, we even get upset with God and try to use Him to get what we really want to worship instead of worshipping Him alone. Here's a few diagnostic questions to check your soul:

1. Who or what do I make sacrifices for?
2. Who or what is most important to me?
3. If I could have any possession or experience that I wanted, what would that be?
4. Who or what makes me the happiest?
5. What is the one person or thing I could not live without?
6. What do I spend my money on?
7. Who or what do I devote my time to?
8. What dominates the thoughts of my mind?
9. When I have extra time, money, or energy, where do I invest it?
10. On a bad day, where do I turn for comfort?

Christian worship is not just a musical style, religious issue, something that happens in a church building, or something that starts and stops, although it does include all of those things. The Bible says, "So whether you eat or drink or whatever you do, do it <u>all</u> for the *glory* of God."[a] In some ways, worship involves every nook and cranny of life.

One of the more insightful sections of Scripture on worship is Hebrews 13:15-17, "Through him then let us continually offer up a sacrifice of praise to God, that is, the fruit of lips that acknowledge his name. Do not neglect to do good and to share what you have, for such sacrifices are pleasing to God. Obey your leaders and submit to them, for they are keeping watch over your souls, as those who will have to give an account. Let them do this with joy and not with groaning, for that would be of no advantage to you."

---

[a] 1 Cor. 6:20, 10:31

In this section we see that worship includes:
1. Praise: Who or what do you praise most passionately and frequently?
2. Proclamation: How commonly and clearly do you confess Jesus Christ in the words you speak, type, and sing?
3. Service: Are you one who serves others with gladness in response to God so faithfully serving you? Or are you someone who prefers to be served rather than to serve? Do you serve when it is inconvenient or unnoticed, or when you are unmotivated?
4. Love: Are you an active participant in the life of your church and community? Do you give your time, talent, and treasure to share God's love in tangible ways with others?
5. Generosity: For whom or what do you sacrifice your time, health, emotion, money, and energy? What do these acts of worship reveal about what you have chosen to deify in your life?
6. Submission: Are you submissive to Godly authority or do you tend to ignore or rebel against Godly authority (e.g., parent, teacher, pastor, or boss)?

WHO WORSHIPS GOD?

Everyone is a worshipper, but not everyone worships God. What makes Christian worship unique is that we worship only God in the ways that God determines. Worship is something that God does and is Godly.

First, God worships. While on the earth, Jesus said, "And now, Father, glorify me in your own presence with the glory that I had with you before the world existed."[a] For all of eternity, Jesus is saying that the Father and Son (along with the Spirit) lived together in loving relationship, unified, and glorifying one another.

Second, divine beings worship God in Heaven. Reporting his visit into Heaven while still on the earth, John says, "I was in the Spirit, and behold, a throne stood in heaven, with one seated on the throne....before the throne were burning seven torches of fire, which are the seven spirits of God...around the throne, on each side of the throne, are four living creatures, full of eyes in front and behind: the first living creature like a lion, the second living creature like an ox, the third living creature with the face of a man, and the fourth living creature like an eagle in flight. And the four living creatures, each of them with six wings, are full of eyes all around and within, day and night they never cease to say, 'Holy, holy, holy, is the Lord God Almighty, who was and is and is to come!'"[b] Right now, there is a world we do not see in the unseen realm that is as real as the world we do see in the seen realm. Right now, in God's presence, are divine beings, including angels and other persons, who are worshipping God.

Third, departed Christians who have gone from earth to Heaven worship God along with the divine beings. In the section of verses, at the same worship event

---

[a] John 17:5 [b] Rev. 4:2-8

WORSHIP: GOD TRANSFORMS

that the divine beings participated in, "whenever the living creatures give glory and honor and thanks to him who is seated on the throne, who lives forever and ever, the twenty-four elders fall down before him who is seated on the throne and worship him who lives forever and ever. They cast their crowns before the throne, saying, 'Worthy are you, our Lord and God, to receive glory and honor and power, for you created all things, and by your will they existed and were created.'"[a]

Fourth, Spirit-filled Christians worship on earth. Jesus said in a conversation about worship with a confused Samaritan woman who worshipped the wrong god in the wrong way as part of a cult, "the hour is coming, and is now here, when the true worshipers will worship the Father in spirit and truth, for the Father is seeking such people to worship him. God is spirit, and those who worship him must worship in spirit and truth."[b] Paul also tells us "we...worship by the Spirit of God".[c] The Holy Spirit connects our worship on earth with the worship of God in Heaven. When we are filled with the Spirit in worship, the two realms are reuniting in the sight of God. This explains why the power of Heaven sometimes falls down on people as they worship – it is a sign pointing to the reality of worship in the unseen realm and builds our faith that one day we will join divine beings and departed saints together forever as one family living in one reality when Heaven comes to earth and everyone and everything worships only God together forever!

WHAT IS IDOLATRY?

Worship is war.

When we worship God, we are engaged in spiritual warfare against the demonic realm. We read of Jesus Christ, "the devil took him to a very high mountain and showed him all the kingdoms of the world and their glory. And he said to him, 'All these I will give you, if you will fall down and worship me.'" Then Jesus said to him, "Be gone, Satan! For it is written, 'You shall worship the Lord your God and him only shall you serve.'"[d] Both the Father and Satan offered Jesus the same opportunity - to sit at their right-hand ruling and reigning over a kingdom in power. The difference was that Satan offered the pleasure path, and the Father offered the pain path. Jesus' choice was an act of war, as He would either chose to worship Satan and war against the Father or choose to worship the Father and war against Satan.

We make the same choice every day. Jesus saw all of the collective sinful temptation that everyone was facing on planet earth. Today, technology and the internet allow us to do the same. We can see global sex, fame, power, money, possessions, and pleasures in an instant and this is all a demonic war for the soul of the world as Satan wants to be worshipped through idolatry.

God creates, and Satan counterfeits. The counterfeit of worship is idolatry.

---

[a] Rev. 4:9-11 [b] John 4:23-34 [c] Phil. 3:3 [d] Matt. 4:8-10

Every human being—at every moment of their life, today and into eternity—is unceasingly doing either the former or the latter. On this point N. T. Wright says, "Christians are not defined by skin colour, by gender, by geographical location, or even, shockingly, by their good behaviour. Nor are they defined by the particular type of religious feelings they may have. They are defined in terms of the god they worship. That's why we say the Creed at the heart of our regular liturgies: we are defined as the people who believe in this god. All other definitions of the church are open to distortion. We need theology, we need doctrine, because if we don't have it something else will come in to take its place. And any other defining marks of the church will move us in the direction of idolatry."[2]

Christian counselor David Powlison says, "Idolatry is by far the most frequently discussed problem in the Scriptures."[3] While idolatry is manifested externally, it originates internally with people who, "have taken their idols into their hearts."[a] Before people see an idol with their eyes, hold it with their hands, or speak of it with their lips, they have taken it into their heart. This violates the first two of the Ten Commandments, choosing something as a functional god longed for in their heart and then worshiping.

Martin Luther's insights on idolatry are among the most perceptive the world has ever known:

"Many a one thinks that he has God and everything in abundance when he has money and, possessions; he trusts in them and boasts of them with such firmness and assurance as to care for no one. Lo, such a man also has a god, Mammon by name, i.e., money and possessions, on which he sets all his heart, and which is also the most common idol on earth...So, too, whoever trusts and boasts that he possesses great skill, prudence, power, favor, friendship, and honor has also a god, but not this true and only God...Therefore I repeat that the chief explanation of this point is that to have a god is to have something in which the heart entirely trusts...Thus it is with all idolatry; for it consists not merely in erecting an image and worshiping it, but rather in the heart...Ask and examine your heart diligently, and you will find whether it cleaves to God alone or not. If you have a heart that can expect of Him nothing but what is good, especially in want and distress, and that, moreover, renounces and forsakes everything that is not God, then you have the only true God. If, on the contrary, it cleaves to anything else, of which it expects more good and help than of God, and does not take refuge in Him, but in adversity flees from Him, then you have an idol, another god."[4]

One of the great evils of idolatry is that, if we idolize, we must also demonize, as Jonathan Edwards rightly taught in *The Nature of True Virtue*. If we idolize our gender, we must demonize the other gender. If we idolize our nation, we must demonize other nations. If we idolize our political party, we must demonize other political parties. If we idolize our socioeconomic class, we must demonize other

---

[a] Ez. 14:1–8

classes. If we idolize our family, we must demonize other families. If we idolize our theological system, we must demonize other theological systems. If we idolize our church, we must demonize other churches. This explains the great polarities and acrimonies that plague every society.

WHAT IS WORSHIPPING THE CREATOR VS WORSHIPPING CREATION?

God is the Creator of everyone and everything. God is independent, everyone and everything else is dependent upon God. Everyone and everything exist to glorify God. When we fail to worship the Creator, our only option is to worship the created.

When it comes to worship, there are only two options. One, we worship the Maker of all. Two, we worship something made by God, or people, like another person, pleasure, or sex. Romans 1:25-28, 32 says, "they exchanged the truth about God for a lie and worshiped and served the creature rather than the Creator, who is blessed forever! Amen. For this reason, God gave them up to dishonorable passions. For their women exchanged natural relations for those that are contrary to nature; and the men likewise gave up natural relations with women and were consumed with passion for one another, men committing shameless acts with men and receiving in themselves the due penalty for their error...God gave them up to a debased mind to do what ought not to be done. Though they know God's righteous decree that those who practice such things deserve to die, they not only do them but give approval to those who practice them." God made us male and female, marriage for one man and one woman, and sex for marriage. When we accept our God-given gender, God's design for marriage, and reserve sex solely for marriage, we are worshippers of the Creator, enjoying His creation. When we reject our God-given gender, redefine marriage, and have sex outside of marriage, we are idolaters worshipping creation instead of the Creator. These timeless words are perhaps timelier than ever.

Paul says that underlying idolatry is the lie and Jesus names Satan "the father of lies."[5]

The truth is two-ism where Creator and creation are separate, and creation is subject to the Creator. Visually, you can think of this in terms of two circles with one being God the Creator and the other containing all of creation.

The lie is one-ism, also called monism. One-ism is the pagan and idolatrous denial of distinction between Creator and creation, and/or a denial that there is a Creator. This is a refusal of binary thinking that makes distinctions and divisions. One-ism is the eradication of boundaries and differences to bring opposites together as one. The materialistic form of one-ism is atheism. Spiritual one-ism is also often called New Age, New Spirituality, or Integrative Spirituality. According to spiritual one-ism, the universe is a living organism with a spiritual force present within everything. Thus, everything is interconnected by the life force or the world soul. This life force manifests as spiritual beings (Christians realize these are demons) that manipulate the course of world events. These spirits can be influenced to serve people by using the ancient magical arts. Humans possess divine power unlimited by any deity. Consciousness can be altered through the practice of rite and ritual. Magic is the manipulation of objects, substances, spirit entities, and minds, including humans and demons, by word (ritual, incantations, curses, spells, etc.) and objects (charms, amulets, crystals, herbs, potions, wands, candles, etc.)

Visually, you can think of this in terms of one circle in which everything is contained and interconnected as one. Often, the circle itself serves as the defining symbol of pagan idolatry. This includes the yantra in Hindu worship, the mandala circle of dharma and Dharmacakra in Buddhist and Taoist worship, the sun cross of Wiccans (who also gather in a circle), and Native American medicine wheels, dream catchers, and drum circles. A well-known expression of one-ism is found in the popular song from The Lion King, "the circle of life."

Monism or one-ism is a religion. Although not always formal like Christianity, it is a view of the world that rejects dualistic thinking.

What God creates, Satan counterfeits. Satan creates nothing, but he does counterfeit, corrupt, and co-opt what God creates. The lie is that there is no difference or distinction in value between what God creates and Satan counterfeits. Here are some examples:

God Creates	**Satan Counterfeits**
God	Satan
angels	demons
obedience	rebellion
truth	lies
two genders	gender spectrum
people and animals	no distinction between human and animal life
Spirit-filled	demon-possessed
cleansing	defilement
humility	pride
forgiveness	bitterness
worship	idolatry
peace	fear
unity	division
shepherds	wolves
God-esteem	self-esteem
covenant with God	inner vow with self
spirit	flesh
freedom	slavery
life	death
Church	world
Kingdom	Hell

WORSHIP: GOD TRANSFORMS

As a worldview, one-ism is antithetical to biblical two-ism. Christians think in terms of black and white (binary thinking). Non-Christians think in terms of shades of gray. Biblical thinking is binary thinking.

When we do not worship the Creator, we end up worshipping created things. This essential truth explains why so many social, culture, moral, and religious conflicts are ultimately spiritual warfare and the war between worshipping God the Creator or worshipping creation as a god. Plainly stated, everything from radical environmentalism to radical animal rights activism, gender confusion, the redefinition of marriage, pornography and all sexual sin, along with all religious and spiritual activity apart from the Holy Spirit is all paganism and idolatry. The world we live in is deeply and profoundly spiritual, but not of the Holy Spirit.

HOW ARE REGENERATION AND WORSHIP RELATED?

One of the most curious things we read in the Bible is how much religious people hated Jesus. They killed God, wrongly thinking that they were worshipping God in doing so. They worshipped power, control, money, and their religious traditions instead of Jesus. The opposite of religion is regeneration. Religion is what people create. Regeneration is what God does to make us a new creation. To worship God, we don't need religion, we need regeneration.

In John 3, a man named Nicodemus came to meet with Jesus. Nicodemus was a devoutly religious man. As a Pharisee, he was among the holiest of men. Jesus said to him, "Truly, truly, I say to you, unless one is born again he cannot see the kingdom of God." This confused Nicodemus, so Jesus explained that there are two births. The first birth is our physical birth where we are physically alive but spiritually dead. The second birth is our spiritual birth whereby God the Holy Spirit causes us to be born again so that we are both physically and spiritually alive. Nicodemus considered himself spiritually alive by virtue of his religion, spirituality, theology, and morality. But he was likely astounded when Jesus told him plainly, "You must be born again."[a]

Nicodemus was much like people today who know some theological truth, have been baptized, attend religious meetings, live a moral life, believe in God, devote time to serving others, and even give some of their income to spiritual causes and organizations, but who need to be born again. Why? Because they are living out of their old nature solely by their will and effort rather than out of a new nature by the power of the Holy Spirit. John Piper says:

"What Nicodemus needs, and what you and I need, is not religion but life. The point of referring to new birth is that birth brings a new life into the world. In one sense, of course, Nicodemus is alive. He is breathing, thinking, feeling, acting. He is a human created in God's image. But evidently, Jesus thinks he's dead. There is no spiritual life in Nicodemus. Spiritually, he is unborn. He needs life, not more

---

[a] John 3:7

DOCTRINE

religious activities or more religious zeal. He has plenty of that."[6]

Being born again is theologically summarized as the doctrine of regeneration, which is the biblical teaching that salvation includes both God's work for us at the cross of Jesus and in us by the Holy Spirit which leads to God's work through us in a life of fruitful living. To say it another way, regeneration is not a separate work of the Holy Spirit added to the saving work of Jesus; rather, it is the subjective actualization of Jesus' work.

While the word regeneration appears only twice in the Bible[a], it is described in both the Old and New Testaments by a constellation of images. Each signifies a permanent, unalterable change in someone at his or her deepest level.

The Old Testament frequently speaks of regeneration in terms of deep work in the heart, our total inner self, so that a new life flows from a new heart empowered by the Holy Spirit, just as Jesus explained to Nicodemus.[b]

Like the Old Testament, the New Testament speaks on many occasions of being born again.[c] Other images include "partakers of the divine nature," "new creation," "new man," "alive together with Christ," and "created in Christ Jesus."[d]

Three very important truths summarize regeneration in the New Testament. First, regeneration is done to ill-deserving, not just undeserving, sinners.[e] Regeneration is a gift of grace, "He saved us, not because of works done by us in righteousness, but according to his own mercy, by the washing of regeneration and renewal of the Holy Spirit."[f] Second, regeneration is something God the Holy Spirit does for us.[g] Therefore, unless God accomplishes regeneration in people, it is impossible for them to live as worshipers of God. Third, without regeneration there is no possibility of eternal life in God's Kingdom.[h]

Accompanying the new birth are 10 soul-transforming, life-changing, and eternity-altering occurrences.

1. Regenerated people have their Creator as their new Lord, thereby displacing all other false and functional lords who had previously ruled over them.[i]
2. Regenerated people are new creations transformed at the deepest levels of their existence to begin living a new life. People being renamed upon conversion, so that Saul becomes Paul and Simon becomes Peter, illustrates the new birth.[k]
3. Regenerated people have a new identity from which to live their new life because their old identity no longer defines them.[m]
4. Regenerated people have a new mind that enables them to enjoy Scripture and thus to begin to think God's truthful thoughts after Him.[n]

---

[a] Matt. 19:28; Titus 3:5 [b] Deut. 30:6; Jer. 24:7, 31:31–33, 32:39–40; Ezek. 11:19–20, 36:26–27 [c] 1 John 1:13; 1 Pet. 1:3, 23; 1 John 5:1 [d] 2 Pet. 1:4; 2 Cor. 5:17; Eph. 2:15, 4:24; Eph. 2:5; Col. 2:13; Eph. 2:10 [e] Eph. 2:1–5 [f] Titus 3:5 [g] John 3:5-8 [h] John 3:3, 5; cf. 1 Cor. 2:6–16 [i] 1 Cor. 12:3b; 1 John 5:18 [k] 2 Cor. 5:17; Gal. 6:15 [m] Eph. 4:22-24 [n] Rom. 7:22; 1 Cor. 2:14–16; 1 Pet. 2:2

5. Regenerated people have new emotions so that they love God, fellow Christians, strangers, and even their enemies.[a]
6. Regenerated people have new desires for holiness, and no longer is their deepest appetite for sin and folly.[b]
7. Regenerated people enjoy a new community with other Christians.[c]
8. Regenerated people live by a new power to follow God by the Holy Spirit's enabling.[d]
9. Regenerated people enjoy a new freedom to no longer tolerate, manage, excuse, or accept their sin but rather to put it to death and live free from habitually besetting sin.[e]
10. Regenerated people live a new life that is not perfect but is increasingly becoming Godlier.[f]

In some ways our new birth is like our physical birth. At birth, babies cry, move, hunger, trust their parent to protect and provide for them, enjoy human comfort, and begin to grow. Similarly, newly born-again people cry out to God in prayer, move out in new life, hunger for the Scriptures, trust God as Father, enjoy God's family the church, and begin to grow spiritually, maturing in their imaging of God. One theologian explains regeneration in terms of how Christians become restored into the image of God:

"It is in Christ that people, formerly conformed to the world's image (Rom. 1:18–32), begin to be transformed into God's image (Rom. 8:28–30; 12:2; 2 Cor. 3:18; 4:4) …This process of transformation into the divine image will be completed at the end of history, when Christians will be resurrected and fully reflect God's image in Christ (1 Cor. 15:45–54; Phil. 3:20–21). They will be resurrected by the Spirit-imparting power of the risen Christ. Since it was the Spirit who raised Jesus from the dead (Rom. 1:4), so the Spirit of Christ will raise Christians from the dead at the end of the age…The Spirit's work in people will enable them to be restored and revere the Lord and resemble his image, so that God will be glorified in and through them."[7]

Only through the regenerating and ongoing empowering ministry of the Holy Spirit can we worship, until one day in our glorified resurrected state we will image God perfectly as unceasing worshipers. This is exactly what Jesus meant when He said, "God is spirit, and those who worship him must worship in spirit and truth."[g]

Commenting on this verse, a theologian says,

"The terms 'spirit' and 'truth' are joined later in the expression 'Spirit of truth,' referring to the Holy Spirit (see 14:17; 15:26; 16:13; cf. 1 John 4:6; 5:6; see also 2 Thess. 2:13…the present reference therefore seems to point John's readers ultimately to worship in the Holy Spirit. Thus, true worship is not a matter of geographical location (worship in a church building), physical posture (kneeling

---

[a] 1 John 4:7 [b] Ps. 37:4; Rom. 7:4-6; Gal. 5:16–17 [c] 1 John 1:3 [d] Rom. 8:4–13 [e] Rom. 6:6; 7:6 [f] Gal. 5:19–23 [g] John 4:24

or standing), or following a particular liturgy or external rituals (cf. Matt. 6:5–13); it is a matter of the heart and of the Spirit...As Stibbe...puts it, 'True worship is paternal in focus (the Father), personal in origin (the Son), and pneumatic in character (the Spirit).'"[8]

For a born-again person with the Spirit, worshipping God is what they want to do at the deepest level of their new nature. Psalm 37:4 says, "Delight yourself in the LORD, and he will give you the desires of your heart." Practically, this means that as we enjoy and delight in who God is, what He has done, and what He will do for us, our regenerated hearts share in the same desires of God. Subsequently, unlike religion, which is based on fear that forces people to do what they do not want to do, regeneration is based on love and new lives of worship, which is exactly what the new heart wants to do at the deepest level. The result is ever-growing, never-ending, ever-worshiping, passionate joy! For the Christian, worshipping God in all of life is not something we have to do but something we get to do and something we want to do! Indeed, sinful temptations do come, and the way we overcome those lesser and weaker desires is by feeding our greater and stronger desires for God and godliness in our new nature by the Spirit's power.

WHAT DOES GOD REQUIRE IN CORPORATE CHURCH WORSHIP?

The New Testament is clear that God's people are to gather regularly for corporate worship. This is apparent by the frequent use of the Greek word *ekklesia*, which simply means a gathered assembly of God's people.[a] Likewise, Hebrews 10:24-25 commands, "Let us consider how to stir up one another to love and good works, not neglecting to meet together, as is the habit of some, but encouraging one another."

When God's people gather, it is incumbent upon the church leaders to do three things.

1. Forbid What God Forbids

Throughout the Old and New Testaments, people who profess to worship the God of the Bible do so in ways that He forbids and are rebuked.

In Deuteronomy 12:4, God points to how other religions worship their demon-gods and commands, "You shall not worship the Lord your God in that way." The second commandment in Exodus 20:4-6 also forbids idolatry, the worship of any created thing or seeking to reduce God to something that is made. The Puritans were particularly serious about this commandment, which explains why they rightly forbade the portrayal of God the Father in artwork in the form of anyone or anything created, such as an old man with a beard. From more recent history, much of the controversy surrounding the book The Shack involved a portrayal of

---

[a] 1 Cor. 10:31

God the Father as a woman, which is a violation of the second commandment.

The New Testament church at Corinth is forbidden from worshiping with members of other religions because doing so is to entertain demons.[a] Christians should have evangelistic friendships with members of other religions, but we must never participate in the practices of other religions because they worship different and demonic gods.

2. *Employ Biblical Methods*

Not only are we to worship the right God, but we are also to worship in the right way.

God-centered.[b] Worship is for God. While this may seem obvious, sadly it is not obvious to all people. God-centered worship is about hearing a message that reveals, from the Bible, who God is and what He has done and is doing for and with us; singing songs about who God is and what He does; and judging the quality of worship based upon whether it accords with the Scriptures and whether we have met with God.

Intelligible.[c] Words spoken should be in the language of the hearers (unlike, for example, the old Catholic Latin Mass or the Protestant preacher who uses so many Greek words that the average person is altogether lost), and any technical words used are explained so that everyone knows what they mean. Defining theological terms is important because, in addition to being God-centered, worship is meant to build up God's people. The Bible itself is an example of this; the New Testament was not originally written in the normal street-level vernacular of the average person so that it could be understood by as many as possible.

Seeker-sensitive.[d] Since non-Christians do attend church (which is a good thing), we need to help them understand who Jesus is and what he has done so that they can become Christians. This is a way the church practices hospitality which means welcoming the outsider in.

Unselfish.[e] If people want to express their personal response to God in a way that draws undue attention to themselves and distracts others from responding to God, then they should do that kind of thing at home, in private, because the meeting is for corporate, not just individual, response to God.

Orderly.[f] The meeting flows in such a way that God's people are able to hear God's Word and respond without distraction. Feedback on the audio speakers; musicians who cannot keep time; singers who cannot keep pitch; long, awkward pauses because no one knows what is happening next; and people speaking in tongues or prophesying out of turn in a way that the Bible forbids all contribute to disorder.

Missional.[g] The meeting fits the culture in which it takes place. This includes seating on a pew, chair or on the floor, when a church meets, for how long, what kind of music is sung, and what technology is used. These things should reflect the

---

[a] 1 Cor. 10:14-22 [b] Matt. 4:8-10 [c] 1 Cor. 14:1-12 [d] 1 Cor. 14:20-25 [e] 1 Cor. 14:26 [f] 1 Cor. 14:40 [g] 1 Cor. 9:19-23

DOCTRINE

culture in which God's people are gathering so that there is no cultural imperialism imposed on one culture from another. This does not mean that features from other cultures or eras cannot be used in the service, such as singing ancient hymns, but it does mean such things are used because they help God's people to meet with God.

3. Do What Scripture Commands

There are certain elements that Scripture prescribes for gathered corporate worship services. Many theologians refer to these as the elements of corporate worship, and they include the following:

1) Preaching[a]
2) Sacraments of baptism and the Lord's Table[b]
3) Prayer[c]
4) Reading Scripture[d]
5) Financial giving[e]
6) Singing and music[f]

It is significant to stress that essentially all Bible-believing Christians agree on these basic biblical concepts.

Regarding how God is to be worshiped, God must be worshiped as He wishes, not as we wish. This explains why God judges those who seek to worship Him with either sinful forms externally[g] or sinful hearts internally.[h] When it comes to worship, which is all of life, the God of the Bible cares about both what we do and why we do it. In Genesis 4, the brothers Cain and Abel bring their worship offerings to God and, while what is in their hands is acceptable, Cain's offering is rejected because what is in his heart is unacceptable to God—he was jealous of his brother.[i]

D. A. Carson has said, "We cannot imagine that the church gathers for worship on Sunday morning if by this we mean that we then engage in something that we have not been engaging in the rest of the week. New-covenant worship terminology prescribes constant 'worship.'"[9]

God, in His great wisdom, has given clear principles and practices to guide the corporate worship of His people. However, He has not given His people clear methods or an order of service. According to Don Carson, "We have no detailed first-century evidence of an entire Christian service."[10] Furthermore, "the New Testament documents do not themselves provide a 'model service.'"[11] John Frame has also said, "we know very little of the church's liturgy in the first century."[12]

Therefore, while God is very clear on the principles and practices to govern corporate worship, He has left it up to church leaders led by the Holy Spirit to determine the methods used to implement them.

Regarding the worship of God by His people, here are some things the Bible

---

[a] 2 Tim. 4:2 [b] Matt. 28:19; 1 Cor. 11:17-34 [c] 1 Tim. 2:1 [d] 1 Tim. 4:13 [e] 2 Cor. 8-9 [f] Col. 3:16 [g] Lev. 10:1-2; Isa. 1:11-17; Jer. 7:9-10; Ez. 8-9 [h] Gen. 4; Isa. 1:11-17; Jer. 7:9-10; Mic. 6:6-8 [i] 1 John 3:12

WORSHIP: GOD TRANSFORMS

does reveal:
1. Heartfelt internally[a]
2. Holy forms externally[b]; Prostrate face down[c]
3. Dancing[d]
4. Clapping[e]
5. Reverence[f]
6. Bowing[g]
7. Kneeling[h]
8. Laying on of hands[i]
9. Lifting hands[k]
10. Falling down[m]
11. Playing musical instruments[n]
12. Writing new worship songs[o]
13. Singing loudly[p]
14. Kneeling[q]
15. Standing[r]
16. Sitting[s]

---

[a] Gen. 4; Deut. 11:16, 30:17; Is. 1:11-17, 29:13; Jer. 7:9-10; Micah 6:6-8; Matt. 15:8; Mark 7:6; 1 Cor. 14:25 [b] Lev. 10:1-2; Deut. 12:31; 1 Kings 11:33; Dan. 3; Is. 1:11-17; Ez. 8-9; Jer. 7:9-10 [c] Num. 24:4,16, Deut. 9:18, 9:25; 1 Kings 18:39; 1 Chron. 29:20; Isaiah 15:3; Dan. 2:46, 8:17 [d] 2 Sam. 6:14; Job 21:11; Eccl. 3:4; Jer. 31:4, 31:13; Matt. 11:7 [e] Job 21:5; Psalm 47:1, 98:8; Isaiah 55:12 [f] Neh. 5:15; Psalm 5:7; Mal. 2:5; 2 Cor. 7:1; Eph. 5:21; Col. 3:22; Heb. 12:28; 1 Peter 3:2; Rev. 11:18 [g] Gen. 19:1, 24:26, 24:48, 24:52, 27:29, 47:31; Ex. 4:31, 12:27; Num. 22:31; Deut. 26:10; 2 Sam. 9:8; 1 Kings 1:47; 2 Kings 5:18, 17:16, 21:21; 2 Chron. 29:28; 29:30; Psalm 5:7, 38:6, 66:4, 95:6, 138:2, 145:14, 146:8, 45:14, 45:23, 49:23, 58:5, 66:23; Lam. 2:10; Ezekiel 8:16; Dan. 10:15; Micah 5:13, 6:6; Matt. 2:11; Luke 24:5; John 19:30; Phil. 2:10 [h] 1 Kings 8:54; Psalm 22:29; Job 40:4; Eph. 3:14 [i] Matt. 19:13; Mark 5:23, 10:16; Luke 20:19; Acts 8:18-19, 9:12, 9:17, 28:8; 1 Tim. 5:22; 2 Tim. 1:6; Heb. 6:2 [k] Psalm 28:2, 63:4, 76:5, 119:48, 134:2; Lamentations 2:19; 3:41-42; 1 Timothy 2:8 [m] Dan. 3:4-7; 1 Cor. 14:22; Rev. 3:7-10, 4:9-11 [n] 1 Sam. 16:15-18; 18:6; 1 Chron. 15:16, 16:42, 23:5; 2 Chron. 5:13, 7:6, 23:13, 29:26-27, 34:12; Neh. 12:36; Psalm 45:8, 98:4; Psalm 150 [o] Psalm 33:3; 40:3; 96:1; 98:1; 144:9, 149:1; Isaiah 42:10; Rev. 5:9, 14:3 [p] Psalm 5:11, 9:2, 9:11, 13:6; Acts 16:25; Rom. 15:9; 1 Cor. 14:15; Eph. 5:18-20; Col. 3:16; Heb. 2:12; James 5:13; Rev. 14:3, 15:3 [q] Isaiah 45:23; Rom. 14:9; Phil. 2:10 [r] Num. 5:16; Deut. 10:6-9, 19:16-17; 1 Kings 19:11; 1 Chron. 23:28-31; Psalm 24:3; 26:12; Hab. 3:2 [s] Psalm 110:1; Lam. 3:27-28; Micah 4:4, 7:8; Zech. 3:10

17. Shouting Amen[a]
18. Serving with your spiritual gift(s)[b]
19. Giving tithes and offerings[c]

A biblically-informed Christian definition of worship includes both adoration and action. John Frame says:

"In Scripture, there are two groups of Hebrew and Greek terms that are translated 'worship.' The first group refers to 'labor' or 'service'...The second group of terms means literally 'bowing' or 'bending the knee,' hence 'paying homage, honoring the worth of someone else.' The English term worship, from worth, has the same connotation. From the first group of terms we may conclude that worship is active. It is something we do, a verb...From the second group of terms, we learn that worship is honoring someone superior to ourselves."[13]

This brings us to stewardship as worship.

WHAT IS A STEWARD?

God came into history as the man Jesus Christ. He left the riches and glory of His heavenly kingdom for poverty and humility.

Jesus' life was perfectly stewarded. Vocationally, He spent most of His life working an honest job as a carpenter. Financially, although poor, Jesus paid His tithes and taxes while giving generously to those in need. Jesus' public ministry included doing the works the Father had given Him to do, "I glorified you on earth, having accomplished the work that you gave me to do."[d]

On the cross, Jesus became the most generous giver that the world has ever known. There, He took our sin, condemnation, and death, and gave us His righteousness, salvation, and life. Following His resurrection, Jesus continues to be generous, giving us the Holy Spirit and spiritual gifts, and is preparing for us a Kingdom in which we will enjoy His generosity together with Him forever.

The early church was marked by generous stewardship because they followed the example of Jesus. Randy Alcorn reminds us of "the Jerusalem converts who eagerly sold their possessions to give to the needy (Acts 2:45; 4:32-35). And the Ephesian occultists, who proved their conversion was authentic when they burned their magic books, worth today what would be millions of dollars (Acts 19:19)."[14]

Christians and non-Christians alike celebrate Jesus' birth every year by giving gifts in the tradition of the Magi, who brought gifts to Jesus as a young boy.

---

[a] Deut. 27:15-26; I Ch. 16:36; Neh. 5:13, 8:6; Psalm 41:13; 72:19, 89:52, 106:48; Jer.11:5, 28:6; Rom. 1:25, 9:5, 11:36, 15:33, 16:27; I Cor. 16:24; Gal. 1:5, 6:18; Eph. 3:21; Phil. 4:20, 4:23; I Tim. 1:17; 6:16; 2 Tim. 4:18; Heb.13:21; I Peter 4:11, 5:11; 2 Peter 3:18; Jude 1:25; Rev. 1:6, 1:7, 3:14, 5:14, 7:12, 19:4, 22:20-21 [b] I Cor. 12:8-10, 12:28-30; Rom. 12:6-8; Eph. 4:11; I Peter 4:11
[c] Ex. 25:2, 35:22, 36:5; I Chron. 29-3-4; 2 Chron. 24:10; Prov. 3:9; Mal. 3:10; Acts 4:34-35; 2 Cor. 8-9 [d] John 17:4

Generally speaking, there are two ways to see our life and possessions. One is through the perspective of ownership, whereby I and my life and possessions belong to me alone. The other is through the perspective of stewardship, whereby I and my life and possessions belong to God and are to be invested for His purposes.

In Titus 1:7, Paul speaks of leaders serving as "God's steward" of the church. Similarly, 1 Peter 4:10 commands every Christian to be "good stewards of God's varied grace." Randy Alcorn describes his own learning about being a steward, "If God was the owner, I was the manager. I needed to adopt a steward's mentality toward the assets. He had entrusted – not given – to me. A steward manages assets for the owner's benefit. The steward carries no sense of entitlement to the assets he manages. It's his job to find out what the owner wants done with his assets, then carry out his will."[15]

Four traits distinguish a steward:

1. I belong to the Lord. This is exactly what Paul says reminding Christians that we "belong to Jesus Christ."[a]
2. Everything I have belongs to the Lord. The Bible recognizes private property ownership, which explains why it forbids stealing. Above all, the Bible teaches that God alone is the ultimate owner of everything, because it comes from Him and is ruled over by Him. God's ownership includes all wealth: "The silver is mine, and the gold is mine, declares the LORD of hosts."[b] God's ownership extends to the natural resources we cultivate for wealth, "For every beast of the forest is mine, the cattle on a thousand hills."[c] Even the abilities we use to earn a living are gifted to us by God and are to be humbly used, "Beware lest you say in your heart, 'My power and the might of my hand have gotten me this wealth.' You shall remember the LORD your God, for it is he who gives you power to get wealth."[d]
3. Everything I have is a gift from the Lord. Paul says, "For who sees anything different in you? What do you have that you did not receive? If then you received it, why do you boast as if you did not receive it?"[e] And just in case anything has been overlooked, Jesus' brother reminds us, "Do not be deceived, my beloved brothers. Every good gift and every perfect gift is from above, coming down from the Father of lights with whom there is no variation or shadow due to change."[f]
4. I want to manage God's resources wisely. Since God is the owner, and I am the manager, I want to steward God's resources in the way that God wants. Practically, this means the air we breathe, the food we eat, money we make, words we speak, days we live, and everything else is a gracious gift from our loving God for us to manage, "Each of you should use whatever gift you have received to serve others, as faithful stewards of God's grace in its

---

[a] Rom. 1:6 [b] Hag. 2:8 [c] Psalm 50:10 [d] Deut. 8:17–18 [e] 1 Cor. 4:7 [f] James 1:16–17

various forms."[a]

Practically, stewards have a very distinct mentality. Rather than wondering how they should spend their time, talent, and treasure, they ask how they should invest God's time, talent, and treasure. This means, as an example, that rather than asking why they should give their money to God or wondering how much of their money they should give to God, they instead prayerfully consider how much of God's money He wants them to keep as well as what He wants done with that portion not used for bills and such.

HOW DO WE WORSHIP WITH OUR TIME, TALENT, AND TREASURE?

Jesus devoted roughly 25 percent of his words in the Gospels to the resources God has entrusted to our stewardship. This includes some 28 passages in the Gospels. In the Old and New Testaments combined, there are over 800 verses on the subject, addressing topics ranging from planning and budgeting, to saving and investing, to debt and tithing. Furthermore, money and wealth and possessions are among the greatest idols in our culture, and there is simply no way to be a disciple of Jesus apart from learning to worship God. That worship includes the stewardship of time, talents, and treasures as the average person has around 27,000 days on the earth during which time, they will speak 400,000-800,000 words.

Time

God has meaningful and purposeful things for His people to accomplish during their life on the earth.[a] To accomplish this, we must always seek God's priorities for our life and remain devoted to them and balance our work and Sabbath so that we can steward our time well. R. C. Sproul says, "Time is the great leveler. It is one resource that is allocated in absolute egalitarian terms. Every living person has the same number of hours to use in every day. Busy people are not given a special bonus added on to the hours of the day. The clock plays no favorites."[16]

The opening pages of the Bible reveal that for six days God worked, and on the seventh day God rested from His work. The Ten Commandments establish a rhythm for us patterned after God's, with a seven-day week marked by six days of work and one day of Sabbath.[b]

Work

Until roughly 30 years of age, Jesus worked as a carpenter. For the remaining roughly three years of his life, Jesus said He was about his Father's work.[c] Jesus' ministry work included exhausting preaching, teaching, demon-confronting, feeding, healing, traveling by foot, and more.

---

[a] 1 Peter 4:10 [b] Eph. 2:10 [c] Ex. 20:11 [d] John 4:34; 5:17, 36

WORSHIP: GOD TRANSFORMS

Both the Old and New Testaments have much to say about work including: God made us to work, work hard, find some satisfaction in our work, provide sustenance by our work, and work by the grace that God gives us.[a] Any work done unto the Lord is an act of worship that God rewards, "Whatever you do, work heartily, as for the Lord and not for men, knowing that from the Lord you will receive the inheritance as your reward. You are serving the Lord Christ."[b]

To sabbath is to rest from one's labor. The first Sabbath day was a Saturday and was enjoyed by God.[c] The first recorded command for humans to sabbath is in Exodus 16:23, and honoring the Sabbath is listed as the fourth commandment.[d]

Regarding the particular day of the Sabbath, some have maintained that it should be celebrated on Saturday like the Hebrews did, the final day of their week. However, the early church abruptly changed the day of worship to Sunday to commemorate the resurrection of Jesus from death[e] on that first day of the new week[f], which was also called the Lord's day.[g]

Sunday remained a workday in the early church until Emperor Constantine instituted it as an official day of rest in AD 321. In America, there was a debate as to whether the Jewish Sabbath of Saturday or the Christian Sabbath of Sunday should be recognized, and the compromise was to keep both, which is why we have two-day weekends.

Sadly, for some, the Sabbath has become a religious idol. Attempts have been made to rob the Sabbath of its worship and joy by carefully mandating what can and cannot be done. However, Jesus seemed to have intentionally lived in public view in order to serve as a model of the Sabbath contrary to that given by legalistic teachers. For example, Jesus healed on the Sabbath, taught on the Sabbath, and promoted evangelism on the Sabbath.[h] Furthermore, our true Sabbath is not found in a day but ultimately in a saving relationship with Jesus, where we can rest from trying to earn our salvation and find rest in his finished work.[i] Therefore, the Sabbath is not a law for believers to obey but instead a grace to enjoy.

Talent

During his life on earth, Jesus was empowered by the Holy Spirit to do ministry. Jesus said that one day, Christians would do even greater ministry than He did.[k] While this does not mean that Christians are greater than Jesus, it does mean that Christians who are gifted and empowered by the Holy Spirit can minister to more people than Jesus could, because there are a few billion professing Christians today spread across the earth. Therefore, our personal ministry is the continuation of Jesus' ministry.

---

[a] Gen. 2:15; Prov. 18:9; 21:25; Eccles. 3:22; 2 Thess. 3:10; 1 Cor. 15:10 [b] Col. 3:23–24 [c] Gen. 2:2 [d] Ex. 20:8–11 [e] Matt. 28:1; Mark 16:1–2; Luke 24:1; John 20:1 [f] Acts 20:7; 1 Cor. 16:2 [g] Rev. 1:10 [h] Matt. 12:1–14; John 9:1–17; Mark 6:1–2; John 7:21–24 [i] Matt. 11:28–30; Rom. 4:5; Col. 2:16–17 [k] John 14:12

In 1 Corinthians 12, a pivotal exposition of the work of the Spirit in believers, Paul summarizes an astonishing variety of manifestations of the Spirit. The common translation of verse 1, "spiritual gifts," is not quite right because the word "gifts" is not in the Greek original of this verse. A better translation is "Now concerning what comes from the Spirit".[a] Paul speaks of "spirituals" which focuses on the things of the Spirit, and how the Spirit moves forward the mission of Jesus through the followers of Jesus.

Verse 4 speaks of gifts (*charismata*), enduring abilities you have that the Spirit can pick up, animate, magnify, and repurpose to carry on the work of Jesus. This is any Spirit-empowered ability that is used in any ministry of the church. We see a list of gifts in Romans 12:6-8. While there are many different kinds of gifts ranging from quite supernatural (working of miracles) to quite natural (administration), all are Spirit-empowered abilities used to continue the mission of Jesus.

Verse 5 goes on to speak of services or ministries (*diakonia*), the place or role or office where believers are called by God to serve inside and/or outside the church. We see a typical list of services in Ephesians 4:11. There are many others inside the church services or roles, such as elder, deacon, worship leader, or children's teacher, as well as community services done outside the church.

Verse 6 speaks of workings or activities (*energema*) the Spirit does. It is a very general reference to all sorts of empowering things the Spirit does in and through believers.

Finally, in verse 7, he speaks of manifestations (*phanerosis*) of the Spirit and gives a list of them in verses 8-11. In addition to the variety of gifts, services, and workings, there are manifestations or appearances of the Spirit in Jesus' followers so we can worship God, serve His people and fulfill our mission of making disciples of all nations. They are bestowed by God through the empowerment of His Spirit and must be exercised in love by following biblical principles and guidelines (1 Cor. 13-14). They are all connected to the fruit of the Spirit (Gal. 5:21-22).

These are not the enduring gifts which a person has as in verse 4, but manifestations which can occur in any believer at any time as the Spirit wills. There are manifestations of prophecy and there are also people who prophesy regularly enough that they are called prophets. Here Paul is speaking of the first category of manifestations.

Paul does not want us to be ignorant of the rich diversity of the Spirit's work which may be through life-long abilities, newly given abilities, or momentary manifestations. Paul's point in listing this rich diversity is to highlight the unity brought by the empowering, unifying presence of the Spirit.

The Spirit works in and through people, individually as Christians and corporately as the Church, by utilizing both our life-long abilities and newly given

---

[a] 1 Cor. 12:1 (Holman Christian Standard Bible.) See also 1 Cor. 14:1, 37

abilities (often called spiritual gifts), which together we will refer to as talents. Our talents are God-given opportunities to do good as an act of worship. Non-Christians have their natural abilities and only Christians are spiritual, meaning animated or made alive by the Holy Spirit. The Holy Spirit connects us and our talents with full Spirit empowerment. Wayne Grudem captures this well when he defines spiritual gifts as "any ability that is empowered by the Holy Spirit and used in any ministry of the church."[17]

The New Testament has many lists of the wide variety of talents or "spirituals." 1 Corinthians 12:8-10 lists the manifestations of wisdom, knowledge, faith, healing, miracles, prophecy, discerning of spirits, tongues, and the interpretation of tongues. 1 Corinthians 12:28-30 lists the talents of serving as an apostle, prophesying, teaching, performing miracles, healing, helping, administrating, speaking in tongues, and interpreting tongues. Romans 12:6-8 lists gifts of prophesying, serving, teaching, exhorting, giving, leading, and showing mercy. Ephesians 4:11 lists serving as an apostle, prophesying, evangelizing, pastoring, and teaching. And 1 Peter 4:11 distinguishes between speaking and serving gifts, as some people minister primarily with their words while others do so with their works.

Since these lists all differ, there is no complete list of talents that exists in the New Testament. Therefore, we are not to regard these lists as exhaustive. In fact, the point of the New Testament seems to be to use whatever talent (lifelong or new endowment) one has wisely for the cause of the Gospel.

There has been no shortage of controversy regarding the so-called "sign gifts" — tongues, miracles, and prophecy—and whether they are to be practiced by the Church today. The following chart outlines the basic positions without getting into great detail, which would require another book to be written on the subject. We will simply say here that we hold the continuationist position.

Cessationist	Functional Cessationist	Continuationist	Word-Faith
Supernatural gifts, especially the speaking gifts (tongues, miracles, and prophecy) functioned only in the early church and are not to be practiced today. God speaks today but only in Scripture. Contemporary "revelations" do not come from God.	Supernatural gifts are given to every generation and may continue to speak but the abuses are so rampant that it is better to avoid them. It is safer to rely solely on the Bible and Spirit-empowered wisdom.	Supernatural gifts are given to every generation. Contemporary revelations are valued but always secondary to Scripture. Supernatural manifestations are sought but must show the fruit of the Spirit.	Supernatural gifts are given to every generation. God's Kingdom is a present reality with immediate healing and prosperity for anyone who exercises a faith confession. Contemporary revelations are highly valued.

Treasure

Jesus stressed that we either worship our wealth or worship with our wealth, "No one can serve two masters, for either he will hate the one and love the other, or he will be devoted to the one and despise the other. You cannot serve God and money."[a]

Money is either a tool or an idol. When wealth is an idol, the "trap" of the "love of money" is worshiped in pursuit of other perceived blessings, such as comfort, security, status, and power. However, "godliness with contentment is great gain, for we brought nothing into the world, and we cannot take anything out of the world. But if we have food and clothing, with these we will be content. But those who desire to be rich fall into temptation, into a snare, into many senseless and harmful desires that plunge people into ruin and destruction. For the love of money is a root of all kinds of evils. It is through this craving that some have wandered away from the faith and pierced themselves with many pangs."[b]

The Bible speaks of many financial sins that accompany money idolatry. These include being continually torn between whether to obey God at financial loss or disobey God in order to retain wealth (as with the rich young ruler)[c], giving from pride so that others will be impressed with your generosity and praise you[d], getting into the slavery of debt[e], enviously coveting the success and possessions of others rather than rejoicing with them[f], a diminished fear of the Lord[g], laziness[h], not providing for one's family[i] poor financial planning leading to poverty[k], not leaving a generous financial legacy to your children and grandchildren[m], becoming a heretic because it is profitable[n], becoming selfish and therefore a bad friend[o], and robbing God by not giving to the cause of ministry.[p]

If we love money, we use God and people. If we love God, we are free to use money to love God and people.

Paul speaks of worshiping with our money, "I have received full payment, and more. I am well supplied, having received from Epaphroditus the gifts you sent, a fragrant offering, a sacrifice acceptable and pleasing to God."[q]

Jesus was rich in Heaven, poor on earth, and is rich right now in Heaven. Therefore, someone can be like Jesus whether they are rich or poor. To help you grow as a worshiper with wealth rather than as a worshiper of wealth, five principles are helpful.

1. God takes our worst and gives His best

In coming to the earth and going to the cross, God took our worst (sin) and gave us His best (Son). John 3:16 says, "God so loved the world that he gave his one and only Son, that whoever believes in him shall not perish but have eternal life."

2. Your wallet is God's scalpel for heart surgery

Sometimes the fastest way to change your heart is to change your budget, "For where your treasure is, there your heart will be also."[r]

---

[a] Matt. 6:24 [b] 1 Tim. 6:6-10 [c] Luke 18:18-30 [d] Matt. 6:1-4 [e] Prov. 22:7 [f] Eccles. 4:4 [g] Prov. 15:16 [h] Prov. 13:4 [i] 1 Tim. 5:8 [k] Prov. 15:21-22; 21:5 [m] Prov. 13:22; 19:14 [n] 1 Tim. 6:3-10 [o] James 4:1-4 [p] Mal. 3:8-10 [q] Phil. 4:18 [r] Matt. 6:21

3. Firstfruits grows faith

When we give to God our first and best, we are thanking Him for what we have, prioritizing our lives to be God-centered, and trusting Him to provide for the rest of our needs, "Honor the LORD with your wealth and with the firstfruits of all your produce…"[a]

4. You cannot take it with you, but you can send it ahead

All of the things that we own in this life will stay behind when we go to the Kingdom of Heaven. But good stewards can send eternal rewards ahead, "Do not lay up for yourselves treasures on earth, where moth and rust destroy and where thieves break in and steal, but lay up for yourselves treasures in heaven, where neither moth nor rust destroys and where thieves do not break in and steal."[b]

5. Giving is a blessing

Every parent or grandparent who has given a gift to a child knows that they are blessed to watch the child be blessed because giving is a blessing. Christians do not give to get a blessing. Christians give knowing that the blessing is the giving, "It is more blessed to give than to receive."[c] This blessing of giving includes forgiving others as a giver is also a forgiver.

SHOULD CHRISTIANS TITHE?

Tithe literally means "tenth." In the Old Testament, the tithe referred to God's people giving the first 10 percent of their gross income (also called "firstfruits") to God to fund the Levite priests' ministry.[d] There were additional tithes and offerings required of God's people, including 10 percent paid for festivals to build community and for celebration, 3.3 percent given to help the poor, crop gleanings collected for the poor and aliens, and other occasional additional tithes above and beyond regular giving.[e] Therefore, the total "mandatory" Old Testament tithe resulted in over 25 percent of a family's gross income going to God and ministry.

In the New Testament, financial giving among God's people focuses on grace, generosity, the heart, and not actual percentages of one's income. The word tithe is rarely used in the New Testament, and when it is, it is usually mentioned negatively in rebuking religious types such as the Pharisees who gave their money to God but not their hearts and lives.

It cannot be overstated that when we give to God, we are not deciding how much of our wealth to give. Rather, we are determining how much of God's wealth we are keeping for our own uses, "But who am I, and what is my people, that we should be able thus to offer willingly? For all things come from you, and of your

---

[a] Prov. 3:9 [b] Matt. 6:19-20 [c] Acts 20:35 [d] Num. 18:21-29, 27:30 [e] Deut. 12:10-11, 17-18, 14:22-27; Deut. 14:28-29; Lev. 19:9-10; Neh. 10:32-33

own have we given you."[a]

Perhaps the most thorough teaching in all the New Testament on giving is found in 2 Corinthians 8–9, where we discover eight principles regarding generous giving.[18]

1. Generous giving is sacrificial.[b] Paul says that the Macedonian Christians were experiencing severe affliction and extreme poverty but responded with abundant joy and overflowing generosity.
2. Generous giving is something that some people are spiritually gifted for.[c] Those with the gift of giving should teach and model it with love as with all other aspects of Christian discipleship.
3. Generous giving is a Gospel issue.[d] Christians are to enjoy being generous givers because doing so is a response to and reflection of Jesus' gift of salvation to them.
4. Generous giving encourages churches to share with other churches and ministries in need.[e] This includes such things as helping churches in impoverished nations, new church plants, and churches filled with new converts and college students.
5. Generous giving is motivated by friendly competition.[f] Paul challenged the wealthier Corinthian church, for example, to match the financial giving of the impoverished Macedonian church.
6. Generous giving is about sowing and reaping.[g] Unlike prosperity theology, which encourages people to give to God so that they might get more money, generosity theology aims to sow, or invest, in ministries that will reap a gospel reward of converts to Jesus and mature disciples. Therefore, the sowing and reaping that the Bible speaks of is not necessarily personal as much as it is missional.
7. Generous giving is one of many evidences that someone is truly a Christian.[h] Paul's point is that if someone has truly received the generous grace of the Gospel of Jesus Christ, he or she will be generous.
8. Generous giving promotes the worship of Jesus as God. This is among the ultimate goals of generous giving—seeing as many people as possible enjoy the generosity of God's grace and respond in worshipful joy. Paul says this repeatedly at the close of his lengthy teaching on generous giving:
    - You will be enriched in every way to be generous in every way, which through us will produce thanksgiving to God.
    - For the ministry of this service is not only supplying the needs of the saints but is also overflowing in many thanksgivings to God.
    - By their approval of this service, they will glorify God because of your submission flowing from your confession of the gospel of Christ, and the generosity of your contribution for them and for all others.

---

[a] 1 Chron. 29:14 [b] 2 Cor. 8:1–6, 10–12 [c] 2 Cor. 8:7 [d] 2 Cor. 8:8–9 [e] 2 Cor. 8:13–15 [f] 2 Cor. 9:1–5 [g] 2 Cor. 9:6–12 [h] 2 Cor. 9:13–14

- Thanks be to God for His inexpressible gift!

Our capacity can be increased every year which means that seeking to increase the percentage of one's giving to the Lord each year is a good life goal. For the Christian, we should seek to be as excited to give God our time, talent, and treasure as we are our sin since all we are and all we have belongs to Him!

QUESTIONS FOR PERSONAL JOURNALING AND/OR SMALL GROUP DISCUSSION

1. Who or what is truly most important in your life?
2. What is your most memorable worship experience in the presence of God?
3. Looking at your past, can you see anything in hindsight that was an idol for you? How did that harm you?
4. Is there anyone or anything you are currently idolizing or demonizing? How can that stop?
5. Is there any aspect of your life that includes non-Christian spiritual practices that need to be stopped?
6. What practical things can you do to keep your heart clean before God (e.g. prayer, singing, Bible reading, church attendance, etc.?)
7. How is your worship of God away from church in places such as your home and work?
8. How can you be more actively engaged in a local church family?
9. Who should you be inviting to church with you?
10. What are the top changes you have experienced since becoming a Christian?
11. How do you worship God with your time?
12. How do you worship God with your talent?
13. How do you worship God with your treasure?

CHAPTER 12: KINGDOM

"GOD REIGNS"

Your kingdom come, your will be done, on earth as it is in heaven.
MATTHEW 6:10

Our world is constantly frustrating, disappointing, and exhausting. No matter how much money we spend, time we invest, wars we wage, elections we hold, and educations we fund, nothing cures our cursed, crooked, corrupted planet.

God made the world "very good". We've made it very bad.

Every once in a while, we get our hopes up only to see them dashed. A war is won that gives hope of peace and prosperity that never comes to pass. A politician rises to power with a vision that inspires hope in us that a better day is on the horizon, yet it's all a mirage.

In the old Peanuts cartoons, Lucy would hold a football for Charlie Brown to kick. With great hope, Charlie Brown would run up to the ball, only to have Lucy pull it away at the last minute sending him flying into the air before landing painfully on his back. The pursuit of a better life in this world is pretty much the exact same experience for every generation.

Because God made us to live in a perfect environment with peace in us, and prosperity around us, our hearts remain restless.[a] Longing for Heaven, we keep going on vacations, moving houses, and exploring the outdoors...to no avail. So, we push our longings out past this life. In his book *Heaven*, Randy Alcorn says

---

[a] Eccl. 3:11 (NLT)

that anthropologists tell us that every culture has some concept of a better life after death. While these visions vary, they reveal that we were made for more, never feel quite at home on this planet, and are all hoping to find our way Home somehow someday.

WHAT HAPPENS WHEN WE DIE?

Losing someone you know, and love, is perhaps the most painful experience in life. In those seasons of loss, something in us simply knows that something has gone terribly wrong as what we are experiencing is unnatural. Having been to numerous funerals as pastors, we have seen the grieving family and friends respond in one of six ways.

One, some people don't know what to believe or say and so they echo pithy statements from greeting cards meant to make people feel better. Examples include, "they are in a better place now", "they are with the Big Guy upstairs", and "they are standing in line at the Pearly Gates". Rather than providing any real hope, these are often well-intended ways that people are saying they have no idea what happens after you die, but they hope it gets worked out somehow.

Two, some people do not believe in life after death and so their grief is final. Without anything beyond the eternal horizon, the loss of life becomes bitter without any hope of getting better. Naturalism is the belief that you are only a physical body without a spiritual soul, and that, once you die, there is nothing more. Not surprisingly, even the most hardened naturalists find it psychologically devastating to accept the logical conclusion of their own beliefs. Subsequently, they try to live on forever through the memory of others, their offspring, or their efforts to change the world in some way that their mark on it remains after their death with such things as foundation, cause, or memorial.

Three, some people believe in a concept of Heaven, but not Hell, and assume that once you die, you get to go to Heaven. Universalism is the belief that, to go to Heaven, you don't need to repent of sin and trust Jesus, but simply die. When pressed, universalists struggle to explain the fairness of the worst people living their entire lives harming others without ever changing and being rewarded eternally. While it sounds nice at first, universalism makes it hard to get excited about living in a home between Genghis Khan and Stalin, with unrepentant pedophiles, sexual predators, and sociopaths as our roommates forever.

Four, some people believe in the concept of purgatory. A bit like an airport, it's the place where you wait as you travel from earth to Heaven. For Catholics, purgatory is a place or state in which those who died in the grace of God expiate their unforgiven sins by being punished before being admitted to Heaven. Practically, this would mean that we need to add to Jesus' work for our sins and contradicts the fact God made us "alive together with him [Jesus], having forgiven us all our trespasses, by canceling the record of debt that stood against us with its legal demands. This he set aside, nailing it to the cross."[a]

Five, people who believe in reincarnation claim that, after you die, you will come back repeatedly until you have paid off your karmic debt, trapped in a cycle of rebirth where the only hope is that after millions of attempts, you finally get it right and escape into the eternal oneness (Nirvana), which is the end of all personhood. Many Americans follow their personally devised versions of neo-paganism, Tibetan Buddhism, Kabala, and Gnosticism. They reject most of the disciplines and beliefs of the original religions in favor of some sort of wishful hope that they are doing it right and that in their next life they will be ascended masters of the universe. Reincarnation cannot solve the sin problem for the simple reason that, even if you could live multiple lives, you would not be paying off your old sin as fast as you would be adding on new sin, and you would thus return as a lower life form every time, which means when you die you have nothing to look forward to forever but increasing doom.

Six, Bible-believing Christians grieve the loss of someone they love, but with the reassurance of eternal life, resurrection of the dead, and reunion of God's entire Forever Family. This is grieving God's heart, "Brothers and sisters, we do not want you to be uninformed about those who sleep in death, so that you do not grieve like the rest of mankind, who have no hope."[b]

God created humans as thinking, feeling, moral persons made up of spirit and body tightly joined together.[c] Death is not normal or natural, but an enemy, the consequence of sin.[d] Death is the tearing apart of these two intertwined parts, the end of relationship with loved ones, and the cessation of life on this earth. The body goes to the grave and the spirit goes into an afterlife[e] to face judgment.[f] The Bible is clear that there will one day be a bodily resurrection for everyone to either eternal life with God or eternal condemnation apart from Him in Hell.[g]

Christians believe our eternal status depends on our relationship with Jesus Christ. We really believe that "God so loved the world, that he gave his only Son, that whoever believes in him should not perish but have eternal life...whoever believes in the Son has eternal life; whoever does not obey the Son shall not see life, but the wrath of God remains on him."[h]

Upon death, a believer's spirit immediately goes to Heaven to be with God.[i] Some, like the Seventh Day Adventists, cannot see how a soul can exist without a body. They mistakenly believe that the soul sleeps unconsciously between the death of the body and its resurrection on judgment day. Others believe the soul exists in God's memory until it is "re-membered" at the end of the age. Such existence in the divine database doesn't fit with John's vision of the souls of the martyrs crying out with a loud voice, "How long before you will judge and avenge our blood on those who dwell on the earth?"[k] Paul's confidence that death will be

---

[a] Col. 2:13-14 [b] 1 Thess. 4:13 NIV [c] Gen. 2:7 [d] Gen. 2:17; Rom. 5:12 [e] Ps. 104:29, 146:4; Eccles. 3:20–21, 12:7; James 2:26 [f] Heb. 9:2 [g] Dan. 12:2; Matt. 25:46 [h] John 3:16, 36 [i] 2 Cor. 5:1–10; Phil. 1:23 [k] Rev. 6:10

"far better" than fruitful work here on earth can hardly mean only a long nap with Jesus.[a]

Jesus gives us a picture in Luke 16:19–31 of existence after death. Lazarus, the godly beggar, goes to be with Abraham, while the self-indulgent rich man is in a place of torment. His deeds show that he does not love God.[b] The rich man, self-absorbed in life and now in death, sees Lazarus only as an instrument of his comfort. His sinning continues in the afterlife. There is neither repentance for his injustice nor the expectation that he can get out of torment now that he is dead.

Jesus, who has come back from death and is thus the expert on what awaits us on the other side, was emphatically clear that a day of judgment is coming when everyone will rise from their graves and stand before Him for eternal sentencing to either worship in His kingdom or suffer in His Hell.[c]

At the final judgment, all—even you—will stand before Jesus. Jesus' followers, whose names are written in the Book of Life, will be with him forever. The Bible could not be clearer: "If anyone's name was not found written in the book of life, he was thrown into the lake of fire."[d]

WHAT IS THE KINGDOM OF GOD?

At its simplest, the Kingdom of God is about God ruling as King over everyone and everything forever, bringing His rule and reign to bear on every inch of creation for all eternity. This is the result of God's mission to rescue and renew his sin-marred creation. Jesus not only saves our souls; He's King over all kings and Lord over all lords, establishing His rule and reign over all, defeating the human and divine evil powers, bringing perfect order to all, enacting justice, and being worshiped as Lord.

God's kingdom is both a journey and a destination, both a rescue operation in this broken world and a perfect outcome in the new earth to come, both already started and not yet finished. This distinction is incredibly important. When the already-ness of the kingdom is overly stressed, the result is an over-realized eschatology. In this case, the presence and power of sin are not fully accounted for, and there is a naive belief that life should be enjoyed with health and wealth, as if the kingdom has already been fully unveiled, and a sort of simplistic optimism sets in. Conversely, when the not-yet-ness of the Kingdom is overly stressed, the result is an underrealized eschatology. In this case, sin seems to be at least as powerful as the Gospel and there is little hope or enthusiasm for evangelism, church planting, or opposing injustice in the world, and a sort of hopeless fatalism sets in. The world is seen as a hopeless mess without the Kingdom of God showing up much in any power until the Second Coming of Christ.

God does not want us to be naïve, as if the Kingdom is fully here. And God

---

[a] Phil. 1:23 [b] 1 John 3:10, 4:8–21 [c] John 5:21–30 [d] Rev. 20:15

KINGDOM: GOD REIGNS

does not want us to be hopeless, as if the Kingdom has not yet begun. The Kingdom has come with Jesus and is coming again with Jesus' Second Coming. God will work His rescue, not by obliterating the physical earth but by recreating it. He will use humans, who are part of the problem but become, by grace, part of the solution, to bless, redeem, and restore. In all this, we are not observers of a divine drama but participants helping with the redemption, each playing the role God has assigned for us to play in making the invisible Kingdom visible.

Despite our sin, which ruined the world God made, He inaugurated His Kingdom rescue mission by calling the Gentile Abraham, blessing him, and making him the father of an offspring and a nation through whom all the sin-ruined families would be blessed.[a] Again, God works through a man, Abraham, who is part of the problem but is made part of the solution. God promised Abraham a plot of land that had previously been the garden of Eden as a place from which the nations would be blessed.

But things did not go well. Abraham, and then his son Isaac and his grandson Jacob, increasingly failed to be faithful to the covenant call. The Kingdom family found themselves exiled in the demonic kingdom of Egypt. In an ironic twist, the rescuers needed to be rescued. So, God in His faithfulness brought them back to ensure the continuation of his kingdom plan. As a response, Exodus 15 sings the triumph of God's Kingdom over the pagan power of the defeated king, the gods of Egypt, and the dark forces behind the counterfeit kingdom.[b] At Mount Sinai, God's people were once again reminded of their Kingdom role among the nations as His, "treasured possession among all peoples, for all the earth is mine; and you shall be to me a kingdom of priests and a holy nation."[c] As such, they existed to bring His glory to the whole earth. But despite God's gift of a beautiful land[d], they longed to return to Egypt;[e] they preferred slavery to freedom and a pagan earthly kingdom to his perfect heavenly Kingdom. Despite God's command[f], the people turned back to the defeated gods and continually preferred a kingdom of darkness.[g]

The glory of God's kingdom comes briefly in the rule of David and in the promise of the Messiah's coming as the Kingdom king.[h] Nonetheless, David's very serious sin ruins the glorious reign[i], and conflict rules through the rest of his time on the throne. In the following years, they constantly worship and serve other gods, powerful demonic spiritual beings, and the twin evils of idolatry and injustice dominate in the land. The whole nation goes into exile in Babylon until God rescues them.

Upon their rescue from Babylon, God tells Israel they will see the return of the Lord to Zion, which is the Bible's language for God's Kingdom. This is not just a vision for redeemed Jerusalem but for all nations because "all the ends of the

---

[a] Gen. 12:1-3 [b] Ex. 12:12; Num. 33:4; Zeph. 2:11 [c] Ex. 19:5-6 [d] Ex. 3:8-9; Num.13 [e] Num. 14:3-10 [f] Ex. 20:3, 23:13-33 [g] Ex. 32 [h] 2 Sam. 7:1-17; Psalm 89 [i] 2 Samuel 11-12

DOCTRINE

earth shall see the salvation of our God."[a] Instead of seeing a king in splendid robes of glory, though, they will see the battered and mangled body of a servant who bears pain and torture, who is wounded for our transgressions, who takes the chastisement for our sins, and who died for our sins only to rise again and make the many righteous.[b]

The Kingdom hope is revealed repeatedly in the Old Testament through Israel and the Messiah. The psalmist paints a mysterious vision of a coming king who will break the nations with a rod of iron and make them the Lord's heritage.[c] The psalmist promises that the king will cry, "My God, my God, why have you forsaken me?" as they pierce his hands and feet.[d] Because of this Messiah King, not only Israel but all the nations were promised inclusion in worshiping God alone, for the Lord rules over the nations as the King of Kings. He will shatter kings on the day of His wrath.[e] He is to be feared and praised above all gods.[f]

The Old Testament kingdom hope is that God will work His rescue mission in and through Israel to all nations. God's Messiah will bring righteousness amidst injustice, beauty amidst devastation, peace amidst conflict, unity amidst division, forgiveness amidst sin, healing amidst sickness, and worship amidst idolatry. The King will defeat the evil powers, reverse the curse, give fullness of life in place of death, and restore harmony to all creation. Tragically, many of the Jews had lost sight of this universal hope. They were expecting God to send a king who would lead a military uprising to free them from Roman rule. They wrongly believed that they would then be vindicated so they could enjoy the exclusive blessings of being God's people.

When Jesus came, He repeated the prophets' calls for repentance of sin and turning back to God. For the selfish and proudly religious, Jesus' message of humble repentance was not enticing. In Jesus' first coming, the seeds of the kingdom were scattered, but the soil in the hearts of many was not good, and they did not respond in faith.[g] Likewise, when Jesus told His disciples that he would be killed, they refused to believe it[h], preferring a messiah who would conquer their enemies so they could sit on thrones beside him.[i]

Jesus' Kingdom message is a reiteration of the same themes God has continually revealed to his people throughout the Old Testament. The Kingdom message is that Jesus is Immanuel, God with us.[k] Spiritual death, the ruptured relationship with God, can be healed through His atoning death alone.[m] The internal destruction sin has brought to our hearts can be renewed through the power of His Spirit.[n] The real enemy conquered by His victory is not political but sin and the god of this world, Satan himself, along with the spiritual forces

---

[a] Isa. 52:8-10 [b] Isa. 52:14-53:12 [c] Psalm 2:8-9 [d] Psalm 22 [e] Psalm 110 [f] Psalm 95:3; 96:4-5; 97:7-9; 135:5; 136:2; 138:1 [g] Matt. 13 [h] Matt. 16:21-23, 17:22-23 [i] Matt. 20:17-28 [k] Matt. 1:23; 28:20; John 1:14-18 [m] 2 Cor. 5:14-15; Eph. 2:1, 4-6; Col. 2:13 [n] John 1:13; 3:5-8; 2 Cor. 5:17; Titus 3:5

of darkness.[a] Jesus formed a new movement, the Church, a redeemed people from every nationality and ethnicity, who will come into the unity of the Spirit to participate in God's rescue mission to the whole world.[b]

Jesus' resurrection prefigures our resurrection.[c] In Jesus' death and resurrection, not only is the price of our sin paid, and our life after death secured, but the eternal life of God has truly come to this cursed earth with the coming of the King, God's Kingdom has come into this world.[d] Because of King Jesus, there will be physical life again after a period of physical death.[e]

Indeed, creation comes from God, belongs to God, and will be restored by God in his Kingdom. The Bible is a story told in beginning-middle-beginning format. The opening book of the Bible, Genesis, begins with two chapters of creation, followed by a chapter of judgment for sin. Likewise, the closing book of the Bible, Revelation, ends with two chapters of new creation preceded by final judgment for sin as God returns to His original design plan for His Kingdom.

HOW IS OUR KING JESUS CHRIST A LION AND LAMB?

A kingdom is the extent of the rule of a king. The Kingdom of God is ruled by King Jesus over all.

The Old Testament prophesied that Jesus would rule in glory with a king's scepter and come in humility riding on a donkey.[f] Jesus' mocking enemies revealed His Kingship when they pressed a crown of thorns into His head and hung over it the sign, "Jesus of Nazareth, the King of the Jews."[g]

Following His resurrection and ascension to Heaven, Jesus is revealed throughout Revelation no less than 45 times to be seated upon a throne, ruling and reigning as sovereign Lord over all. Truth and judgment come from this throne while worship, praise, glory, and adoration will go to His throne. By placing the throne of Jesus Christ at the center of creation and history, John is radically displacing humanity; the goal of redemption and Kingdom is to orient all worship toward God alone.

Most Christians view Jesus Christ as either Lion or Lamb and not both. Those of us with more lamb personalities will focus on the parts of the Bible where Jesus was meek, kind, patient, loving, and appears more passive if not even timid. Those of us with more lion personalities will focus on the parts of the Bible where Jesus was strong, firm, urgent, controversial, and appears more active, if not aggressive.

Are you more of a lion or a lamb? Do you see Jesus more as a Lion or a Lamb?

The Bible presents Jesus as both a Lion and a Lamb. Looking into eternity and

---

[a] John 12:31-32, 16:11; Col. 2:15; Heb. 2:14 [b] Matt. 28:16-20; Acts 1:5-8
[c] 1 Cor. 15:12-57 [d] John 3:16, 5:24, 6:40; 2 Cor. 4:10-11 [e] 1 Cor. 15:44-46; 2 Cor. 5:1-8 [f] Gen. 49:10; Zech. 9:9 cf. John 12:14-15 [g] Matt. 27:37; Mark 15:26; Luke 23:38; John 19:19

the realities of Heaven and Hell, Revelation 5:5-6 says, "Weep no more; behold, the Lion of the tribe of Judah, the Root of David, has conquered, so that he can open the scroll and its seven seals. And between the throne and the four living creatures and among the elders I saw a Lamb standing, as though it had been slain, with seven horns and with seven eyes, which are the seven spirits of God sent out into all the earth."

A lion is the king of the jungle. A lion eats whatever it wants—buffalo, hogs, and even elephants or alligators. A male lion lives in a pride or pack with mainly females and children and will go to war against anything that threatens his pack. Sometimes Jesus is a Lion. Examples include His repeated wars with Satan, fights with demonic religious leaders, and making a whip to attack money changers at the Temple for exchanging the worship of God for the demon god of money, Mammon. As a lion, Jesus Christ is tough.

Lambs are meek creatures who stick together with their flock because they are very social animals. Lambs are vulnerable and so comforting and safe that we invite children to count them at night until they fall asleep. Lambs eat grass and are not a threat to any animal or human. We witness Jesus as lamb in His tender love for women, children, the outcast, and suffering. Examples include the healing of Jairus' daughter, forgiving the sinful Samaritan woman at the well, weeping at the death of His friend Lazarus, and tenderly caring for His mother Mary from the cross. As a lamb, Jesus is tender.

Those who see Jesus more as Lion struggle with God forgiving and saving some people they struggle to forgive. Those who see Jesus more as Lamb struggle with God not loving, saving, and forgiving everyone forever.

Jesus is both tough as a Lion and tender as a Lamb. In Heaven, King Jesus will rule as a tender Lamb. In Hell, King Jesus will rule as a tough Lion.

One soldier is a good example of tough and tender. He serves in an elite military unit that goes on secret missions to kill drug cartel leaders, demonic military dictators, and terrorists. In combat, he is a fiercely ruthless lion. Upon arriving home from a mission, his young daughter plans special tea parties to welcome him. On one occasion, his daughter demanded he sit down for the tea party immediately after arriving home from a mission while still wearing his combat gear. Imagine a giant man covered in the sweat and dirt of battle sitting on a little chair in a pink room with a little girl in a dress eating cookies and drinking tea. That man is both as tough as a lion and as tender as a lamb. He fights to protect those he loves. This soldier loves Jesus who is perfectly lion and lamb forever as He rules both Hell to protect His people and Heaven to bless His people.

WHAT JUDGMENT AWAITS CHRISTIANS AT THE END OF THIS LIFE?

Christians will not be judged at the end of this life in the same way that non-Christians will be. The Bible teaches this truth clearly and repeatedly. Jesus said,

"Truly, truly, I say to you, whoever hears my word and believes him who sent me has eternal life. He does not come into judgment, but has passed from death to life."[a] Paul says, "There is therefore now no condemnation for those who are in Christ Jesus."[b] Simply stated, in Christ, all sin is forgiven having been judged at Jesus' cross.[c] Subsequently, Christians are members of the family of God now and forever.

Nonetheless, Christians will be judged at the end of this life in a way that is different from the judgment of non-Christians. This life, and what we do and do not do with it, matters greatly. The Holy Spirit has given every Christian time, talent, and treasure that they are to steward well for the Kingdom. The Christian's judgment is a day of assessment when "we must all appear before the judgment seat of Christ, so that each one may receive what is due for what he has done in the body, whether good or evil."[d]

This theme of accountability and reward runs all through Scripture as a continual reminder not to waste our life but rather steward it in light of eternity.[e]

To illustrate this concept, Jesus tells a Kingdom story in which He gives believers 10 minas, a large amount of money, and commands them to do business with it.[f] The servant who brings 10 more minas receives authority over 10 cities in the kingdom, while the servant who brings five minas receives authority over five. The last servant, who hides his mina from fear of the master, typifies someone who does not have a grace relationship with Jesus. Though his description of the Master shows that he does not know God at all, God in His lavish grace still endows him with a mina, a large amount of money. The point of Jesus' story is that if we are truly Christians and know the love of our Master, we should faithfully invest our lives in the service of His Kingdom. The quality of work we do will be revealed and tested in the end, and only work that survives Jesus' evaluation will be worthy of a reward. Positively, our day of testing can be a day of great rejoicing when we hear Jesus declare, "Well done," if we are faithful stewards in this life.

Negatively, some Christians will be grieved by the lack of reward given to them. Paul says, "If anyone's work is burned up, he will suffer loss, though he himself will be saved, but only as through fire."[g] The Bible is clear that there are eternal consequences for believers doing both good and evil.[h]

Those who love Jesus will strive to be like Him. Because we are God's workmanship, created for good works, we should do them.[i] The Bible repeatedly exhorts us to "make every effort" to be faithful to God's calling.[k]

We are children of God with the full right of inheritance. Participation in the Kingdom is already ours, not because of what we have done for God, but because

---

[a] John 5:24 [b] Rom. 8:1 [c] Col. 2:13; 1 John 2:12 [d] 2 Cor. 5:10 [e] Matt. 24:45-47, 25:14-30; Luke 12:42-48, 16:1-13, 17:7-10, 19:12-27; Rom. 2:16, 14:10; 1 Cor. 3:8-15, 4:5, 9:17-27; Col. 3:23-25; 1 Tim. 2:3-6; 2 Tim. 4:8; 1 Pet. 1:7; 5:4; Rev. 4:4, 10, 22:12 [f] Luke 19:12-27 [g] 1 Cor. 3:15 [h] 2 Cor. 5:10 [i] Eph. 2:10 [k] Luke 13:24; Rom. 14:19; Eph. 4:3; Heb. 4:11, 12:14; 2 Pet. 1:5-10, 3:14

of what God has done for us. We should respond by being trustworthy. Bit by bit, we learn and grow in faithfulness with the small kingdom works he has entrusted to us. We know that God is a Father whose love for and devotion to His children is purely by grace and will never change. Still, as a good Father, He also gives chores and responsibilities to each of His children to help them mature and grow so that He can entrust to them increasingly important things; in the Kingdom, He rewards the children who are faithful in this life in ways that He does not reward the children who are unfaithful in this life.[a]

WHAT JUDGMENT AWAITS NON-CHRISTIANS AT THE END OF THIS LIFE?

When a great injustice has occurred, there is cheering when justice is served. This explains why joy rises when a dangerous criminal is captured, or a demonic dictator is toppled. Because God made us in His image with a conscience, we long for righteousness where wrongs are made right.

Romans 2 is one chapter of the Bible that deals in depth with the blessings and benefits for God's judgment. Human judgment and justice are usually imperfect because they're generally only known in part and have biases. Making matters worse, to some degree we are all guilty of the very things we judge others for doing, "Therefore you have no excuse, O man, every one of you who judges. For in passing judgment on another you condemn yourself, because you, the judge, practice the very same things."[b] We tend to see the sin of others much more clearly than our own. Thankfully, there is a day coming when God will perfectly judge everyone, "on the day of wrath when God's righteous judgment will be revealed."[c]

The reason God has not yet had the final judgment is not because He is indifferent, but rather He is patient, giving sinners ample opportunity to trust in the Savior, "Or do you presume on the riches of his kindness and forbearance and patience, not knowing that God's kindness is meant to lead you to repentance? But because of your hard and impenitent heart you are storing up wrath for yourself on the day of wrath when God's righteous judgment will be revealed."[d]

Just as Jesus said that believers store up treasures for themselves in Heaven by their works in the Spirit, so Paul says that unbelievers similarly store up wrath for themselves in Hell by their works of the flesh. Paul even uses the same Greek word as Jesus to contrast the judgment of believers and unbelievers.[e] Paul concludes by saying of God, "He will render to each one according to his works: to those who by patience in well-doing seek for glory and honor and immortality, he will give eternal life; but for those who are self-seeking and do not obey the truth, but obey unrighteousness, there will be wrath and fury...For God shows no partiality."[f]

---

[a] Luke 16:10-12, 19:17-19 [b] Rom. 2:1 [c] Rom. 2:5 [d] Rom. 2:4-5 [e] Matt. 6:19; Rom. 2:5 [f] Rom. 2:6-8,11

Jesus said, "Whoever believes in the Son has eternal life; whoever does not obey the Son shall not see life, but the wrath of God remains on him."[a] The new creation can be new only if everyone in it loves God and obeys Him. There can be no sin or sinners. They must be separated out. In the Kingdom, the twin sins of idolatry and injustice will be transformed into obedience of Jesus' twin commands to love God and neighbor.[b]

A day is coming when God will judge the living and the dead[c] through the Son.[d] When the Son of Man's throne arrives on the earth, all will stand before Him for judgment.[e] From the beginning of creation[f] to the end[g], the Bible makes it clear that the basis of God's judgment is our deeds.[h]

There are degrees of punishment in Hell like there are degrees of reward in Heaven. Jesus told the people of Capernaum that it would be worse for them in the judgment than for Sodom.[i] The one who sins knowingly and willfully will receive a more severe beating than the one who did not know.[k] Both in life and in Hell, some sins receive more severe punishment, because that is just.[m] This fits the scriptural teaching that some sins are qualitatively worse than others in that the depth of their evil and the damage that ensues is greater. Jesus illustrated this when he told Pilate, "He who delivered me over to you has the greater sin."[n]

WHAT DOES SCRIPTURE TEACH ABOUT HEAVEN?

Most people don't know much about Heaven, and what they think is often just plain wrong. Based upon some bad religious art on the Sistine Chapel, the average person thinks of Heaven as the boring place where we're all chubby babies sitting on clouds wearing diapers plunking harps for all eternity pretending that we like it.

Satan got kicked out of Heaven and he's been bitter ever since. He came to Heaven on earth, Eden, to get humanity kicked out of Heaven as well. Ever since, Satan has undertaken an incredibly effective fake news campaign to misrepresent Heaven and Hell and encourage folks to seek to create their own little Heaven on earth without God. We all seek to be happy and healthy, and that should lead us to God and Heaven rather than Satan and rebellion.

According to the Bible, there is one reality ruled by God over two realms. One realm is the spirit world where God, divine beings (including angels), and departed saints live right now. The other realm is the physical world where human

---

[a] John 3:36 [b] Deut. 6:5, 10:12, 30:6; Lev. 19:18; Matt. 22:37-40; Mark 12:30-31; Luke 10:27; Rom. 13:9-10, 15:2; Gal. 5:14, 6:10; James 2:8 [c] Acts 10:42; 2 Tim. 4:1; 1 Pet. 4:5 [d] Ps. 2:12; Mark 14:62; John 5:22; Acts 17:31 [e] Matt. 25:31-46; Rev. 20:11-15 [f] Gen. 2:15-17 [g] Rev. 20:12-13 [h] Jer. 17:10; 32:19; Matt. 16:27; Rom. 2:6; Gal. 6:7-8; Rev. 2:23; 22:12 [i] Matt. 11:21-24 [k] Luke 12:47-48 [m] Num. 15:22-30; Lev. 4:1-35, 5:15-19; Matt. 18:6; 1 Tim. 5:8; James 3:1; 1 John 5:16-18 [n] John 19:11

beings live right now.

Originally, these two realms were connected. The Garden of Eden in Genesis was literally Heaven on earth where the unseen realm and seen realm connected. This explains why Adam and Eve met with God there, were not shocked when a divine being showed up (Satan), and saw an angel keep them from the Tree of Life once they sinned. Once we sinned, the realms were disconnected. So, upon death, the two parts of our being are also disconnected. Our body goes into the ground awaiting resurrection. Our soul goes to be with God.

The apostle Paul says this is "far better" than our current life on earth and all we have is "gain" to look forward to being "at home with the Lord".[a] So, if someone loves Jesus and dies today, they are with Jesus in the spiritual Heaven. That, however, is not their final destination. When Jesus returns to earth, He brings Heaven to earth with Him to restore things to how they were before sin entered the world. Those who love Jesus will be joined to their resurrection bodies to live forever on the New Earth. Far too many people think of Heaven only in terms of the intermediate spiritual state, and not the earthy physical reality that God has planned for all eternity.

Right now, Heaven exists in the unseen realm and is just as real as the world we occupy in the seen realm. Much like a Zoom call, Isaiah, Ezekiel, and John all got to communicate with Heaven and see what was happening there. For example, Revelation 6:9-11 says, "I saw...the souls of those who had been slain for the word of God and for the witness they had borne. They cried out with a loud voice, 'O Sovereign Lord, holy and true, how long before you will judge and avenge our blood on those who dwell on the earth?' Then they were each given a white robe and told to rest a little longer..."

The departed Christians right now are consciously aware of what is happening both in Heaven and on earth. Additionally, they communicate with God and one another. This is an amazing insight.

Even more amazing is that people whose soul is with God, and whose body is in the ground on earth, are given clothes to wear – namely white robes. This seems to indicate that they have physical bodies of some kind.

We tend to think of Heaven, our abode between death and return to the New Earth, as a solely spiritual place without any physical bodies. But we know that there is at least one person in the unseen realm of the spiritual Heaven right now in a body – Jesus Christ.[b] Also, we know that Enoch and Elijah in the Bible never died and were taken into Heaven still alive, which would put the total of people in bodies in Heaven right now at three or more. Additionally, when Moses and Elijah came down to visit with Jesus and Peter on the Mount of Transfiguration, they seemed to show up in bodies. This leaves open at least the possibility that a believer in Jesus Christ who dies could occupy a temporary body of some kind until they raise from death in their eternal body.

[a] 2 Cor. 5:8; Phil. 1:21-23 [b] Acts 1:11

KINGDOM: GOD REIGNS

When we think of Heaven, we need to stop thinking about leaving this planet and instead think about what it will be like when Jesus' prayer is answered, and the Kingdom of Heaven comes to earth, and God's will is done from one end of the cosmos to the other. God does not abandon His design plan from creation. God will not be defeated, dissuaded, or distracted. God remains focused on going back to where He started and sticking with His plan to have human life flourishing on earth and ruled by Heaven which comes to earth.

Even though we change, and Heaven and earth change, God does not change, and God does not change His plan for His people and His planet. This explains why the Bible uses lots of words like restore, redeem, resurrect, renew, etc. Acts 3:21 looks forward to "the time for restoring all the things about which God spoke by the mouth of his holy prophets". God will go back to where He started to lift the curse, sentence Satan, raise the dead, and make the realm of Eden in the unseen world visible in the seen realm of earth. He will overtake and liberate all that has been cursed by our sin to be cured by His Son.

The analogy that Paul uses for life as we experience it right now is childbirth. We've never met a woman who likes the process of childbirth. We've met many women who love the child they birthed. For this Christian, this life of screaming, weeping, stressing, and pushing is our version of birth where God will bring new, beautiful, and worthwhile life on the other side. Like childbirth, this painful process is worth the new life birthed on the other side of all the pain. For the Christian, this frames our love for Heaven and infuses our present pain with incredible meaning as one day we will have the same joy as a new mom holding her baby.

Right now, there is a place called Heaven that exists in the unseen realm. Living there are God, divine beings including angels, and departed saints who loved Jesus in their life on earth. When you die, you go there to be with them if you love Jesus. Theologians call this the "intermediate heaven".

One day, maybe in hours or centuries, Jesus Christ will return to this sin-cursed, tear-soaked world with Heaven as the King and everyone and everything in His Kingdom make the big move to New Earth. Just as Jesus brought Heaven and earth together at His first coming, He will bring the New Heaven and New Earth together at His Second Coming.[a]

For the Christian, dying is really just moving. Like any move, it's important to do some research so you can prepare yourself for your new home, get directions (which is basically following Jesus, who is the way home) and pushing through the hassles of this life to move to your Forever Home in Heaven.

There are six ways that the Bible describes Heaven, which the Bible often calls the New Earth: Sabbath, Kingdom, City, Home, Garden, and Party. For starters, you will need to use your imagination. When we are kids, it seems we can think in creative and faith-filled categories a lot easier than adults do, "The disciples came to Jesus, saying, 'Who is the greatest in the kingdom of heaven?' And calling to

---

[a] Is. 65:17; 2 Pet. 3:13; Rev. 21:1-3

him a child, he put him in the midst of them and said, 'Truly, I say to you, unless you turn and become like children, you will never enter the kingdom of heaven.'"[a]

Jesus is clear – to get ready for Heaven, you need a childlike faith. Childish faith is immature, irresponsible, and weak. Childlike faith is simple and strong, trusting the Father who is good for His promises.

Heaven is a Sabbath

Everyone wants Heaven, seeing it as a place of self-indulgent happiness. Only those who know and love Jesus want to be with God doing the things He loves, which is what Heaven, the New Earth, is. The context of Hebrews 4 is that some folks had faith in God, and they would enjoy the eternal rest of Heaven. Others, sadly, wanted Heaven but not God and are spoken of in terms of "fall" and "disobedience". The same is sadly true today. The truth is Heaven is not just a place, it's also a person named Jesus. Apart from Jesus, there is no place like Heaven. Apart from Jesus, no one makes it to the real Heaven.

Hebrews 4 reflects back on the Exodus. There, Joshua and Caleb, acting like the president and vice president, are leading the people from Egypt to the Promised Land.[b] Having been in Egypt for over 400 years, they became slaves and had not had a day off for maybe generations. God supernaturally delivered them with plagues, death, a parted sea, and manna food delivered daily. A nation of perhaps a few million, they wandered in the wilderness for some 40 years, grumbling and sick of living a homeless life of walking and camping. Honestly, we'd fare no better.

The author of Hebrews uses the Exodus as an analogy for our life. God supernaturally delivered us through the resurrection of Jesus, defeated our Pharaoh of Satan and slavery to sin, and promises us an eternal home and rest. Yet here we are stuck wandering around this forsaken planet wondering when we finally get to go Home. The key, Hebrews says, is that we have "faith" in the "good news" about Jesus Christ and keep following God through our desert.

Those who do not understand the real Heaven try to make their version of Heaven on earth in vain. The Israelites who were given the fourth Commandment in Exodus 20 about the Sabbath are spoken of in Hebrews 4. These are the same people who got drunk, had crazy naughty parties, and worshipped a golden calf, which was likely some crazy cult concept that they borrowed from their slavery in Egypt.

In Heaven, the New Earth, our eternal home, we will get to do the same things we enjoy on our Sabbath in this life. There will be sports, music, learning, reading books, art, crafts, swimming, hikes, pets, cooking, parties, baking, solitude, hikes, fishing, gardening, playing games, travel, adventure, surfing, and, yes, napping, just like Jesus who took a nap on the earth to set an example for us on how to

---

[a] Matt. 18:1-3 [b] Num. 14:24,30

KINGDOM: GOD REIGNS

Sabbath. Heaven and Earth were together before sin and are rejoined after sin. The same kind of stuff that Adam and Eve got to enjoy before sin entered the world is the same kind of stuff that we will get to enjoy once sin has been ripped from the world.

Heaven is a Kingdom

This world does not need another political party.

This world does not need another political candidate.

This world does not need another election.

This world does not need another theory of government for yet another national experiment.

What this world does need is one benevolent ruler filled with grace – funded with unlimited resources and fueled by the desire to glorify God by doing good for people.

Jesus Christ will return to the earth as King of Kings and establish a Kingdom that never ends. Following Him into this world will be the entire Kingdom of the unseen realm with departed saints and divine beings (including angels) in His wake.[a]

In the Kingdom of Heaven, no one will be hungry, no one will be homeless, and no one will be helpless.

In the Kingdom of Heaven, there will be no war, no worry, and no weariness.

In the Kingdom of Heaven, there will be no sin, suffering, or shame.

In the Kingdom of Heaven, there will be no tears, trials, or troubles.

In the Kingdom of Heaven, there will be no pollution, politics, or problems.

Everyone who has been frustrated with this world, angry at their government, voted in an election, said something stupid on social media, marched in a protest, signed a petition, or shed a tear really truly wants the Second Coming of Jesus Christ whether they know it or not. This world is the problem. This means the solution has to come from another world into this world. His name is King Jesus.

Heaven is a City

What are the most amazing cities you have traveled to? What cities are on your bucket list to visit some day?

Heaven is the fullness of human ability unleashed once the curse is lifted to live in. The New Jerusalem City of God that comes down from Heaven is a prototype for the kind of cities God welcomes us to build and explore on our planet and beyond it into the galaxies that need to be explored and will be open for human dominion and settling into great global and galactic cities.[b] Yes, the Star Trek and Star Wars fans are onto something...

---

[a] 2 Sam. 7:12-13; Heb. 11:16 [b] Heb. 11:10

DOCTRINE

The storyline of the Bible opens with the Garden of Eden (meaning paradise) that is a realm where God and divine beings live and ends with a city coming down from Heaven with the Garden of Eden in that city. Imagine what a perfect city will be like made by God for human flourishing without sin or the curse and you are starting to lean into eternity. In the ancient cities, they were protected by a wall and people had to pass through a gate to enter. You were only allowed to enter if your name was on the list of official residents. The same is true of God's eternal City of Heaven. If you belong to Jesus Christ, then your name is already written in the Lamb's book of life. If you have not turned from your sin and trusted in Jesus Christ, then you need to do that right now and become a Christian to have your name added to the eternal guest list in the City of God.[a]

Heaven is a Home

How many homes have you lived in? What is your favorite home you have ever lived in? If there was one home, or hotel, that you've ever seen and could live in, what would it be?

For most people, the biggest investment of our lifetime is our home. The place where we make the most memories, organize the most activities, and celebrate the most holidays.

A home is two things – people and a place. On one particularly low day after moving our family to another state, one of our children said they missed "home". They were looking back to where they used to live and wanted to go back. I asked them if going back to their old house minus their family would still feel like "home". They said no, because home is both a people and a place. Even if they were in the same place, minus the people they call family, it would not be home. Our child was experiencing the same thing that every Christian does in this life. We have left our home in God's presence in Eden, but we've not yet moved into our forever Heavenly Home with God's people in God's presence. Life on this planet is lived in a body and a home for our body that are both rentals we won't be in forever.[b]

We were made to be at home together with God our Father as a family. Everyone who has bought a home, moved, stayed in a hotel, gone camping, done a home improvement project, watched a home improvement show on tv, or gone through an open house for a home up for sale is actually looking forward to Heaven which is our home and the Father's House.

Heaven is a Garden

Being outdoors in a beautiful environment simply makes you feel closer to God. This is why we go on vacations, hike mountains, swim lakes, raft rivers, play golf, and plant gardens.

---

[a] Rev. 21:23-27 [b] John 14:1-3; 2 Cor. 5:1

KINGDOM: GOD REIGNS

Before God made people, He made a garden for us to live in. Eden means paradise, and we feel at home in beautiful outdoor spaces because that was our original home. The garden of Eden is a realm in which God and other divine beings (including angels) met with our first parents as the connection point between the Kingdom of Heaven in the unseen realm and the Kingdom of Earth in the seen realm. That garden and realm continue to exist, although we have lost access to it. When Jesus died on the cross, one of the thieves dying at His side repented of his sin and received Jesus as his Savior. He was then told by Jesus that upon death he would be taken to "paradise" which means garden and was likely the same place that Adam and Eve were kicked out of.

When Jesus returns, Revelation reveals that He will bring the paradise garden of Eden with Him. God's original plan for this planet has not been ruined by Satan and sin but will be restored by our King and His Kingdom. Eternity will begin as history did – with God ruling from a garden on the earth seated on a throne with the tree of life open for people to be healed from the curse and live together forever on the earth in physical bodies.[a]

The next time you see a sunrise or sunset, jump into a lake, hike up a mountain, plant a garden, put flowers in your home, enjoy the leaves of fall, feel a breeze, step into a river, or feel the cool grass or warm sand under your feet, remind yourself that the best is yet to come.

Heaven is a Party

In John 2, Jesus begins His public ministry changing water into wine at a wedding party.

Why?

The miracles of God point to the Kingdom of God. The reason Jesus did His first miracle at a wedding party is because the Kingdom of God is the last and best wedding party.[b] Revelation 19 previews the final wedding in history, ushering in eternity as Jesus returns to rule the earth as a kingly groom, with the church being loved and cared for like a bride. The entire scene that ushers in forever is the most epic party that kicks off the party that never ends.

You were made for that party. Everyone who celebrates a birthday, loves the holidays, buys a cake, blows a kazoo, grills at a tailgate party, cheers at a concert, hosts a dinner party, smiles at a wedding, wears the jersey of their favorite team, or shows up for the inauguration of their candidate is someone who, deep down, wants Jesus to come back and throw a party...whether they know it or not.

Earth is the shadow of Heaven. The parties we throw are shadows of the Party that is Heaven. Sadly, the Devil has done a good job lying about Heaven and convincing folks that Hell is where the party is, and that Heaven is where the party

---

[a] Gen. 2:8; cf. Rev. 22:1-2 [b] Matt. 22:1-2

poopers are. Nothing could be further from the truth.

The problem is that it's easy to equate religious people and Heaven. This equation, however, is flawed. When on the earth, Jesus kept going to parties and having people throw parties when He showed up, including kids. Jesus has the perfect sense of humor and tells us that this life has some tears, but that Heaven is a party of laughing and rejoicing: "Blessed are you who weep now, for you shall laugh...Rejoice in that day, and leap for joy, for behold, your reward is great in heaven..."[a]

When the Bible uses the word "joy" some 200 times, and throws in the word "laugh" some 40 times, it reminds us that laughing is practice for Heaven. Martin Luther once said, "If you're not allowed to laugh in heaven, I don't want to go there."[1]

A cheerless, critical, boring Christian is a bad advertisement for Heaven, which is the party that never ends!

WHAT DOES SCRIPTURE TEACH ABOUT HELL?

Jesus talks about Hell more than anyone else in all of Scripture. Jesus' words come in the context of the rest of Scripture, which says that God "desires all people to be saved and to come to the knowledge of the truth."[b] Furthermore, He "is patient toward you, not wishing that any should perish, but that all should reach repentance."[c]

Despite God's love for and patience with sinners, it is a horrid mistake to dismiss the Bible's clear teachings on Hell. Richard Niebuhr characterized the ongoing attempt of liberal Christians to deny Hell as "a God without wrath brought men without sin into a kingdom without judgment through the ministrations of a Christ without a cross."[2] Jesus said more about Hell than about any other topic. Amazingly, 13 percent of his sayings are about Hell and judgment; more than half of His parables relate to the eternal judgment of sinners.[3]

The Bible does not give us a detailed exposition of hell, but there are many descriptions of the fate of its inhabitants in that place of eternal punishment. They include (1) fire;[d] (2) darkness;[e] (3) punishment;[f] (4) exclusion from God's presence;[g] (5) restlessness;[h] (6) second death;[i] and (7) weeping and gnashing of teeth.[k]

Admittedly, there is a long discussion among Christians regarding how literally to take these descriptions. Evangelicals usually follow John Calvin in seeing them as metaphorical figures trying to describe the indescribable.[4] These evangelical

---

[a] Luke 6:21,23 [b] 1 Tim. 2:4 [c] 2 Pet. 3:9 [d] Matt. 13:42, 50; 18:8, 9; Rev. 19:20, 20:14-15 [e] Matt. 25:30; Jude 13 [f] Rev. 14:10-11 [g] Matt. 7:23; 25:41; Luke 16:19ff.; 2 Thess. 1:9 [h] Rev. 14:11 [i] Rev. 2:11; 20:6, 14; 21:8 [k] Matt. 13:42, 50, 22:12-13, 24:51, 25:30; Luke 13:28

Christians don't decrease the severity but only the specificity of the descriptions.

The Bible's portrait of Hell is nothing like the mocking cartoon caricatures drawn by Matt Groening or Gary Larson. Likewise, Hell is not a fun place where sinners get to live out their sinful pleasures, as if Satan rules over Hell and sin can be pursued without inhibition. This erroneous view of Satan ruling in Hell comes not from Scripture but from Puritan John Milton's Paradise Lost, which has the devil arrogantly declaring, "Better to reign in hell, then serve in Heav'n."[5] But Satan will not reign there. Hell is a place of punishment that God prepared for the devil and his angels.[a] It is where the beast and the false prophet and those who worship them will drink the wine of God's wrath, poured full strength into the cup of His anger, and he will be tormented with fire and sulfur in the presence of the holy angels and in the presence of the Lamb. And the smoke of their torment goes up forever and ever, and they have no rest, day or night.[b]

At the end of the age, the devil will be "thrown into the lake of fire and sulfur where the beast and the false prophet were, and they will be tormented day and night forever and ever."[c] Hell will be ruled by Jesus, and human and demon alike, including Satan, will be tormented there continually.

Hell is real and terrible. It is eternal. There is no possibility of amnesty or reprieve. Daniel says that some of the dead will be resurrected "to shame and everlasting contempt."[d] Jesus says, "Depart from me, you cursed, into the eternal fire prepared for the devil and his angels...And these will go away into eternal punishment."[e]

Paul tells us, "God considers it just to repay with affliction those who afflict you, and to grant relief to you who are afflicted as well as to us, when the Lord Jesus is revealed from heaven with his mighty angels in flaming fire, inflicting vengeance on those who do not know God and on those who do not obey the gospel of our Lord Jesus. They will suffer the punishment of eternal destruction, away from the presence of the Lord and from the glory of his might."[f]

Perhaps the clearest and most gripping depiction of Hell in all of Scripture is the frequent mention of Hell as "Gehenna." The name refers to an area outside of the city of Jerusalem where idolatry and horrendous sin, including child sacrifice, were practiced.[g] Gehenna was a place so despised and cursed by God's people that they turned it into the city dump where feces, refuse, and the dead bodies of criminals were stacked. Jesus spoke of Gehenna as the hellish final home of the wicked.[h] Since Gehenna is described as a fiery abyss[i], clearly it is also the lake of fire[k] to which all the Godless will ultimately be eternally sentenced[m], together with Satan, demons, and unrepentant sinners.[n] So, when the Bible speaks of Hell

---

[a] Matt. 25:41 [b] Rev. 14:10-11 [c] Rev. 20:10 [d] Dan. 12:2 [e] Matt. 25:41, 46 [f] 2 Thess. 1:6-9 [g] 2 Kings 16:3, 21:6; 2 Chron. 28:3, 33:6; Jer. 19:56, 32:35 [h] Matt. 5:22; 10:28; 18:9 [i] Mark 9:43 [k] Matt. 13:42, 50 [m] Matt. 23:15, 33 [n] Matt. 25:41; Rev. 19:20, 20:10, 14, 15

DOCTRINE

as a place where the fire is not quenched and the worm does not die, the original hearers would easily have remembered Gehenna, where this reality was ever present outside of their city.[a]

Our attitude toward Hell should be the same as that of the Father, who takes no pleasure in the death of the wicked but begs them to turn from their evil ways.[b] Jesus joins the Father's compassionate yearning as He weeps over Jerusalem.[c] Paul also has "great sorrow and unceasing anguish in my heart. For I could wish that I myself were accursed and cut off from Christ for the sake of my brothers, my kinsmen according to the flesh."[d] Furthermore, he "did not cease night or day to admonish everyone with tears."[e]

Feeling as he ought about Hell, Charles Spurgeon rightly began his sermon on the eternal conscious torment of the wicked in Hell this way: "Beloved, these are such weighty things that while I dwell upon them I feel far more inclined to sit down and weep than to stand up and speak to you."[6]

WHAT ARE SOME OF THE MAJOR OBJECTIONS TO THE DOCTRINE OF HELL?

The thought of Hell is rightly concerning to anyone who believes the painful eternity that the Bible promises for those who die apart from faith in Jesus Christ. Therefore, we will answer some of the major objections to Hell in an effort to bring clarity to those who have concerns.

Hell is Unloving

In a very important sense, God doesn't send anyone to Hell. The only ones there are those who have rejected His revelation, choosing to suppress the truth He made plain to them, refusing His kindness that leads them to repentance.[f]

God made people in His image, after His likeness, with the power to say no and to reject the universal revelation of Himself. Subsequently, sinners have no one to blame but themselves if they are damned.

To get to Hell, someone must reject the God who shows them his goodness[g] and out of love for all "gives to all mankind life and breath and everything";[h] reject the Spirit who "convicts the world concerning sin and righteousness and judgment";[i] and reject the crucified Son who said, "I, when I am lifted up from the earth, will draw all people to myself."[k] Obviously, God has been exceedingly gracious to sinners.

The Lausanne Covenant (1974)[7], an evangelical manifesto that is one of the most influential documents in Christendom, puts it this way:

---

[a] Isa. 66:24; Mark 9:47-48 [b] Ezek. 18:23, 33:11; 1 Tim. 2:4; 2 Pet. 3:9 [c] Jer. 31:20; Hos. 11:8; Matt. 23:37-38; Luke 19:41-44 [d] Rom. 9:2-3 [e] Acts 20:31; cf. Acts 20:19-20; Phil. 3:18 [f] Rom. 2:4 [g] Acts 14:17 [h] Acts 17:25 [i] John 16:8 [k] John 12:32

KINGDOM: GOD REIGNS

All men and women are perishing because of sin, but God loves everyone, not wishing that any should perish but that all should repent. Yet those who reject Christ repudiate the joy of salvation and condemn themselves to eternal separation from God. To proclaim Jesus as "the Saviour of the world" is not to affirm that all people are either automatically or ultimately saved, still less to affirm that all religions offer salvation in Christ. Rather it is to proclaim God's love for a world of sinners and to invite everyone to respond to him as Saviour and Lord in the wholehearted personal commitment of repentance and faith. Jesus Christ has been exalted above every other name; we long for the day when every knee shall bow to him and every tongue shall confess him Lord.[8]

People who reject Jesus in this life will not rejoice in Him after this life. Revelation tells us that all sinners flee from the vision of Jesus precisely because they do not desire Him.[a]

Unrepentant sinners hide from Him, even preferring death to seeing the face of Jesus.[b] Even when faced with the unmistakable reality of Jesus, they "did not repent of the works of their hands nor give up worshiping demons and idols of gold and silver and bronze and stone and wood, which cannot see or hear or walk, nor did they repent of their murders or their sorceries or their sexual immorality or their thefts."[c]

Hell is only for those who persistently reject the real God in favor of false gods. So, in the end, people get to be with the god they love. To paraphrase C. S. Lewis, either people will say to God, "Thy will be done," or God will say to them, "Thy will be done."[9] Not only is God loving, but he is also just. Heaven and Hell are the result of his love and justice.

Hell is Intolerant

Everyone draws lines. We do not let drunk people drive. We do not let smokers light up in hospitals. We do not let sex offenders teach children at school. We do not let 30-year-old men marry 15-year-old girls. We do not let people lacking eyesight join the military and shoot guns. Why? Because we know these things are wrong. So wrong that we deem them intolerable. The question is not will lines be drawn but rather who draws them and where?

The truth is, we are all intolerant of some people and their actions, which is why we have doors on our homes and locks on those doors. God has the same right, which is why He has a door on His Kingdom Home, and that door is Jesus Christ. Those who pass through the door are part of the family, and are welcome to enter in. Those who are not part of the family do not enter in for the same reason that strangers and enemies are not welcome at your home.

It might surprise you that, even as the Bible speaks of God in terms of holiness, love, justice, and mercy, it never suggests tolerance as one of His attributes.

---

[a] Rev. 20:11 [b] Rev. 6:15–17 [c] Rev. 9:20–21

DOCTRINE

A simple English word search of the entire Bible in the most popular English translations shows few if any appearances of the word tolerance. The handful of times it does appear in various translations, it is used pejoratively to describe an evil done by God's people as they "tolerate" things such as sexual sin[a] and false teaching.[b] The New Living Translation speaks of God not tolerating other religions[c], injustice[d], sinful behavior[e], or teaching based on the beliefs of other religions.[f] Reading the Bible does not support the conclusion that the God of the Bible is tolerant.

God is not tolerant of people who don't like the way of Jesus. He is completely committed to a new earth where no one will have to be on guard against idolatry and injustice. The new earth will include a redeemed community that reflects the character of God, who is "merciful and gracious, slow to anger, and abounding in steadfast love and faithfulness, keeping steadfast love for thousands, forgiving iniquity and transgression and sin, but who will by no means clear the guilty."[g] So, it will be a place where community will be characterized by "compassionate hearts, kindness, humility, meekness, and patience...[and] love, which binds everything together in perfect harmony."[h]

A loving God protects His children from sin and evil by separating them. In this way, God is a father who is tolerant of all who obey Him and are safe for His children. But He is intolerant of those who sin against Him and do evil to His children. Subsequently, God is intolerant in a way that is like our own cultural intolerances of those who drink and drive, steal, rape, and murder; we, too, demonstrate our intolerance by separating such people from society. To call such actions on God's part intolerant is shameful, because tolerance would denote both approval and support of evil.[10]

Hell is Unjust

Some argue that the punishment of sinners is annihilation because it would be unjust for our short lives to result in eternal punishment. Annihilationism means that after someone dies apart from faith, they suffer for a fitting period of time and then simply cease to exist so that Hell is not eternal in duration. In question is the nature and length of the punishment.

Despite having proponents who are otherwise fine Bible teachers (such as John Stott)[11], annihilationism is simply not what the Bible teaches. Daniel 12:2 says, "Many of those who sleep in the dust of the earth shall awake, some to everlasting life, and some to shame and everlasting contempt." Jesus teaches the same thing and speaks of those who "will go away into eternal punishment, but the righteous into eternal life."[i] Grammatically, there is no difference here between the length of time mentioned for life and that for punishment; rather, there is simply eternal life and eternal death.

---

[a] 1 Cor. 5:1 [b] Rev. 2:20 [c] Exod. 20:5; Deut. 5:9 [d] 2 Chron. 19:7; Mic. 6:11 [e] Ps. 5:4, 101:5 [f] Rev. 2:14 [g] Ex. 34:6-7 [h] Col. 3:12-14 [i] Matt. 25:46

KINGDOM: GOD REIGNS

The Bible tells us that "the smoke of their torment goes up forever and ever, and they have no rest, day or night, these worshipers of the beast and its image"[a] and "they will be tormented day and night forever and ever."[b] The word forever (Greek *aion*) means unending. This word is used to describe the blessedness of God[c], Jesus after His resurrection[d], the presence of God[e], and God Himself.[f] As uncomfortable as some may be with it, it also describes eternal, conscious punishment.

The key arguments for annihilationism are (1) the nature of fire (which consumes), (2) the use of the word destroy, which means "the extinction of being," (3) the concept of justice, whereby God punishes "according to what they had done,"[g] and (4) the passages that speak of God triumphing over evil, so that God is all in all and reconciles all things to Himself.[h] We'll address each point in turn.

First, fire does consume but only things that are inherently destructible. For example, if you put metal in a fire, it burns forever, but it does not cease to exist.[i] Humans, like angels, are created for unending existence; hence their contempt and punishment are forever and ever. Thus, the result of the unpardonable sin is eternal punishment.[k] Hebrews 6:1-2 establishes "eternal judgment" as an "elementary" or fundamental and essential "doctrine of Christ".

Second, the English words "destroy" and "destruction" do seem to indicate the end of existence. If so, passages such as Matthew 10:28 and Philippians 3:19 that describe the destiny of the wicked with these words would mean that these people would cease to exist. However, the Greek words (noun *olethros*; verb *apollumi*) never mean the end of existence. In the three parables in Luke 15, the coin, the sheep, and the son are "lost." Likewise, destroyed wineskins do not cease to exist but become useless.[m]

Jesus says, "For whoever would save his life will lose it, but whoever loses his life for my sake will save it."[n] The lost life continues. The people upon whom "sudden destruction will come" at the end of the age still appear before the judgment seat.[o] The temptations of riches that "plunge people into ruin and destruction" ruin them but do not end their existence.[p]

Paul explains the meaning of "the punishment of eternal destruction" as being "away from the presence of the Lord."[q] This rules out the idea that destruction means "extinction." Only those who exist can be excluded from God's presence.

The point of the destruction of the wicked is that they are wrecked, ruined, and useless. Thus, destruction is a sudden loss of all that gives worth and meaning to existence. Those who are destroyed are like the prodigal son: far from home and father. They continue to exist but are broken in spirit, miserable, and without hope in that state.

---

[a] Rev. 14:11 [b] Rev. 20:10 [c] Rom. 1:25 [d] Rev. 1:18 [e] 1 Pet. 1:25 [f] Rev. 4:9; 20:10 [g] Rev. 20:12 [h] E.g., 1 Cor. 15:28; Col. 1:20 [i] Zech. 13:9; Mal. 3:3; Rev. 3:18 [k] Mark 3:29 [m] Matt. 9:17 [n] Luke 9:24 [o] 1 Thess. 5:3 [p] 1 Tim. 6:9 [q] 2 Thess. 1:9

This is why the Bible speaks of Hell as conscious, eternal punishment.

Many object that eternal punishment for sin of a few decades is unjust. But we have already explained that the parable of the rich man shows that the sinning of those who reject God and His ways continues after death.

One summary of the Bible's teaching on the pain of Hell says:

Those in hell suffer intense and excruciating pain. This pain is likely both emotional/spiritual and physical (John 5:28–29). Hell is a fate worse than being drowned in the sea (Mark 9:42). It is worse than any earthly suffering—even being maimed (Matt. 5:29–30; Mark 9:43). The suffering never ends (Matt. 25:41; Mark 9:48). The wicked will be "burned with unquenchable fire" (Matt. 3:12). Those in hell will be thrown into the fiery furnace and will experience unimaginable sorrow, regret, remorse, and pain. The fire produces the pain described as "weeping and gnashing of teeth" (Matt. 8:12; 13:42, 50; 22:13; 24:51; 25:30). The intensity of the suffering seems to be according to the wickedness of the person's behavior (Rom. 2:5–8). Hell is utterly fearful and dreadful (Heb. 10:27–31). This punishment is depicted as "coming misery," "eating flesh with fire," and the "day of slaughter" (James 5:1–5). Those in hell will feel the full force of God's fury and wrath (Rev. 14:10). They will be "tormented" with fire (14:10–11). This suffering is best understood as endless since the "smoke of their torment rises forever and ever" (14:11). This suffering is constant because it is said that those in hell "will have no rest day or night" (14:11) and "will be tormented day and night forever and ever" (20:10).[12]

Third, we have already supported the points that humans are created to live forever, and their rebellion and rejection of God continues as long as they themselves do. Thus, continued exclusion from God's fellowship is fully appropriate and just.

Fourth, there are passages teaching that Christ will "reconcile to himself all things, whether on earth or in heaven, making peace by the blood of his cross."[a]

If this were the only passage in Scripture speaking to the issue, we would have to believe in some sort of universal saving reconciliation with God. But the eternal punishment passages require us to adopt the understanding that the peace spoken of is not a peace of salvation for all sinners but, rather, peace that comes by God triumphing over all sinners. The enemies will be conquered, and their destructive agenda destroyed. The new earth will be a place of only peace and godliness because the enemies have been crushed and removed forever.

In summary, annihilationism is not biblical. For this reason, it was condemned by the Second Council of Constantinople (AD 553) and the Fifth Lateran Council (1513).

Hell is Temporary

Today, though, it is becoming popular to hope that sinners will eventually

---

[a] Col. 1:20

repent and everyone will end up in Heaven. This is universal reconciliation, the ancient view of Origen. However, there is not a shred of evidence for post-mortem repentance. The continual teaching of the Bible is that we die once and are then judged, without any second chance at salvation. As one clear example, Hebrews 9:27 says, "It is appointed for man to die once, and after that comes judgment."

At the end of the discussion, we must admit the total irrationality of those who resist and refuse the grace of Jesus Christ. Any attempt to make sense of their rebellion will have to remain a mystery. But we never stop trying to persuade them to receive forgiveness and new life through the crucified and resurrected Lord Jesus because, among other reasons, the conscious eternal torments of Hell await the unrepentant.

DO PEOPLE WHO HAVE NEVER HEARD ABOUT JESUS GO TO HELL?

Jesus said, "No one comes to the Father except through me."[a] Peter preached, "There is salvation in no one else, for there is no other name under heaven given among men by which we must be saved."[b]

The conclusion is simple: there is only one way to the Father and that is through Jesus Christ. All other religious roads lead to false gods and a real Hell.

But there are many ways to Jesus. While the norm is responding to the preached Word of God[c], there are biblical examples as well as life experiences where God gives special revelation of the Messiah to unsaved people in other forms, including direct speech, dreams, and visions. God called Abraham directly.[d] He gave Pharaoh dreams.[e] He spoke to the treacherous prophet Balaam in a vision so that he prophesied about the Messiah.[f] He appeared to Cornelius in a vision, which resulted in his being saved.[g]

I (Gerry) once talked with a Chinese man who was a brilliant university student and a rising member of the Communist party. In the ruthlessness of the Communist system, he sensed there was a kindness somewhere, which he longed for. One night as he slept, a shining person appeared in a vision, saying in Chinese, "I am who you are looking for. My name is 'Gospel,'" with the last word in English. The young man had never heard the word Gospel before but soon found it in his dictionary. He is now a Christian pastor with a very effective ministry. There are many such stories. The reality is that anyone who is searching and willing to respond to the goodness of God as Cornelius did will receive special revelation. God is perfectly able to bypass the "normal" channels to accomplish His purposes.

No one who comes to the Lord will be cast out.[h] As Paul says, "The Scripture says, 'Everyone who believes in him will not be put to shame.' For there is no distinction between Jew and Greek; for the same Lord is Lord of all, bestowing his

---

[a] John 14:6 [b] Acts 4:12 [c] Rom. 10:13-15 [d] Gen. 12:1-3 [e] Gen. 40-41 [f] Num. 24:4, 16-19 [g] Acts 10:3-6 [h] John 6:37

riches on all who call on him. For 'everyone who calls on the name of the Lord will be saved.'"[a]

Therefore, while there is no salvation apart from faith in Jesus Christ, there is also no reason to overlook the creativity of God to get the Gospel out. His creativity includes using us to preach the Gospel to the ends of the earth as pioneering missionaries to unreached people groups and generous givers to ministries that translate the Bible into new languages.

DO UNBORN BABIES AND YOUNG CHILDREN GO TO HEAVEN?

The loss of a child is deeply personal and painful. The eternal fate of unborn children and infants is a mystery that has always haunted the Church. There are six options available as possible answers:
1. All babies are reprobate sinners and thus immediately banned from Heaven, awaiting the final eternal judgment for their sin nature inherited from Adam and sentenced to Hell.
2. All babies are elect by God and thus immediately translated into God's presence in Heaven upon death.
3. God chooses whom He saves and damns, therefore some babies are taken to Heaven and the rest are left to spend eternity in Hell.
4. All babies are innocent until they reach the age of accountability, therefore all children who die before the age of accountability go to Heaven.
5. All babies who are baptized into a covenant family are part of the New Covenant and therefore go to Heaven upon death.
6. God is both the Father and Son who make the decision about salvation, the Spirit can save from the womb, and the decision is ultimately the Lord's, whom we trust by faith.

There are three towering truths that help frame our understanding of infant life:
1. We are sinners from our mother's womb.[b]
2. God knows us and is intimately involved with us from our mother's womb.[c]
3. God can and does save people from their mother's womb.[d]

Isaiah[e] and Jeremiah[f] were both called by God for prophetic ministry from their mothers' wombs. John the Baptizer was promised to "be filled with the Holy Spirit, even from his mother's womb."[g]

Long before ultrasounds, our Creator God saw exactly what happens in the womb. Additionally, Jesus Christ, who became a baby, also loves children and said Heaven was for kids.[h]

---

[a] Rom. 10:11-13 [b] Ps. 51:5 (NLT) [c] Ps. 139:13-16 (NLT) [d] Psalm 22:9-10 (NKJV) [e] Isa. 49:1-7 [f] Jer. 1:4-5 [g] Luke 1:15 [h] Luke 18:15-17

For parents who have lost a child, the Gospel of Jesus Christ is a great comfort. God is a Father, and Jesus Christ is the Son of God. When the Son of God died on the cross, the Father experienced exactly what it feels like to lose a beloved child.

Regarding what happens to a child after they die, and whether or not they go to Heaven, the most common Scripture given to answer that question is from the Old Testament. There, David is the father of a beloved child who died.[a]

David was in mourning, pleading with God to spare the life of his child who was very ill. David was in the pit of despair, so grieved that others wondered if he was suicidal. Yet, David stopped grieving and quickly moved on with his life once the child died. Why?

David had hope for his deceased child on the other side of death, and so should we.

God is a Father and to become a Christian is to be adopted into His family as His child. This is how everyone is saved, young and old. Ultimately, God the Father determines which children He will spiritually adopt into His family. The Father decides. And that is good news. Since He is a loving Father, our hearts should be at peace trusting Him for the eternity of our child in the same way we are trusting Him for our own eternity.

Pastor Charles Spurgeon (1834–1892) said, "I cannot conceive it possible of him [Jesus] as the loving and tender one, that when he shall sit to judge all nations, he should put the little ones on the left hand, and should banish them for ever from his presence."[13]

AM I GOING TO HELL?

After explaining Heaven and Hell, the closing verses of the Bible say, "Come!" as an invitation for all who desire to receive God's saving grace as a gift. The Gospel says that Jesus is Immanuel, God with us. Jesus died and rose and is exalted in Heaven. If you repent of sin, change your mind about who or what is Lord of your life, and believe, trusting that you can stake your life and eternity on the truth of what God says, then you will receive full forgiveness of all sin, new life in and by the Holy Spirit, membership in the church of Jesus Christ, a meaningful part in His rescue mission in the world, and citizenship in His kingdom. You will be with Jesus and His people now and forever.

We want this for you, and we would be unloving if we finished this book without seeking to ensure that you are a Christian.

Have you confessed your sins to Jesus Christ, seeking forgiveness and salvation? If not, asking Jesus to forgive your sin as your Savior, and leading you through life as your Lord is what you should do in prayer right now!

---

[a] 2 Sam. 12:15–23

HOW CAN I LIVE FOR HEAVEN IN A WORLD GOING TO HELL?

When all is said and done, only two cultures will remain – the cultures of Heaven and Hell. Today, you live between the two and experience a bit of each every day. The decisions you make every day either pull Hell up into your life (e.g. bitterness, lies, pride, hard-heartedness), or invite Heaven down into your life (e.g. forgiveness, truth, humility, tender-heartedness). For this to happen, we must be intentional in all our decision-making by first ensuring you have, "Set your minds on things that are above, not on things that are on earth."[a] Once we have seen things from the perspective of God's culture in Heaven, we are then ready to respond in the Spirit and live Kingdom down rather than Hell up. Jesus taught us to pray and live exactly this way, "Your kingdom come, your will be done, on earth as it is in heaven."[b]

Until we get to the Kingdom of Heaven, we have to endure some hellish days here on earth. Heaven is coming, hell is ending, so trust Jesus who is coming and keep on going. For the unbeliever, this life is your Heaven and what awaits you is Hell. For the believer, this life is your hell and what awaits you is Heaven. As Winston Churchill is believed to have famously said, "If you're going through hell, keep going…"

QUESTIONS FOR PERSONAL JOURNALING AND/OR SMALL GROUP DISCUSSION

1. Has your view of Heaven and hell changed in your life? How?
2. What are you most looking forward to in the Kingdom of God?
3. What about life in our world is most frustrating for you and the thing you are anxious to see fixed in eternity?
4. How does the promise of eternal rewards help you persevere in seeking to do what is right in this life no matter the outcome?
5. What changes should come in your life to live more Kingdom down in alignment with the culture of Heaven?
6. Who do you need to talk to about Jesus in hopes of being together with them in the Kingdom of Heaven?
7. Do you see Jesus more as a Lion or Lamb? Why?
8. Which imagery of the Kingdom of Heaven do you find most exciting (Sabbath, Kingdom, City, Home, Garden, Party)?
9. Do you believe in the literal conscious eternal torments of Hell? Why or why not?
10. Which departed believers are you most looking forward to a reunion with in the Kingdom of Heaven?

---

[a] Col. 3:2 [b] Matt. 6:10

NOTES

CHAPTER 1: TRINITY
1. Robert H. Stein, "Fatherhood of God," Evangelical Dictionary of Biblical Theology, Baker Reference Library (Grand Rapids: Baker Book House, 1996), 247.
2. Gen. 19:24; Ps. 45:6-7; Isa. 48:16-17; Hos. 1:6-7; Zech. 3:2; and Mal. 3:1-2 are some of the other Old Testament passages where two beings are distinguished and both are called Lord or divine.
3. John 17 is one of the clearest examples of this. In Jesus' High Priestly Prayer, we are given an opportunity to listen in on the prayerful communication within the Trinity.
4. Cf. Matt. 1:20-23.
5. J. I. Packer, "Trinity," Concise Theology: A Guide to Historic Christian Beliefs (Carol Stream, IL: Tyndale, 1993), 40.
6. Rom. 8:3-4, 15-17; 1 Cor. 1:4-7; 2:4-5; 6:11, 19-20; 2 Cor. 1:21-22; Gal. 3:1-5; Eph. 1:17; 2:18,20-22; Phil. 3:3; Col. 3:16; 1 Thess. 1:4-5; 2 Thess. 2:13.]: See Gordon D. Fee, God's Empowering Presence: The Holy Spirit in the Letters of Paul (Peabody, MA: Hendrickson, 1994), 48n39.
7. See Sinclair B. Ferguson, A Heart for God (Colorado Springs: NavPress, 1985), 18-37.
8. Wayne Grudem, Systematic Theology: An Introduction to Biblical Doctrine (Grand Rapids, MI: Zondervan, 1994), 231.
9. United Pentecostal Church International, "Oneness of God," http://www.upci.org/about.asp.
10. See Stanley J. Grenz, David Guretzki, and Cherith Fee Nording, "Councils," Pocket Dictionary of Theological Terms (Downers Grove, IL: InterVarsity, 1999), 15.
11. E.A. Park, quoted in Augustus Hopkins Strong, Systematic Theology (Old Tappan, NJ: Revell, 1907), 304.
12. Timothy Keller, The Reason for God: Belief in an Age of Skepticism (New York: Penguin, 2008), 214.]

CHAPTER 2: REVELATION
1. Driscoll, M (2019). Christians Might Be Crazy: Answering the Top 7 Objections to Christianity. Dunham & Company, 140].
2. Ibid.
3. F. F. Bruce, The New Testament Documents: Are They Reliable? (Grand Rapids, MI: Eerdmans, 1981), 22.
4. Walter A. Elwell and Barry J. Beitzel, Baker Encyclopedia of the Bible (Grand Rapids, MI: Baker, 1988), 301.

5. J.I. Packer, God Has Spoken: Revelation and the Bible, 3rd ed. (Grand Rapids, MI: Baker, 2000), 109.
6. Glenn W. Barker, William L. Lane, and J. Ramsey Michaels, The New Testament Speaks (New York: Harper & Row, 1969), 29.
7. United Methodist Church, The Book of Discipline of the United Methodist Church (Nashville: Abingdon, 2004), 77.
8. John Foxe, Foxe's Book of Martyrs (Charleston, SC: Forgotten Books, 2007), 234.
9. United Bible Society, "Statistical Summary of Languages with the Scriptures," 2008, http://www.ubs-translations.org/about_us/#c165.
10. The Standard Bible Society, "Translation Philosophy," 2009, http://www.esv.org/translation/philosophy.
11. Crossway, "The ESV Bible Reaches Five-Year Milestone," September 26, 2006, http://www.crossway.org/page/news.2006.09.26.
12. Driscoll, M (2019). Christians Might Be Crazy: Answering the Top 7 Objections to Christianity. Dunham & Company, 142].
13. http://www.equip.org/article/the-bibliographical-test-updated/
14. Driscoll, M (2019). Christians Might Be Crazy: Answering the Top 7 Objections to Christianity. Dunham & Company,144.
15. Craig L. Bomber, (2004-03-01), Making Sense of the New Testament: Three Crucial Questions (Kindle Locations 237–238). Baker Publishing Group. Kindle Edition.
16. Ibid., Kindle Locations 242–244. In his note on this point, Blomberg says, "The standard scholarly introduction to New Testament textual criticism, from which these and many other data may be gleaned, is Kurt Aland and Barbara Aland, The Text of the New Testament, 2d ed. (Grand Rapids: Eerdmans, 1989). For a far briefer survey, requiring no technical knowledge of the field, see David A. Black, New Testament Textual Criticism: A Concise Guide (Grand Rapids: Baker, 1994)."
17. Driscoll, M (2019). Christians Might Be Crazy: Answering the Top 7 Objections to Christianity. Dunham & Company, 144].
18. http://www.phrases.org.uk/meanings/give-a-man-a-fsh.html.
19. When Critics Ask, by Norman Geisler and Thomas Howe, is very helpful in doing this (Grand Rapids, MI: Baker, 1992).
20. For further reading, see The Big Book of Bible Difficulties: Clear and Concise Answers from Genesis to Revelation, by Norman L. Geisler; When Critics Ask: A Popular Handbook on Bible Difficulties, by Norman L. Geisler and Thomas Howe; New International Encyclopedia of Bible Difficulties, by Gleason L. Archer Jr.; Alleged Discrepancies of the Bible, by John Haley.
21. Daniel B. Wallace, "First-Century Fragment of Mark's Gospel Found!" March 22, 2012, http://danielbwallace.com/2012/03/22/frst-century-fragment-of-marks-gospel-found/.
22. Dan Brown, The Da Vinci Code (New York: Anchor Books, 2003), 251.

NOTES

23. Ibid, 259.
24. Craig L. Blomberg, "Jesus of Nazareth: How Historians Can Know Him and Why It Matters" (Deerfield, IL: Christ on Campus Initiative, 2008), http://tgc-documents.s3.amazonaws.com/cci/Blomberg.pdf, 25–26.
25. N. T. Wright, The Resurrection of the Son of God (Minneapolis: Fortress Press, 2003), 76.
26. Edwin Yamauchi, "Easter: Myth, Hallucination, or History?" Christianity Today, March 15, 1974 and March 29, 1974, 4–7, 12–16.
27. Ibid.
28. Ibid.
29. Lee Strobel, The Case for the Real Jesus (Grand Rapids, MI: Zondervan, 2007), 174–75; and Bruce M. Metzger, Historical and Literary Studies: Pagan, Jewish, and Christian (Grand Rapids, Eerdmans, 1968), 11.
30. J. I. Packer, "Hermeneutics and Biblical Authority," Themelios 1.1 (Autumn 1975): 11. Also see http://s3.amazonaws.com/tgc-documents/journal-issues/1.1_Packer.pdf.
31. See John Wenham, Christ and the Bible, 3rd ed. (Grand Rapids, MI: Baker, 1994), 170–71.
32. John Elder, Prophets, Idols, and Diggers: Scientific Proof of Bible History (New York: Bobbs-Merrill, 1960), 16.
33. Frederick C. Grant, An Introduction to New Testament Thought (New York: Abingdon-Cokesbury Press, 1950), 75.
34. See Bryant Wood, Jericho and Archaeology, https://www.youtube.com/watch?v=nJNjhnTe4B0 For good answers to questions about specific biblical "contradictions," see Gleason L. Archer Jr., New International Encyclopedia of Bible Difficulties (Grand Rapids, MI: Zondervan, 2001).
35. Driscoll, M (2019). Christians Might Be Crazy: Answering the Top 7 Objections to Christianity. Dunham & Company,153].

CHAPTER 3: CREATION

1. Alvin Plantinga, Where the Conflict Really Lies: Science, Religion, and Naturalism, Oxford University Press, 2011. Thomas Nagel, Mind and Cosmos: Why the Materialist Neo-Darwinian Conception of Nature Is Almost Certainly False, Oxford University Press, 2012. Nagel is an atheist who realizes the limitations of naturalism.
2. See Martin Luther, "Lectures on Genesis Chapters 1–5," in Luther's Works, American Edition, 55 vols. ed. Jaroslav Pelikan and Helmut T. Lehmann (Philadelphia: Muehlenberg and Fortress; St. Louis: Concordia, 1955–1986), 1:6.
3. See Michael J. Behe, Darwin's Black Box: The Biochemical Challenge to Evolution (New York: Free Press, 2006).
4. Steve Paulson, "The Believer" (interview with Francis Collins), Salon.com, 3, http://salon.com/books/int/2006/08/07/

collins/index2.html.

5. Fred Hoyle, quoted in Alvin Plantinga, "The Dawkins Confusion," Books & Culture 13, no. 2 (March/ April 2007): 21, http://www.christianitytoday.com/bc/2007/002/1.21.html.
6. Historic creationism is best articulated by John Sailhamer in Genesis Unbound: A Provocative New Look at the Creation Account (Dawson Media; 2nd edition, 2011), esp. pp. 44–45, and The Pentateuch as Narrative (Grand Rapids, MI: Zondervan, 1992), 81–100. Sailhamer sees the central idea as telling the story of humanity rather than the story of cosmos. He let the text itself define key terms like land and day.
7. Proponents include Creation Ministries International; http://creation.com; Henry Morris, Institute for Creation Research, http://www.icr.org; Ken Hamm, Answers in Genesis, https://answersingenesis.org.
8. E.g., see Westminster Theological Seminary's statement regarding the days of creation: http://www. wts.edu/about/beliefs/statements/creation.html.
9. Scientific American, August, 1954.
10. Carl Sagan, Cosmos (New York: Random House, 1980), 1.
11. Richard Dawkins, The Blind Watchmaker (New York: Norton, 1996), 6, emphasis in original.
12. Antony Flew, There Is a God: How the World's Most Notorious Atheist Changed His Mind (New York: HarperCollins, 2007).
13. Thomas Nagel, Mind and Cosmos: Why the Materialist Neo-Darwinian Conception of Nature is Almost Certainly False, Oxford University Press, 2012.
14. Steve Paulson, "The Believer," interview with Francis Collins, Salon.com, 3, http://salon.com/books/ int/2006/08/07/collins/index2.html.
15. Stephen Hawking and Roger Penrose, The Nature of Space and Time (Princeton, NJ: Princeton University Press, 1996), 20.
16. Quoted in Alvin Plantinga, "The Dawkins Confusion," Books & Culture 13 (March/April 2007): 21.
17. Quoted in Francis S. Collins, The Language of God: A Scientist Presents Evidence for Belief (New York: Free Press, 2006), 75.
18. Ibid.
19. Richard Lewontin, "Billions and Billions of Demons," The New York Review of Books, January 9, 1997, 150.
20. Ibid.
21. "Free People from Superstition," Freethought Today, April 2000, http://www.ffrf.org/fttoday/2000/april2000/weinberg.html.
22. Ibid.
23. "Why You Don't Have Free Will," USA TODAY, 1/1/2012.
24. Thomas Nagel, The Last Word (New York: Oxford University Press, 1997), 135.
25. Francis Collins is an example of a Christian doing just that. In the same

year that atheist Richard Dawkins published The God Delusion (Boston: Houghton Mifflin Harcourt, 2006), Collins published The Language of God. Collins is an eminent research scientist and head of the Human Genome Project. In his book he speaks about how his study of creation led him down a path following the truth until it led him to his Creator, and he converted from atheism to Christianity.

26. See Rodney Stark, For the Glory of God: How Monotheism Led to Reformations, Science, Witch-Hunts and the End of Slavery (Princeton, NJ: Princeton University Press, 2003); Philip Sampson, Six Modern Myths about Christianity and Western Civilization (Downers Grove, IL: InterVarsity, 2001); and Vinoth Ramachandra, Subverting Global Myths (Downers Grove, IL: IVP Academic, 2008).
27. Bertrand Russell, "A Free Man's Worship," in Mysticism and Logic (Mineola, NY: Dover, 2004), 37.
28. Quoted in Henry F. Schaefer III, Science and Christianity: Conflict or Coherence? (Watkinsville, GA: Apollos Trust, 2003), 82.
29. N. T. Wright, Simply Christian: Why Christianity Makes Sense (New York: HarperCollins, 2006), 60–61.
30. Ibid., 61.
31. Ibid., 62.
32. Ibid.
33. Ibid., 65.

CHAPTER 4: IMAGE

1. Sinclair Ferguson, "Image of God," in New Dictionary of Theology, ed. Sinclair Ferguson, David Wright, and J. I. Packer (Downers Grove, IL: InterVarsity, 1988), 328.
2. Strassner, K. (2009). Opening up Genesis (pp. 25–26). Leominster: Day One Publications.
3. Piper, J. (1995). Future grace (p. 76). Sisters, OR: Multnomah Publishers.
4. The same Hebrew word for "one" is used for a husband and wife in Gen. 2:24 and for the Trinity in Deut. 6:4.
5. The following material is largely summarized from William Dyrness, Themes in Old Testament Theology (Downers Grove, IL: InterVarsity, 1979), 79–96.
6. Many current atheists follow the classic expression, B. F. Skinner, Beyond Freedom and Dignity.
7. Abraham J. Heschel, Who Is Man? (Stanford, CA: Stanford University Press, 1965), 7–8.
8. See Christian Smith and Melinda Lundquist Denton, Soul Searching: The Religious and Spiritual Lives of American Teenagers (New York: Oxford University Press, 2009), 162ff., 166.
9. Paul Ramsey, Basic Christian Ethics (Louisville, KY: Westminster, 1950), 250, emphasis in original.

10. For another helpful summary of these views see Millard J. Erickson, Christian Theology (Grand Rapids, MI: Baker, 1998), 517–36.
11. See Douglas Considine, ed., Van Nostrand's Scientific Encyclopedia, 5th ed. (New York: Van Nostrand Reinhold, 1976), 943; Keith L. Moore and T. V. N. Persaud, Before We Are Born: Essentials of Embryology and Birth Defects, 6th ed. (Philadelphia: W. B. Saunders, 2001), 2; Bruce M. Carlson, Patten's Foundations of Embryology, 6th ed. (New York: McGraw-Hill, 1996), 3; Jan Langman, Medical Embryology, 3rd ed. (Baltimore: Williams & Wilkins, 1975), 3; Ronan O'Rahilly and Fabiola Müller, Human Embryology and Teratology, 2nd ed. (New York: Wiley-Liss, 1996), 8, 29.
12. Robert P. George and Christopher Tollefsen, Embryo: A Defense of Human Life (New York: Doubleday, 2008), 3–4. George is a professor of jurisprudence and director of the James Madison Program in American Ideals and Institutions at Princeton University and a former member of the President's Council on Bioethics. Right-to-life arguments have typically been based explicitly on moral and religious grounds. In Embryo, the authors eschew religious arguments and make a purely scientific and philosophical case that the fetus, from the instant of conception, is a human being, with all the moral and political rights inherent in that status. The authors argue that there is no room for a "moral dualism" that regards being a "person" as merely a stage in a human life span. An embryo does not exist in a "pre-personal" stage that does not merit the inviolable rights otherwise ascribed to persons. Instead, the authors argue, the right not to be intentionally killed is inherent in the fact of being a human being, and that status begins at the moment of conception. Moreover, just as none should be excluded from moral and legal protections based on race, sex, religion, or ethnicity, none should be excluded on the basis of age, size, or stage of biological development.
13. Didache 2.2.
14. To learn more about the history of Planned Parenthood, read George Grant, Grand Illusions: The Legacy of Planned Parenthood (Nashville, TN: Cumberland, 2000).
15. Ernst Rudin, "Eugenic Sterilization: An Urgent Need," The Birth Control Review (April 1933): 102.
16. Leon Whitney, "Selective Sterilization," The Birth Control Review (April 1933): 85.
17. H. Wayne House, "Should Christians Use Birth Control?" Christian Research Institute, http://www.equip.org/site/c.mul1LaMNJrE/b.2717865/k.B30F/DE194.htm.
18. David Goldstein, Suicide Bent: Sangerizing America (St. Paul: Radio Replies Press, 1945), 103.
19. Mark Driscoll, "What do 55 million people have in common?" https://www.foxnews.com/opinion/what-do-55-million-people-have-in-common.

NOTES

20. Ibid.
21. Charles Darwin, The Descent of Man (1871), Volume I, Chapter VI: "On the Affinities and Genealogy of Man," 200–201.
22. D. James Kennedy and Jerry Newcombe, What if Jesus Had Never Been Born? 225.
23. Ibid.
24. D. James Kennedy and Jerry Newcombe, What if Jesus Had Never Been Born? 235.
25. Nancy Pearcey, "Sexual Identity In a Secular Age."
26. Ibid.
27. Ibid.
28. Ibid.
29. Drew Pinsky and S. Mark Young, The Mirror Effect: How Celebrity Narcissism Is Endangering Our Families - And How To Save Them (New York: Harper, 2010), 2–3.
30. Ibid., 11.
31. Ibid., 12.
32. Ibid., 73.
33. Ibid.,15.
34. Martin Luther, "Lectures on Genesis Chapters 1–5," 1:64.

CHAPTER 5: FALL

1. Driscoll, M and G (2019). Win Your War. Charisma House.
2. At the beginning of the Protestant Reformation, Martin Luther had a clear belief in the cosmic battle between God and angels and Satan and demons, including speaking against the demonic in the hymn he penned "A Mighty Fortress is our God". A noted historian on Luther wrote an entire book on Luther's experience with and teaching about the devil.
3. Heiko A Oberman, Luther: Man between God and the Devil (trans. Eileen Walliser-Schwarzbart; New Haven: Yale University Press, 1989), 104. In Table Talk, Luther wrote of the devil more times than the Bible, gospel, grace, and prayer. Footnote: Mark Rogers, "'Deliver Us from the Evil One': Martin Luther on Prayer," Themelios 34, no. 3 (2009): 340. Luther also speaks of multiple visits from the devil including appearing in his room at the Castle of Wartburg, Germany, as Luther sat down to translate the Bible. Startled, Luther grabbed his inkwell and threw it at the devil. For some years following, tourists would be shown the ink well spot on the wall and told the story. But today, the inkwell story is not told to visitors and the ink spot cannot be seen. Some historians believe the ink stain evidence of the devil was painted over, forever hidden, as the story of the devil's visit to that very spot was also removed from the tour and dismissed as silly superstition.
4. https://www.christianpost.com/news/the-night-the-demon-visited.html. Perhaps the painting over of demonic evidence explains the rest of church

history since.

5. William Barclay, ed., The Gospel of Matthew, vol. 1, The Daily Study Bible Series (Philadelphia, PA: The Westminster John Knox Press, 1976), 65.]
6. Scott H. Hendrix, "Legends About Luther," Christian History Magazine-Issue 34: Martin Luther: The Reformer's Early Years (Carol Stream, IL: Christianity Today, 1992).
7. Helmut Thielicke, "The Great Temptation," Christianity Today (Carol Stream, IL: Christianity Today, 1985), 28.
8. Craig S. Keener. Miracles: The Credibility of the New Testament Accounts. 2 vols. Grand Rapids: Baker, 2011. 1,172 pp.
9. One example is the work of Dr. Michael Heiser, whom we will quote throughout this book. Michael S. Heiser. The Unseen Realm: Recovering the Supernatural Worldview of the Bible. Bellingham, WA: Lexham, 2015. 413 pp.
10. Driscoll, M (2019). Christians Might Be Crazy: Answering the Top 7 Objections to Christianity. Dunham & Company.
11. P. K. McCarter Jr., "Sons of God (OT)," ed. Geoffrey W. Bromiley, The International Standard Bible Encyclopedia, Revised (Wm. B. Eerdmans, 1979–1988), 584.
12. Michael S. Heiser, Angels: What the Bible Really Says about God's Heavenly Host (Bellingham, WA: Lexham Press, 2018), 12.
13. "Angels in the OT are often ranged in military and astral ranks known collectively as the heavenly host (Deut. 4:19; 1 Kgs. 22:19), or they are referred to individually as mighty ones. On occasion they intervened in Israel's wars (Judg. 5:20; 2 Kgs. 6:17). They were led by a captain or prince, who appears as chief angel (Josh. 5:14)…In Daniel the national guardian angels are called…princes (Dan. 8:25). The prince of Persia opposes Michael, who is 'one of the chief princes' (Dan. 10:13). Michael is also Israel's guardian angel…" Willem VanGemeren, ed., New International Dictionary of Old Testament Theology and Exegesis (Grand Rapids, MI: Zondervan Publishing House, 1997), 941.
14. D. A. Carson, Christ and Culture Revisited (Grand Rapids, MI: Eerdmans, 2008), 46.
15. Heiser, The Unseen Realm, 44.
16. John Calvin, Institutes of the Christian Religion, 2 vols., ed. John T. McNeill, trans. Ford Lewis Battles (Philadelphia: Westminster, 1960), 2.i.8.39.
17. Cornelius Plantinga Jr., Not the Way It's Supposed to Be: A Breviary of Sin (Grand Rapids, MI: Eerdmans, 1995), 5.
18. Sigmund Freud, Civilization and Its Discontents, trans. Joan Riviere (London: Hogarth, 1963), 58.
19. John Charles Ryle, Holiness: Its Nature, Hindrances, Difficulties, and Roots (Moscow, ID: Charles Nolan, 2002), 4.
20. A. W. Tozer, The Pursuit of God (Radford, VA: Wilder, 2008), 18–19.

NOTES

21. C. S. Lewis, The Screwtape Letters (New York: HarperCollins, 2001), ix.
22. See Thomas Brooks, Precious Remedies against Satan's Devices (Philadelphia: Jonathan Pounder, 1810), 16.
23. William Gurnall, The Christian in Complete Armour (London: William Tegg, 1862), 781.
24. Plantinga, Not the Way It's Supposed to Be, 124, emphasis in original.]
25. Augustine, Confessions, 8.7.
26. J. I. Packer, "Theodicy," in Sinclair B. Ferguson and J. I. Packer, New Dictionary of Theology (Downers Grove, IL: InterVarsity, 2000), 679.
27. C. Stephen Evans, "Theodicy," in Pocket Dictionary of Apologetics and Philosophy of Religion (Downers Grove, IL: InterVarsity, 2002), 114.
28. Packer, "Theodicy," 679.
29. See Edward Welch, "Addictions: New Ways of Seeing, New Ways of Walking Free," Journal of Biblical Counseling 19, no. 3 (2001): 19–30.
30. Plantinga, Not the Way It's Supposed to Be, 68.
31. R. C. Sproul, The Holiness of God (Carol Stream, IL: Tyndale, 2000), 115–16.

CHAPTER 6: COVENANT

1. Paul R. Williamson, Sealed with an Oath: Covenant in God's Unfolding Purpose, New Studies in Biblical Theology (Downers Grove, IL: IVP Academic, 2007), 43.
2. See O. Palmer Robertson, Christ of the Covenants (Phillipsburg, NJ: P&R, 1980), 4.
3. Also helpful is this Bible Project video on covenant: https://www.youtube.com/watch?v=8ferLIsvlmI.
4. Some systematic theologies add a sixth covenant with Adam. They appeal to Hosea 6:7, which is the only place the word covenant is used in connection with Adam. The debate that surrounds this point on such things as a covenant of works in covenantal theology or a dispensation of innocence in dispensational theology is more than we can address in this one chapter on covenant. Still, since the Genesis account of Adam does not speak of him as being in covenant with God, we have chosen not to include the possibility of the Adamic covenant as part of this chapter, but we do acknowledge that there were Adamic commands.
5. Rabbi Harold M. Kamsler, "Hesed—Mercy or Loyalty?" The Jewish Bible Quarterly, vol. 27, no. 3 (1999): 184–85.
6. Sally Lloyd-Jones, The Jesus Storybook Bible: Every Story Whispers His Name (Grand Rapids, MI: Zondervan, 2007), 200.
7. Christopher J. H. Wright, "Covenant: God's Mission through God's People," in The God of Covenant, ed. Alistair I. Wilson and Jamie A. Grant (Nottingham, UK: Inter-Varsity, 2005), 55.
8. Phil. 2:12-13; Tit. 3:8; 2 Pet. 1:5-11.

9. Christopher J. H. Wright, "Covenant: God's Mission through God's People," 65.
10. Ibid., 64.
11. This is an enormously complex issue. For more in-depth study see Thomas R. Schreiner, Forty Questions on the Law (Grand Rapids, MI: Kregel, 2010); Thomas R. Schreiner, The Law and Its Fulfillment: A Pauline Theology of Law (Grand Rapids, MI: Baker, 1993); Frank Thielman, Paul and the Law: A Contextual Approach (Downers Grove, IL: InterVarsity, 1994); Frank Thielman, The Law and the New Testament: The Question of Continuity (New York: Crossroad, 1999); Stephen Westerholm, Israel's Law and the Church's Faith: Paul and His Recent Interpreters (Grand Rapids, MI: Eerdmans, 1988); and Greg L. Bahnsen, Walter C. Kaiser Jr., Douglas J. Moo, et al., Five Views on Law and Gospel (Grand Rapids, MI: Zondervan, 1996).

CHAPTER 7: INCARNATION
1. J. I. Packer, Knowing God (Downers Grove, IL: InterVarsity, 1973), 45.
2. Ibid., 53.
3. Dallas Theological Seminary (2004; 2005). Bibliotheca Sacra, vol. 161 (vnp.161.641.75).
4. See Leon Morris, The Gospel According to John, rev. ed., The New International Commentary on the New Testament (Grand Rapids, MI: Eerdmans, 2000), 105–6. The Targums where originally oral paraphrases of the Hebrew Bible which were later written down. Since Jews would not pronounce the Name of God, they substituted phrases like "the Holy One" or "the Name" along with "The Word (Memra)." See Targum Neofiti and the Targum of Jonathan.
5. For an excellent discussion of how there is complexity in the unity of God for first century Jews, see Richard J. Bauckham, Jesus and the God of Israel: God Crucified and Other Studies on the New Testament's Christology of Divine Identity, Eerdmans, 2008.
6. Ron Rhodes, The Counterfeit Christ of the New Age Movement (Grand Rapids, MI: Baker, 1990), 215.
7. John 1:18; George Eldon Ladd, A Theology of the New Testament, rev. ed. (Grand Rapids, MI: Eerdmans, 1993), 278.
8. D. A. Carson, New Bible Commentary: 21st Century Edition, electronic ed. (Downers Grove, IL: InterVarsity, 1994), Mic. 5:1.
9. Roy B. Zuck, ed. A Biblical Theology of the Old Testament (Chicago: Moody, 1991), 66.
10. Jacob Neusner, The Incarnation of God: The Character of Divinity in Formative Judaism (Binghamton, NY: Global Academic, 2001).
11. See Ibid.,12, 17.
12. Ibid., 12.
13. Ibid., 166.

NOTES

14. Suetonius, Life of the Deified Augustus, Chapter 94.
15. D. Martyn Lloyd-Jones, God the Father, God the Son (Wheaton, IL: Crossway, 1996), 264.
16. Ibid., 256-57.
17. James Orr, The Virgin Birth of Christ (New York: Scribner's, 1907), 138.
18. The Apology of Aristides, trans. and ed. Rendel Harris (London: Cambridge University Press, 1893), 25.
19. William A. Jurgens, Faith of the Early Fathers (Collegeville, MN: Liturgical Press, 1998), 42.
20. J. Gresham Machen, The Virgin Birth of Christ (New York: Harper & Brothers, 1930), 269.
21. "Is God Always Superior to Jesus?" Should You Believe in the Trinity? Watch Tower Bible and Tract Society of Pennsylvania, Watchtower Society online ed., http://www.watchtower.org/e/ti/index. htm?article=article_06. htm.
22. Billy Graham, "God's Hand on My Life," Newsweek, March 29, 1999, 65.
23. Quoted in Charles Edmund Deland, The Mis-Trials of Jesus (Boston, MA: Richard G. Badger, 1914), 118-19.
24. Grant R. Osborne, Revelation, Baker Exegetical Commentary on the New Testament (Grand Rapids, MI: Baker Academic, 2002), 789.
25. Sanh. 43a
26. Origen, Contra Cels. 1.38.
27. Flavius Josephus, "Jewish Antiquities," in The New Complete Works of Josephus, trans. William Whiston (Grand Rapids, MI: Kregel, 1999), 18.63.
28. Craig L. Blomberg, Matthew, The New American Commentary (Nashville: Broadman, 1992), 315-16.
29. Athanasius, "Orations Against the Arians," bk. 3, in Richard A. Norris, trans. and ed., The Christological Controversy (Philadelphia: Fortress, 1980), 92-93, emphasis in original.
30. Quoted in G. C. Berkouwer, The Person of Christ, trans. John Vriend (Grand Rapids, MI: Eerdmans, 1954), 94.
31. For example, in 1 Timothy 1:17, Jesus is the King who has the divine attributes of eternality, immortality, invisibility, and is called "the only God." According to other Scriptures, Jesus other divine attributes possessed by him during His life on earth include omnipresence (Ps. 139:7-12; Matt. 28:20), creator (Isa. 37:16; 44:24; John 1:3; Col. 1:16; Heb. 1:2), savior (Joel 2:32; Rom. 10:9-13), and deity as the only God (Isa. 45:21b-23; Phil. 2:10-11).
32. For a more thorough study of this and other issues regarding the Holy Spirit, He Who Gives Life: The Doctrine of the Holy Spirit by Graham A. Cole (Wheaton, IL: Crossway, 2007) is a helpful resource.
33. Packer, Knowing God, 46.
34. Aldous Huxley, The Perennial Philosophy: An Interpretation of the Great Mystics, East and West (New York: HarperCollins, 2004), 49.

35. Geoffrey Parrinder, Avatar and Incarnation: The Divine in Human Form in the World's Religions (Oxford: Oneworld, 1997), 13.
36. See Winfried Corduan, "Jesus: The Avatar I Never Knew," Christian Apologetics Journal 4, no. 2 (2005): 29–44.
37. See Timothy C. Tennent, Christianity at the Religious Roundtable (Grand Rapids, MI: Baker, 2002), 59–60.
38. https://realfaith.com/sermon-series/christians-might-be-crazy/
39. Jonathan Edwards, History of Redemption (Oxford: Oxford University Press, 1793), 312.
40. Lloyd-Jones, God the Father, God the Son, 286–87.
41. Abraham Kuyper, The Work of the Holy Spirit, trans. Henri de Vries (Grand Rapids, MI: Eerdmans, 1975), 97.
42. Gerald F. Hawthorne, The Presence and the Power: The Significance of the Spirit in the Life and Ministry of Jesus (Dallas: Word, 1991), 234.

CHAPTER 8: CROSS

1. Much of the following historical overview of crucifixion is from A&E Television and The History Channel's two-hour special called Crucifixion (March 23, 2008).
2. Suetonius, The Lives of the Caesars, Vesp. 5.4.
3. Josephus, J.W. 7.203.
4. Cicero, Pro Rabirio Perduellionis Reo 5.16.
5. Crucifixion, A&E Television and The History Channel.
6. Crucifixion, A&E Television and The History Channel.
7. Luke 23:34; Luke 23:43; John 19:26-27, Psalm 22:2, Matt. 27:46 cf. Mark 15:34 as this is the only statement from the cross appearing in more than one gospel, John 19:28-29. It is possible that the sponge and wine vinegar were part of the military kit used by soldiers to clean themselves after going to the bathroom in the field, the ancient version of both toilet paper and disinfectant.
8. To learn more about each facet of the cross, see our book Death by Love: Letters from the Cross (Wheaton, IL: Crossway, 2008).

CHAPTER 9: RESURRECTION

1. "Sleep," in Leland Ryken, Jim Wilhoit, et al., Dictionary of Biblical Imagery (Downers Grove, IL: InterVarsity, 2000), 799.
2. See N. T. Wright, The Resurrection of the Son of God (Minneapolis: Fortress Press, 2003), 30–31.
3. Ibid., 31.
4. Ibid.
5. Ibid.
6. Ibid.
7. Ibid., 83.

NOTES

8. Ibid., 32.
9. Aeschylus, Eumenides 647–48, quoted in Wright, Resurrection, 32.
10. Wright, Resurrection, 35.
11. Ibid., 49.
12. Ibid., 53.
13. Ibid.
14. Ibid., 60.
15. Ibid., 76.
16. Ibid., 81–82.
17. Ibid., 82–83.
18. Craig spent two years as a fellow of the Humboldt Foundation studying the resurrection of Jesus Christ at the University of Munich. See William Lane Craig, The Historical Argument for the Resurrection of Jesus During the Deist Controversy (Lewiston, ID: Edwin Mellen, 1985), and Assessing the New Testament Evidence for the Historicity of the Resurrection of Jesus (Lewiston, ID: Edwin Mellen, 1989).
19. William Lane Craig, "Did Jesus Rise from the Dead?" in Jesus Under Fire: Modern Scholarship Reinvents the Historical Jesus, ed. Michael J. Wilkins and J. P. Moreland (Grand Rapids, MI: Zondervan, 1996), 160, emphases in original.
20. Yamauchi has immersed himself in no less than twenty-two languages and is an expert in ancient his- tory, including Old Testament history and biblical archaeology, with an emphasis on the interrelationship between ancient near Eastern cultures and the Bible. He is widely regarded as an expert in ancient history, early church history, and Gnosticism. He has published over eighty articles in more than three dozen scholarly journals and has been awarded eight fellowships. His writing includes contributing chapters to multiple books as well as books on Greece, Babylon, Persia, and ancient Africa.
21. Edwin Yamauchi, "Easter: Myth, Hallucination, or History?" Christianity Today, March 15, 1974 and March 29, 1974, 4–7, 12–16.
22. Ibid.
23. Ibid.
24. See Lee Strobel, The Case for the Real Jesus (Grand Rapids, MI: Zondervan, 2007), 174–75; and Bruce M. Metzger, Historical and Literary Studies: Pagan, Jewish, and Christian (Grand Rapids, Eerdmans, 1968), 11.
25. See Craig, "Did Jesus Rise from the Dead?"
26. James Orr, The Resurrection of Jesus (London: Hodder & Stoughton, 1908), 198.
27. J. P. Moreland, Scaling the Secular City (Grand Rapids, MI: Baker, 1987), 172.
28. Quoted in Richard N. Ostling, "Who Was Jesus?" Time, August 15, 1988, 41.

29. William Lane Craig, The Son Rises: The Historical Evidence for the Resurrection of Jesus (Eugene, OR: Wipf & Stock, 2001), 134.
30. Ibid.
31. Simon Greenleaf, The Testimony of the Evangelists: The Gospels Examined by the Rules of Evidence Administered in Courts of Justice (Grand Rapids, MI: Kregel, 1995), 32.
32. Kenneth Scott Latourette, A History of the Expansion of Christianity, 7 vols., The First Five Centuries (New York: Harper, 1937), 1:59.
33. Lucian, "The Death of Peregrine," in The Works of Lucian of Samosata, trans. H. W. Fowler and F. G. Fowler, vol. 4 (Oxford: Clarendon, 1949), 11–13. Also see Pliny, Letters, trans. William Melmoth, vol. 2 (Cambridge: Harvard University Press, 1935), 10.96.
34. Murray J. Harris, Raised Immortal: Resurrection and Immortality in the New Testament (Grand Rapids, MI: Eerdmans, 1985), 40.
35. Craig, "Did Jesus Rise from the Dead?" 152.
36. Yamauchi, "Easter: Myth, Hallucination, or History?" 4–7.
37. James D. G. Dunn, The Christ and the Spirit (Grand Rapids, MI: Eerdmans, 1998), 67–68.
38. C. F. D. Moule, The Phenomenon of the New Testament (London: SCM Press, 1967), 13, emphasis in original.
39. Flavius Josephus, "Jewish Antiquities," in The New Complete Works of Josephus, trans. William Whiston (Grand Rapids, MI: Kregel, 1999), 18.63–64, emphasis added. There is great controversy about the authenticity of this text. Kostenberger, Andreas J.; Kellum, L. Scott; Quarles, Charles L. (2009). The Cradle, the Cross, and the Crown: An Introduction to the New Testament, pp. 104-108 is an excellent summary of the controversy.
40. Suetonius, Vita Nero 16.11–13.
41. Pliny the Younger, Letters 10.96.1–7.
42. John R. W. Stott, Basic Christianity (Grand Rapids, MI: InterVarsity, 1971), 49.
43. C. Truman Davis, "The Crucifixion of Jesus: The Passion of Christ from a Medical Point of View," Arizona Medicine (March 1965): 183–87.
44. Richard N. Ostling, "Jesus Christ, Plain and Simple," Time, January 10, 1994, 32–33.
45. John Shelby Spong, Resurrection: Myth or Reality? (New York: HarperCollins, 1994), 143.
46. Ibid., 255, emphasis added.
47 See Craig, "Did Jesus Rise from the Dead?" 159–60.
48. C. S. Lewis, Surprised by Joy: The Shape of My Early Life (Orlando: Harcourt Brace, 1955), 201.
49. N. T. Wright, For All God's Worth: True Worship and the Calling of the Church (Grand Rapids, MI: Eerdmans, 1997), 65.

NOTES

CHAPTER 10: CHURCH

1. Bonaparte, Napoleon. At St. Helena, to Count de Motholon. Major General Alfred Pleasonton. Stephen Abbott Northrop, D.D., A Cloud of Witnesses (Portland OR: American Heritage Ministries, 1987; Mantle Ministries, 228 Still Ridge, Bulverde, Texas), pp. 361–362. Vernon C. Grounds, The Reason for Our Hope (Chicago: Moody Press), p. 37. Willard Cantelon, New Money or None? (Plainfield, NJ: Logos International, 1979), p. 246. Quoted from William J. Federer, Great Quotations: A Collection of Passages, Phrases, and Quotations Influencing Early and Modern World History Referenced according to Their Sources in Literature, Memoirs, Letters, Governmental Documents, Speeches, Charters, Court Decisions and Constitutions (St. Louis, MO: AmeriSearch, 2001).
2. William M. Ramsay, The Bearing of Recent Discovery on the Trustworthiness of the New Testament (London: Hodder & Stoughton, 1915), 222.
3. William Lane Craig, "Rediscovering the Historical Jesus: The Evidence for Jesus," Faith and Mission 15, no. 2 (1998): 20.
4. Michael S. Heiser, The Unseen Realm: Recovering the Supernatural Worldview of the Bible (Bellingham, WA: Lexham Press, 2015), 297.
5. T. F. Torrance, Theology in Reconstruction (Grand Rapids, MI: Eerdmans, 1965), 266.
6. R. L. Omanson, "The Church," in Evangelical Dictionary of Theology, ed. Walter A. Elwell (Grand Rapids, MI: Baker, 1984), 231.
7. Ibid.
8. Wayne Grudem, Systematic Theology: An Introduction to Biblical Doctrine (Grand Rapids, MI: Zondervan, 1994), 857.
9. This is what David Murrow speaks of in his book Why Men Hate Going to Church (Nashville: Thomas Nelson, 2004).
10. These three organizational points are adapted from Steve Walker, pastor of Redeemer's Fellowship, Roseburg, OR. The same basic outline can be seen in Luke 24:46–47; Acts 10:39–43; 13:26–39; Rom. 4:22–25; and 1 Cor. 15:1–8.

CHAPTER 11: WORSHIP

1. Harold M. Best, Unceasing Worship: Biblical Perspectives on Worship and the Arts (Downers Grove, IL: InterVarsity, 2003), 23.
2. N. T. Wright, For All God's Worth: True Worship and the Calling of the Church (Grand Rapids, MI: Eerdmans, 1997), 28.
3. David Powlison, "Idols of the Heart and 'Vanity Fair,'" The Journal of Biblical Counseling vol. 13 (Winter 1995): 35. Also available here: http://www.greentreewebster.org/Articles/Idols%20of%20the%20Heart%20(Powlison).pdf.
4. Martin Luther, "The Large Catechism," in The Book of Concord (St. Louis: Concordia, 1921), 3.5–28, http://www.bookofconcord.org/lc-3-

tencommandments.php.
5. Dr. Peter Jones has dedicated much of his adult academic life to the concepts of one-ism and two-ism. We have discussed these matters on multiple occasions, and much of what is shared is a summary of those conversations and his writings. You can find his work at https://truthxchange.com/.
6. John Piper, Finally Alive: What Happens When We Are Born Again (Fearn, Scotland: Christian Focus, 2009), 29.
7. G. K. Beale, We Become What We Worship: A Biblical Theology of Idolatry (Downers Grove, IL: IVP Academic, 2008), 282.
8. G. K. Beale, We Become What We Worship: A Biblical Theology of Idolatry (Downers Grove, IL: IVP Academic, 2008), 82.
9. D. A. Carson, "Worship under the Word," in Worship by the Book, ed. D. A. Carson (Grand Rapids, MI: Zondervan, 2002), 24, emphasis in original.
10. Carson, "Worship under the Word," 21, emphasis in original.
11. Ibid., 21–22.
12. Frame, Worship in Spirit and Truth, 67.
13. John M. Frame, Worship in Spirit and Truth: A Refreshing Study of the Principles and Practice of Biblical Worship (Phillipsburg, NJ: P&R, 1996), 1–2, emphases in original.
14. Randy Alcorn, The Treasure Principle: Discovering the Secret of Joyful Giving (Sisters, OR: Multnomah, 2001), 10.
15. Ibid., 25.
16. R. C. Sproul, "Time Well Spent: Right Now Counts Forever," Tabletalk (September 1997): 4. The article is excerpted here: http://www.sovereigngraceministries.org/Blog/post/Time-Redeemed.aspx.
17. Wayne Grudem, Systematic Theology: An Introduction to Biblical Doctrine (Grand Rapids, MI: Zondervan, 1994), 1016.
18. These points are adapted from John Stott's book The Living Church: Convictions of a Lifelong Pastor (Downers Grove, IL: InterVarsity, 2007).

CHAPTER 12: KINGDOM

1. "Eutychus & His Kin," Christianity Today (Carol Stream, IL: Christianity Today, 1980), 674.]
2. H. Richard Niebuhr, The Kingdom of God in America (New York: Harper & Row, 1937), 193. For a contemporary attempt to explain away hell, see Brian D. McLaren, The Last Word and the Word after That (San Francisco: Jossey-Bass, 2008).
3. John Blanchard, Whatever Happened to Hell? (Durham, England: Evangelical Press, 1993), 128.
4. See John Calvin, Institutes of the Christian Religion, 2 vols., ed. John T. McNeill, trans. Ford Lewis Battles (Philadelphia: Westminster, 1960), 2:1007; (3.25.12). Others who agree that the figures are metaphorical

NOTES

include Billy Graham, Leon Morris, J. I. Packer, Millard Erickson, and D. A. Carson, according to William Crockett, Four Views on Hell (Grand Rapids, MI: Zondervan, 1997), 44–45n6.

5. John Milton, Paradise Lost, bk. 1, ln. 263.
6. Charles Haddon Spurgeon, "The Final Separation," sermon no. 1234, preached in 1875, The Charles H. Spurgeon Library Version 1 (AGES Digital Library, CD-ROM), 353.
7. In July 1974, 2,700 evangelical leaders from 150 countries convened the Lausanne Congress, made up of an unprecedented diversity of nationalities, ethnicities, ages, occupations, and denominational affiliations. Time magazine described it as "possibly the widest-ranging meeting of Christians ever held" ("A Challenge from Evangelicals," Time, August 5, 1974, http://www.time.com/time/magazine/ article/0,9171,879423,00.html). They composed the Lausanne Covenant. In faithfulness to Jesus, it was a direct challenge to the widely held philosophy that Christians do not have the right—let alone the duty—to disturb the honest faith of a Buddhist, a Hindu, or a Jew by evangelizing them.
8. The Lausanne Movement, "The Uniqueness and Universality of Christ" (par. 3) in The Lausanne Covenant, http://www.lausanne.org/covenant/.
9. C. S. Lewis, The Great Divorce (New York: HarperCollins, 2001), 75.
10. C. S. Lewis wrote a brilliant essay refuting the liberal approach to dealing with sin and crime, entitled "The Humanitarian Theory of Punishment," that can be found on the Internet or in God in the Dock: Essays on Theology and Ethics (Grand Rapids, MI: Eerdmans, 1970), 287–300.
11. Evangelical proponents of annihilationism include John Stott, John Wenham, Clark Pinnock, and Edward Fudge. J. I. Packer's excellent article addressing this topic, "Evangelical Annihilationism in Review," Reformation & Revival, vol. 6 (Spring 1997), is available at http://www.the-highway.com/annihilationism_Packer.html.
12. Christopher W. Morgan, "Biblical Theology: Three Pictures of Hell" in Hell Under Fire, ed. Christopher W. Morgan and Robert A. Peterson (Grand Rapids, MI: Zondervan, 2004), 144.
13. https://www.spurgeon.org/resource-library/sermons/infant-salvation

PASTOR MARK DRISCOLL

With Pastor Mark, it's all about Jesus! Mark and his wife Grace have been married and doing vocational ministry together since 1993. They also planted The Trinity Church with their five kids in Scottsdale, Arizona as a family ministry (thetrinitychurch.com) and started Real Faith, a ministry alongside their daughter Ashley that contains a mountain of Bible teaching from Pastor Mark as well as content for women, men, parents, pastors, leaders, Spanish-speakers, and more.

Pastor Mark has been named by *Preaching Magazine* one of the 25 most influential pastors of the past 25 years. He has a bachelor's degree in speech communication from the Edward R. Murrow College of Communication at Washington State University as well as a master's degree in exegetical theology from Western Seminary in Portland, Oregon. For free sermons, answers to questions, Bible teaching, and more, visit **RealFaith.com** or download the **Real Faith app**.

Together, Mark and Grace have authored "Win Your War" and "Real Marriage". Pastor Mark has authored numerous other books including "Spirit-Filled Jesus", "Who Do You Think You Are?", and "Vintage Jesus". Recently, Pastor Mark also released "Pray Like Jesus" with his daughter Ashley Chase as a father-daughter project.

If you have any prayer requests for us, questions for future Ask Pastor Mark or Dear Grace videos, or a testimony regarding how God has used this and other resources to help you learn God's Word, we would love to hear from you at **hello@realfaith.com.**

DR. GERRY BRESHEARS

In addition to serving as a professor of theology at Western Seminary in Portland, Oregon since 1980, Dr. Gerry Breshears is a pastor to pastors and a member of the elder and preaching teams at Grace Community Church in Gresham, Oregon. He gets the honor of teaching and preaching in churches and seminaries across not only the United States but the world including Ukraine, Uganda, Poland, Lebanon, Russia, the Taiwan region, the Netherlands, and the Philippines. He is also a founding board member on The Bible Project.

Upon graduating from the University of New Mexico - Albuquerque in 1968, Gerry started his ministry as a junior high math teacher in Jefferson County, Colorado before God called him to the Philippines to teach at Faith Academy in 1969. After God changed the direction of his life, he did seminary (Denvery Seminary, MDiv, 1975) and his Ph.D. (Fuller Theological Seminary, Ph.D., 1984) to become a missionary church planter and Bible college teacher in the Philippines. Then, God interrupted his life again and brought him to Western Seminary.

In addition to writing the original *Doctrine: What Christians Should Believe* book with Pastor Mark in 2010, Dr. Breshears and Pastor Mark also co-authored *Vintage Jesus* (2008), *Death by Love* (2008), and *Vintage Church* (2009). He also contributed a section called "Spiritual Abuse" to Bev Hislop's *Shepherding Women in Pain: Real Women, Real Issues, and What You Need to Know* in 2020.

He and his wife Sherry have been married since 1968 and have two sons and a daughter. They enjoy collecting kids, so they have a growing number of non-legal (not illegal) children, grandchildren, and great grandchildren. Together, they enjoy ministering and extending hospitality to others. Gerry's hobbies include traveling, hiking, and reading.

IT'S ALL ABOUT JESUS!

REALFAITH.COM

$39.99
ISBN 978-1-7374103-5-5

PRINTED IN PRC